ALEX PRAGER

Silver Lake Drive

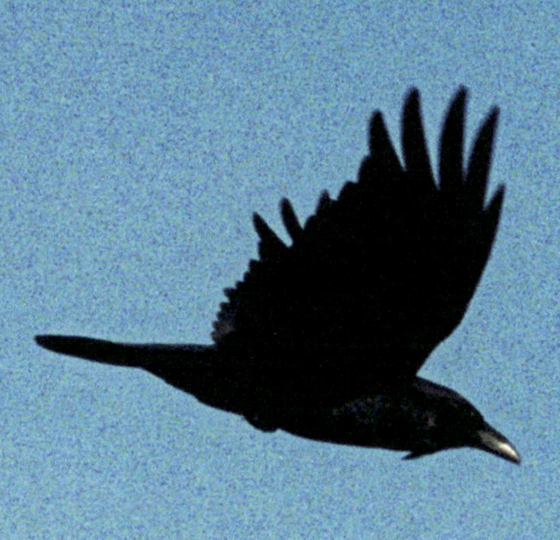

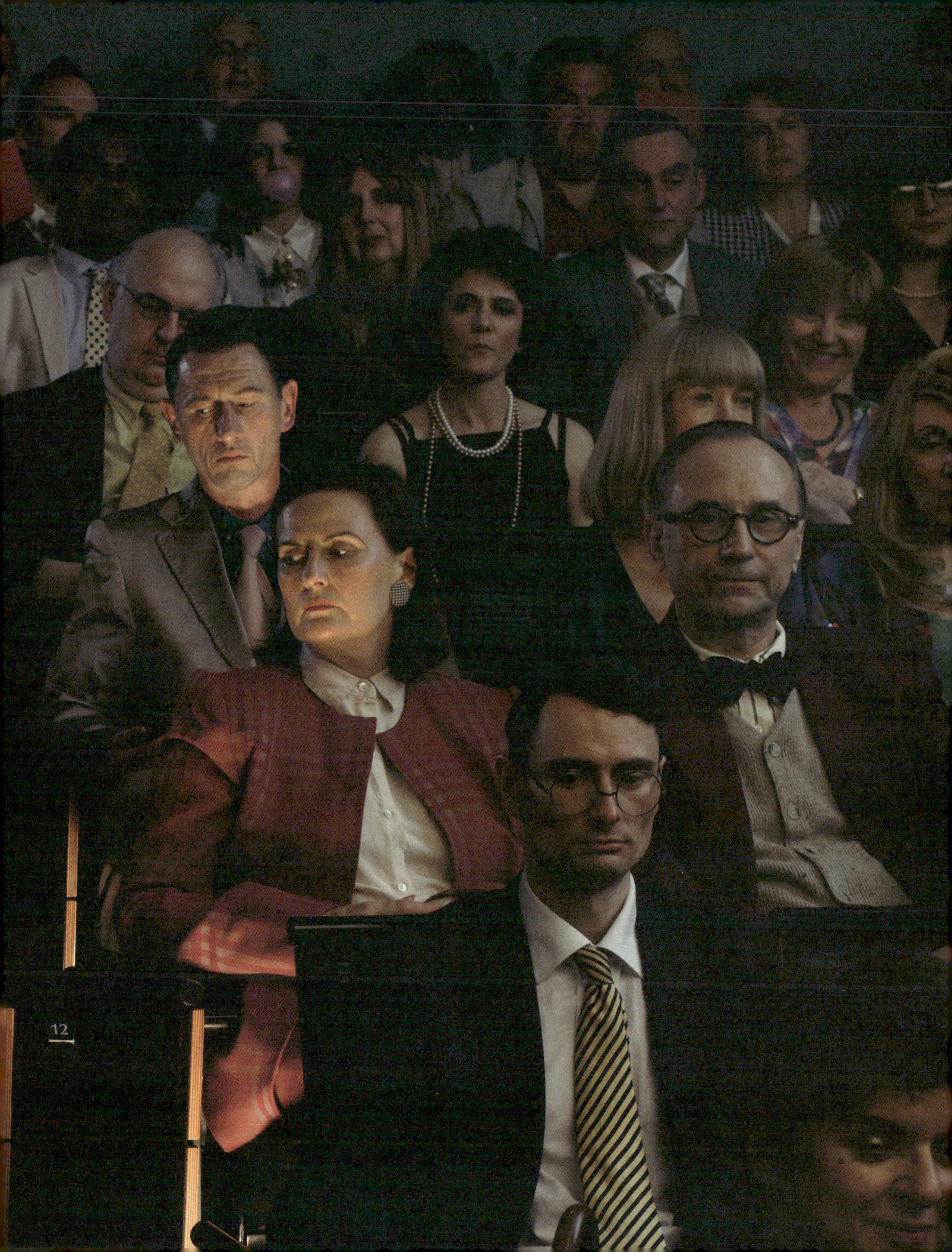

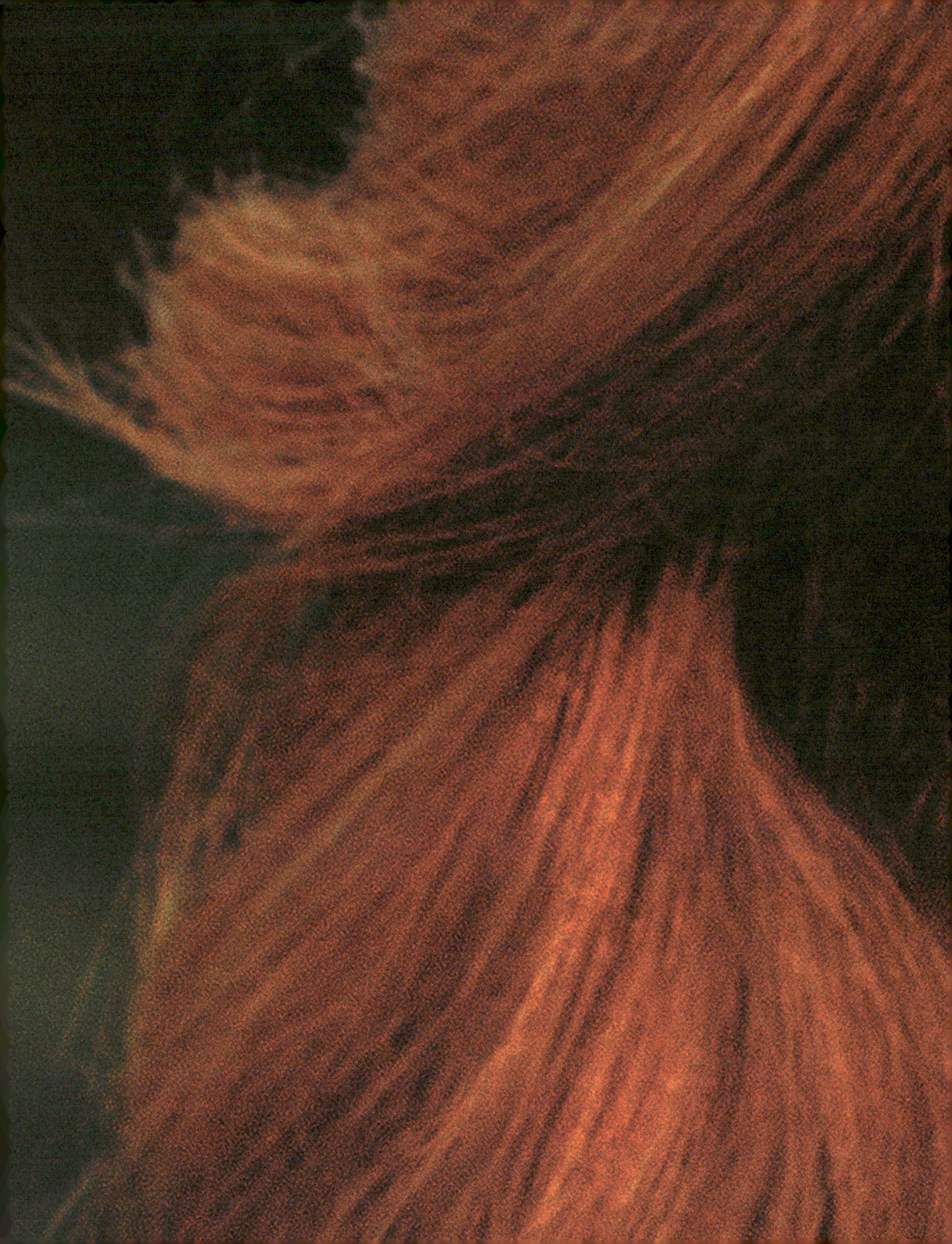

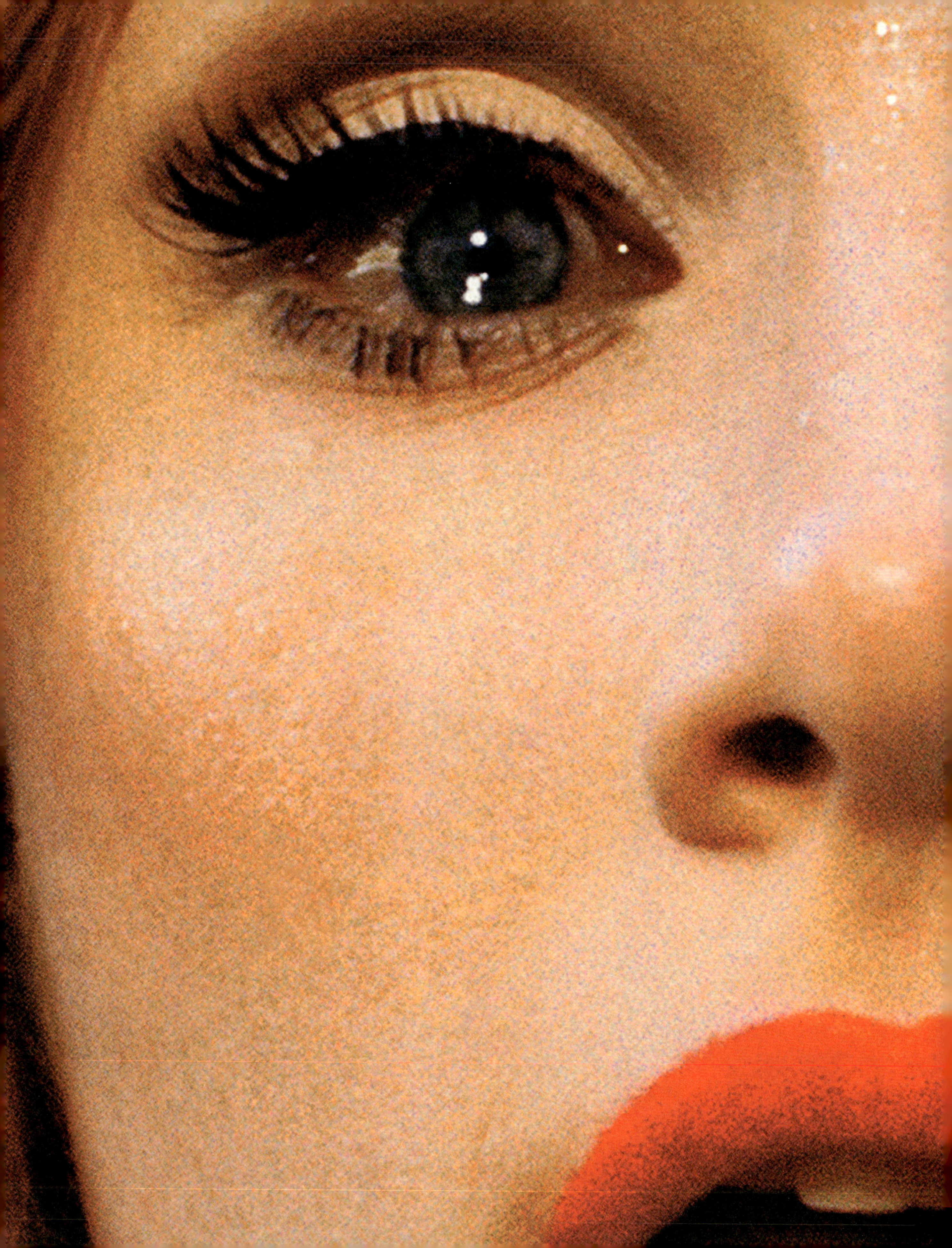

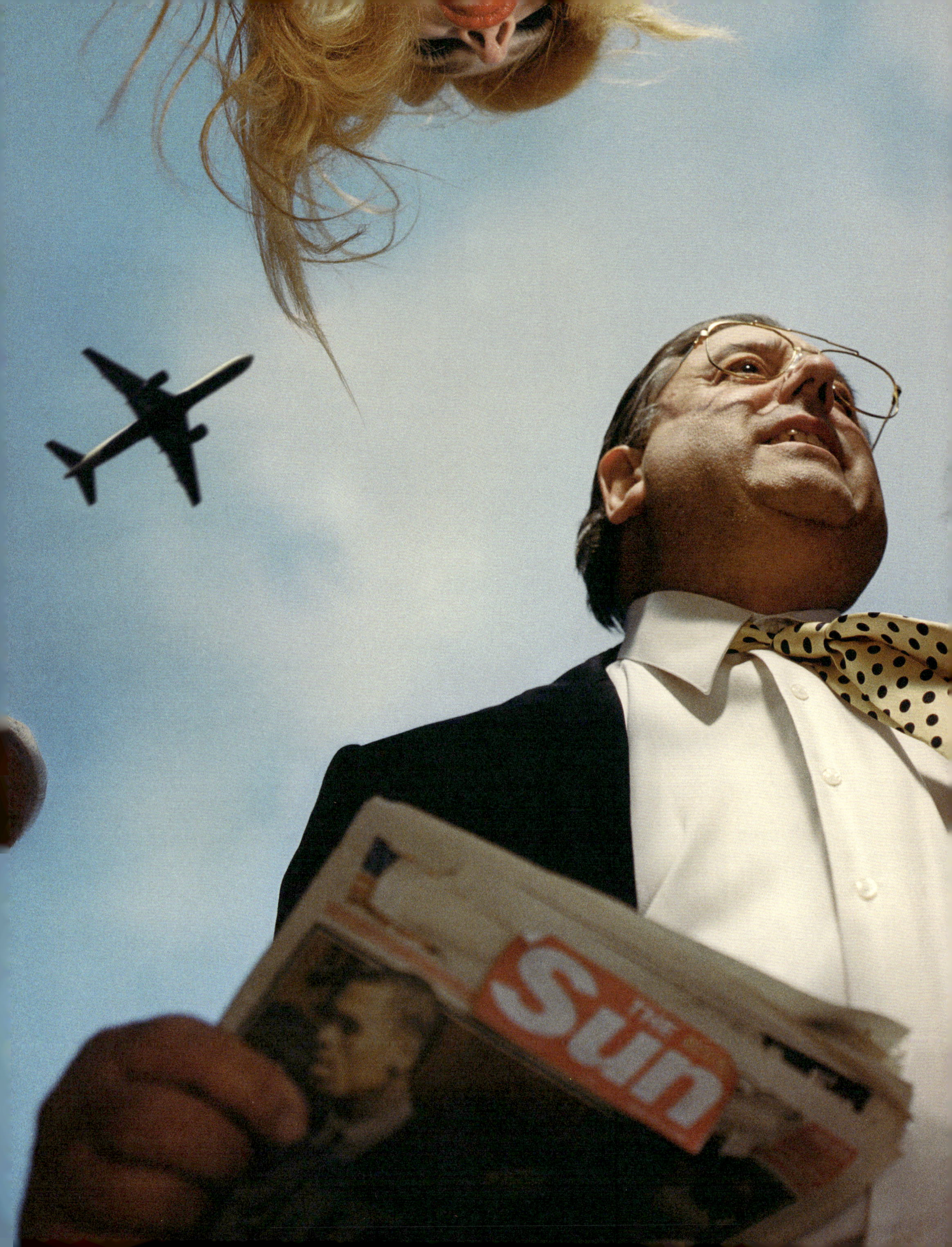

The Sun

ALEX PRAGER

Silver Lake Drive

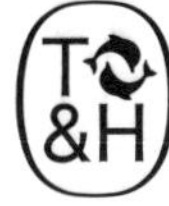

with over 250 illustrations, including 91 plates

Contents

12   *Alex Prager, Double Take*
Michael Govan

74   *Interview with Alex Prager*
Nathalie Herschdorfer

114   *Face in the Crowd*
Clare Grafik

146   *Pretend to Pretend in the Art of Appearances*
Michael Mansfield

202   Behind the Scenes

206   Selected Works

218   Curriculum Vitae

224   Acknowledgments

17 *PART 1*

18 POLYESTER (2007)
32 THE BIG VALLEY (2008)
46 WEEK-END & THE LONG WEEKEND
   (2009–2012)

89 *PART 2*

90 COMPULSION (2012)
122 FACE IN THE CROWD (2013)

145 FILMS

161 *PART 3*

184 LA GRANDE SORTIE (2016)

Alex Prager, Double Take

Michael Govan

Like most, I first encountered an Alex Prager *Face in the Crowd* picture with a double take, being quickly drawn in by the beguiling strangeness of it all. The picture's colours seemed too vivid. The figures – with their intentional facial expressions and clothes worn like costume, implying a not-quite-recent past – suggested many hyper-specific individual narratives. And the gazes of these disconnected characters within a crowd were rarely directed to others; rather they sent my own gaze darting across the composition as if scanning the surface of an Abstract Expressionist painting.

Set in public spaces, from beach to airport to theatre, Prager's crowds are seen from an opportune perspective – from above, like a surveillance camera – an optimal view from which to see the most characters. Occasionally, a single figure will be looking directly up at the camera (a surrogate for both the artist and the viewer), revealing the theatre of the whole enterprise.

Much has already been written about Prager, who was so taken with an image by William Eggleston that she taught herself photography. Initially pursuing a more documentary form, street photography in the vein of early 20th-century masters, she soon realized she could make her own unique contribution to the genre by employing fantasy, artifice, and, like Eggleston, luminous colour.

Prager's photographic and filmic compositions, like Eggleston's photographs, Alfred Hitchcock's films, and Edward Hopper's paintings, reveal the extraordinary lurking within the ordinary. Wreaking havoc with our involuntary voyeurism and our tendency to leap to conclusions about people's characters based on the merest details of their appearances, Prager cues our own fantasies by representing her own.

Perhaps the ideal of a photograph is to capture the reality of a certain moment. But the earliest photography, burdened by its hunger for light, required that its subjects, whether a person or a train, hold still to be photographed. And even the best modern journalistic photography is prized for its storytelling. As critic Susan Sontag has written, 'The camera has the power to catch so-called normal people in such a way as to make them look abnormal. The photographer chooses oddity, chases it, frames it, develops it, titles it' (Susan Sontag, *On Photography*, 1977, p. 34). One of the first and most famous photographic documentarian photographers, Edward Curtis, was known to have paid his Native American subjects to dress in compelling, if inaccurate, costume in what came to be regarded less as ethnographic documentary and more as a simulation of the fantasy of un-modernized societies.

Costume is frequently used in photography, theatre, or cinema to reinforce character, and to suggest a backstory. While Prager's sets, or settings, are often generic, it is her use of costume that most extends her narratives – whether defining a single character, or, as in her crowd photographs, disparate characters that seem even more diverse and theatrical than real crowds. During a recent visit to the artist's mostly nondescript studio-office I was struck by the small but intriguing back room that housed Prager's collection of costumes and accessories. A close look at her pictures reveals that certain costumes show up more than once. It's as if the racks of clothes that Prager has collected since her childhood, visible in vertical slices of colour and pattern, function for her as a great library of archetypal stories and references – or as a painter's assorted brushes, colours, and techniques.

Most of Prager's subjects are not posed like fashion models; rather, like street photography, they seem captured in some kind of motion. Her photographic images are always described as extremely cinematic, often suggesting stills from a much longer narrative. Prager makes specific and intentional references to Hitchcock and many other filmmakers. It wasn't long after she became a photographer that she picked up a video camera to construct her own movies. Prager takes advantage of the abundant access to tools and expertise afforded her by her native city, Los Angeles: Hollywood sets, sound stages, costume and makeup, lighting, actor-extras, and so on. The red carpet and the beaches that appear in a couple of Prager's crowd pictures are both physical localities and signifiers for Hollywood and cinema in general.

While early motion pictures ostensibly added another level of realism to photography through the representation of movement, the art of cinema, practically since its inception, has been described as dreamlike. The film editor assembles fragments of time and space – often indicating multiple viewpoints – in ways that resemble a dream. Cinema developed as a medium just as Sigmund Freud proposed a psychoanalytic dimension to the retelling and *interpretation* of dreams in terms of desire and 'wish fulfilment'. Surrealists, from Salvador Dalí to Maya Deren, later took maximum advantage of cinema's liminal position between the real and the unreal and its ability to manipulate time and space. Similarly, Prager creates a confusion between reality and fantasy by making use of photography and film's precarious balance between documentary and fiction. That's the double take: you have to look at least twice to discern what is what you already know, and what is different.

Prager has sometimes referred to her first video as a 'moving photograph', and uses her moving images to complicate and extend the context of her still images. Often her films emphasize the more surreal dimension of her narratives, defying time and space and gravity, encouraging a more fantastical reading of her still images. Prager's first moving picture, *Despair* from 2010, features a Prager-like woman who is introduced, utterly alone and tearful, talking in a phone booth, which she exits in a hurry into a street occupied by more and more people until she is in a crowd and finds a red door that she goes inside. The camera pans and follows her up through the building, across a top floor, and out of a window, from which she falls slowly, and more happily, in a spotlight and through a sunset, until she disappears – only her red shoes falling to the ground. The short narrative moves from earth to sky, and back, in a progression from reality to dream. Included are references to many other films and narratives, and different kinds of space, from personal to public to ethereal, all compressed into a colourful, hyper-stylized, moving picture the length of a pop song. Some of the clothes and cars might conjure an earlier era, a past before Prager was born. An aeroplane that traverses the bright blue, lightly clouded sky of the title sequence reappears as a portending shadow as the protagonist exits her phone booth; the film's conclusion has her flying as she falls. The brief filmic journey follows despair from isolation, to alienation in a crowd, to a tragic spectacle of release and relief, and then absence – perhaps metaphorically suggesting the anxieties of an artist through the creative act. These may begin in feelings of despair, be forced into the crowd of viewers, and end in momentary ecstasy and even a fantasy of disappearance. In film, psychological anxieties are often explored in the form of a 'dream sequence'. The images in *Despair*, as in all Prager's work, inhabit a space between the real and the imaginary.

'Dream' describes the cinematic-like interplay of memory and imagination that occurs during sleep; 'dream' also describes desire, goal, imagination and beauty, as well as horror and surprise. It is something stuck between the possible and the impossible, the perceived and the fleeting. Similarly, an artwork might be material and yet elusive. Accompanying her *Crowds* series, the artist's video *Face in the Crowd* features a character that looks much like the artist herself, a double, observing the crowd with her hand against a window and also being within that crowd – in the same way one often not only observes, but also sees oneself, in a dream. The transparent pane of glass is like the picture plane, or the Brechtian fourth wall, of the camera, the screen, and the conscious perception of reality and dream. The protagonist is curiously equally alone and disconnected as observer, and among the crowd of disconnected individuals that she observes.

In her most recent film, *La Grande Sortie*, inspired in part by the 1948 ballet film based on the fairytale *The Red Shoes*, Prager explores a similar dynamic of being within and without. The film begins by dwelling on the deliberate ritual of the assembly of an audience, another Prager crowd with all its many embedded narratives. A ballerina begins her performance on stage in a forest suggesting a fairytale. She is then joined by a male partner (prominently wearing a watch that suggests real time), who after a while is suddenly replaced by a woman in the audience whom the ballerina has noticed particularly; the woman is in turn replaced by another man and another woman in similar fashion, as the ballerina gains awareness of other individuals and becomes increasingly frenetically dishevelled. Finally, she disappears in a puff of smoke, her costume left on stage, after looking into the audience and seeing her double, who then departs through the theatre's exit (*sortie*).

The ballerina and her double are perhaps surrogates for the artist Prager herself, who, it seems, is represented in 'cameos' in several of her other works, including *Despair* (which also features an exit door and a disappearance). If this artist's 'grand exit' is more open-ended and less tragic than that of the dancer of *The Red Shoes*, who in choosing art over love exits to her death, it is also a more complex and self-reflexive meditation on the artifice that is art. In confusing the being of the artist and the observer, Prager suggests that an artwork, like a costume, is an externalization of self, engendering a kind of self-awareness, a double take – like a dream where one is both observer and observed.

PART 1

POLYESTER

(2007)

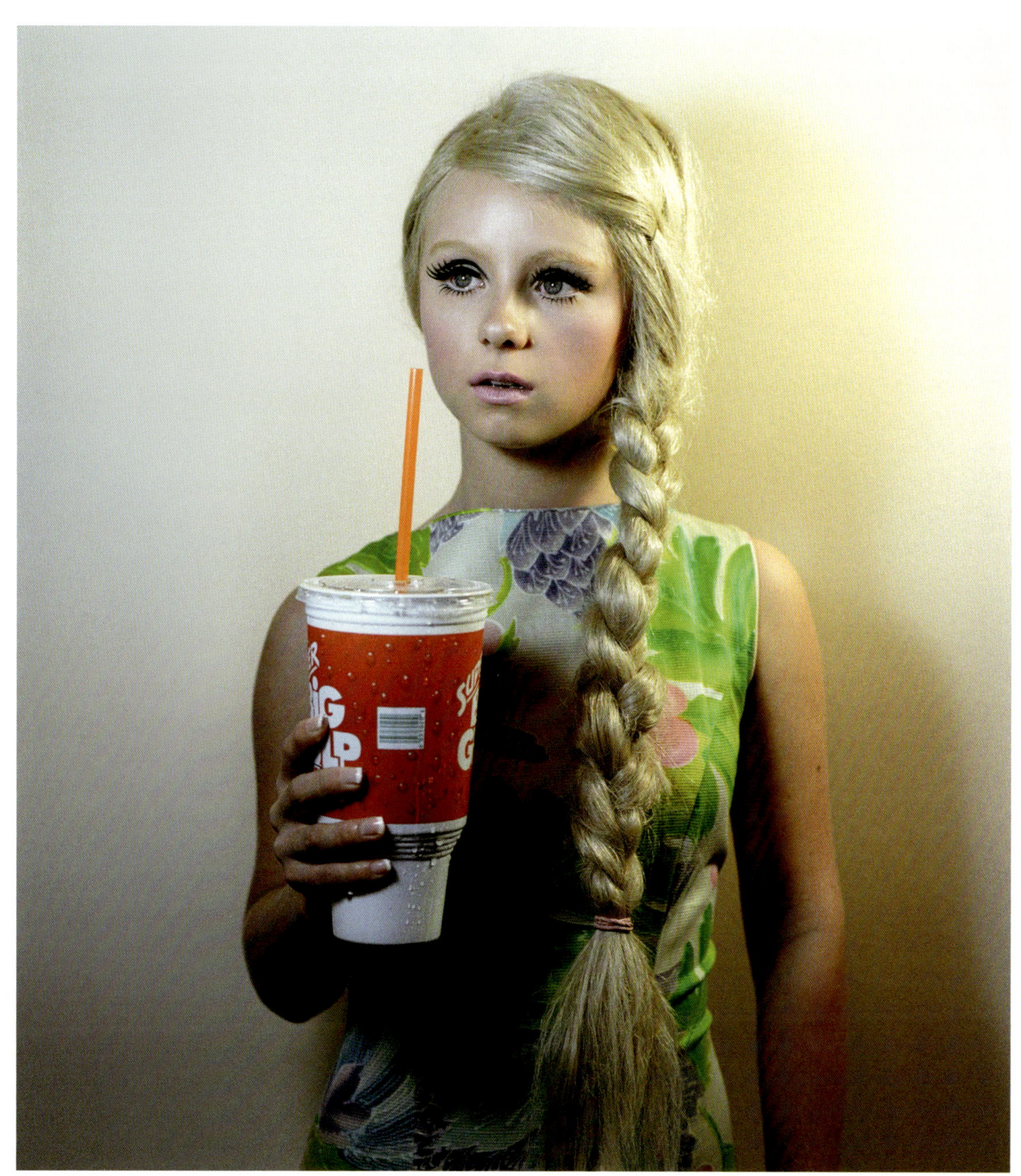
SUPER
BIG
GULP

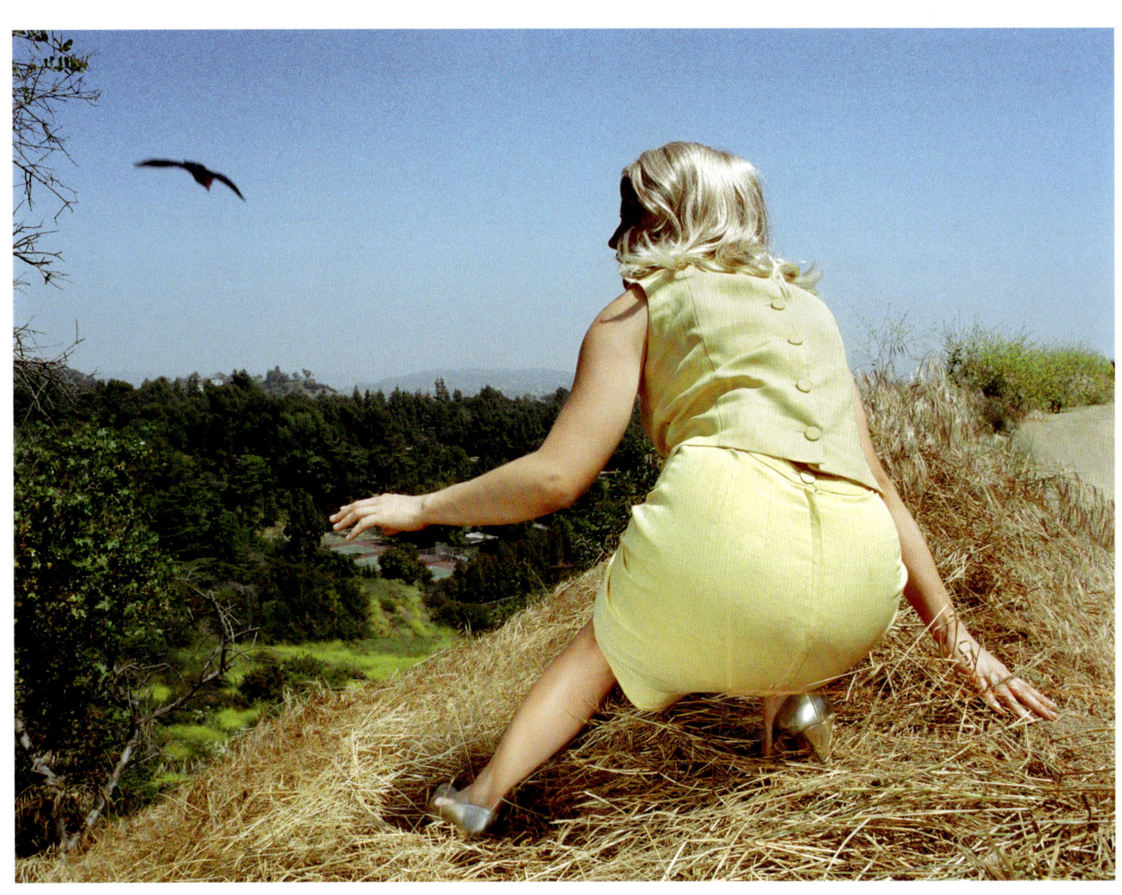

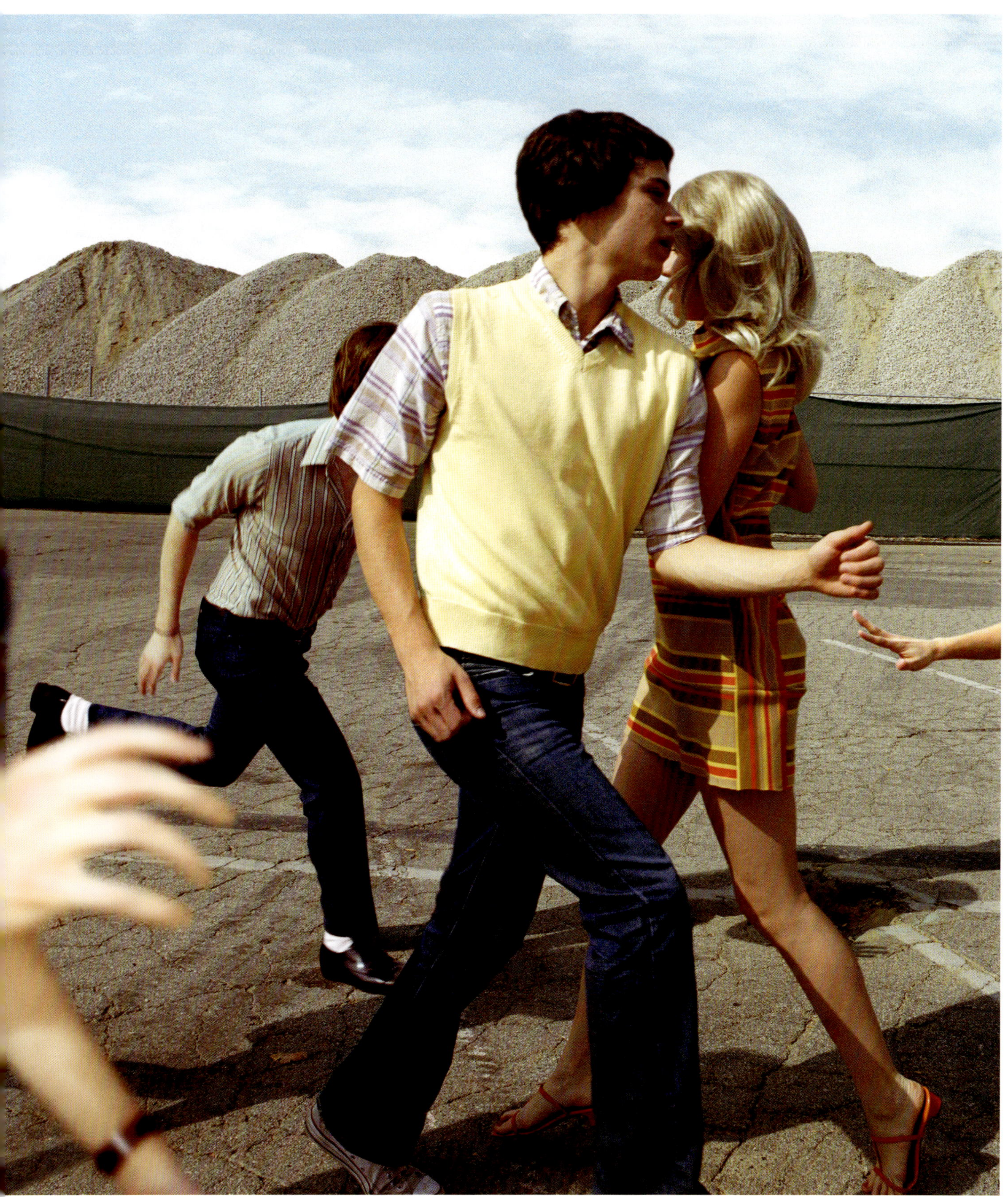

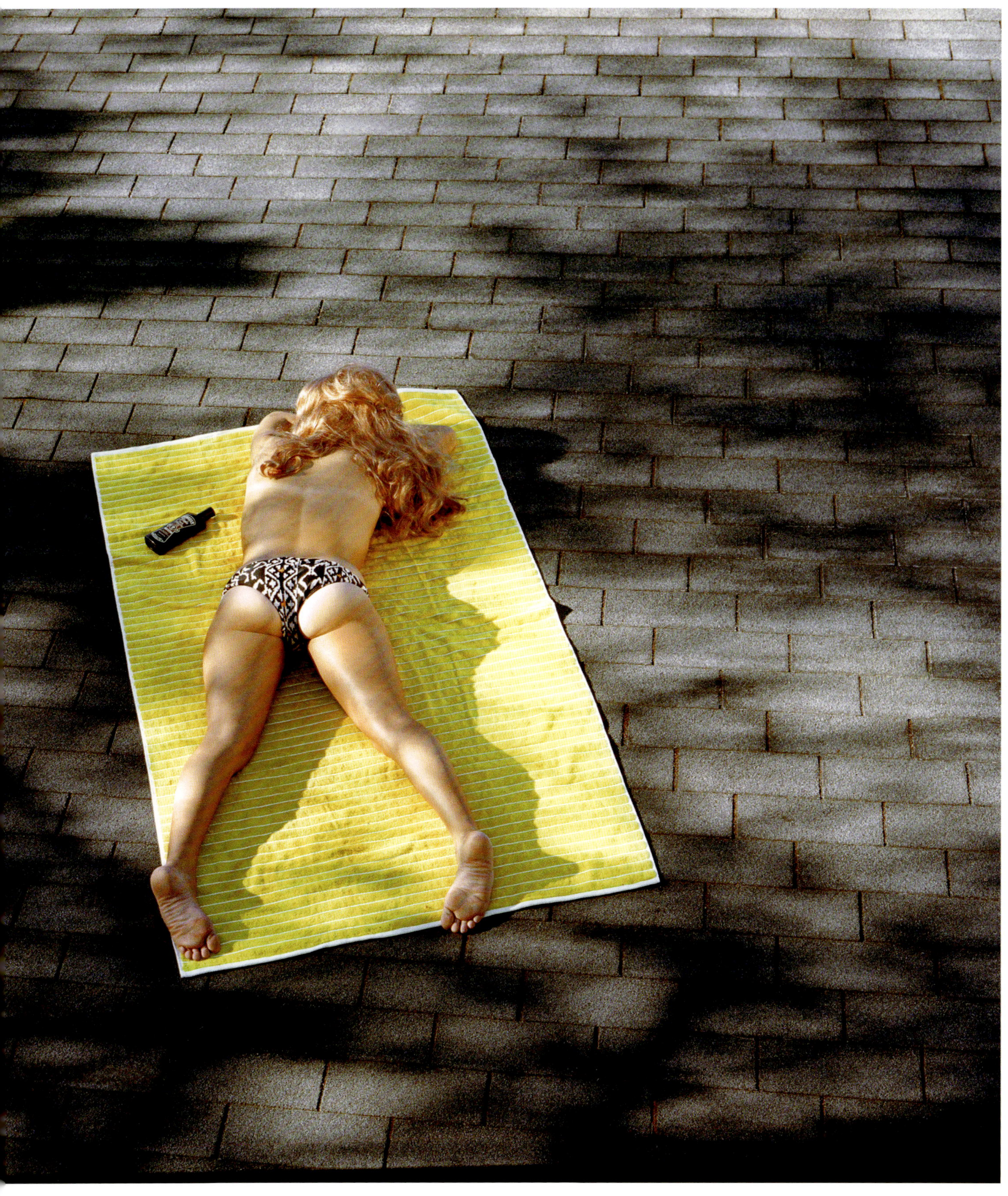

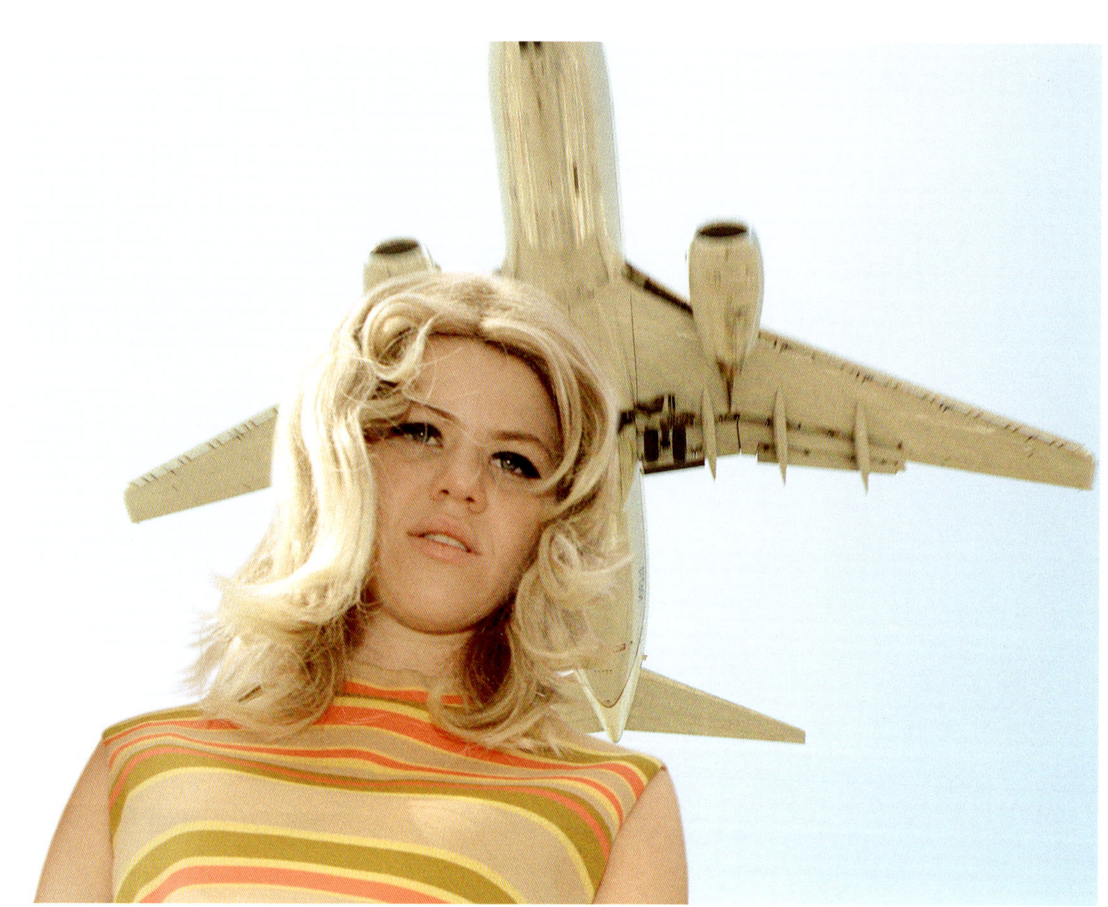

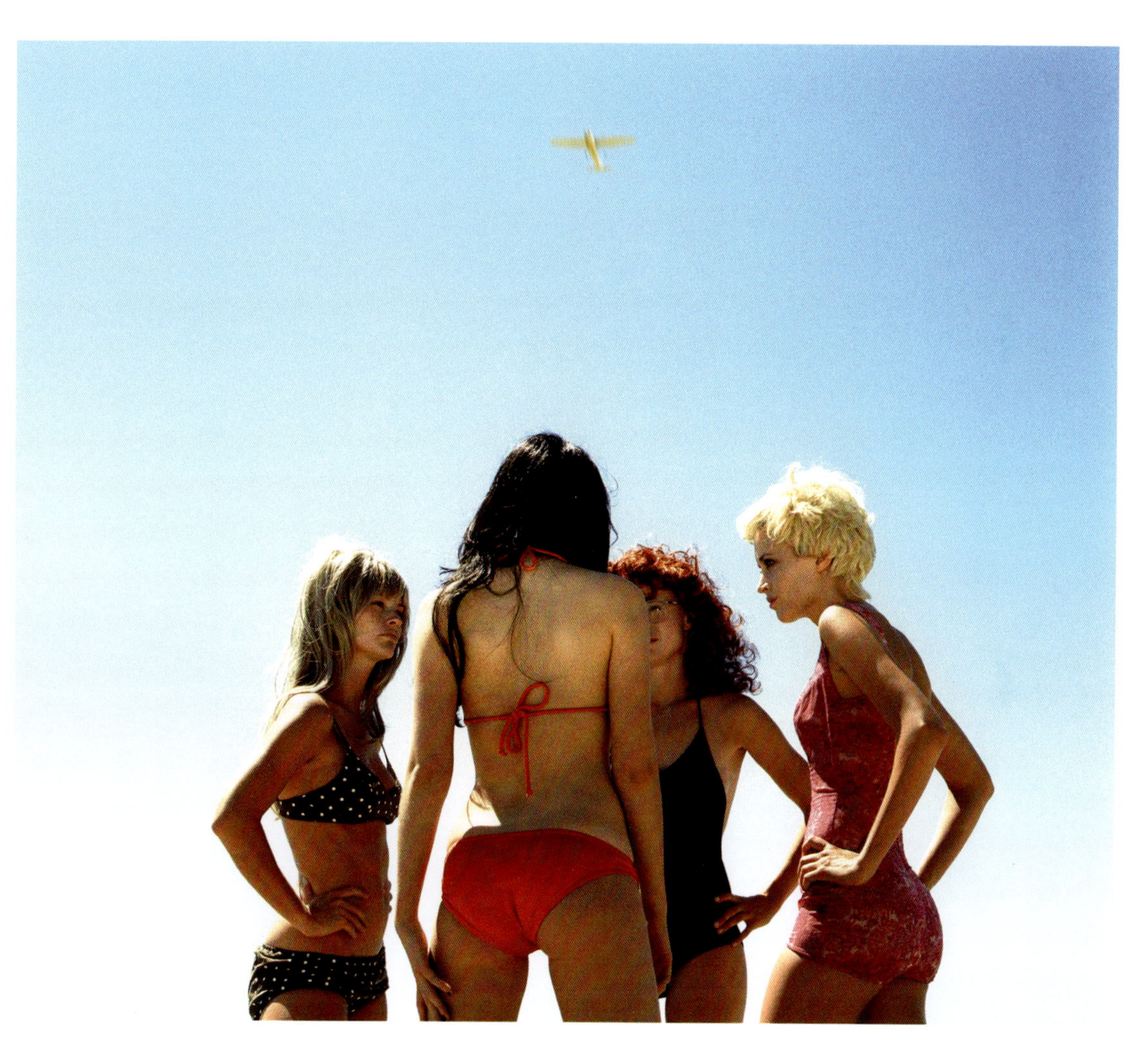

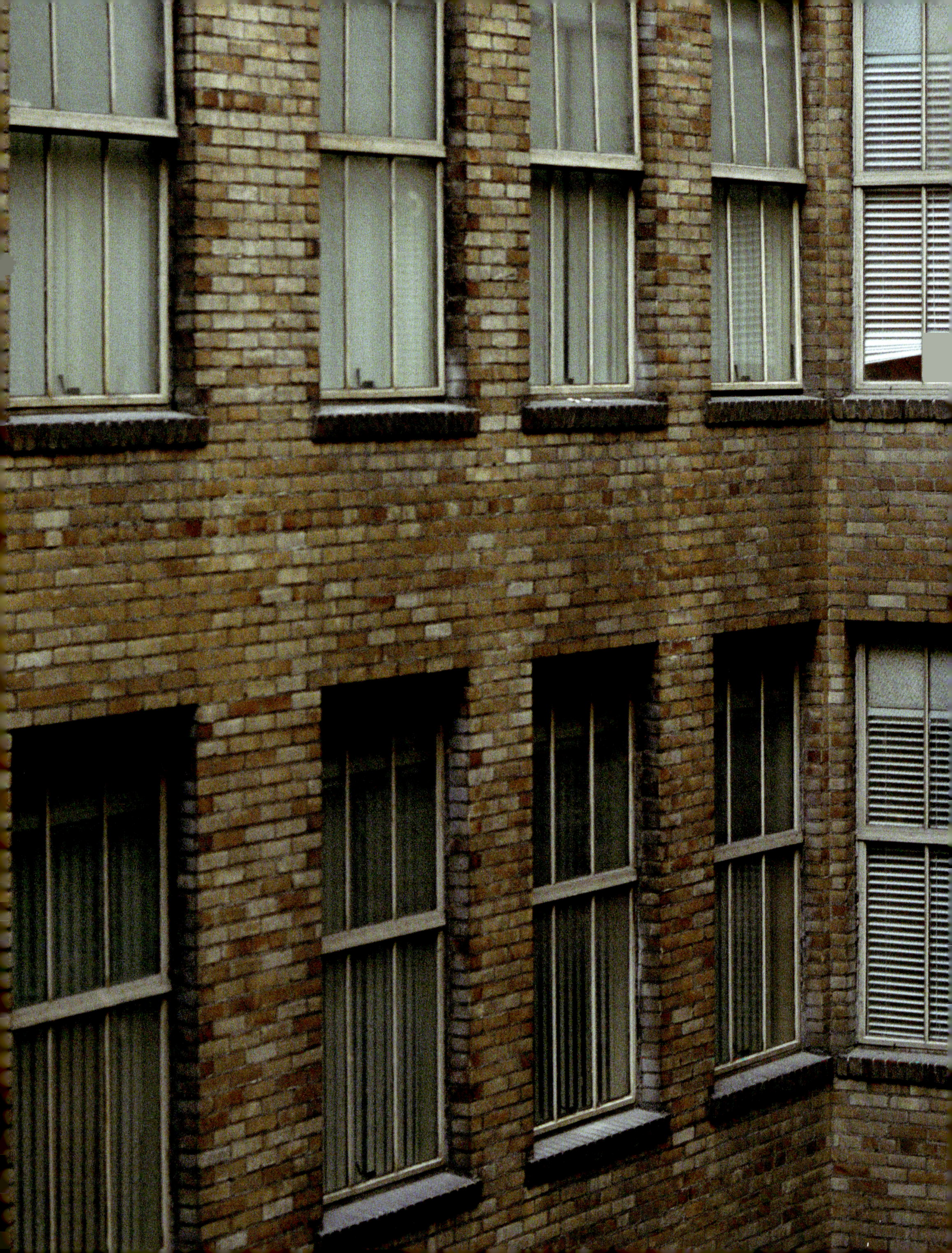

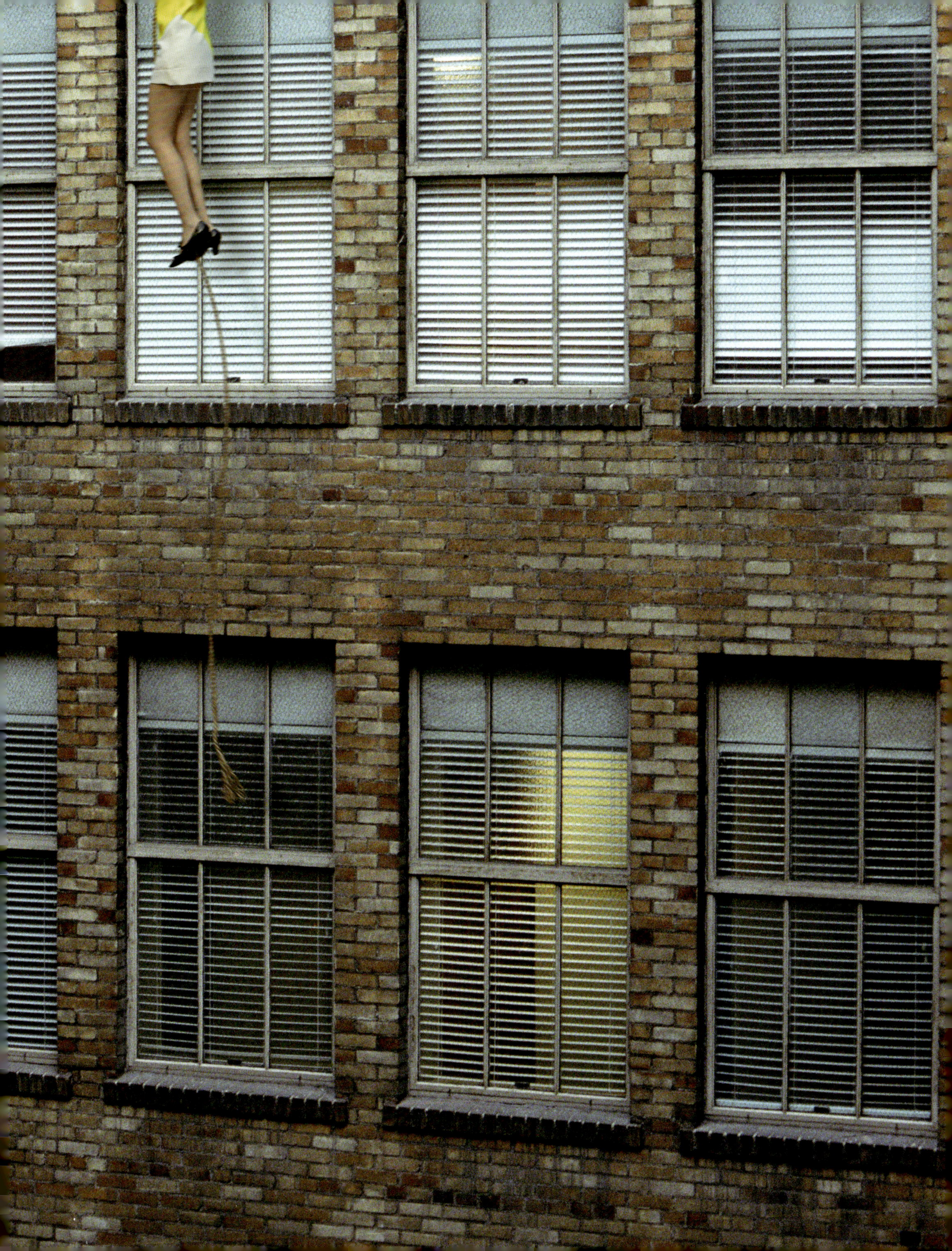

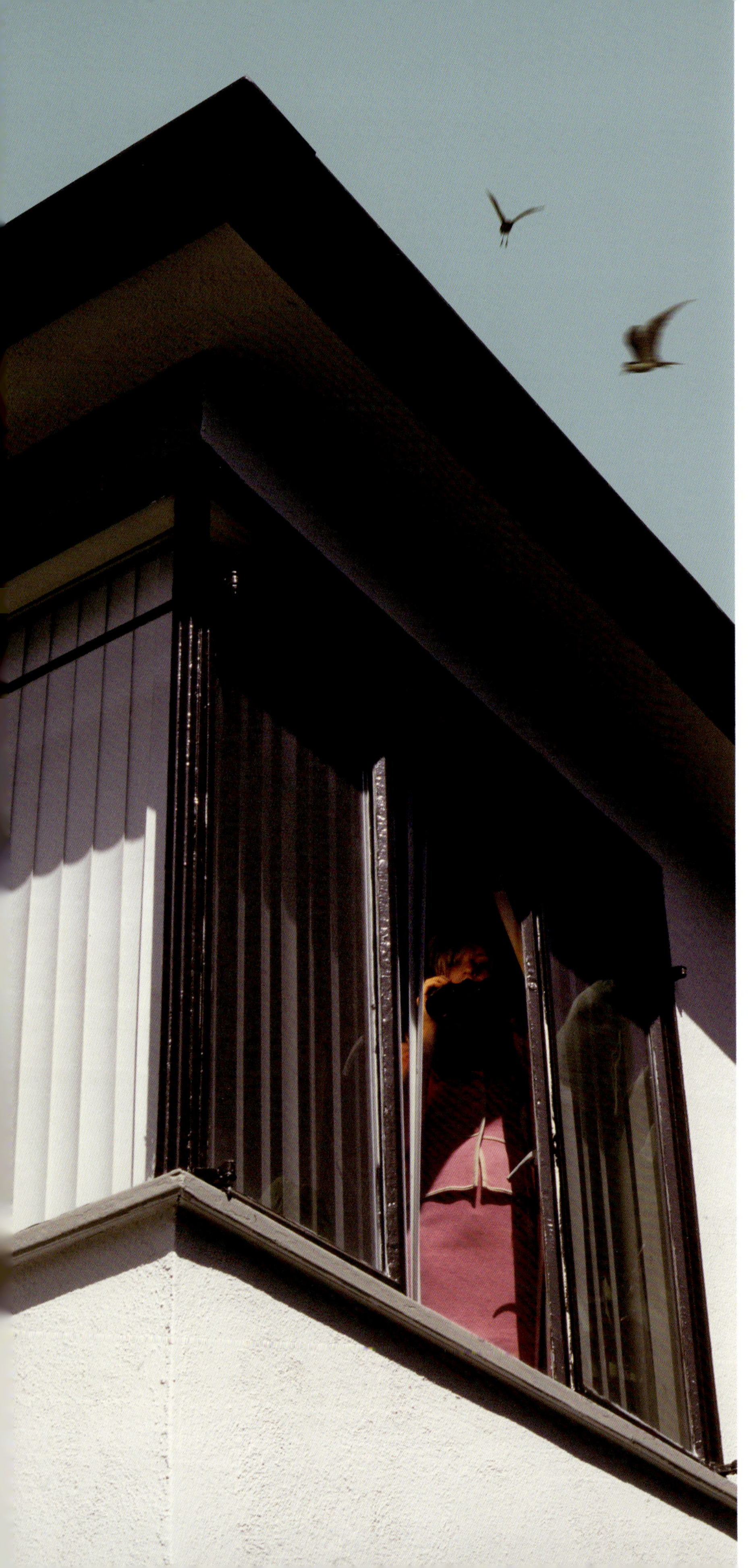

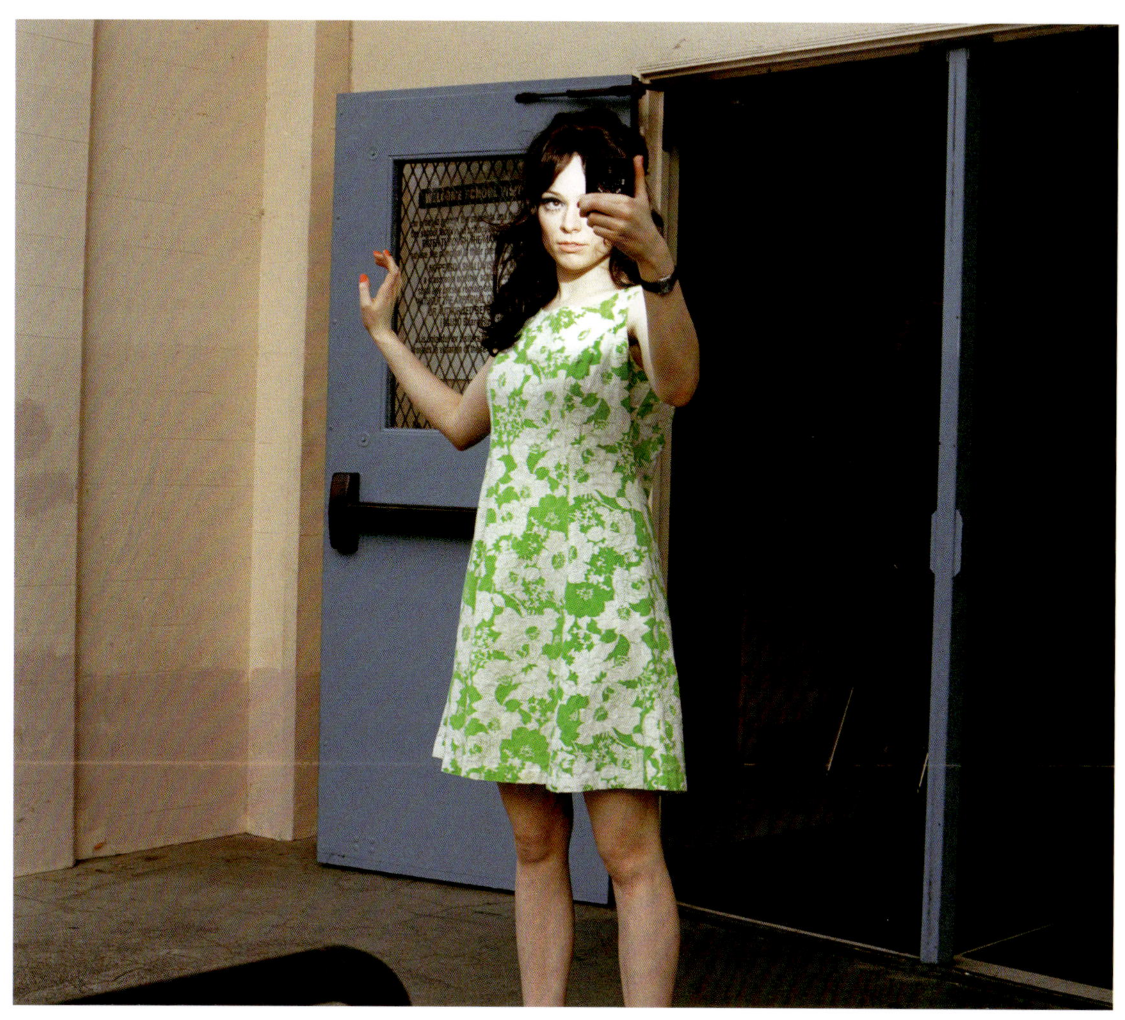

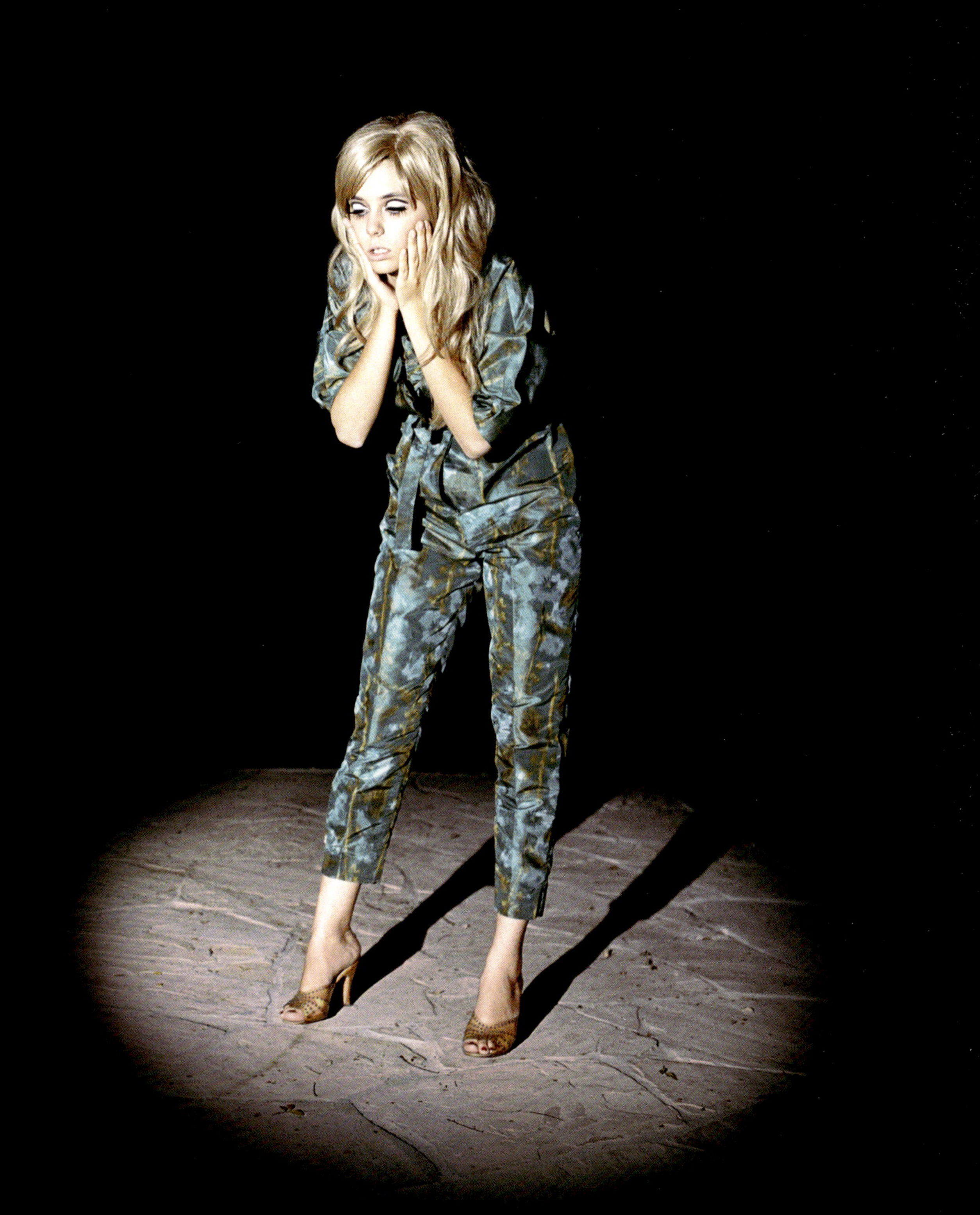

THE BIG VALLEY

(2008)

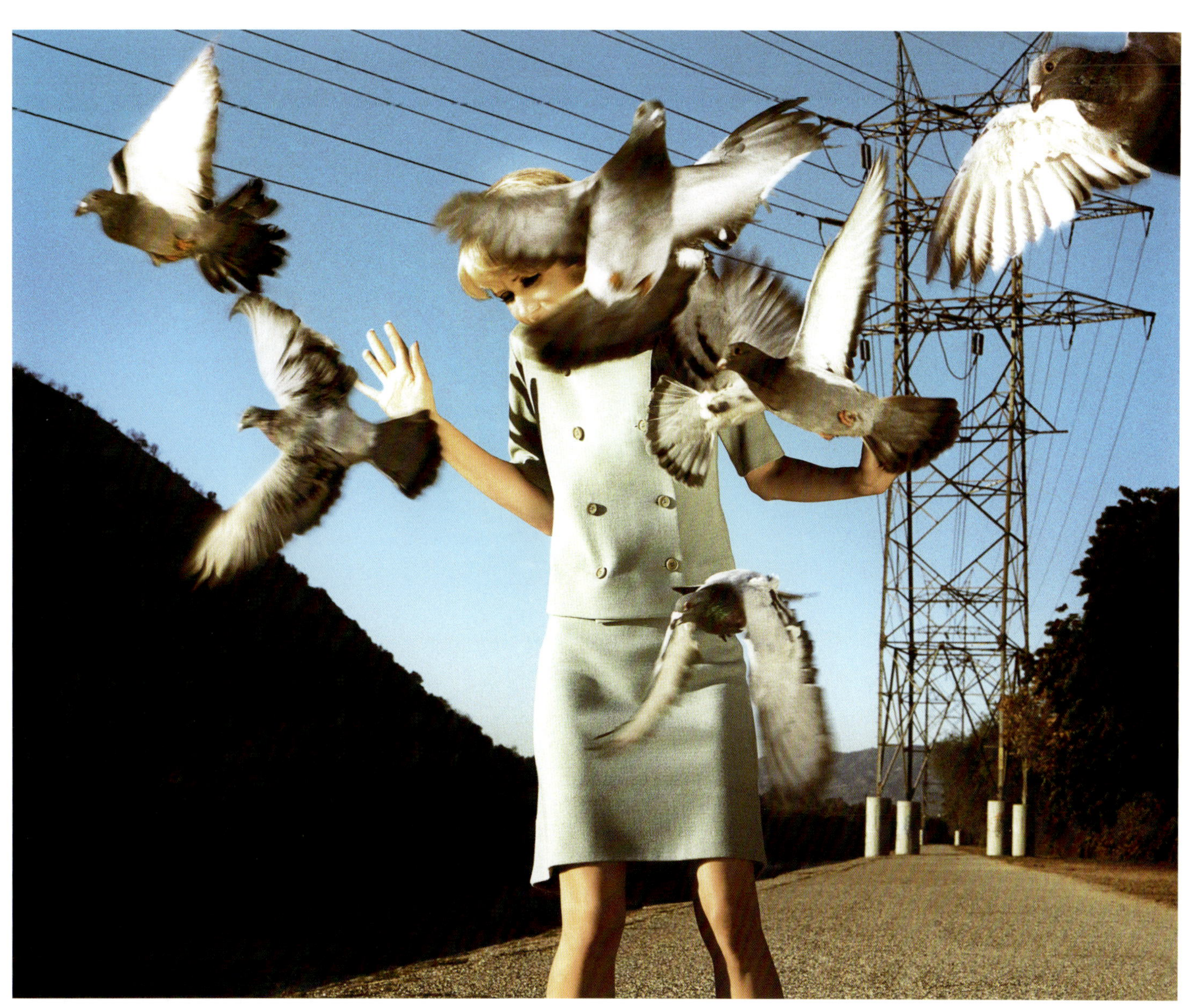

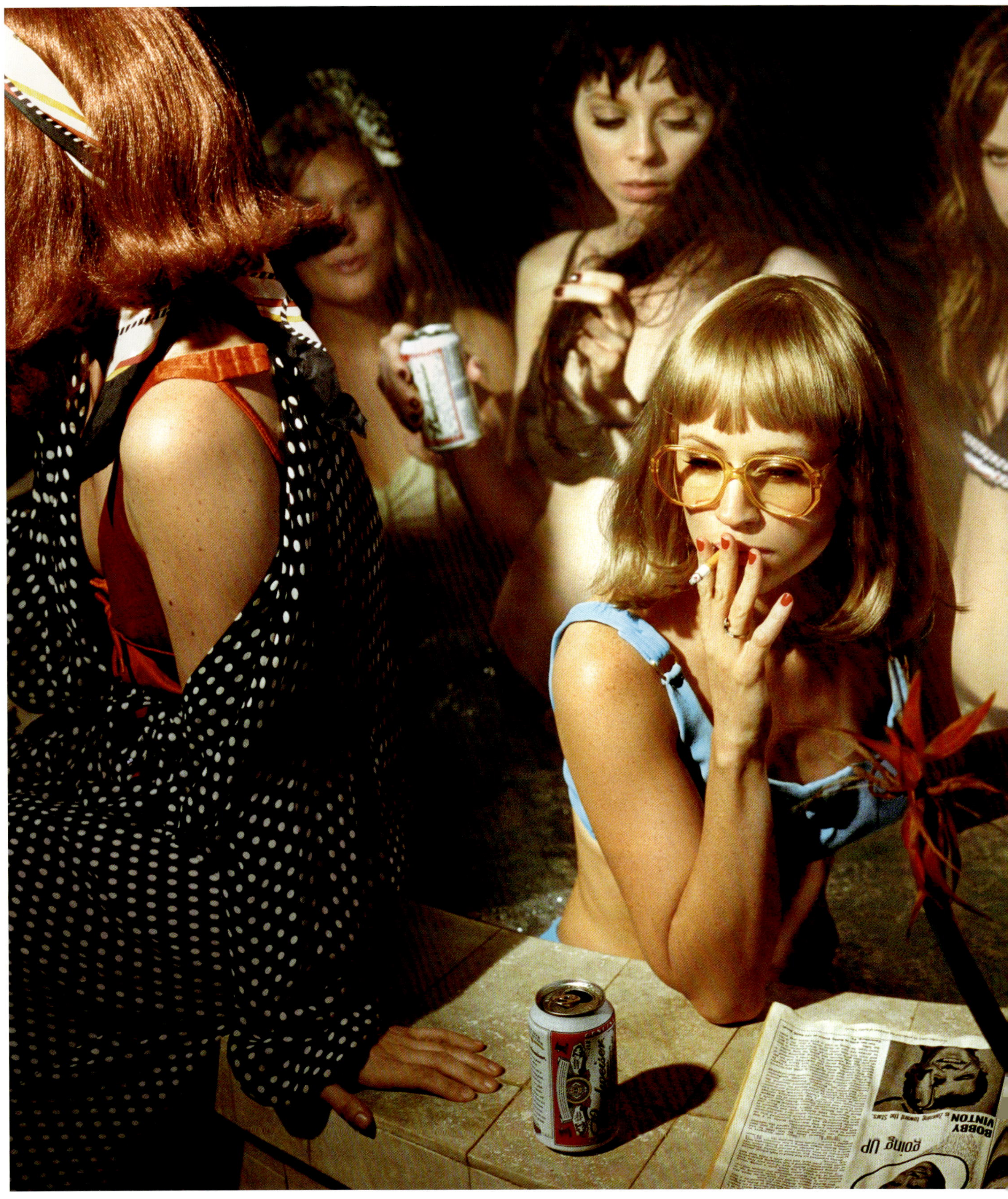
BOBBY VINTON
is zooming toward the stars
going UP

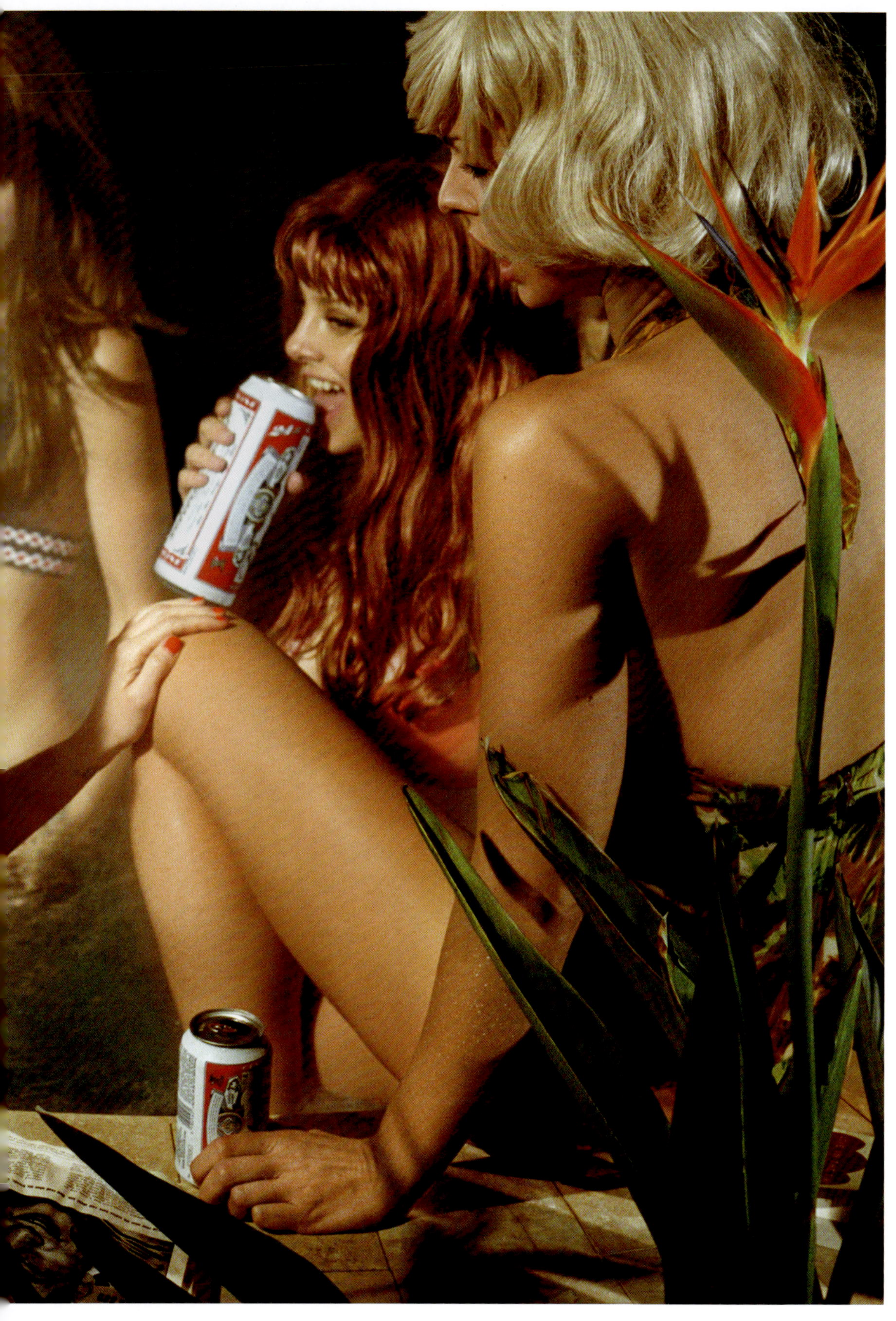

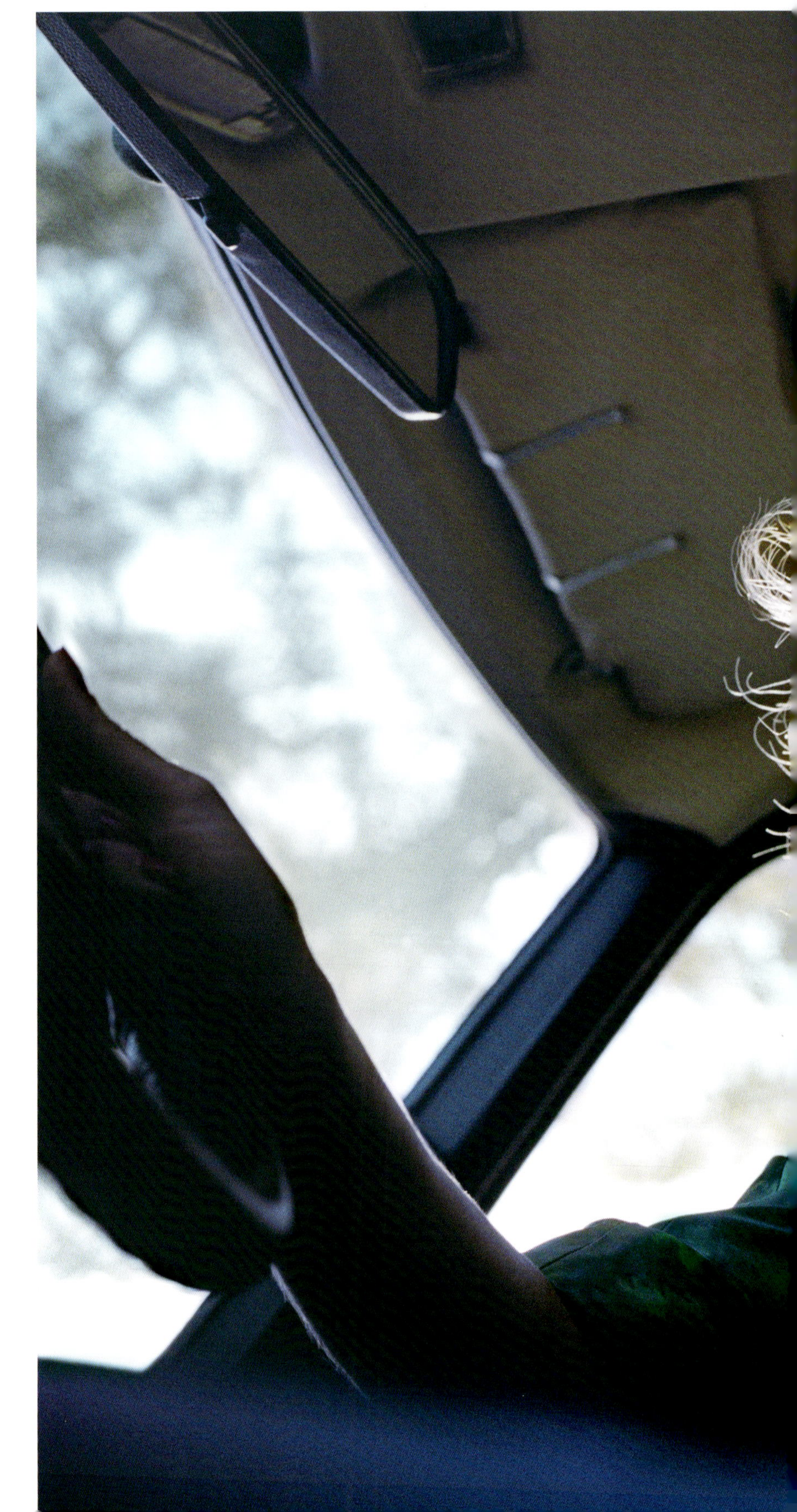

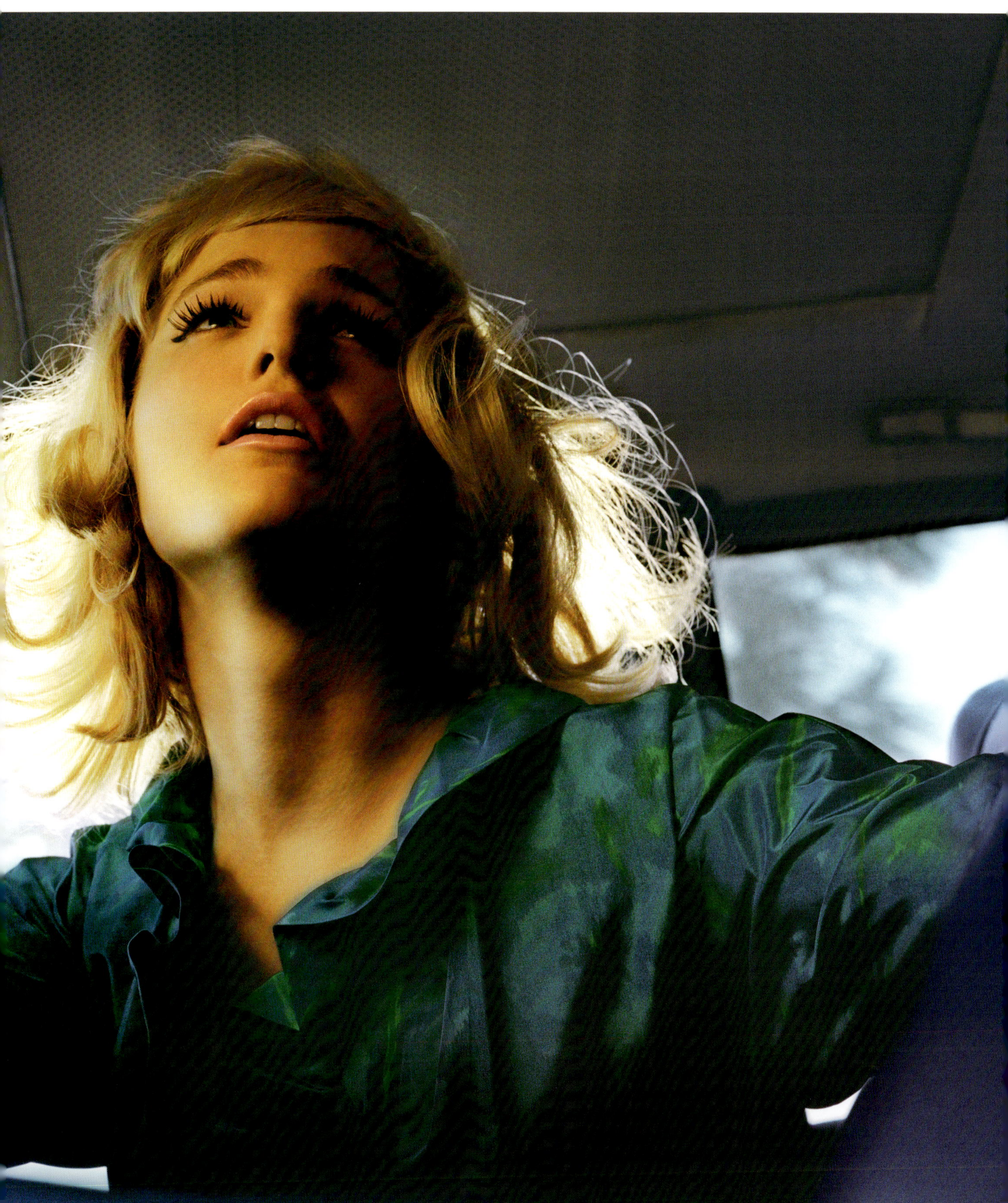

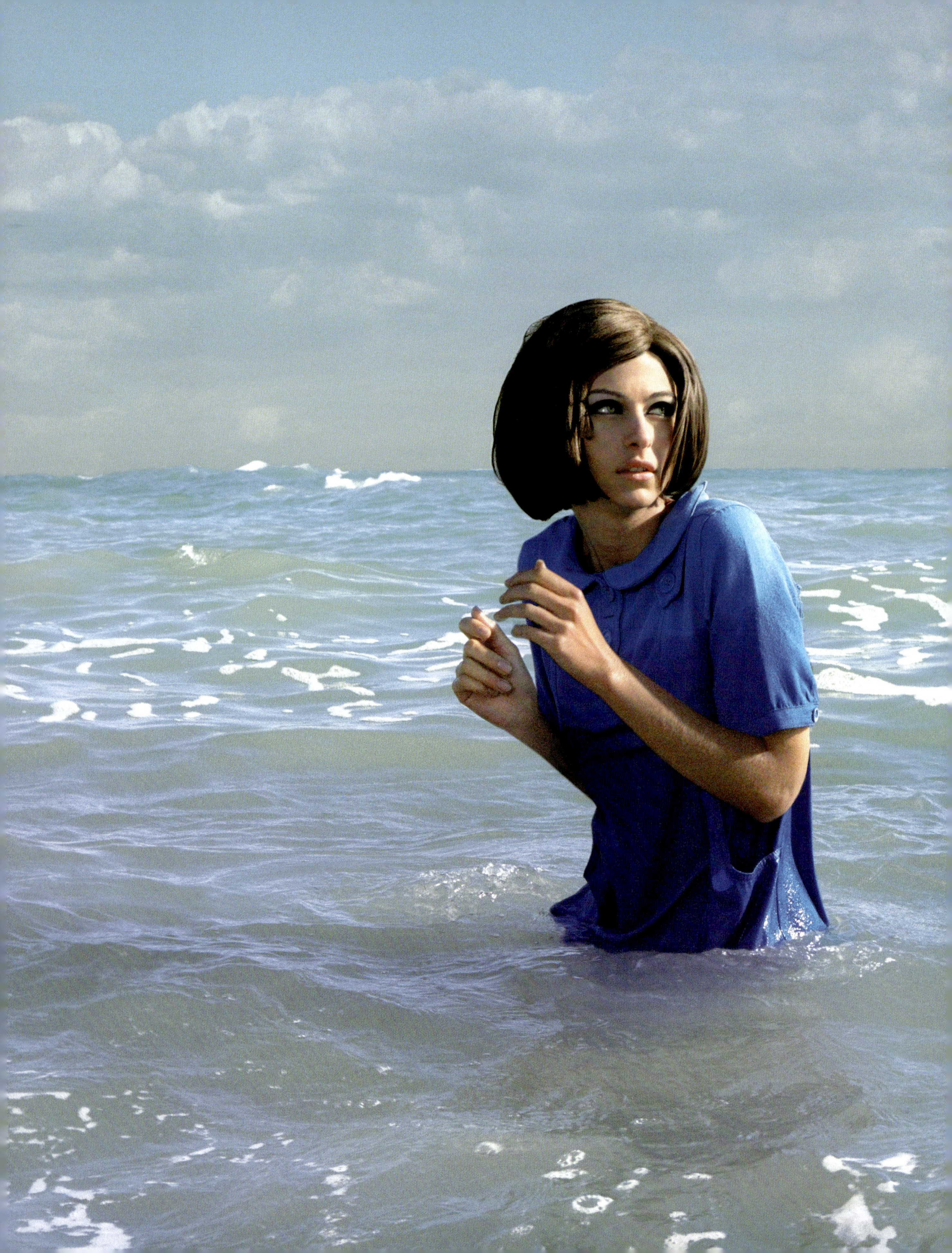

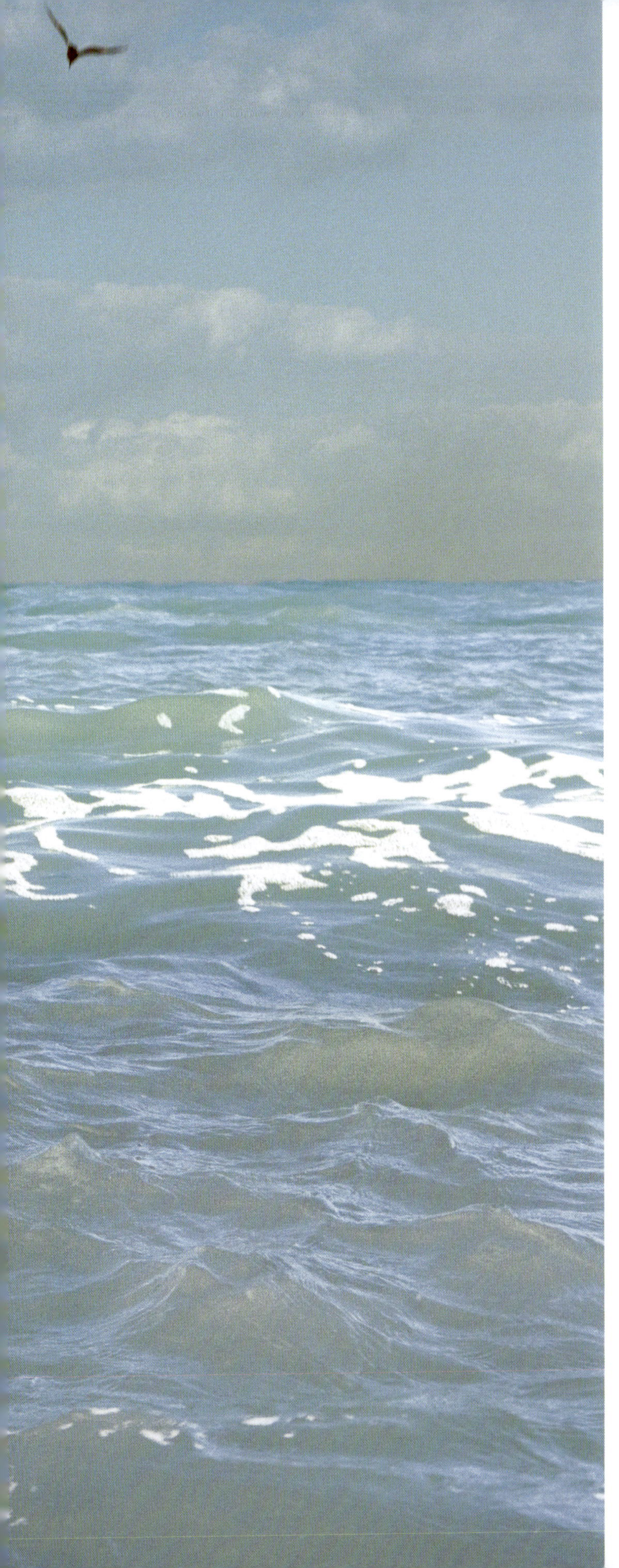

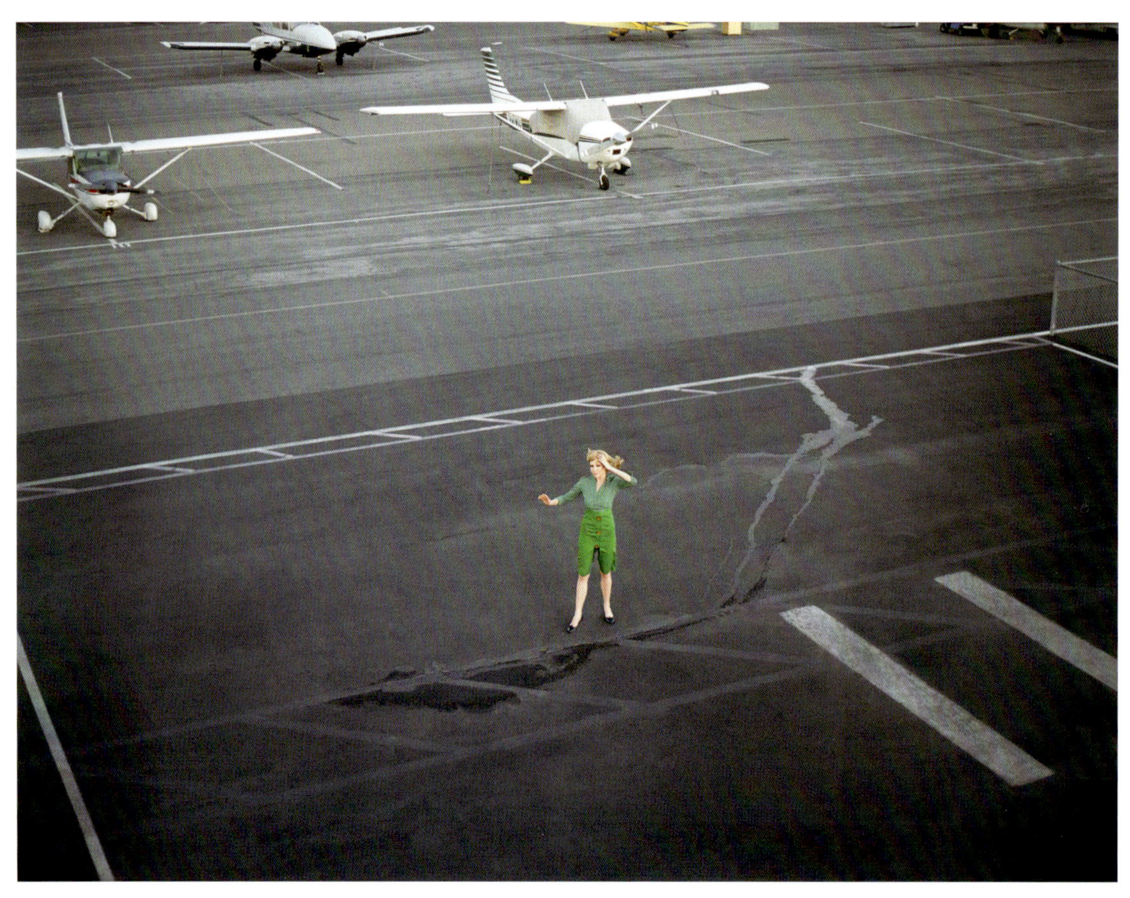

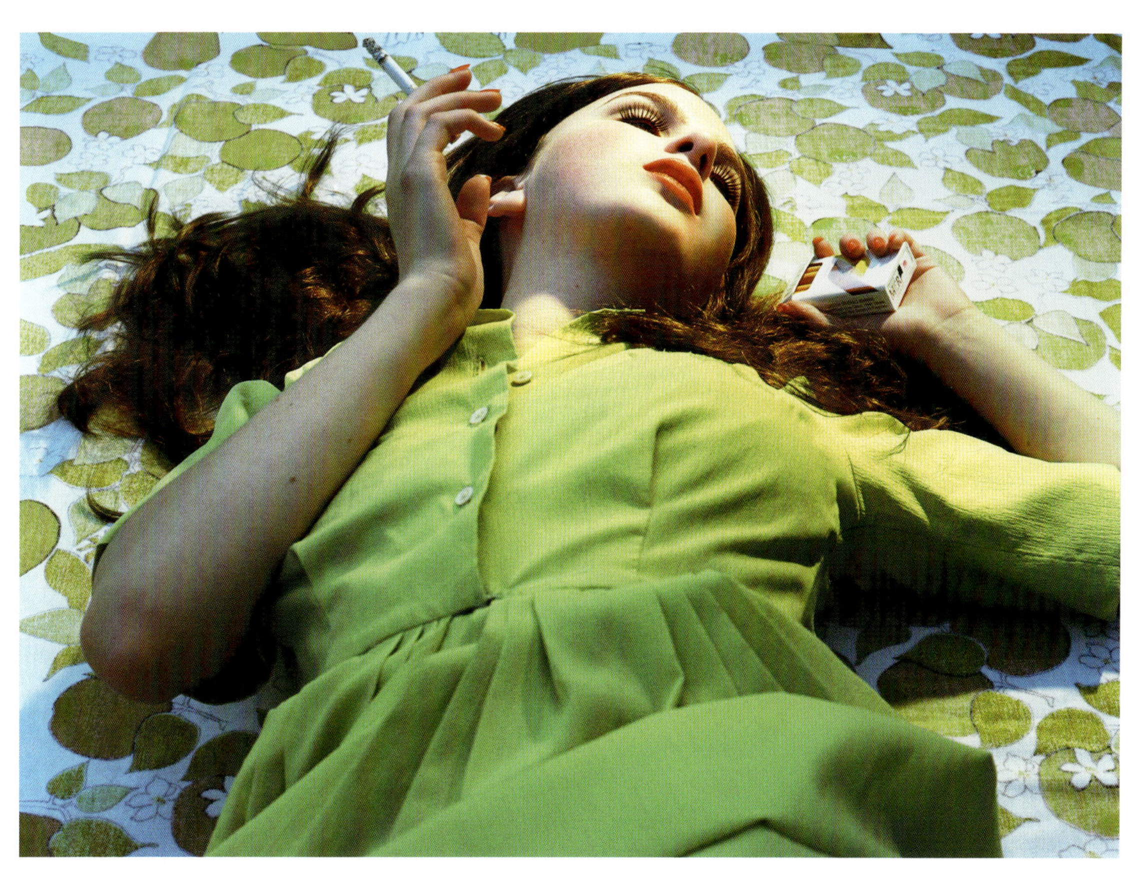

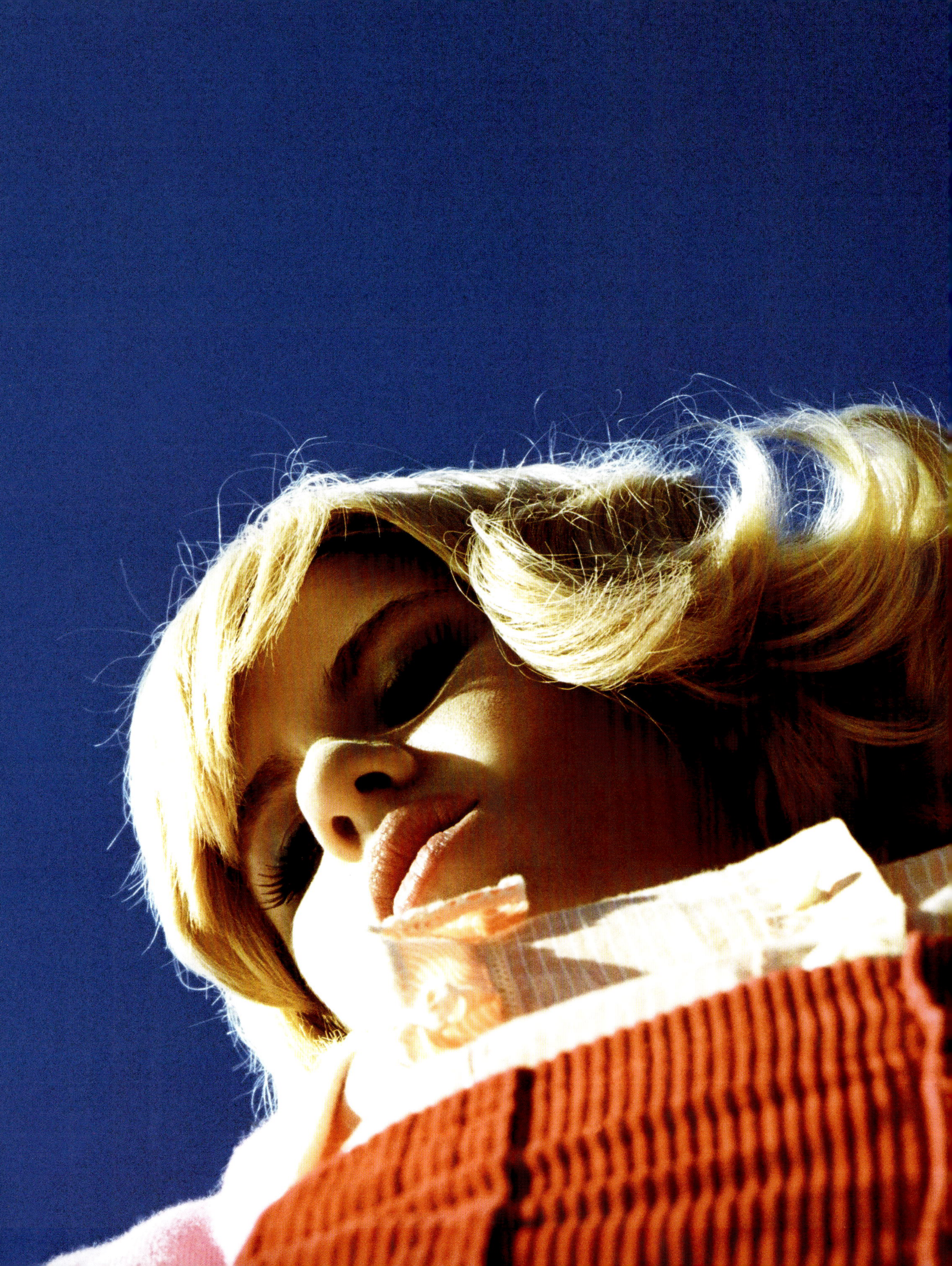

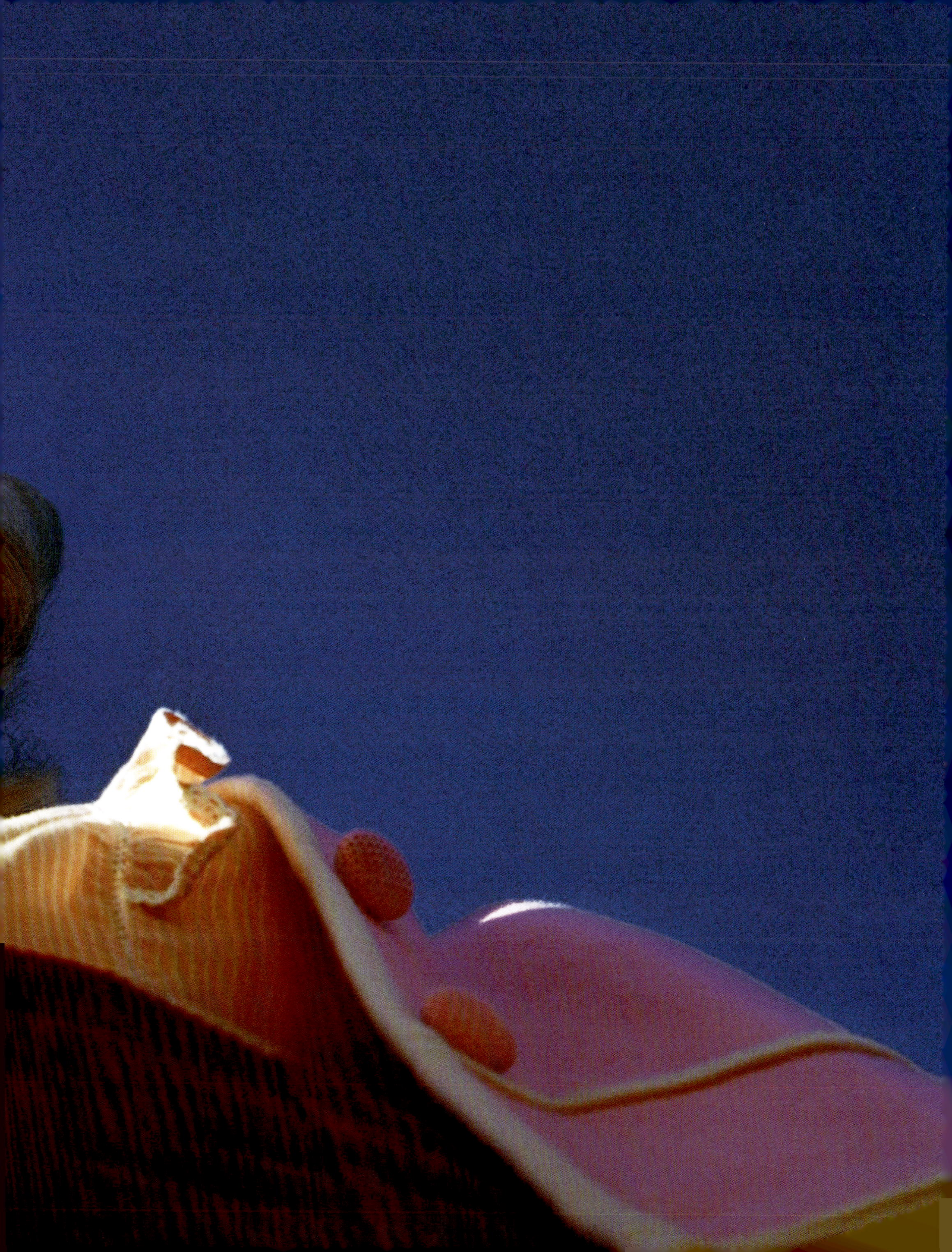

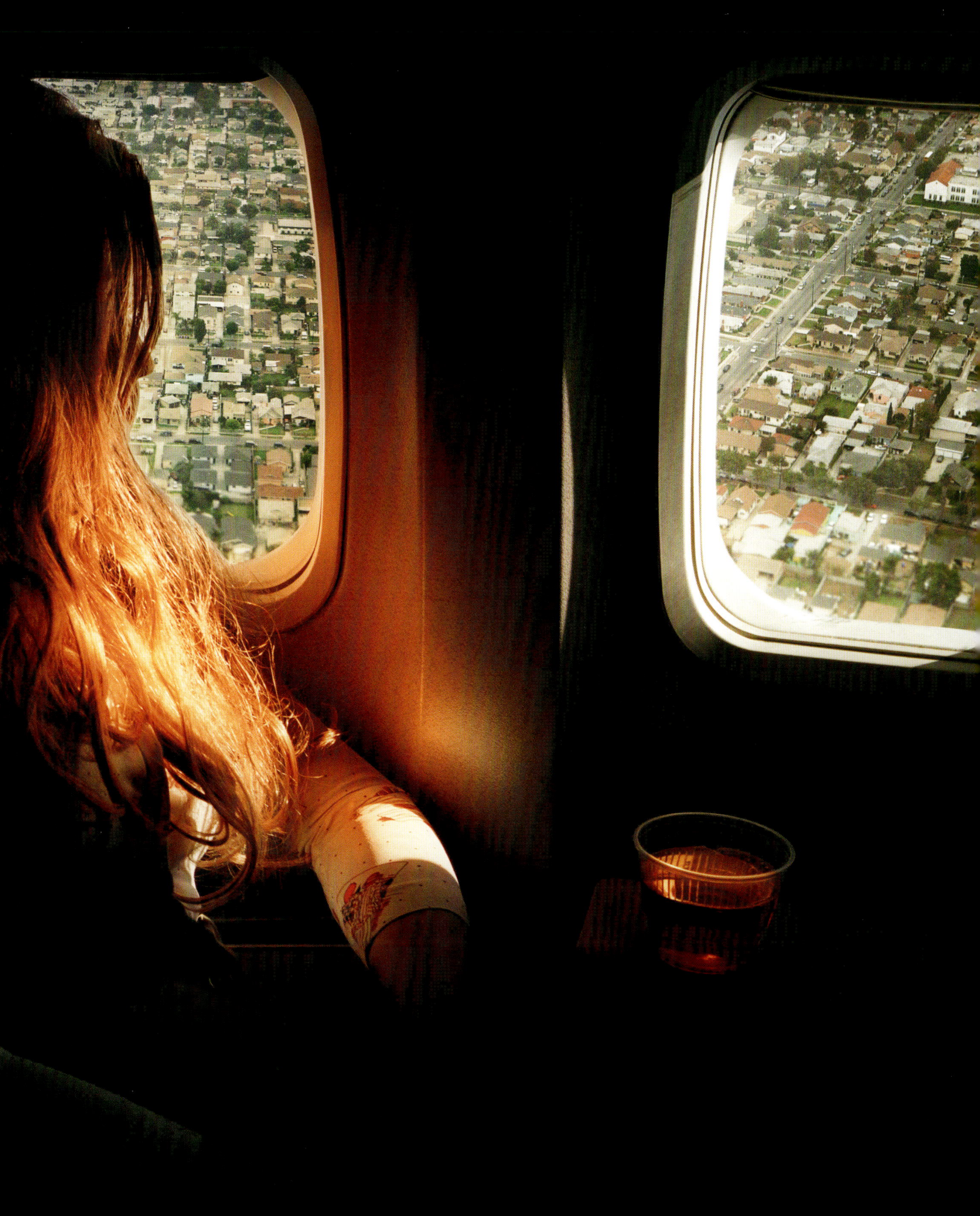

WEEK-END &
THE LONG WEEKEND
(2009—2012)

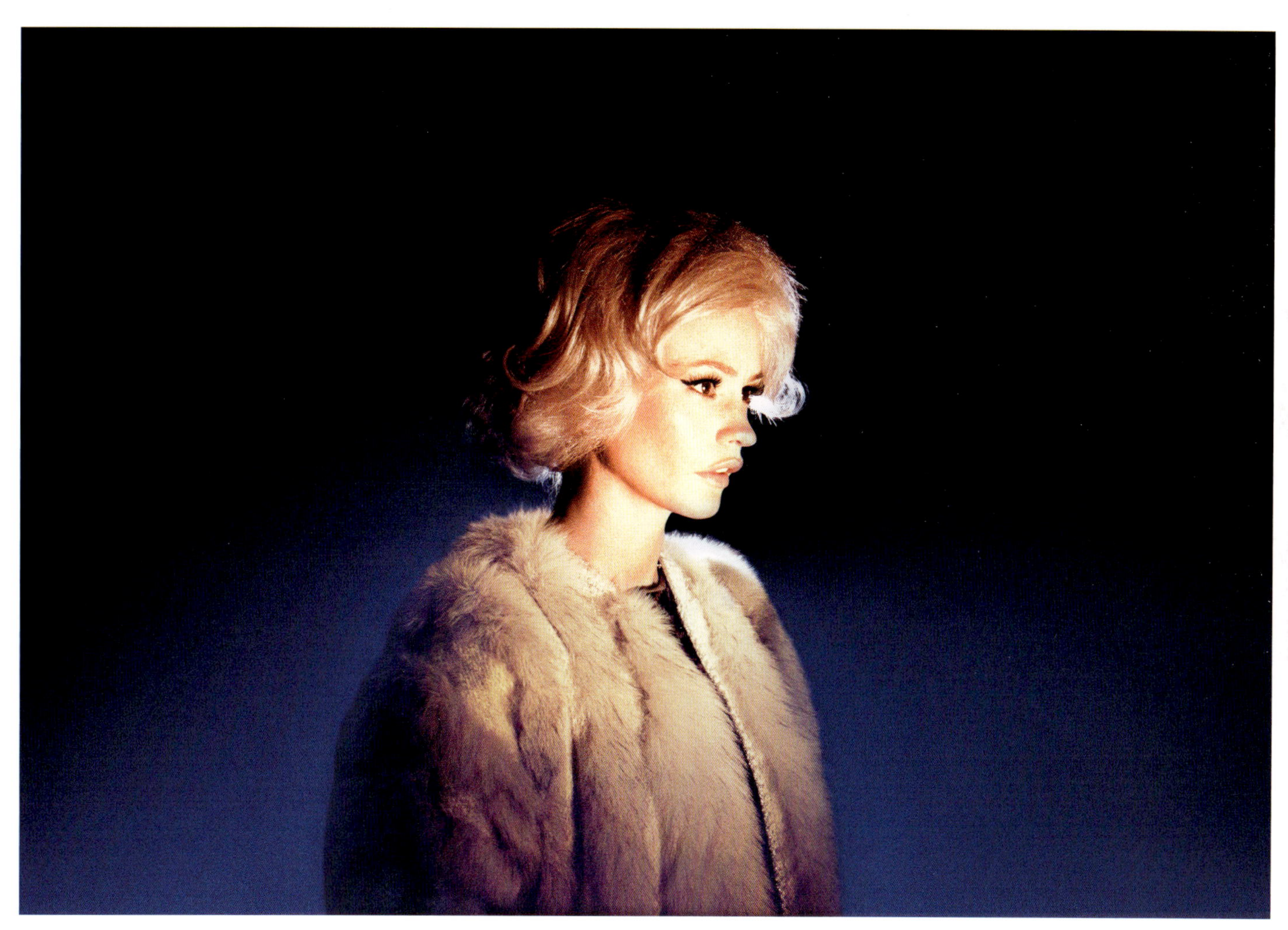

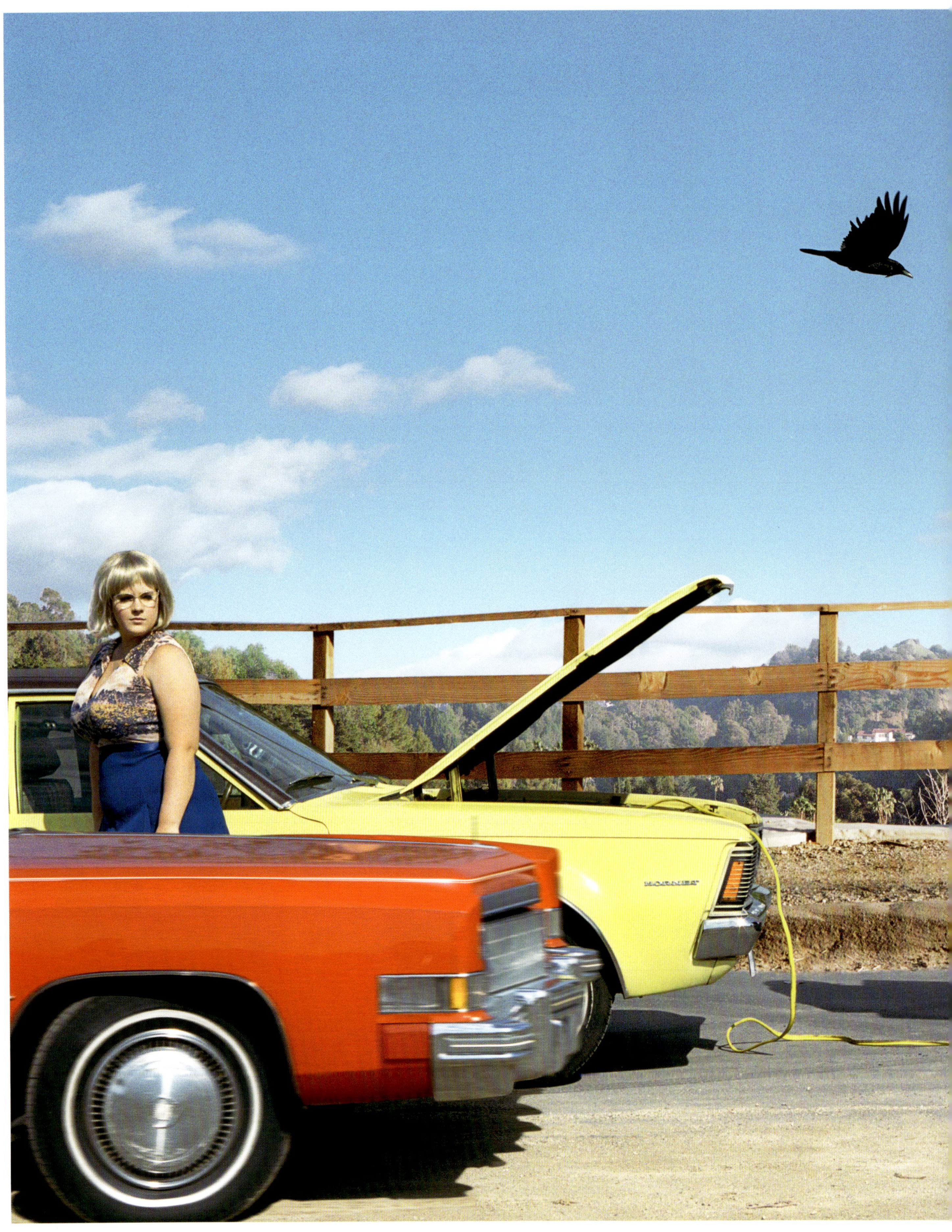

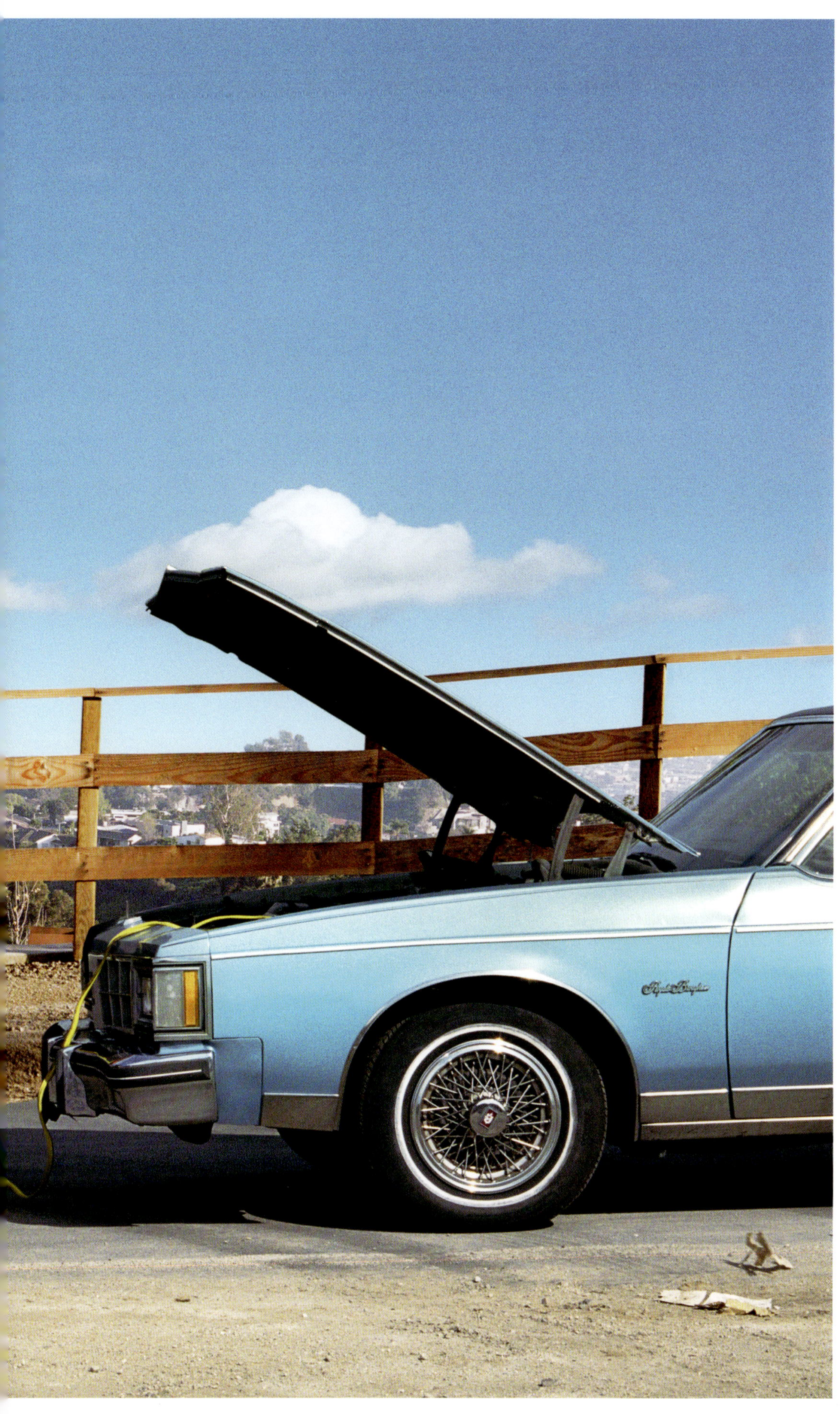

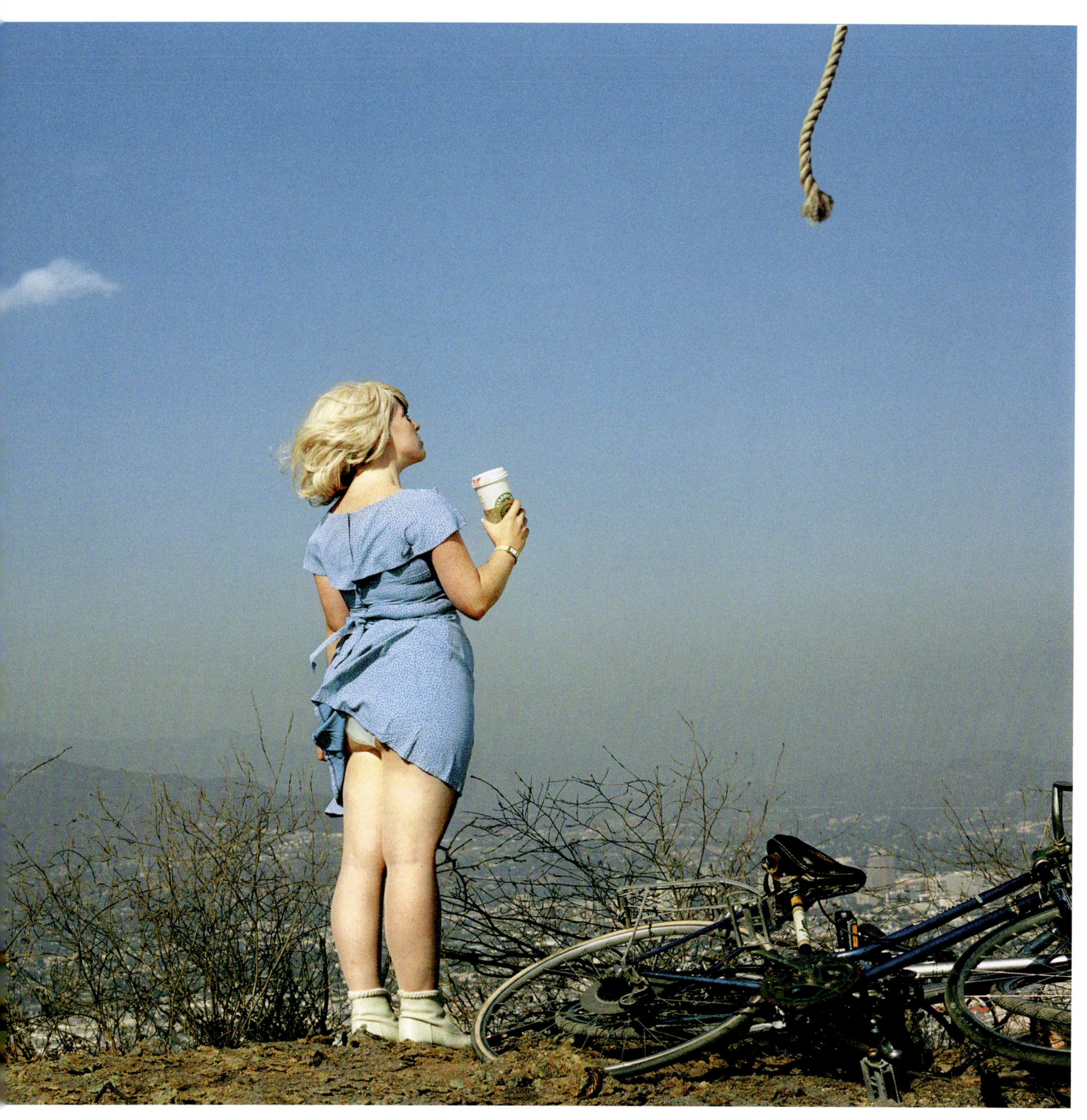

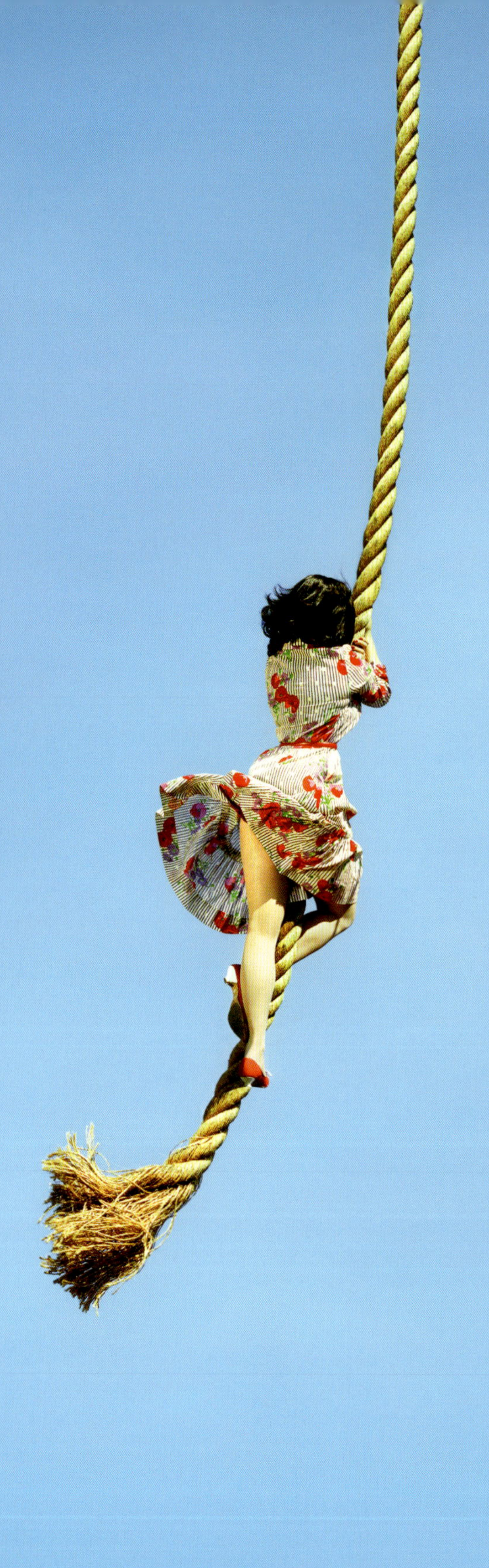

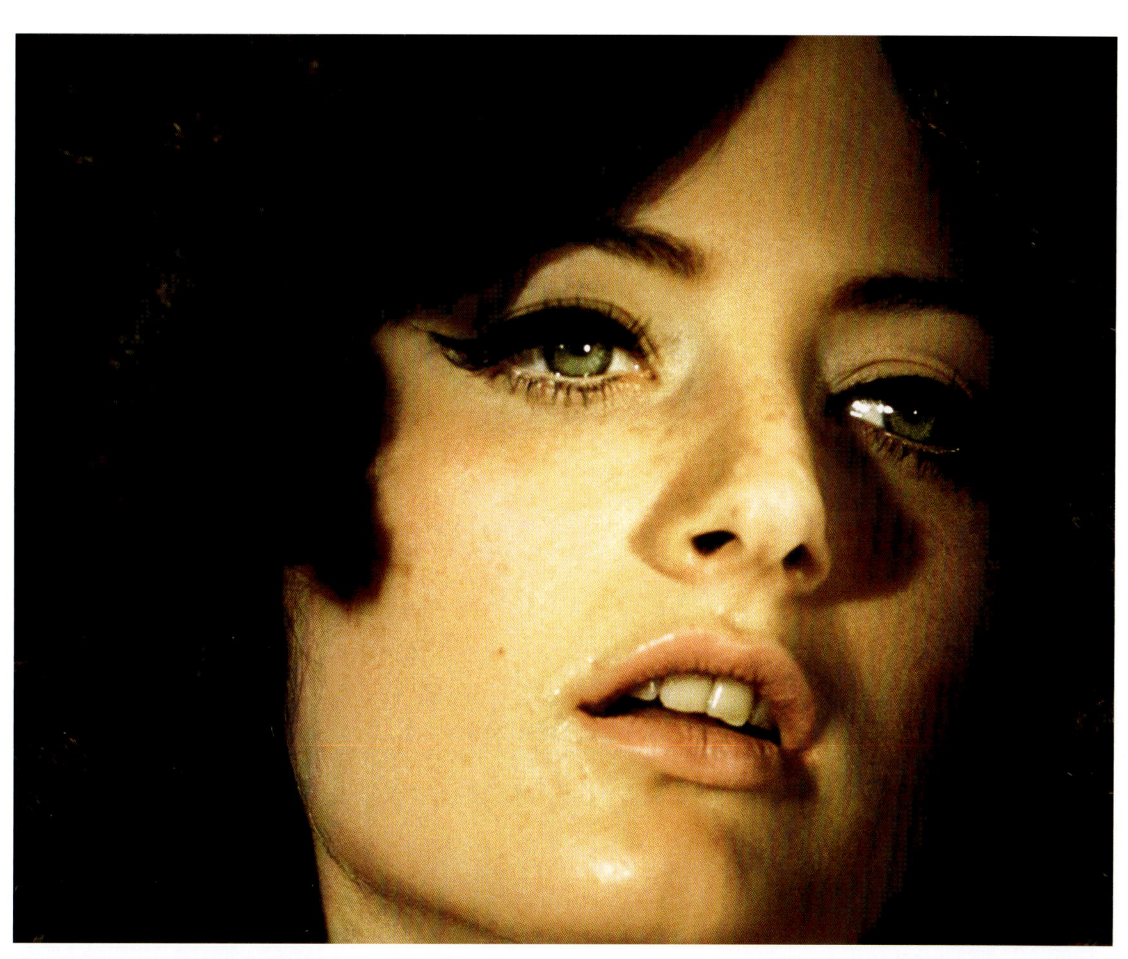

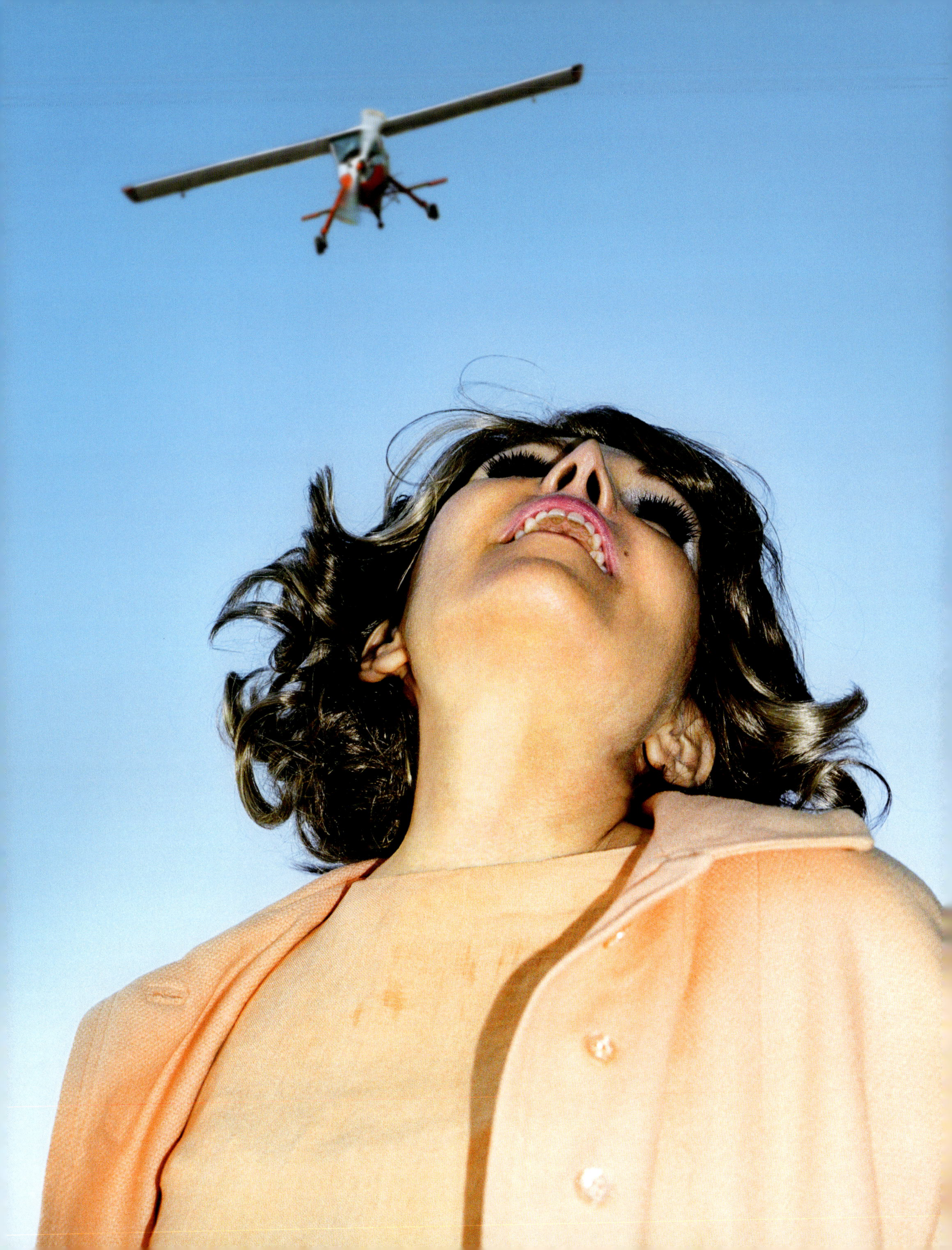

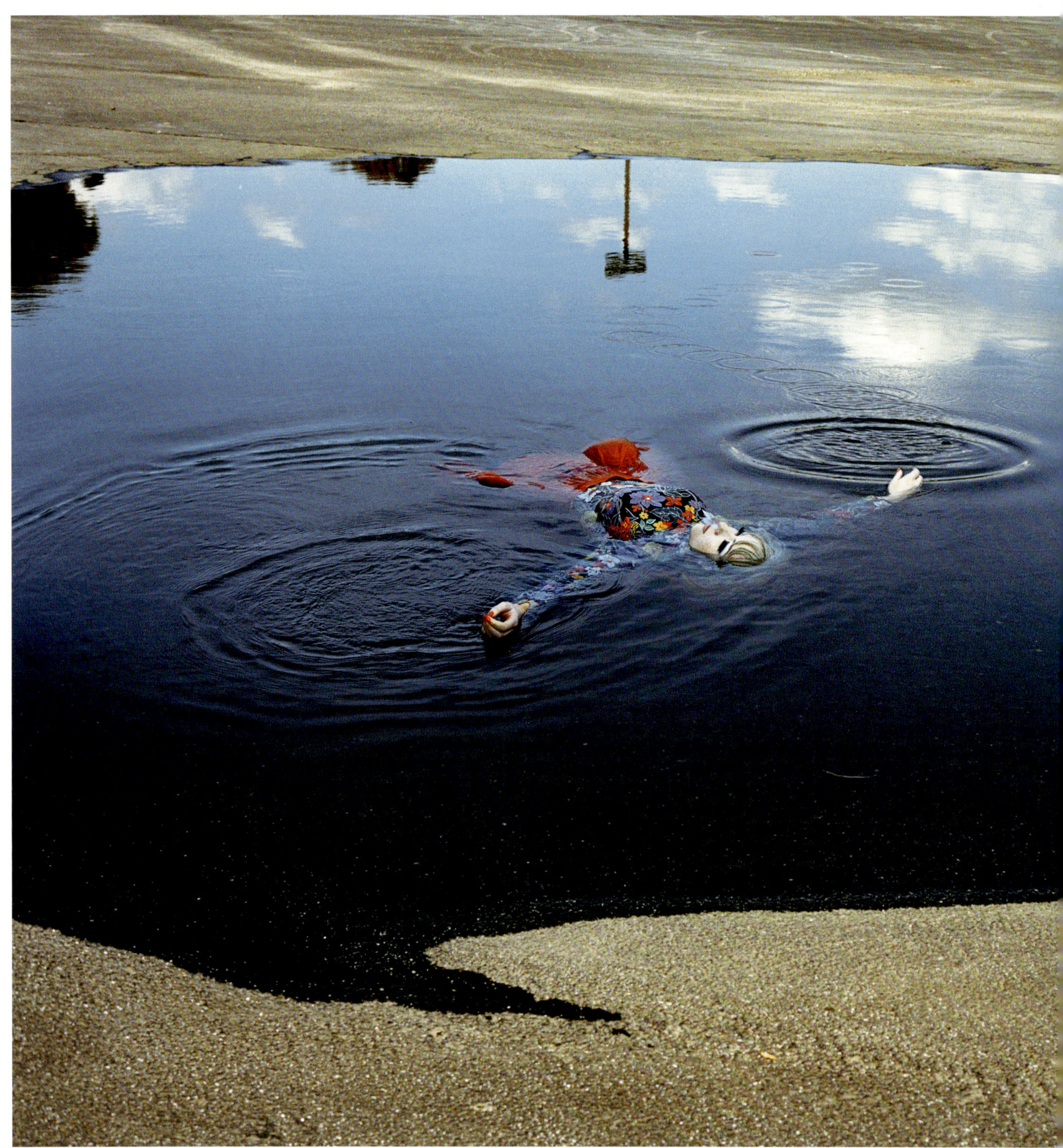

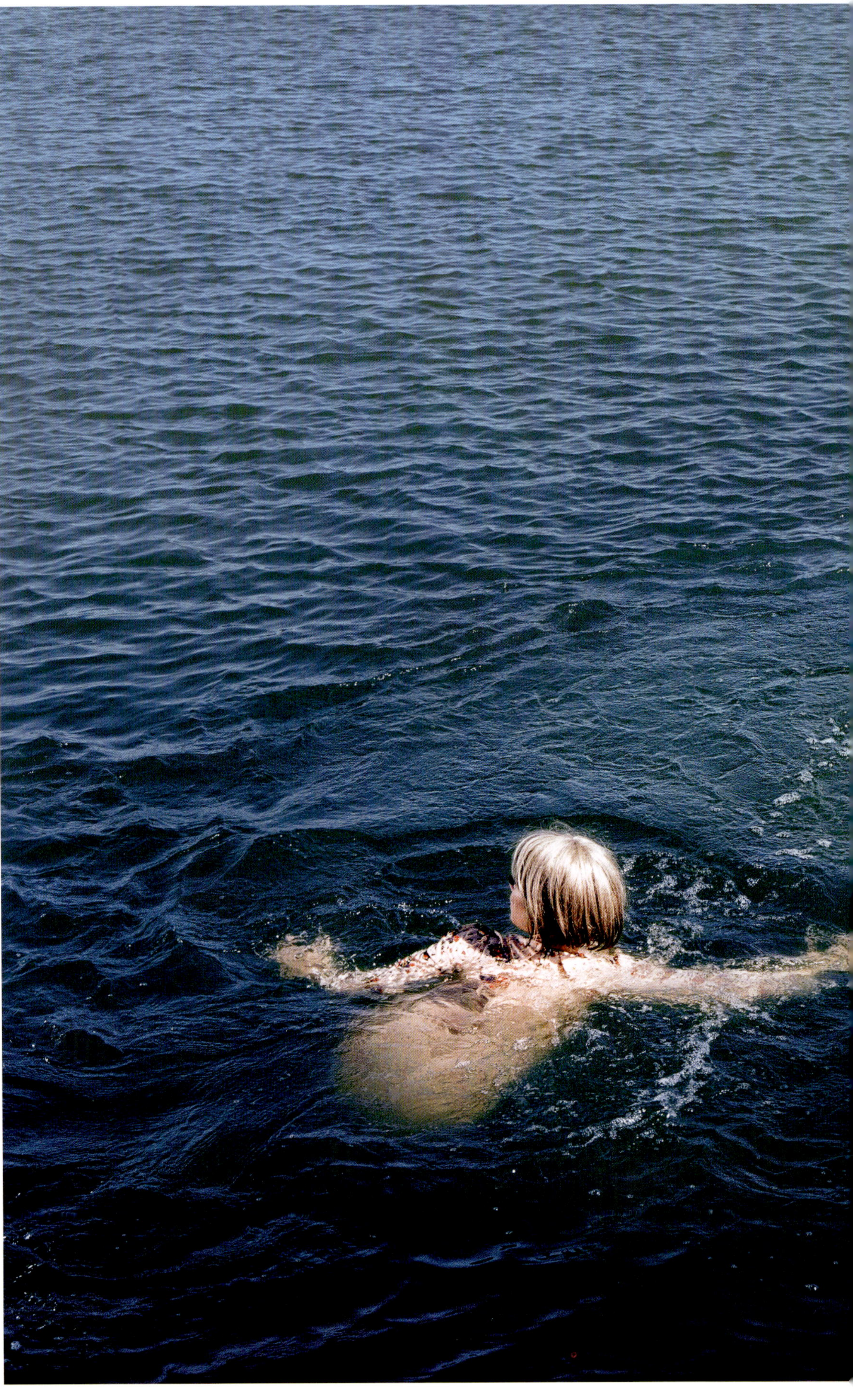

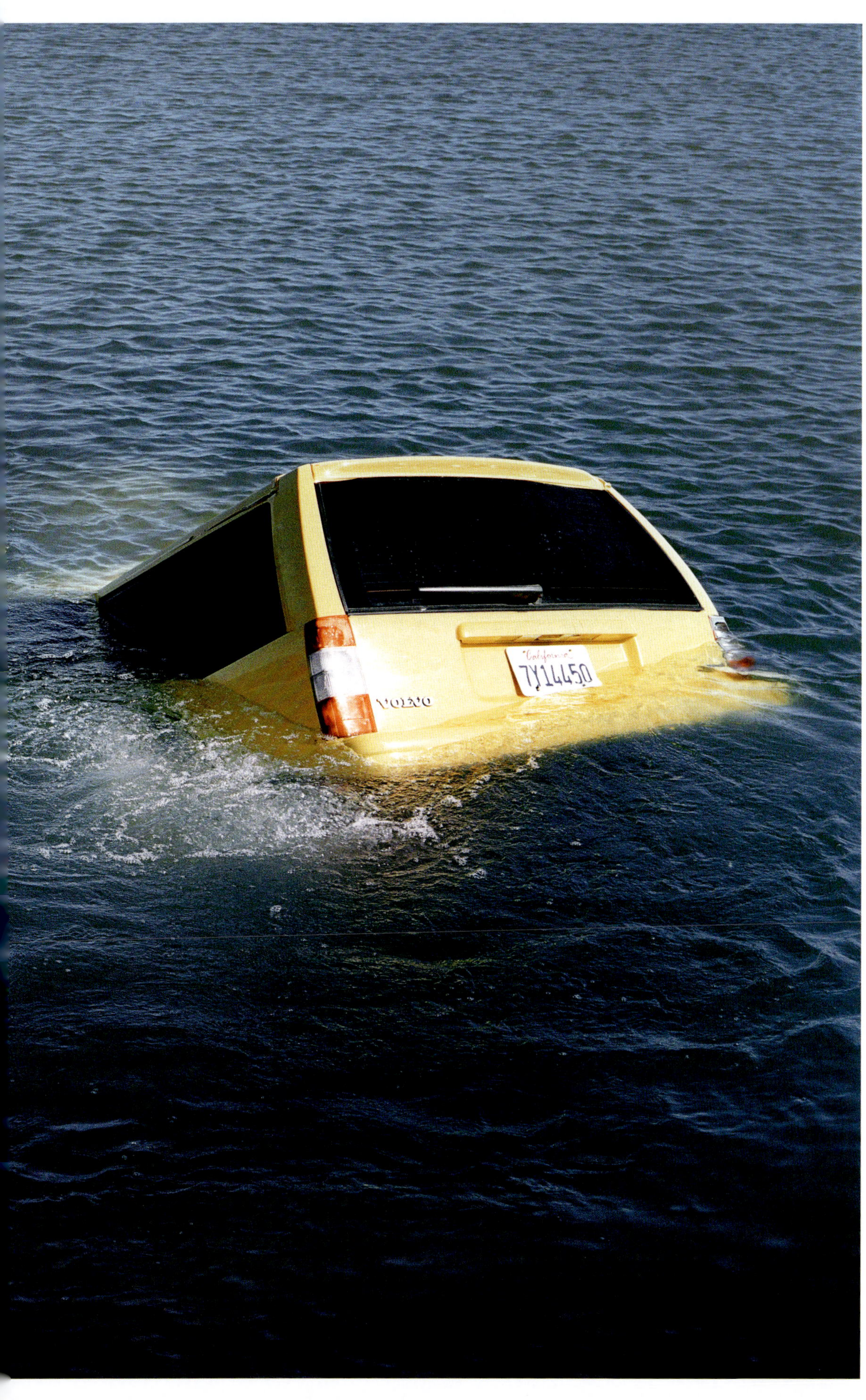
VOLVO
California
7Y14450

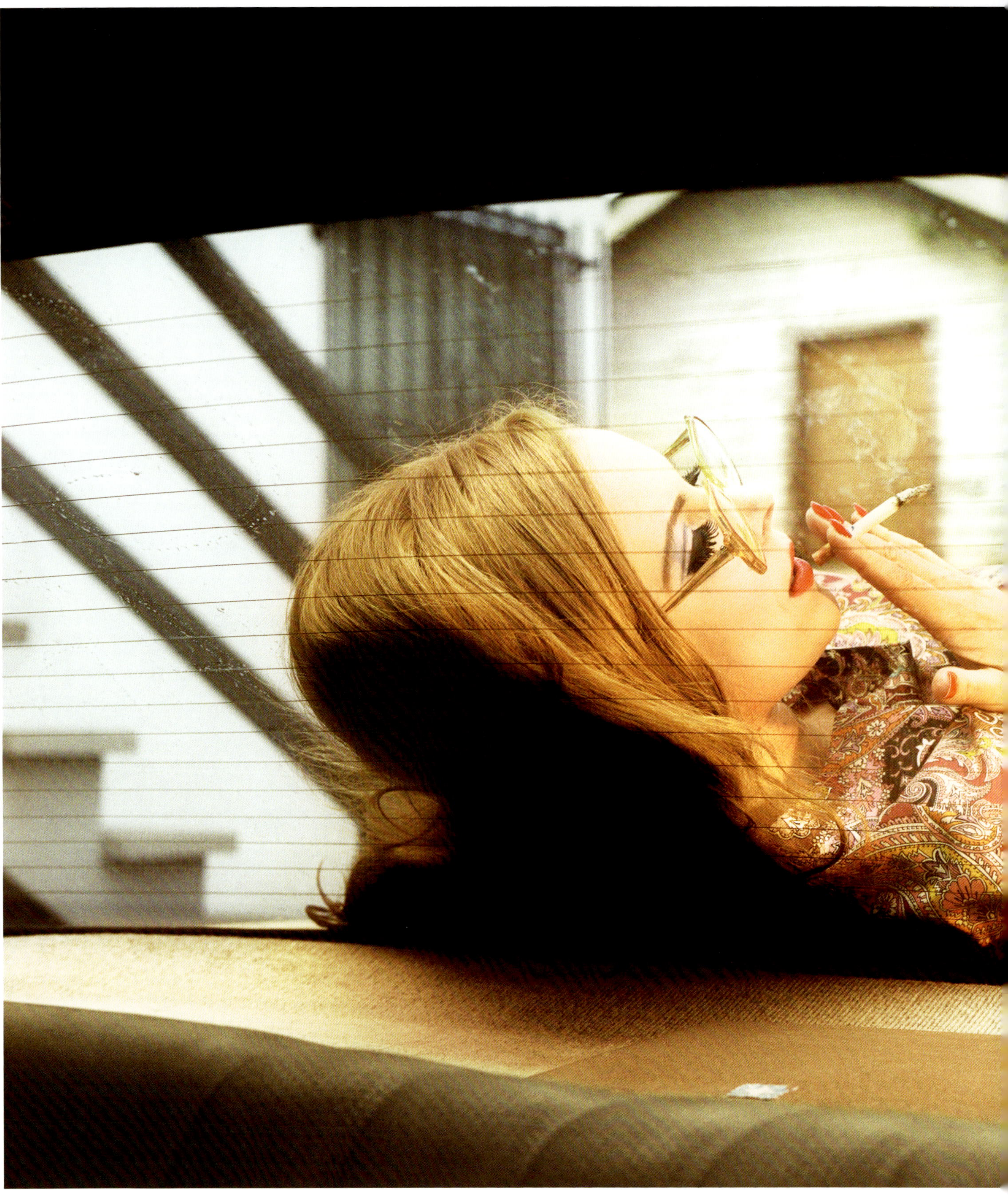

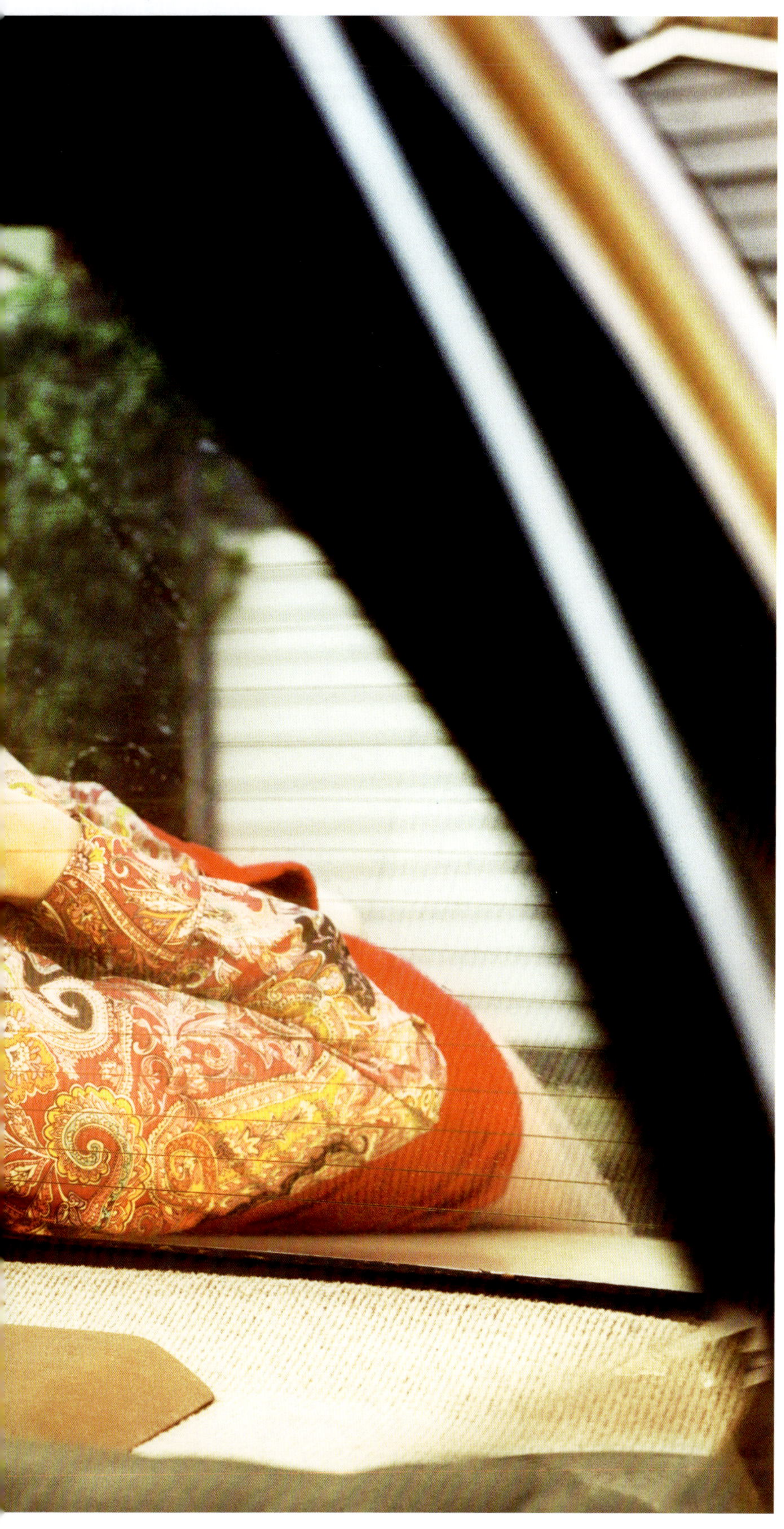

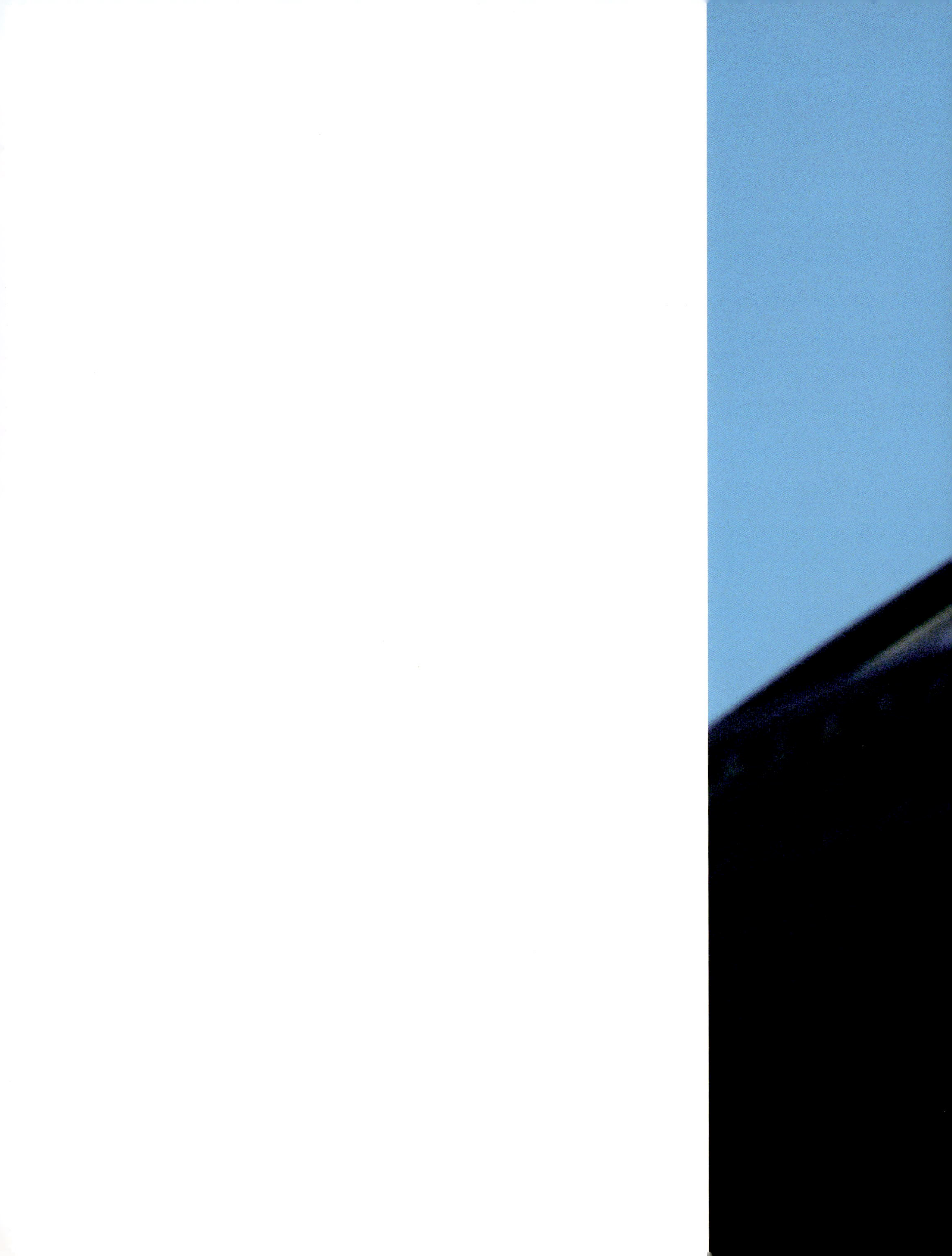

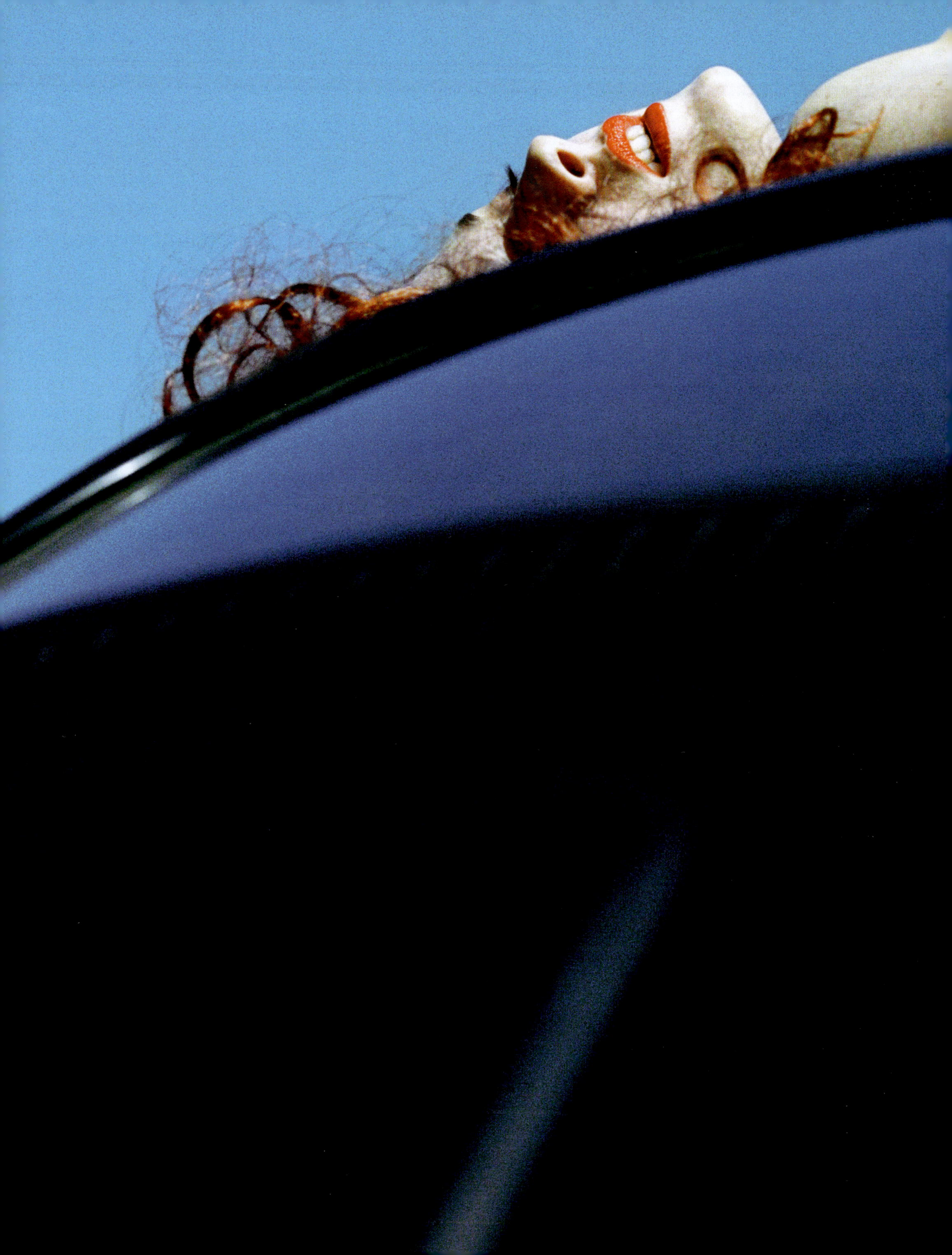

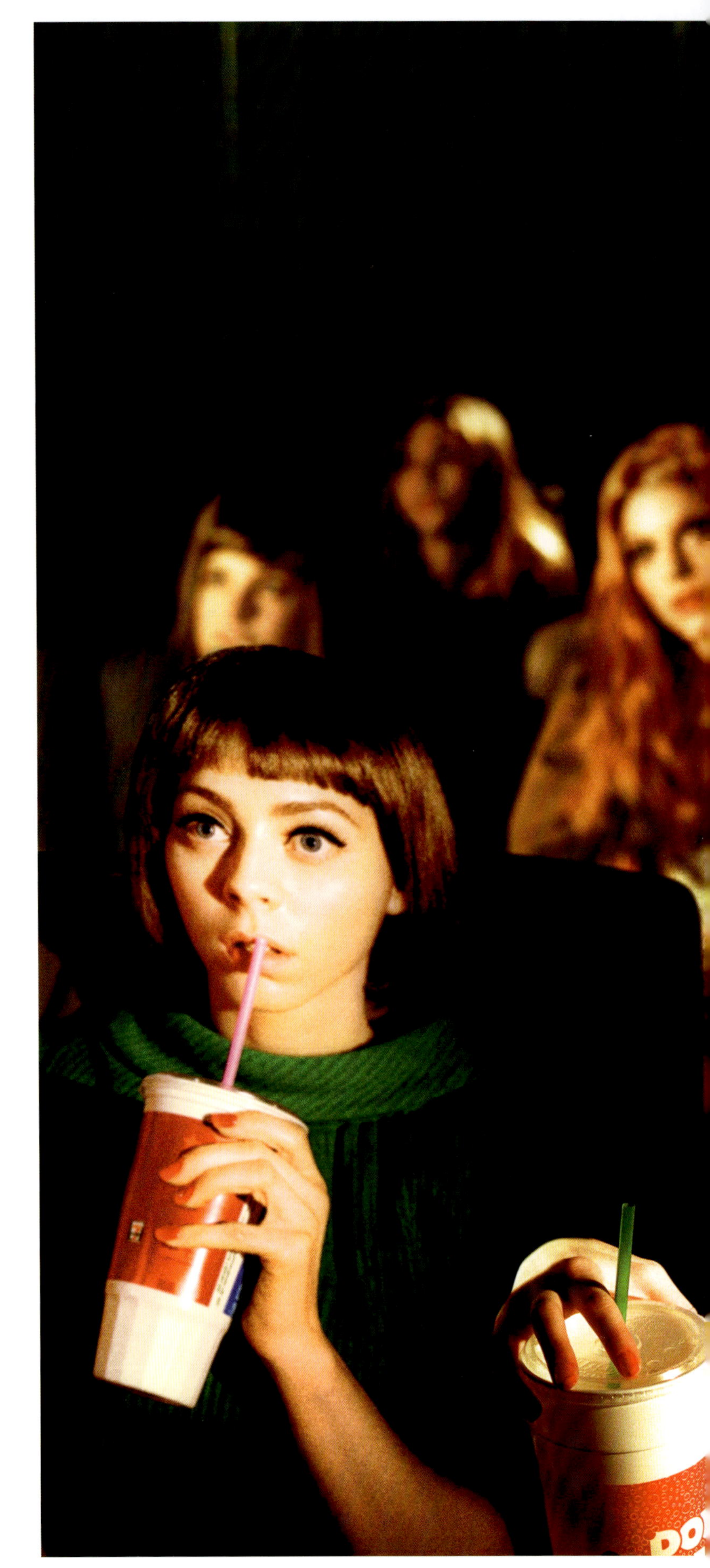

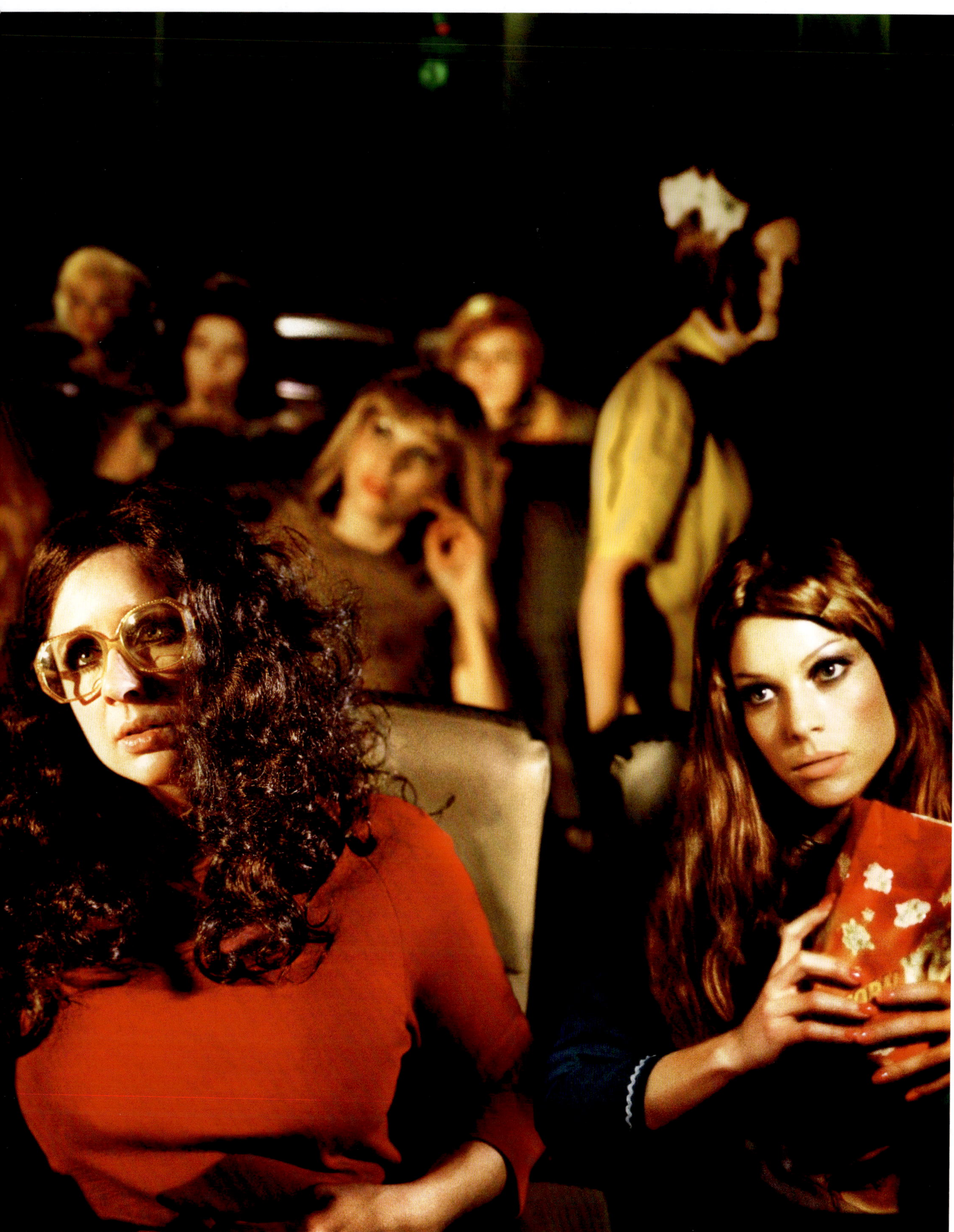

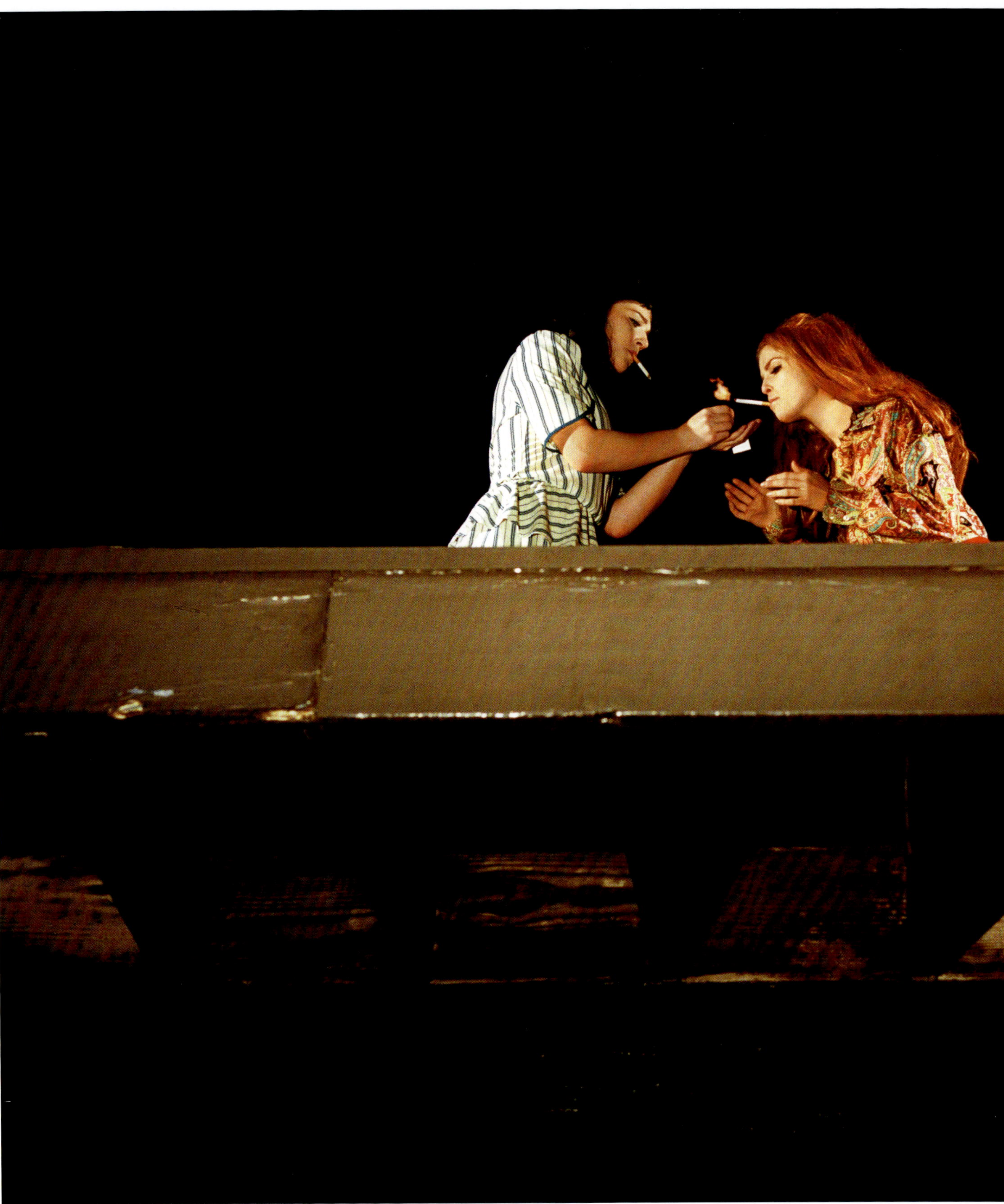

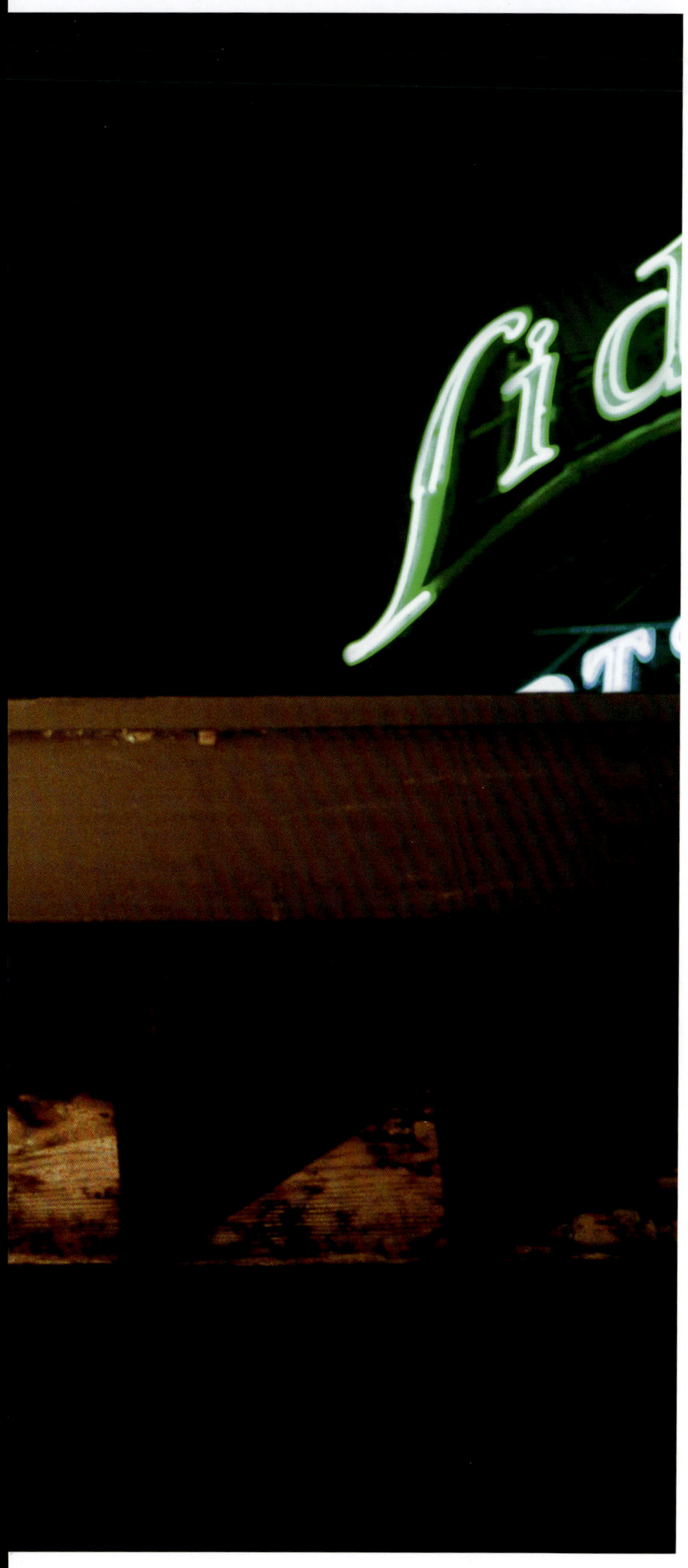

Lid

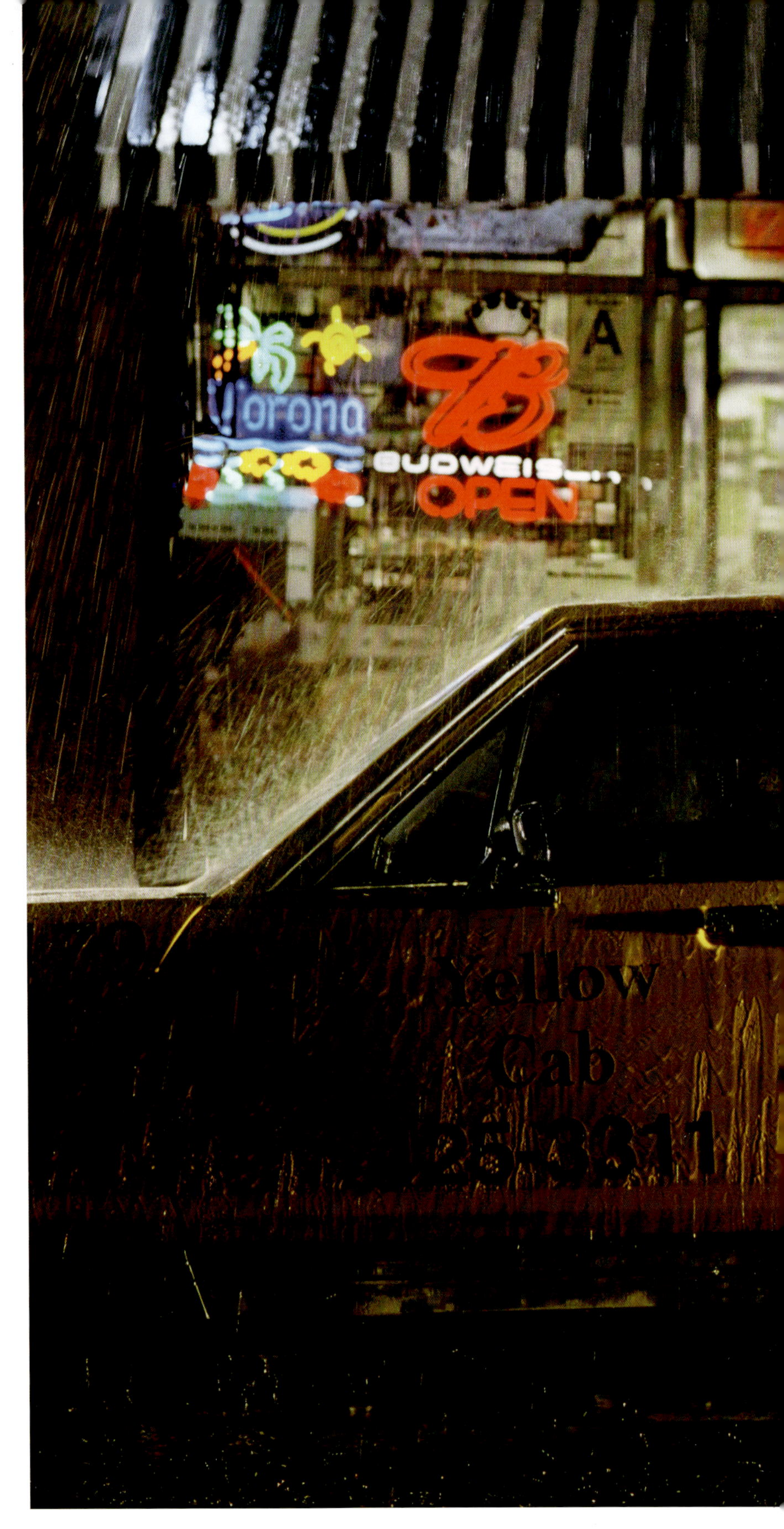
orona
Budweis
OPEN
A
Yellow
Cab

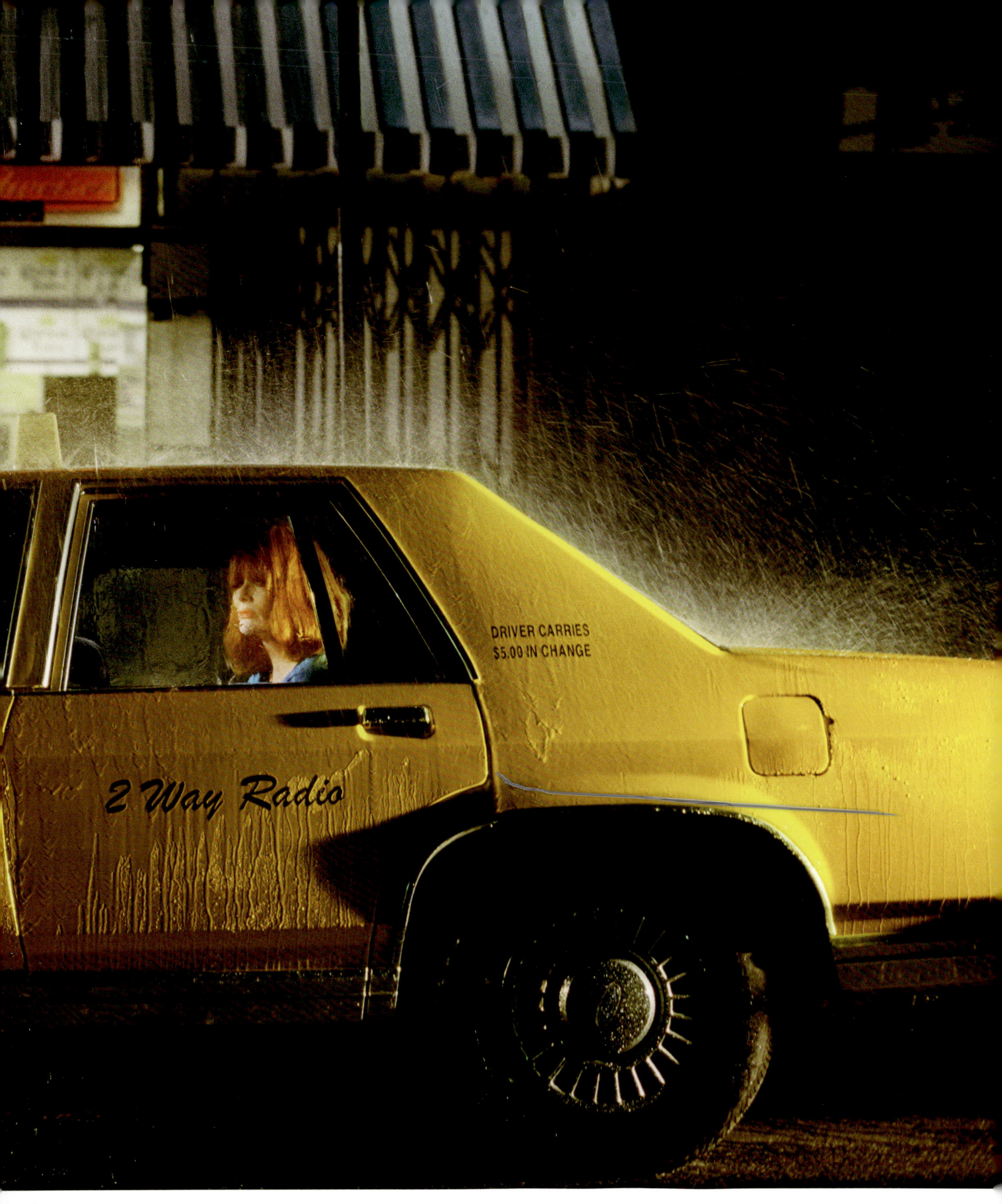
DRIVER CARRIES
$5.00 IN CHANGE
2 Way Radio

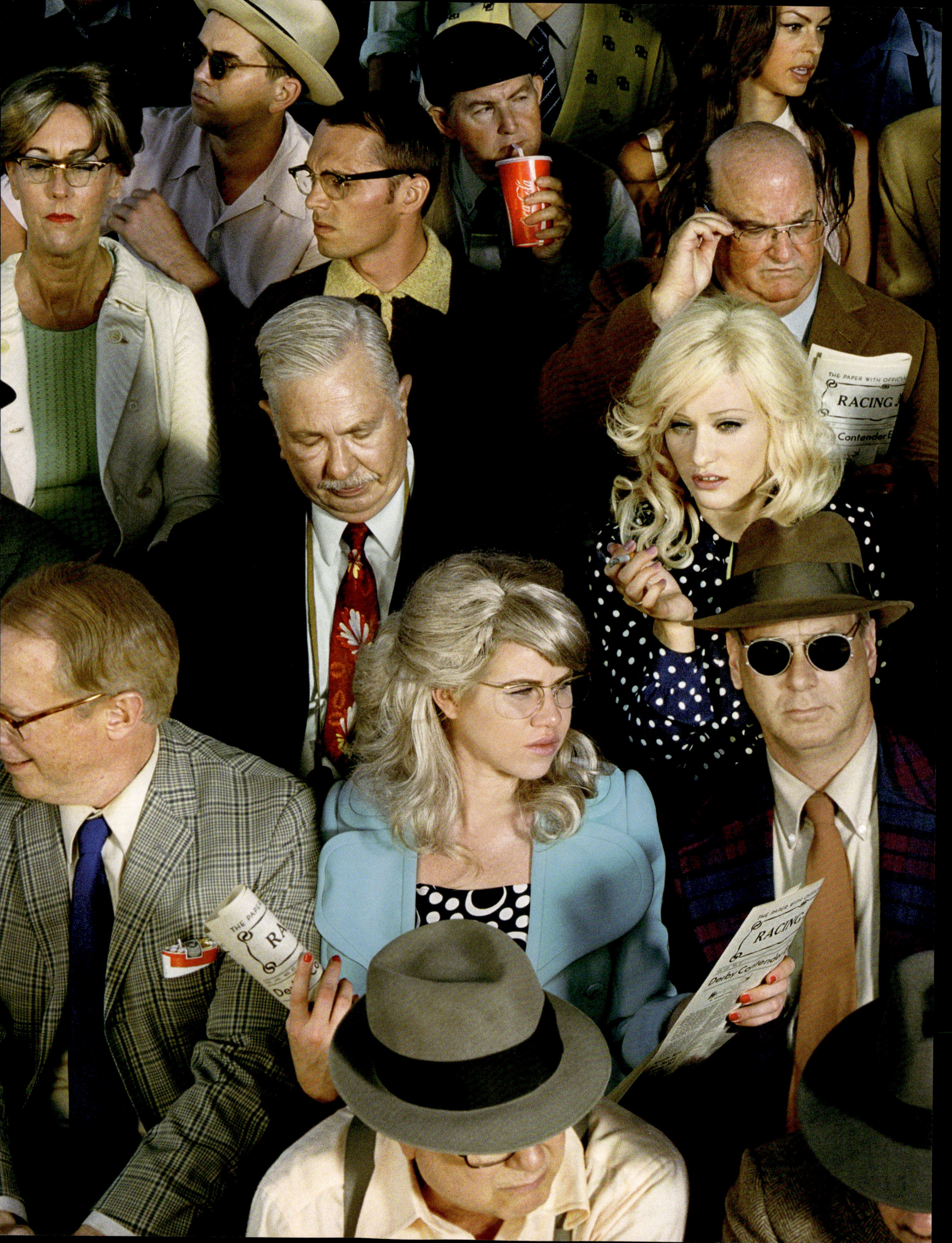
THE PAPER WITH OFFICIAL
RACING
Contender
Derby Contender

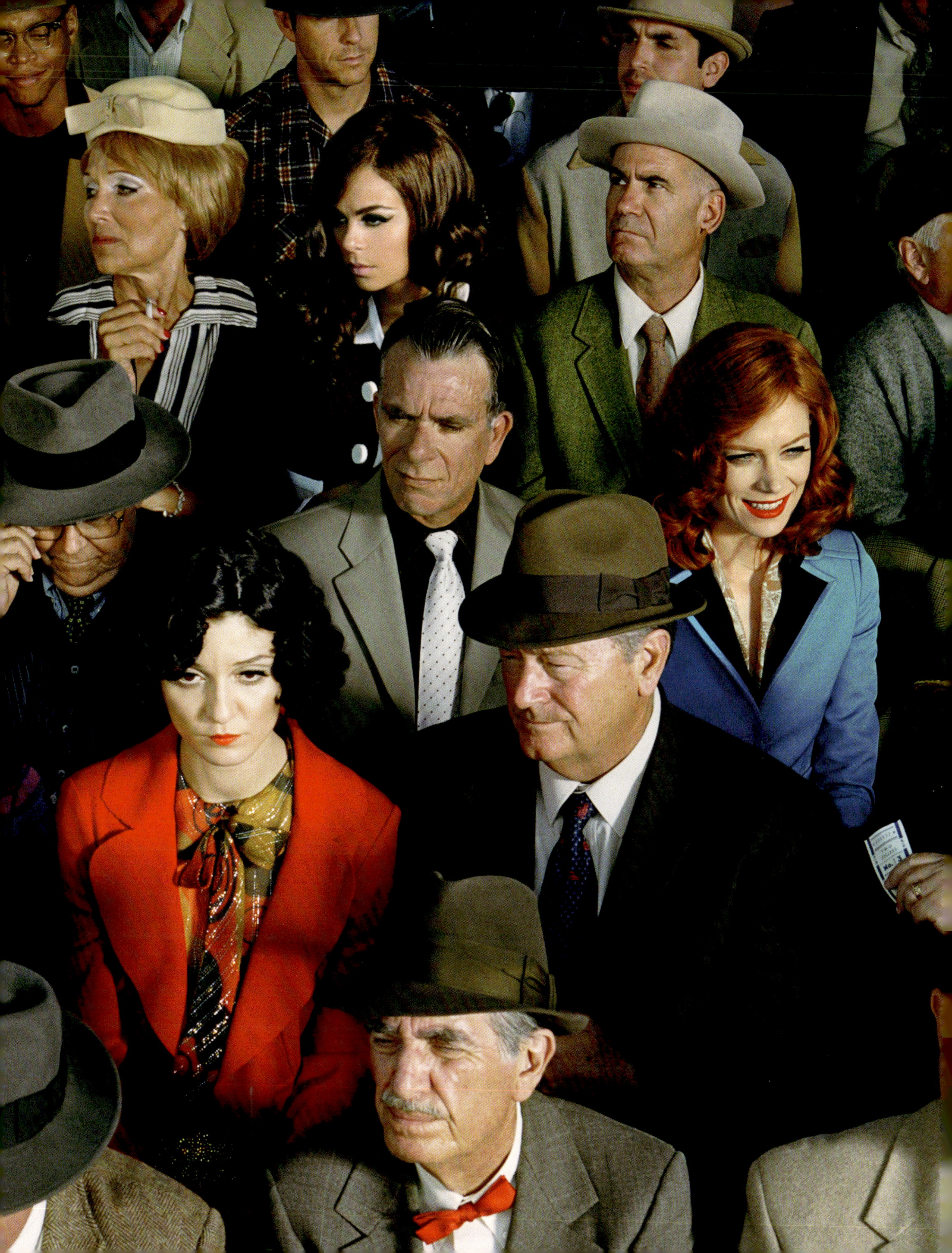

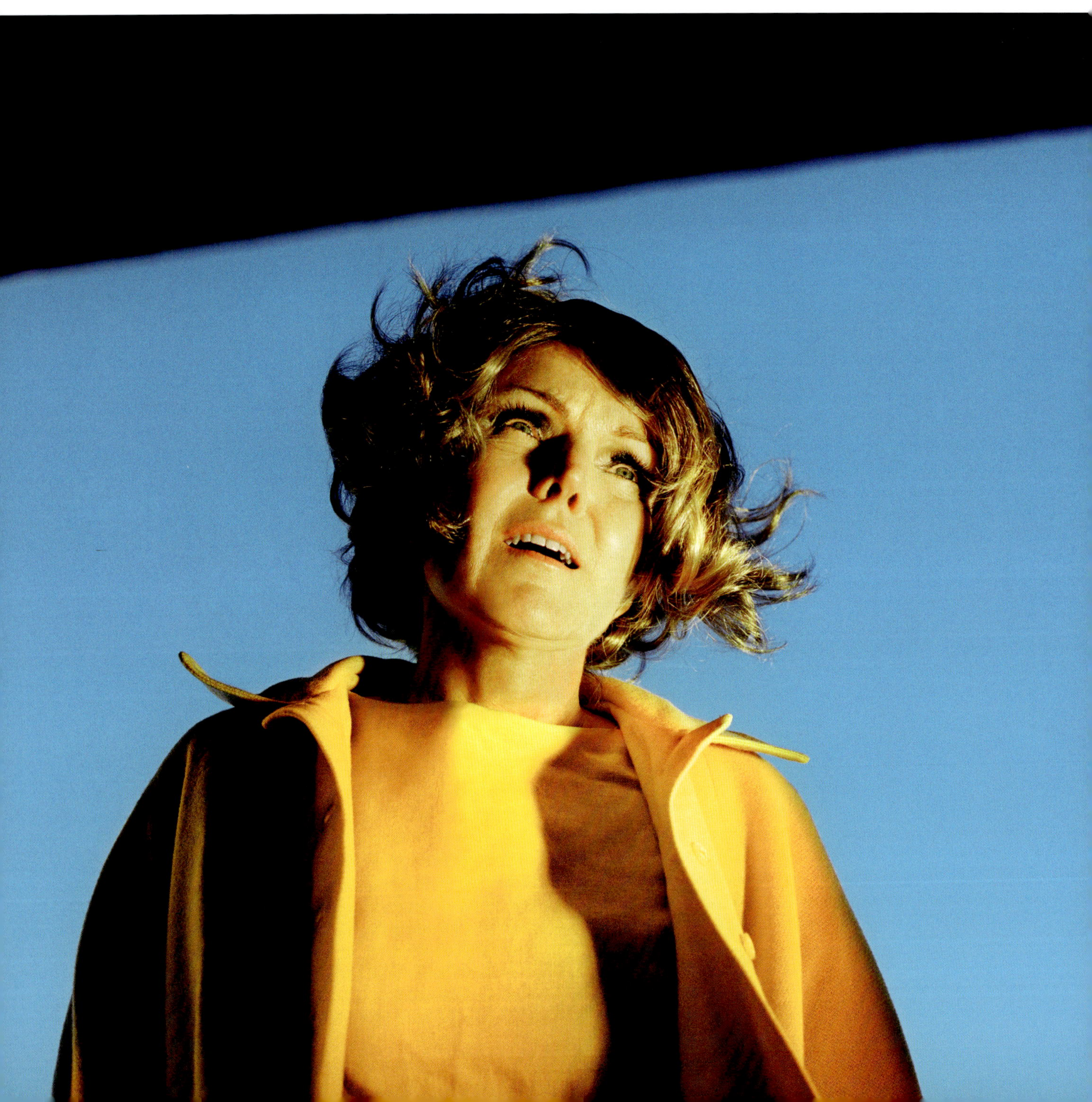

Interview with Alex Prager
Nathalie Herschdorfer

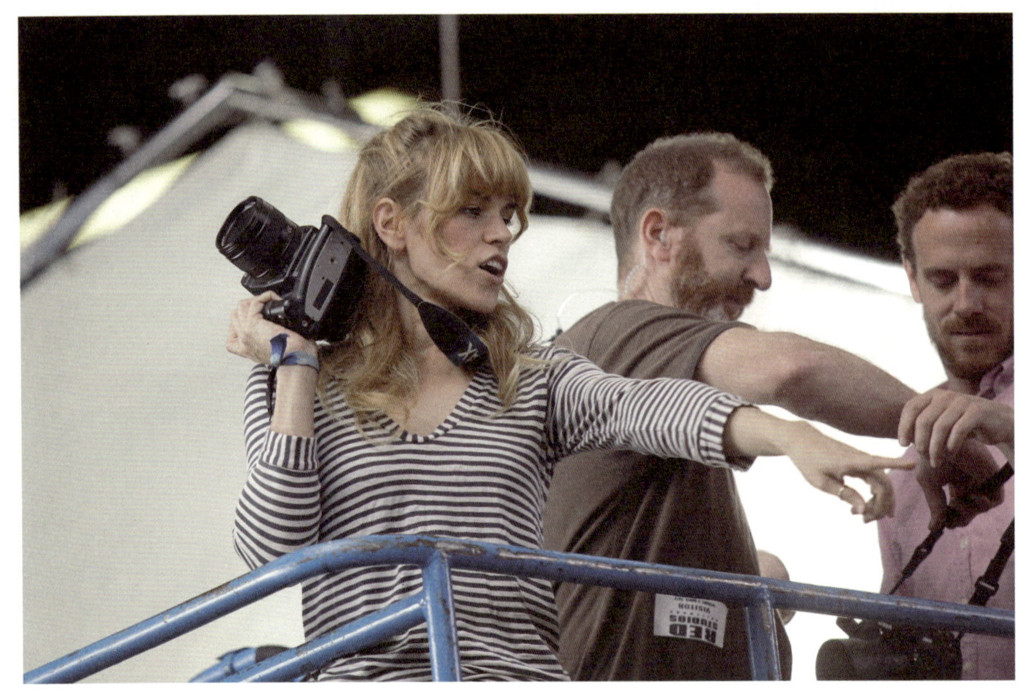

Courtesy of Jeff Vespa, 2013

NH   Was art part of your education as a child?

AP   I wasn't really exposed to much art as a child, but I always
            knew that my mother loved it. Thinking about it today,
            I remember that both my mother and my grandmother liked
            to draw. And, interestingly, my sister is a painter. While
            she was on the phone, my grandmother drew eyes, with
            different expressions and emotions! Although my family
            wasn't in the art world, my grandmother's sister, Wilma,
            was friends with artists, poets, musicians and painters. She
            died very young and I have this idea of her being beauti-
            ful, mysterious, romantic, a kind of muse for artists. When
            I told my grandmother I was going to be a photographer
            she told me for the first time that my grandfather and my
            great-grandfather were photographers. My grandfather had
            a portrait studio in Arizona. My grandparents separated
            early on so I never met him and I didn't know that he had
            been a photographer. When she told me, she brought out
            his old cameras and photographs. I really discovered art
            by myself, though, when I became friends with artists as
            a young adult.

NH Would you say that your education had an impact on your life as an artist?

AP My parents always encouraged me to be independent, from when I was young, and to make my own decisions and to be responsible for them. I don't remember ever being part of any kind of system, and I can see that this has a lot to do with the way I work and the life I live today. My parents were very supportive and somehow they knew that I would be a creative person later in life. They showed me creative avenues that I could take, such as music and dance, although not photography. From when I was 14 until I was 18 years old my parents let me go to Switzerland for the summer. They wanted me to get a different perspective on the world and not just to get a formal education. They realized that the European experience would be valuable to me as an artist. I had a very clear idea about the life I wanted to have – I wanted to be free and not to be part of a class system.

NH You are a self-taught photographer. How did you discover photography? Do you remember the first photograph that had an impact on you?

AP I became a photographer overnight! I visited a William Eggleston exhibition at the J. Paul Getty Museum here in Los Angeles and, looking at his photographs, I had a physical reaction. I was struck by his vision, not only emotionally, but also physically. I remember clearly two specific images, the dirty shoes under the bed and the bicycle. I think I spent hours just by myself in the exhibition. Before I went home, I bought his book, *William Eggleston's Guide*. I looked at the work obsessively. Within a few days, I bought everything I needed to become a professional photographer.

NH   Once you realized that you wanted to be a professional photographer, did you attend any photography classes?

AP   I never went to school, so that wasn't my first thought, but when I came home from the Eggleston exhibition I spoke to my mentor, a dear friend of mine who is a professional painter. He gave me this advice: that if I wanted to be a professional photographer, then for the first two years I shouldn't speak to any other photographers! This way I would be able to develop my own style, and not just learn about all the rules. The second piece of advice was to buy a professional camera, which I had to learn how to use. He said not to get a simple amateur camera because I'd need to replace it with a more advanced one after a year. I followed his advice. I bought a camera – and even slept with it. I was photographing in the street until three in the morning, then I worked in my darkroom until six in the morning so that I could immediately process my films. I had to go to work at 9 a.m. I came back at six and went out again with my camera. At that time, I was reading a lot of technical books, studying lighting and composition by looking at pictures. I had to understand why I was struck by particular photographs.

NH   Did you study specific photographers in these books?

AP   I was obsessed with Diane Arbus, Henri Cartier-Bresson, and Weegee. They were the first photographers I studied. Nobody told me what I should study in photography. Most of my friends were musicians or painters, not photographers. I only learned what I needed to learn to make my photographs. In the first few months, I made portraits in the street, so I studied the works of street photographers such as Brassaï, Martin Parr, Bruce Gilden. I worked in black-and-white and then, after three months, I started shooting in colour. Later on, I got interested in setting up shots with my friends, putting them in specific locations. I studied stage photography, looking at the work of Helmut Newton, Guy Bourdin, Gregory Crewdson, Philip-Lorca diCorcia. I had ideas for my pictures and all I wanted to do was focus on how to make them.

NH   Did you show your photographs to other people?

AP   I started exhibiting my pictures in the laundry room in my
            apartment building. I hung them anonymously. Some of
            them were taken (or stolen!) so it did help me to understand
            what resonated with people. These were my first small
            exhibitions. My first exhibition in a gallery came six months
            after I had bought my first camera, in 2001. I showed a mix
            of colour images (some were staged photographs) and street
            photography. The only ones I sold were the staged images.
            I felt that I had something to offer here. I not only wanted
            to learn more about staged photography, but I also wanted to
            feel challenged. After that first show, I regularly showed my
            portfolio to galleries around Los Angeles, but there was no
            real interest. It didn't stop me making more images, though.

NH   Your work focuses on female characters. Can you tell us
            about these women and their lives?

AP   I focus on women whom I can use to emulate what I am
            going through myself. The stories I've made so far are about
            emotions. My work is about things I have experienced or
            observed. For example, *Face in the Crowd* was about my stage
            fright. I was travelling a lot at one point and I felt alone
            among strangers. *La Grande Sortie* is also about stage fright,
            but on a different level. With this work, I was questioning
            what my reality was, and how I perceived the audience
            and how the audience perceived me on stage. A lot of my
            work is about perception: how the lines between what is
            real and what only feels real, but is actually imagined or
            just perceived, can become blurred. *Compulsion* was born
            at this moment when I was on a freeway and I passed a van
            completely on fire. It could have blown up at any moment.
            Everyone was slowing down on the freeway. It is true that
            we always want to know more about the horrible things
            that happen. With this series I bring this question to light
            – about all the things that go wrong in the world and how
            they affect us as spectators. How much do we really want to
            look away? My projects usually come from a very personal
            place, a place with a mix of emotions, a place of love, fear,
            and isolation. Then I figure out how to show these emotions
            in composition, colour, music...

NH   How did you come to your signature style that can be described as a retro-style?

AP   I think that going back to older times is very interesting because it allows some space. The silent-film era overstylized the makeup in order to tell the darkest stories in the movies. The film-noir period did this too: with murders, deception, affairs, basically just bad people's stories. In order to connect with the people, filmmakers use tricks, lighting, makeup and music. I realized that there is some space between the reality I am trying to describe (I mean, here, contemporary issues) and the nostalgia that provides familiarity and comfort for the viewer. This is my way to engage with an audience. If I just showed reality, then people wouldn't be able to connect with it, because they get enough harsh reality every day. We always think that the past was much better than today. That nostalgic lens gives a softer feeling to the past, and then I can add my reality. I never have a specific era in mind, but more of a timeless feeling that incorporates now and some time from the past. This is how I prefer to engage people with my work. Of course, there is a sense of humour as well. This has been used for a long time, if you think about theatre. It's not a new trick. So there is play and comedy in my work, but I am talking about now, not about the past. I am dealing with the emotions of people. And to capture these emotions, I try to be as honest as possible because people can sense when they are being lied to. It is one thing to use tricks with the camera, lighting, or costumes, but the honesty in the work is very important. I want people to connect with the emotions I have in my stories.

NH   Your work is very precise and has this aesthetic quality because of your technical skills. Does the technical part play an important role in your approach?

AP   The technical part is important: it gives me the freedom to create the image I have in my mind. I never considered myself to be a photographer in the sense that the camera is my only tool. The physicality of things is very important to me. I build my sets, I have a collection of wigs, props, and costumes. So much of what we look at in our world today is unreal, but I want to be honest with my imagery. I love the world of movie props, I'm obsessed with the way people make things in films, where they are working with real elements. I still shoot with film. Every stage is important: preparation, shooting, and post-production.

NH   Can you tell us about the way you work? How do you plan
            a day of shooting with your team and your actors?

AP   Everything is very planned. When I am on set, the pre-
            production is already done, and decisions have been made
            about how I want it to look, what lighting to use, which lens,
            how the camera is supposed to move, the storyboard has
            been written, and the script is clear. We will have gone over
            all the logistics, so when I show up on set, if all is going
            smoothly, I can focus on the purely creative. For me, this
            means focusing on emotions, on the acting, and the energy
            I try to get from the people on set. I use actors and also
            my family, my husband, my mom, my dog, and my friends.
            If I just had actors this would change the dynamic on set.
            I like the weird energy of having 'real' people on set, people
            I know really well. This aspect goes back to my interest in
            street photography, because anything can happen on the
            street, even if you know exactly what angle you are looking
            for. If I shoot on set, with a huge production, I still want to be
            open to all the chaos that can come. People have emotions,
            the crew has their own point of view, some things cannot
            be controlled as so many different things are happening.
            Alfred Hitchcock said that when the storyboard is made,
            the movie is made. I know what he meant. My storyboards
            are quite precise: there is a clear vision in them and I know
            exactly what we are going to do during shooting. And it is
            true that there is no real room for trying other things because
            the schedule is so tight in film production. But the best
            things that happen during filming are usually something
            that nobody planned.

NH   Can you tell us a bit more about the way you prepare before the shooting?

AP   Here is my process: I start with sketches and writings. Usually, I start alone, with a pencil, and then I talk to people. What I sketch is what is on the final picture. If you look at my sketches of *La Grande Sortie*, you will find the whole film. It is exactly what we shot.

NH   How do you distinguish your photography from your film works?

AP   Photographs and films are shot the same day. Motion and stills are made together, one after the other. It doesn't make sense to shoot separately. The actors are warmed up, the lighting is there. The distinction between the two media is very clear. Photographs are much more posed. With the *La Grande Sortie* photographs there is a stillness in isolation. I learned the difference between the photographs and the moving images on *Despair*, the first film I ever made. In order to have the woman in true despair, I needed her to be in her role, feeling all the emotions. I needed the narrative for her to follow. For some images, I don't need moments that have to be moving, it comes from a different kind of energy. There is a stillness that I am looking for, the space in-between. I love working in photography and in film, I still have something to do in both media. The more I do both, the more different they become.

NH   What brought you into filmmaking?

AP   I first shot *Despair* because I didn't know where my
            photography was going. I had reached the point where
            I had done what I intended to do with my photography.
            It was 2008 and I was having an exhibition in London at
            the Michael Hoppen Gallery. At the opening, people asked
            me what happened to the woman in the photographs, right
            before and right after. I wanted to answer these questions
            so I went back to work. I wasn't thinking of making a movie,
            I didn't intend to transition into film and become a filmmaker.
            I was thinking of the before and after as a sequence of
            still images that would tell the story and the emotions
            of my character. And the result was *Despair*. It was probably
            similar to the way people approached film in the early days
            of 'moving pictures'. When I started doing more narrative
            film, it was a new challenge. And when I finished *Despair*,
            I was excited again about photography. The film experience
            opened my eyes to photography once more. It became fresh
            for me again. And I love working in film, because this is
            the art that uses all media: music, installations, sculptures,
            photography, painting, theatre...

NH   Since you come from Los Angeles, I guess that the move
            to films was quite natural for you. Did you have any
            connection with Hollywood that nourished your interest
            in moving pictures?

AP   Because I grew up in Los Angeles, the film industry clearly
            had an influence on me. I've never wanted to be in the film
            industry, but it was around and I was fascinated, certainly.
            Films have always been part of my life from a very young
            age. I watched lots of films on television, the old movie
            channels in particular. I still watch a lot of movies, all kinds
            of movies, old and new. I didn't take photography classes
            and I didn't study films. When I started to work on films
            I watched them all the time. When I became more serious
            about filmmaking, I did a lot of research, not only about
            different directors, but I also wanted to understand how
            a film begins, how techniques are done before, and how they
            evolve. I read loads of books, talked to people and watched
            many 'behind-the-scenes' videos because I love to see how
            different sets are made up. What I've learned is that there
            are a million different ways to make films. Every time a film
            begins the production it means a long journey for all the
            people involved. From pre-production to post-production,
            things evolve constantly. Experiment and invention are part
            of the journey. Every day you might find a need to invent
            something to make a shoot, you may end up with a new
            lens, a new camera, a new system to sharpen your vision.
            Making a film is a very physical job, but it is also very creative:
            experimenting and inventing happen every single day.

NH   Your work is also an homage to Golden Age Hollywood
            motion pictures. Alfred Hitchcock has often been mentioned
            in reference to your work. Are there other filmmakers who
            have been influential in your practice?

AP   The list of names is quite eclectic. I watch a film every day so
            I have a long list of filmmakers in mind: Ingmar Bergman,
            Powell & Pressburger, Howard Hawks, David O. Selznick,
            Jean Renoir, Stanley Kubrick, Sergio Leone, Federico Fellini,
            Sidney Lumet, Steven Spielberg, Christopher Nolan, Quentin
            Tarantino, David Fincher, the Coen brothers... I discovered
            Alfred Hitchcock after people compared our work. The same
            thing happened with Cindy Sherman, whose work I didn't
            know. And the comparison was made very early on. But
            besides filmmakers or photographers, I look at painters:
            John Currin, Lucian Freud, Jenny Saville, Egon Schiele and
            Bruegel the Elder.

NH   Many photographers work by themselves, alone. But the
            way you work, in film and in photography, involves many
            people, not just filmmakers, editors, cinematographers, set
            designers... How large is your staff?

AP   It depends on the size of the set. It can be two people or
            70. It really depends on how many people we need for the
            production we are doing. The way I approach it is that it's all
            about the making. The logistics behind what we are making
            are whatever they need to be in order to make the things we
            are making. For *Face in the Crowd* we had 350 people (I mean
            extras) for the day of the shoot, and the crew to support that
            many people. I constantly speak to my team. I consider them
            to be my family. My work is very collaborative. I feel I am
            the most happy when I am working on a set with my team.
            This is the best version of myself.

NH   This book ends with *La Grande Sortie*. Thinking about this body of work, I have the feeling that you are opening a new chapter here. Does it announce a new cycle?

AP   Yes, I feel that something new is happening in my work. Going through these ten years of work shows me that I have been very productive. But I see from this book that there are some ideas that appear over and over. I was photographing them, filming them in different ways and I think that I was trying to tell the same story, in various ways. It is true that *La Grande Sortie* opened a new door in my work. I would never have thought of a ballet project without Benjamin Millepied's commission. He gave me access to an amazing place, the Paris Opera, and to some of the best dancers in the world. It was definitely good for my work. The same happened with *Touch of Evil*, the 13 films I made for *The New York Times*, and *Sunday*, which was commissioned by *W* magazine. For each of these projects, I had complete freedom. The benefit of having these commissions is that I can test new ideas and experiment. So even if it starts as a commission, I develop these projects as my own work.

NH   In *La Grande Sortie* the tension in the audience is palpable. As in all your works, there is an enigmatic atmosphere that is unresolved for the viewer. Emotional impact always seems important to you.

AP   My film is about a ballerina who hadn't danced onstage for a year. I wanted to explore her fear, the tension of being back on stage. These were the feelings that I had during the making of *La Grande Sortie*. Emotions and instincts are the way I relate to imagery. The moment I am taken by a work, I focus on emotions. When I am watching a movie, I am not analysing the work, I experience emotions. With my work, I am trying to make the world a little more interesting to me and to inspire other people, to connect. If I think back, my life changed forever when I visited the Eggleston show. I was so inspired by the work. It was an emotional shock. It is exciting to be making small steps to inspire other people's lives. For me, art is about communication and getting a response from people.

NH   Looking now at these different series made over ten years, how would you describe your work?

AP   I would say that my work is like film stills that are films that have never been made. I like to use primary colours as much as possible because there is a simplicity that resonates in a different way than in strictly contemporary images. But these colours are always very saturated – Kodachrome, technicolour colours – which gives them a certain feel so we are not sure when they were made. There is a nostalgic feeling running through all of these works that people can relate to, in their personal life. I try to use archetypes, stereotypes and branding that we've seen for decades in American culture to give back that familiar feeling and coax the viewer to sink deeper in.

NH   Do you have a personal project that remains unpublished in a drawer?

AP   Yes, I have one personal project I haven't done yet. Usually I make a project with whatever I shoot. But for some reason this one has not been done. Maybe it will come out of its drawer in the future...

Los Angeles, 2017

PART 2

COMPULSION

(2012)

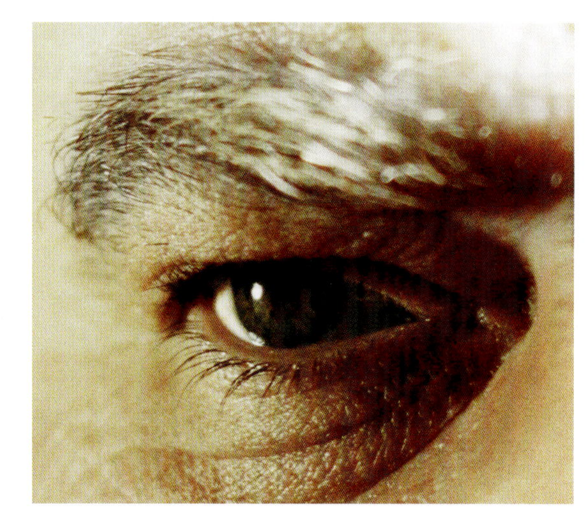

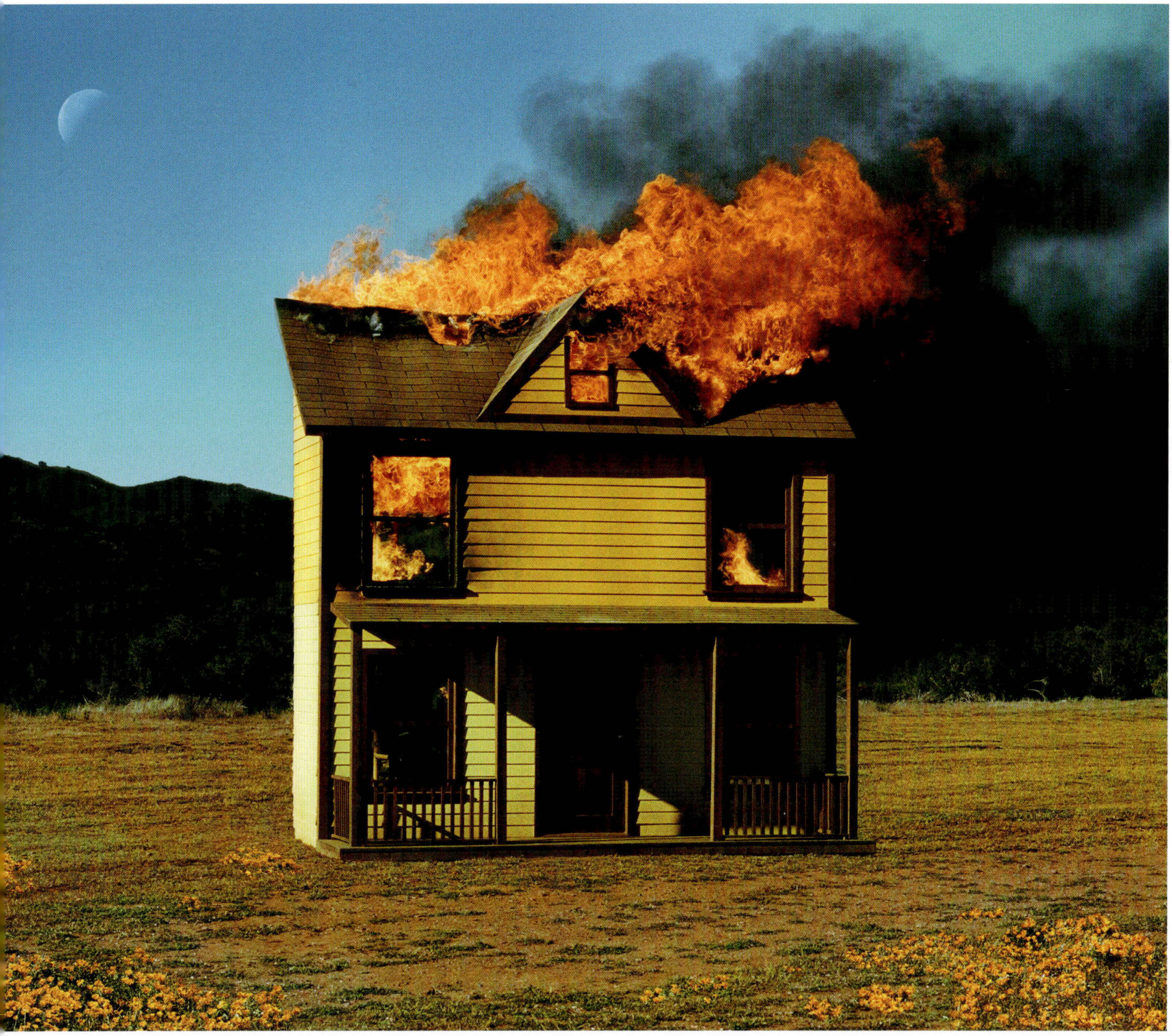

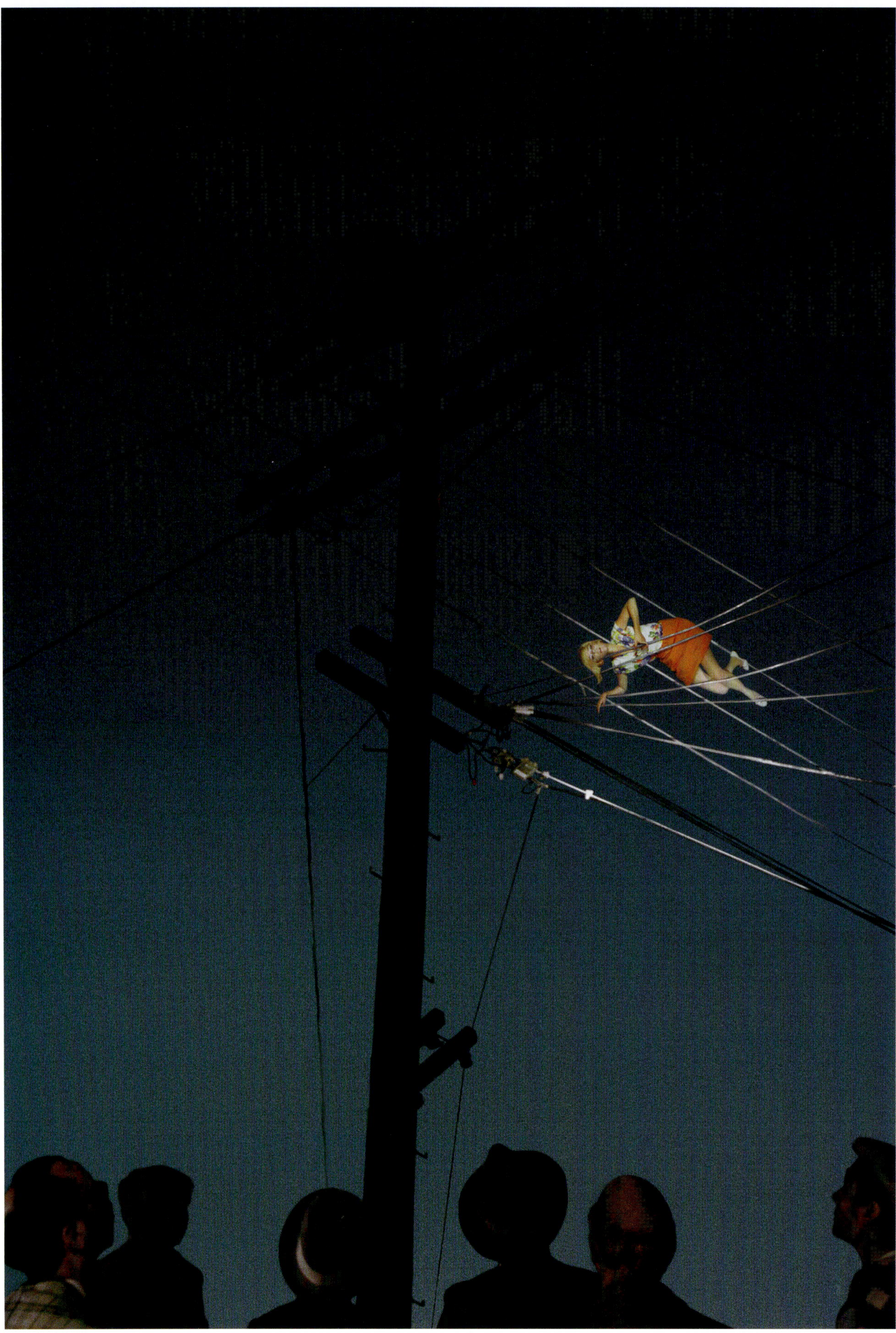

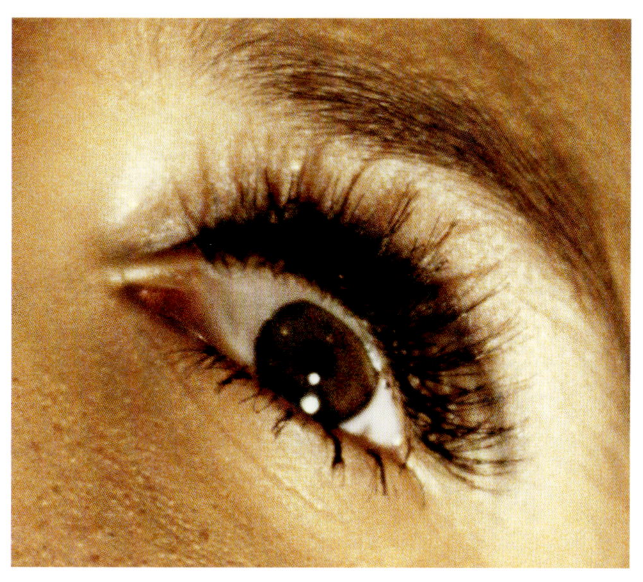

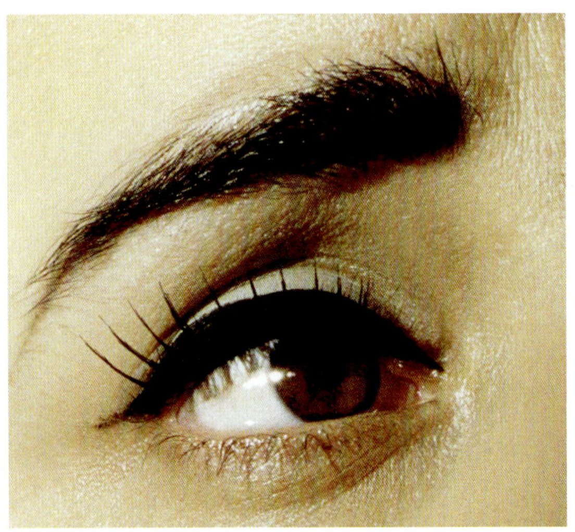
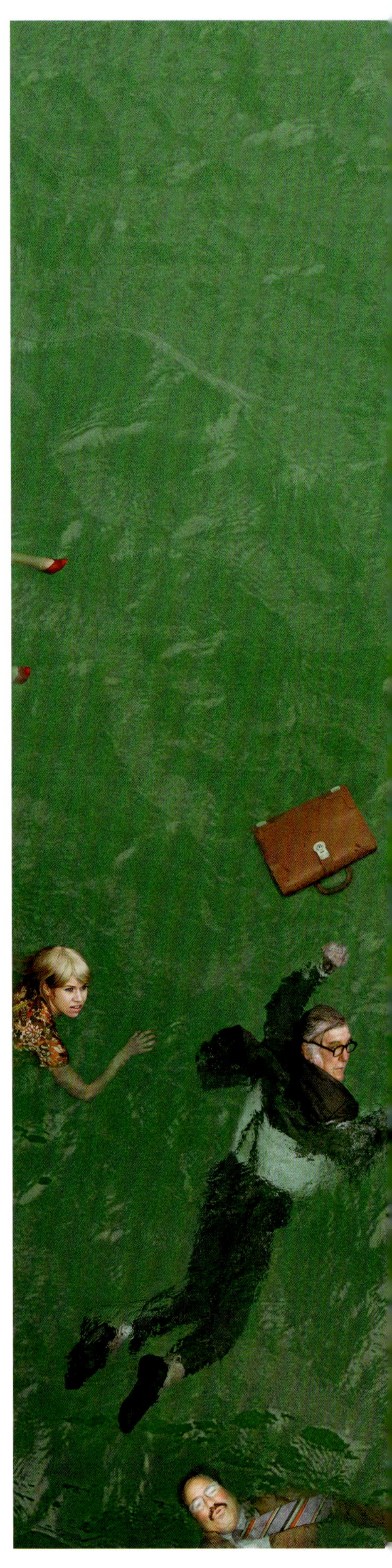

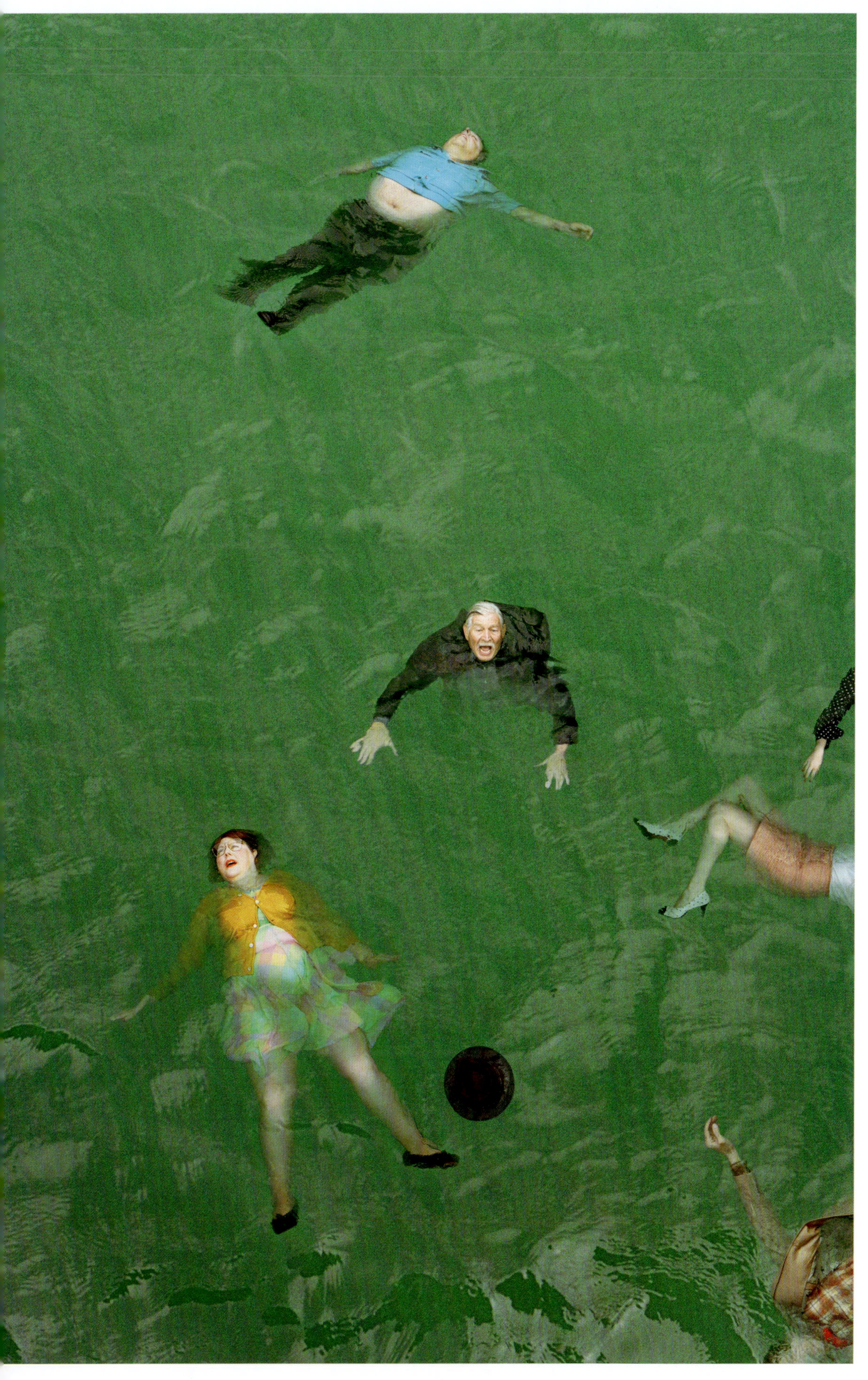

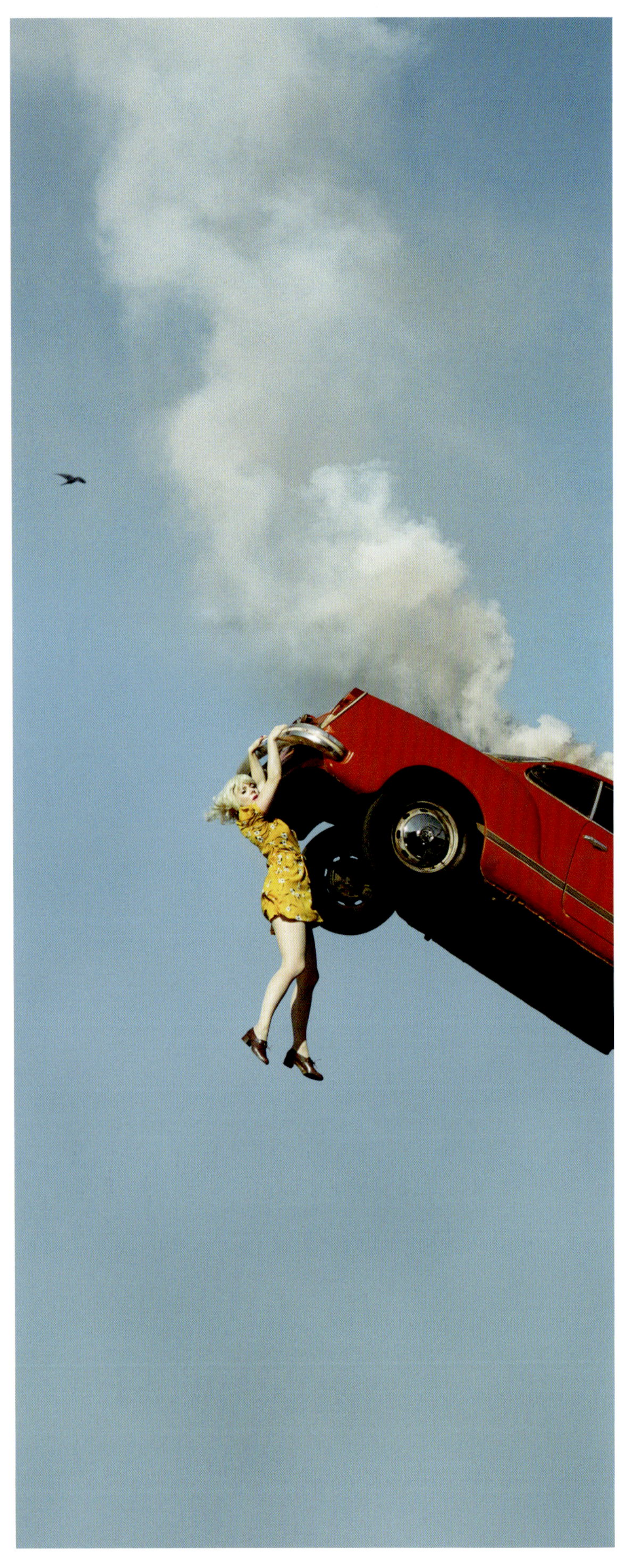

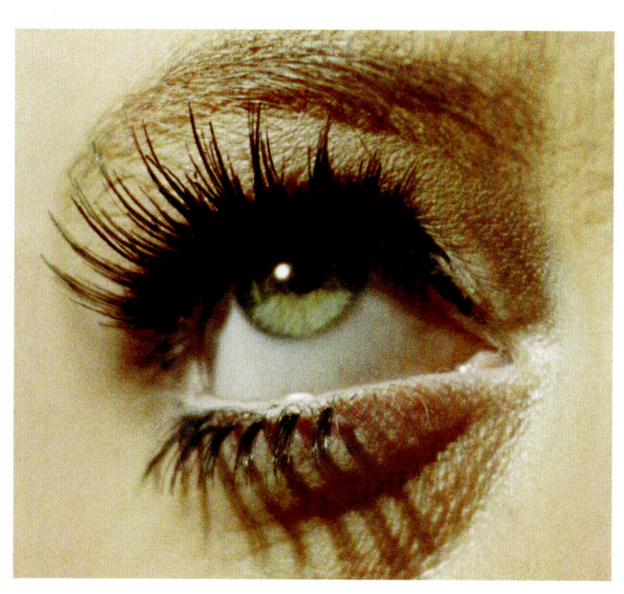

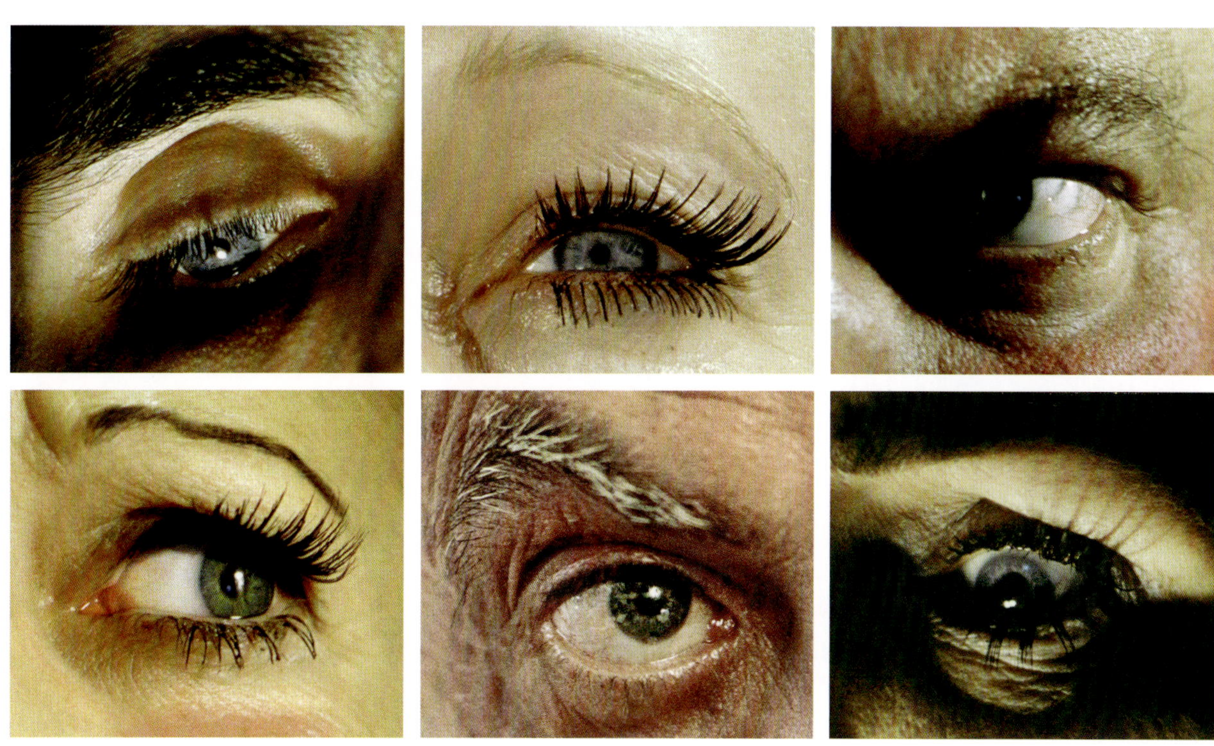

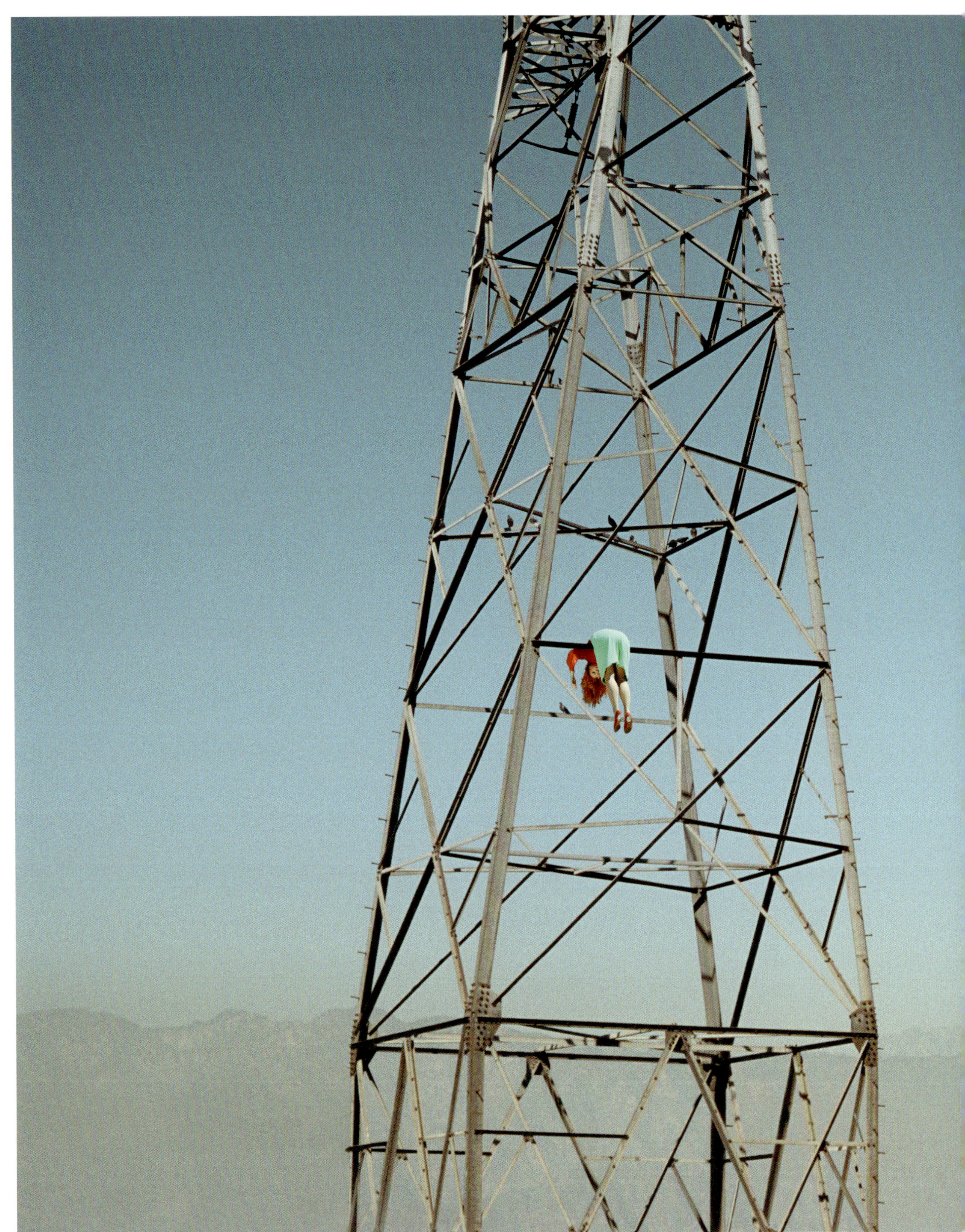

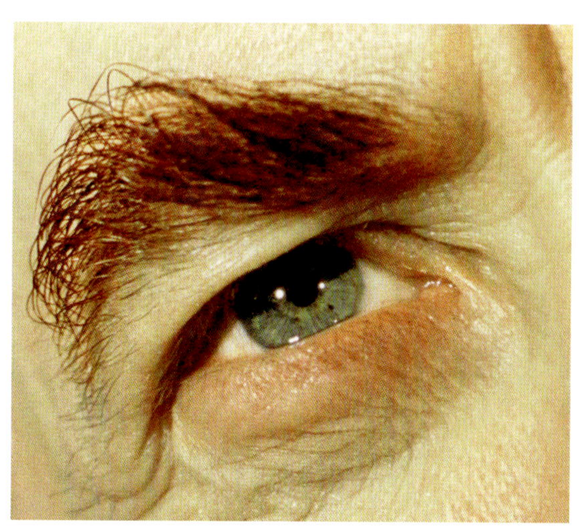

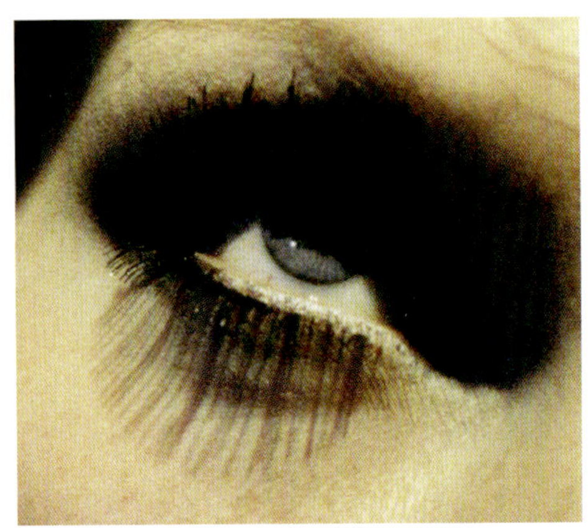

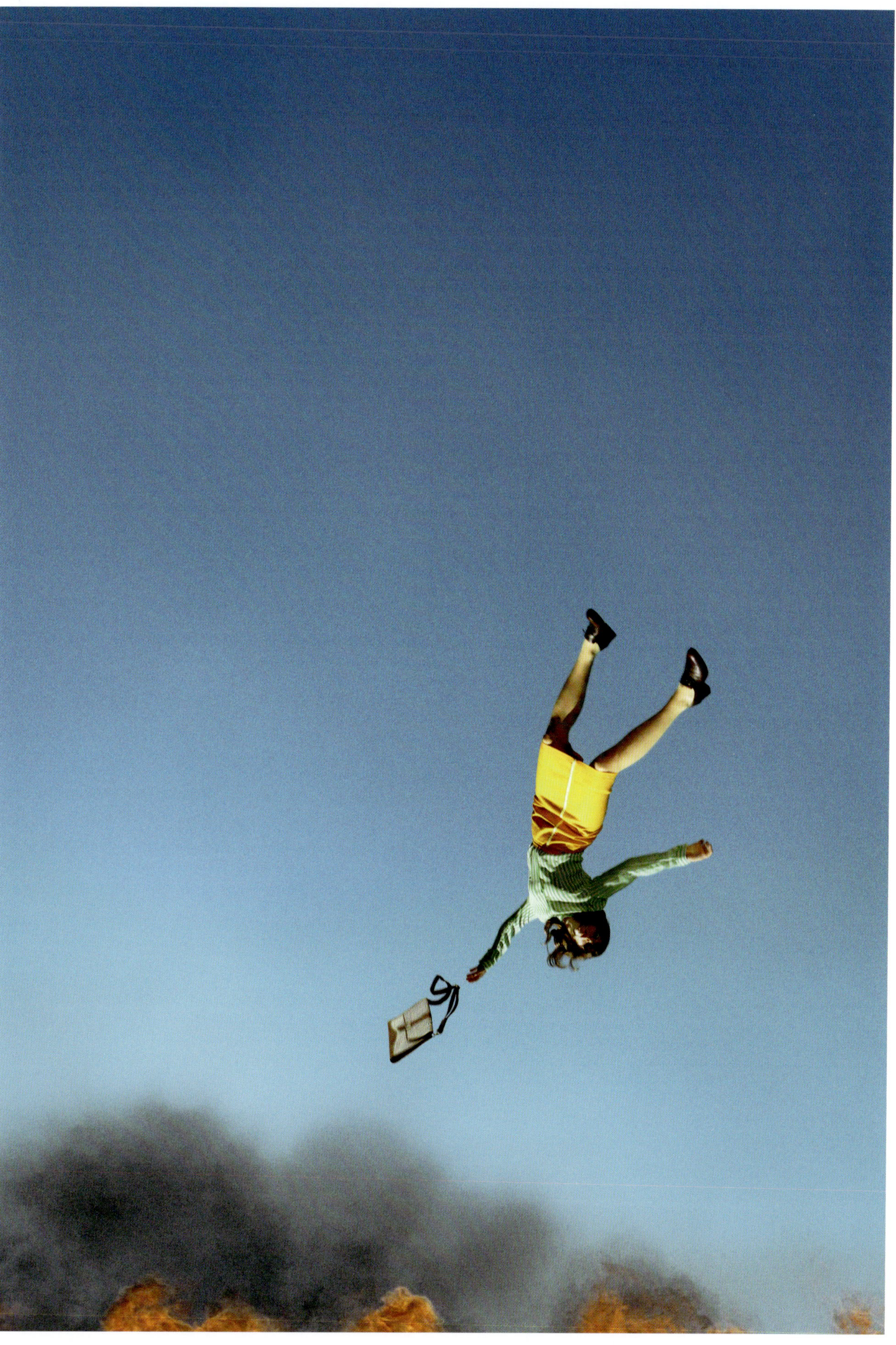

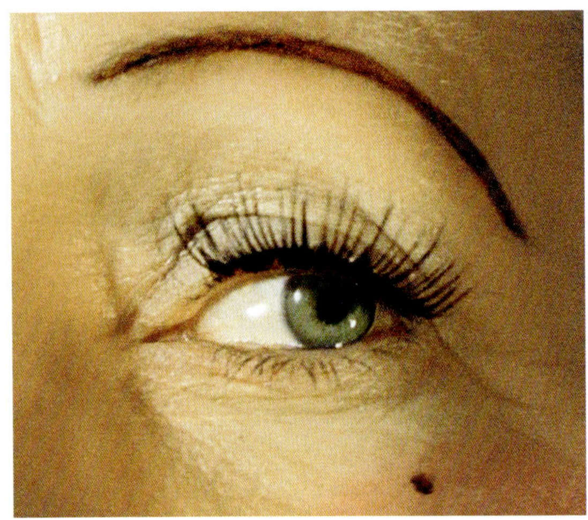

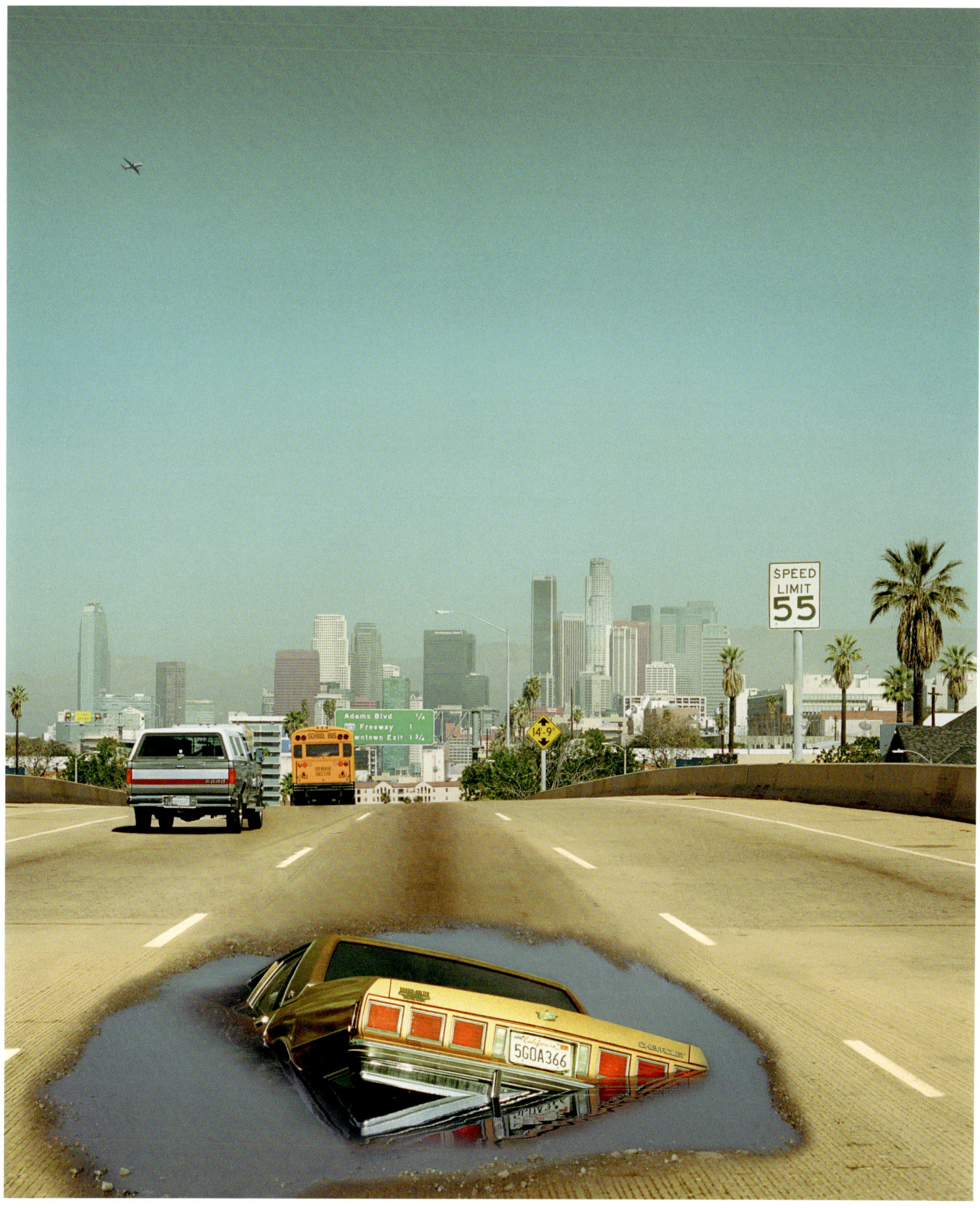

SPEED
LIMIT
55
Adams Blvd   ¼
Freeway   1
wntown Exit 1 ¾
14-9
SCHOOL BUS
FORD
California
5GOA366

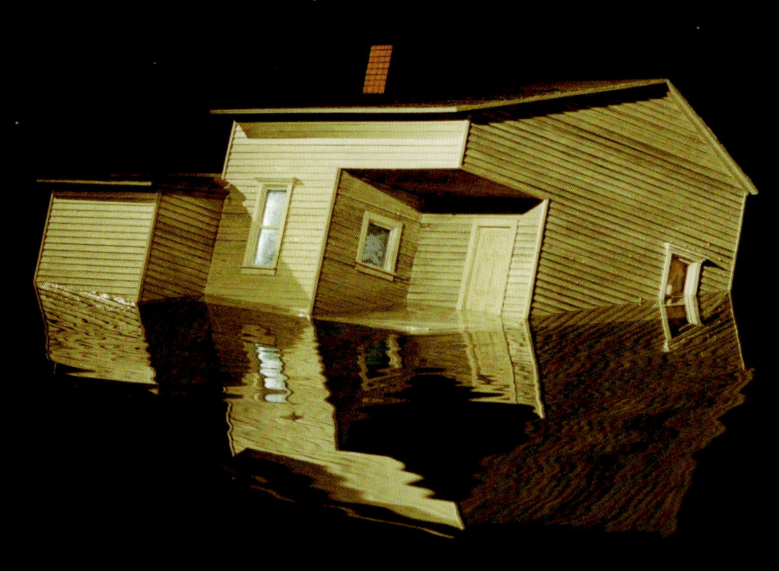

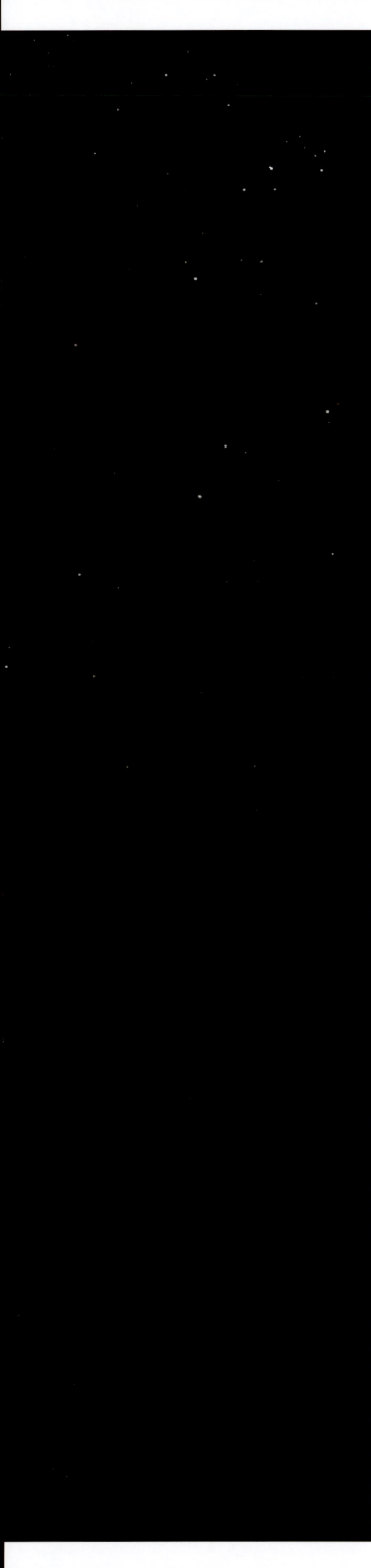

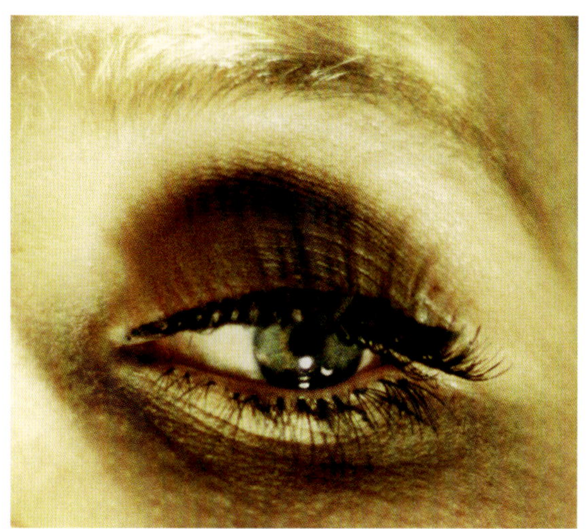

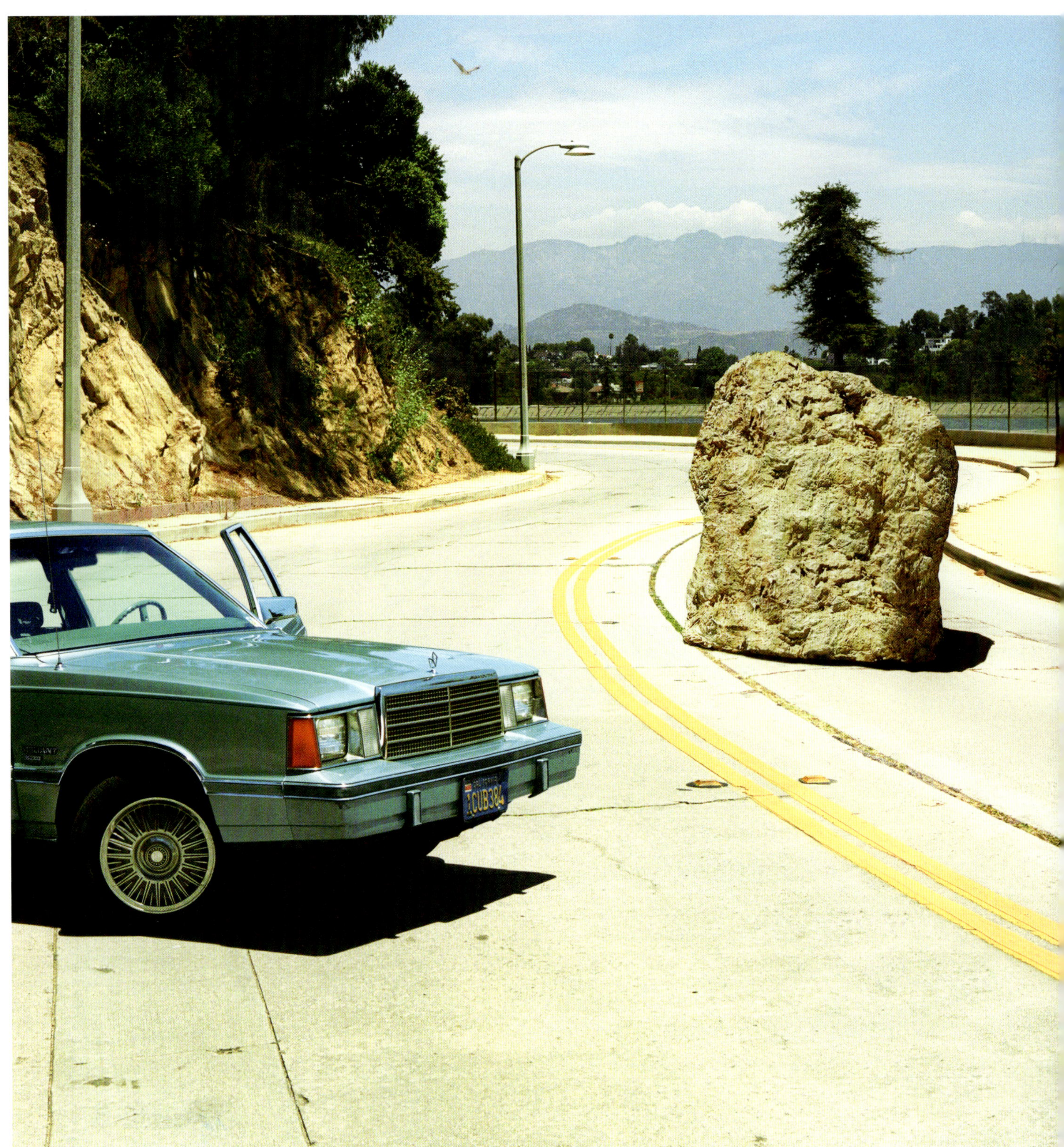

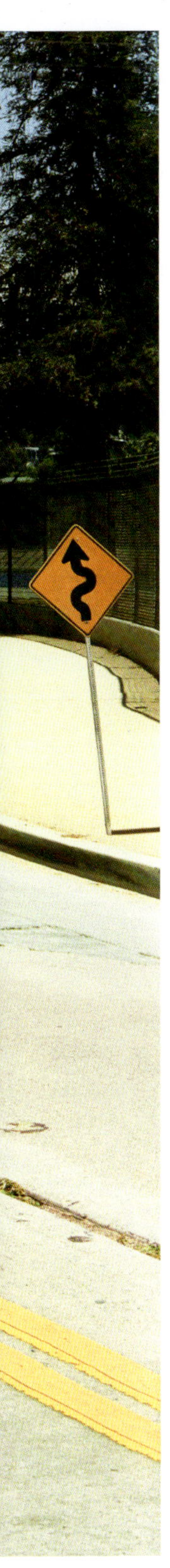

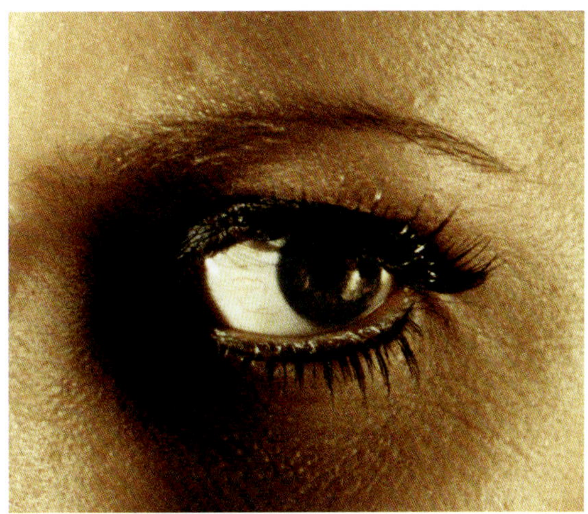

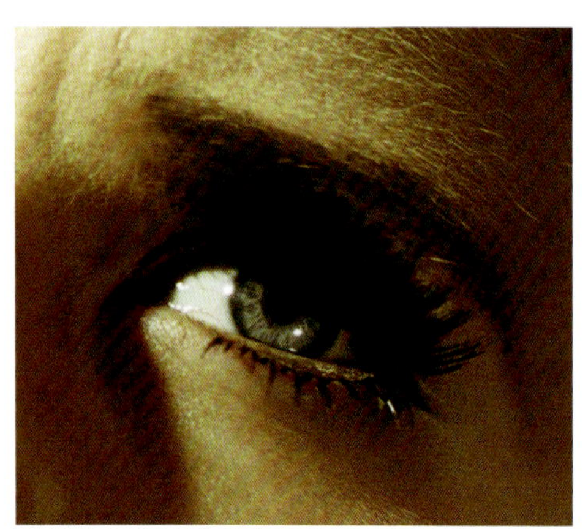
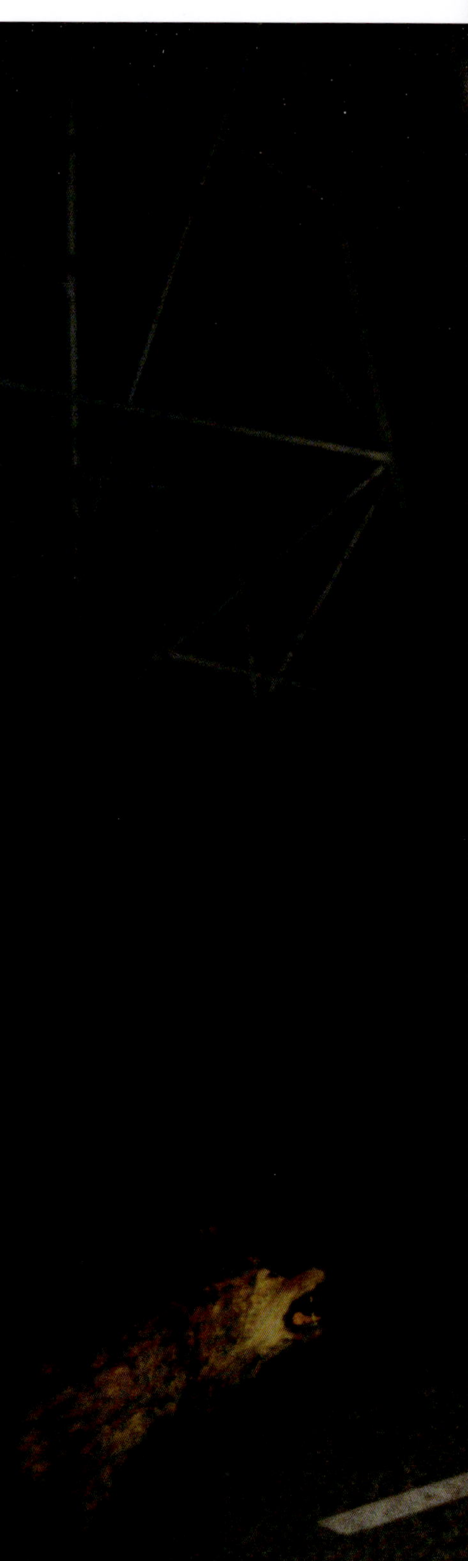

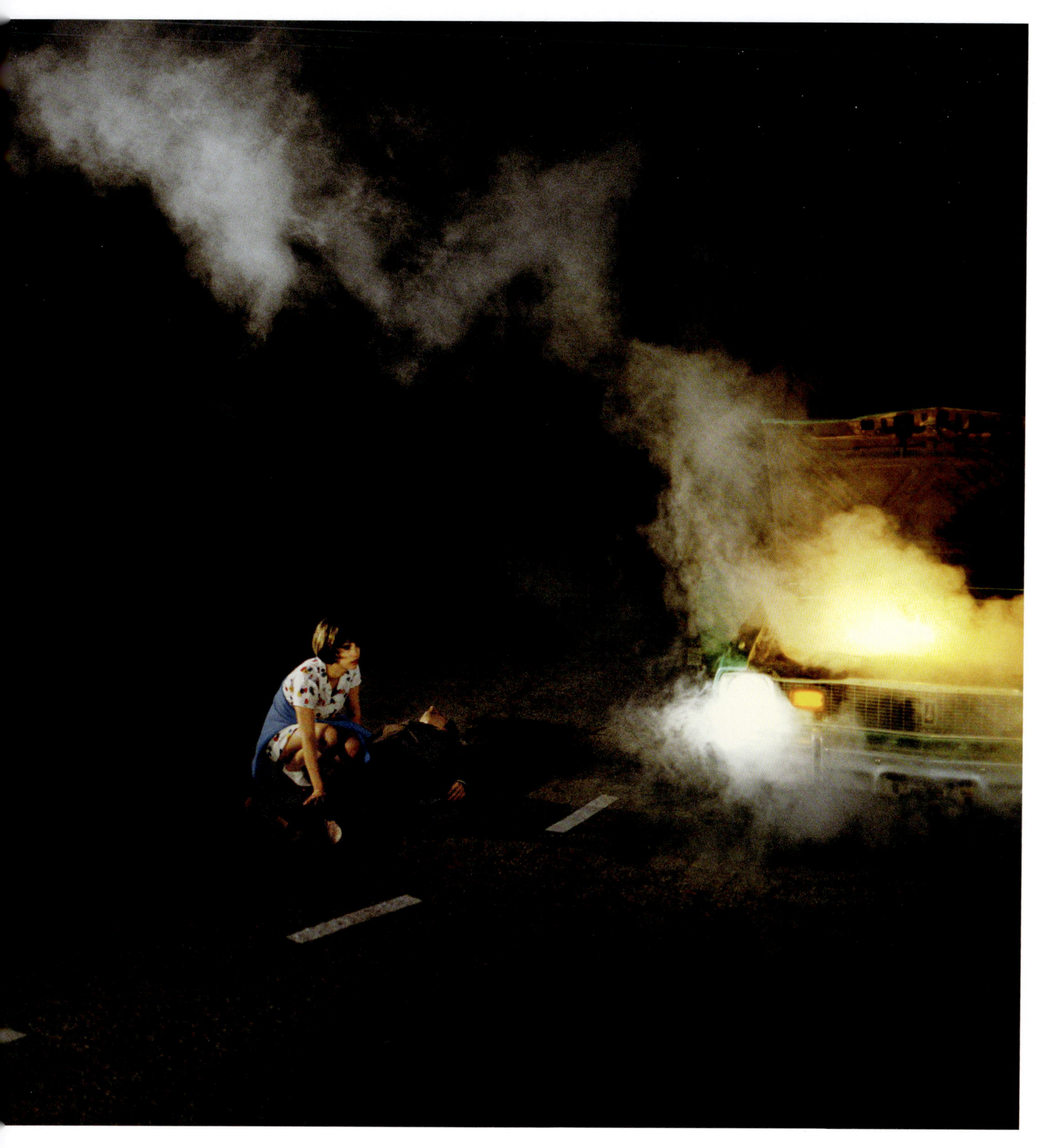

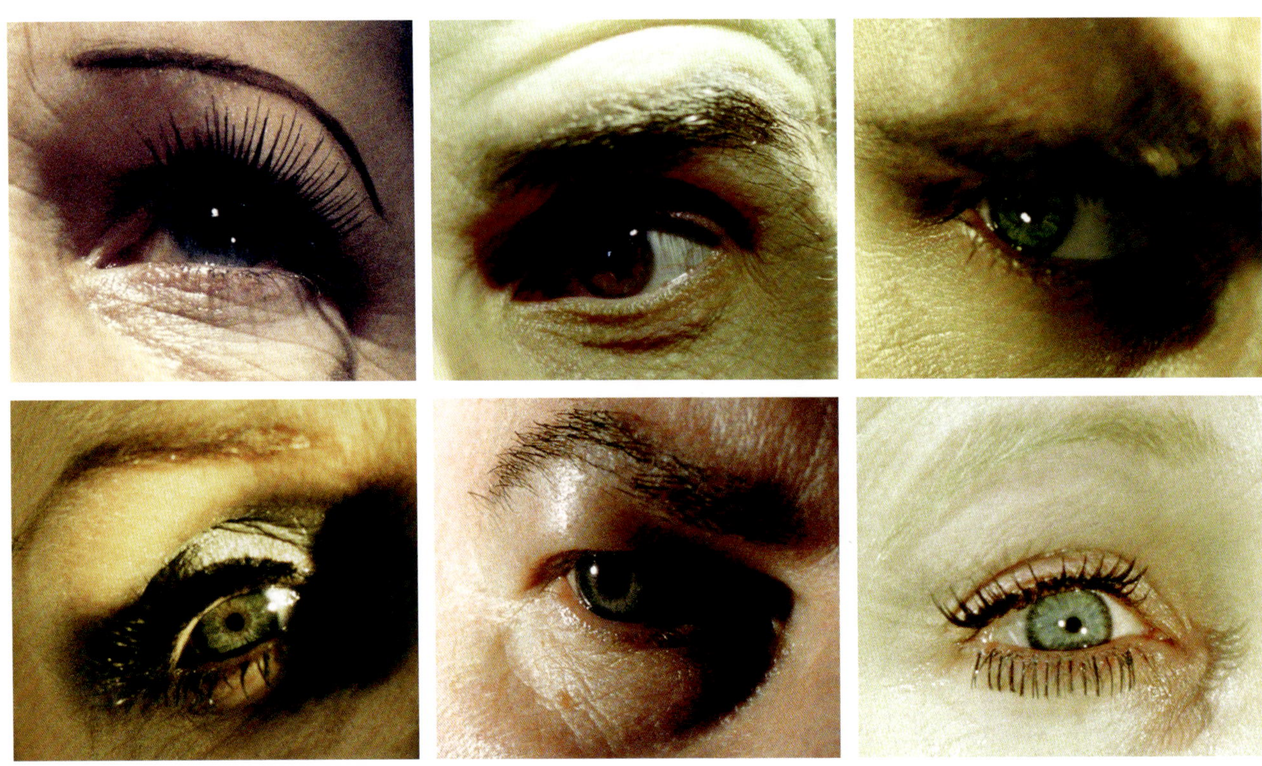

Face in the Crowd
Clare Grafik

The apparition of these faces in the crowd;
Petals on a wet, black bough.[i]

Ezra Pound, 'In a Station of the Metro', 1913

Alex Prager's 2013 exhibition *Face in the Crowd* at the Corcoran Gallery of Art in Washington, D.C. was not only Prager's first solo museum exhibition in the USA, but also marked a decisive step change in practice and ambition in her work. Featuring new photographic images and film work, this substantial exhibition drew upon familiar themes that had been developing in Prager's practice, but it was also a striking and immersive exploration of the contemporary condition – that of the individual and the crowd. This essay will offer a short consideration of how individual and collective identities have been played out in a variety of art-historical – and other – contexts within the modern period, which continues to make it such a rich, creative, ambiguous, and resonant subject today.

There is a well-trammelled pathway through art-historical narratives that leads back to that great French 'painter of modern life', Édouard Manet (1832–1883). Considered to be one of the first artists to address a truly 'modern' subjectivity, Manet chose to turn his attention to the real world he witnessed around him. His paintings – which were roundly rejected by the establishment – absorbed a newly modernized Paris where public spaces, the streets, cafés, and theatres, of the city provided the platform for the urban masses to play out their leisure and working lives. Charles Baudelaire had already provided a positive spin on the perks of this new cosmopolitan culture, particularly for the artist who can watch 'the flow of life move by, majestic and dazzling. He admires the eternal beauty and the astonishing harmony of life in capital cities, a harmony so providentially maintained in the tumult of human liberty'.[ii] Manet's painting *A Bar at the Folies-Bergère* (1882) depicted the bustling interior of the renowned (and notorious) Folies-Bergère music hall. The crowds are picked out in the background through suggestive spots of colour describing anonymous top-hatted gentlemen and women staring through opera glasses at, we imagine, a spectacle on stage. In the foreground, a barmaid stares directly at us out of the canvas with a benign indifference, while her oddly juxtaposed reflection in the mirror behind positions us – the viewer – in the same place as the man we see asking for service. Manet's Paris not only luxuriates in Baudelaire's city of spectacles, but also reminds us that nothing is for free, our view is an exchange, fiscal, gendered; it is both a hall of mirrors and a stage on which everyone is forced to play.

In his influential 1903 text *The Metropolis and Mental Life*, the German sociologist Georg Simmel (1858–1918) identified the ambiguity between the freedom afforded by the city and its impact, stating, 'The individual has become a mere cog in an enormous organization of things and powers which tear from his hands all progress, spirituality, and value in order to transform them from their subjective form into the form of a purely objective life...the metropolis is the genuine arena of this culture which outgrows all personal life.'[iii] Many artists shared a reticence about the dehumanizing effects of the metropolitan landscape; this was exemplified in German Expressionist artist Ernst Ludwig Kirchner's (1880–1938) *Street Scenes* series (1913–1915). These paintings, created in the bustling environs of pre-war Berlin, depict elongated anonymous figures looming towards us. Defined by lurid colours and broad brushstrokes, women dressed in fashionable clothes with mask-like faces walk in groups towards the viewer, while the darkened figure of a man (we suspect, the artist) is often shown walking out of the frame – a figure of futile resistance against the march of progress.

The existential anxiety within these images is a far cry from the romance of the carefree *flâneur*, a figure who influenced the works of another great theoretician of the modern age, Walter Benjamin (1892–1940). It would be Benjamin's *Das Passagen-Werk* (*The Arcades Project*, 1927–1940) that would identify and critique the modern city and its assimilation of consumer culture: 'For the first time, with Baudelaire, Paris becomes the subject of lyric poetry. This poetry is no hymn to the homeland; rather, the gaze of the allegorist, as it falls on the city, is the gaze of the alienated man. It is the gaze of the *flâneur*, whose way of life still conceals behind a mitigating nimbus the coming desolation of the big-city dweller.'[iv] Benjamin also wrote about the effect new technologies, in particular photography and film, had on individual and collective subjectivities and on the work of art. 'The camera introduces us to unconscious optics as does psychoanalysis to unconscious impulses'.[v] Benjamin considered photography to be both radical and totalitarian, rendering the 'cult of the genius', and with it some belief in individualism, obsolete, while offering a multiplicity of viewpoints and fractured identities. In the wake of the First World War, artists such as the Russian constructivist Alexander Rodchenko (1891–1956) and German Dadaist Hannah Höch (1889–1978) would utilize mass-produced images from newspapers into collage works. These often featured images of crowds or 'the masses' as an unstoppable flowing force, using the new angles and aerial viewpoints afforded by the camera to create a sense of dynamism and revolutionary spirit. At the same time pioneering filmworks, both avant-garde and popular, appeared, including Fritz Lang's epic Expressionist film *Metropolis* (1927) and Charlie Chaplin's *Modern Times* (1936). Both films, despite their formal differences, stand as silent-era responses to the effects of industrial labour, political power, and the dehumanization of the urban working class.

It would be in other avant-garde practices that the concept of modern self-identity as a performance would arise. Marcel Duchamp's (1887–1968) female alter ego Mademoiselle Rrose Sélavy (whose name is a pun on the French saying 'Eros, c'est la vie') and Claude Cahun's (1894–1954) Surrealist self-portraits would continue to influence the later feminist practices of the 1960s and 1970s outside their native France.

While much artistic activity later on moved towards the more hermetic concerns of Abstract Expressionism, documentary photography played a central role in the picturing of modern urban life in the mid-20th century. As a medium, and through its various platforms, it allowed for the representation of infinitely more faces, more spectacles, more everyday life, than painting ever could. From the horrors of the Second World War to the Civil Rights movement, it offered the appearance and dissemination of collective experiences on a much wider stage. The street photographer took on the role of latter-day *flâneur*, a detached, predominantly male, observer. Walker Evans' (1903–1975) early candid photographs, 'Subway Portraits' (1938–1941), were black-and-white images of a cross-section of anonymous commuters taken with a hidden camera in New York's underground trains. The ostensible 'ordinariness' of these photographic subjects offered a new and intimate insight into urban experience, at once valourizing and fetishizing the life of the 'everyman'. Evans writes, 'As it happens, you don't see among them the face of a judge or a senator or a bank president. What you do see is at once sobering, startling, and obvious: these are the ladies and gentlemen of the jury'.[vi] Post-war America, in particular, became a fertile subject for photographic narratives about urban life, individuality, and alienation as seen through the eyes of photographers such as Robert Frank (b. 1924) in *The Americans*

(1955-1956) which, as Jack Kerouac stated, 'sucked a sad poem right out of America and onto film'.[vii] As the Beats did through their poetry and writing, Frank's images of crowded streets, mesmerized pedestrians, and isolated subjects spoke of an existential emptiness at the heart of the mass-consumer culture in the atomic age while also offering a stark portrayal of class, gender, and cultural undercurrents in a country at odds with its own self-image.

In the 1960s it would be Pop Art and its assimilation of Hollywood tropes, mass culture, and celebrity that could be said to signal the end of the modernist period. Contemporary preoccupations with individual and collective realities paved the way for other movements of the post-modern era, such as conceptual and feminist art practices where subjectivities were treated as multifarious, political, and contextual. Guy Debord's (1931-1994) influential *The Society of the Spectacle* (1967) considered that all authentic contemporary experience had been replaced by its representation. Describing the image-saturated, mediated world of mass consumerism and celebrity culture – so eloquently co-opted by Andy Warhol (1928-1987) – he stated that 'The spectacle is not a collection of images, but a social relationship among people, mediated by images.'[viii] Debord was highly critical of these new conditions: 'The reigning economic system is a vicious circle of isolation. Its technologies are based on isolation, and they contribute to that same isolation. From automobiles to television, the goods that the spectacular system chooses to produce also serve it as weapons for constantly reinforcing the conditions that engender "lonely crowds".[ix]

While it is these 'lonely crowds' that Alex Prager chooses as her subject matter, *Face in the Crowd* offers redemption to the ever-present sense of dislocation.

For the first time in Prager's work, characters are offered a space to speak before plunging back into the street, the theatre, or the airport hall – back into the muted environs of the photographic space. They ruminate on existential anxieties, every-day fears and personal challenges. Speaking candidly to the camera, one young man recalls a dream: 'I'm standing at the edge of something…and I'll just fall and it always wakes me up and it's always so frightening'; while the central character of the film, actor Elizabeth Banks, stares out at the crowded street through a window, then into the crowd, and reminisces, 'I guess she [her mother] was working a lot so she just wanted me to have lots and lots of things to do with kids my own age – maybe she thought it would help me not notice how often I was actually alone.'

i   Ezra Pound, 'In a Station of the Metro', 1913, from *Personae*, 1926. Reprinted with the permission of the publishers: Faber and Faber Ltd (for UK edition); New Directions Publishing Corp, New York (for US and other language editions).

ii   Charles Baudelaire, *The Painter of Modern Life (Le Peintre de la vie moderne)*, 1863 in Baudelaire, *Selected Writings on Art and Artists,* Cambridge University Press, Cambridge, 1981, translation and introduction by P. E. Charvet, p. 400.

iii   Georg Simmel, *The Metropolis and Mental Life (Die Grosstädte und das Geistesleben)*, 1903 in *The Sociology of Georg Simmel*, adapted by D. Weinstein from the translation by Kurt Wolff, Free Press, New York, 1950, p. 422.

iv   Walter Benjamin, *The Arcades Project (Das Passagen-Werk)*, 1927–1940, Harvard University Press, Cambridge, Mass., 1999, prepared on the basis of the German volume edited by Rolf Tiedemann, translation by Kevin McLaughlin and Howard Eiland, p. 10.

v   Walter Benjamin, *The Work of Art in the Age of Mechanical Reproduction (Das Kunstwerk im Zeitalter seiner technischen Reproduzierbarkeit)*, 1935 in *Illuminations*, Schocken Books, New York, 1969, edited by Hannah Arendt and translation by Harry Zohn, p. 237.

vi   Walker Evans, 'The Unposed Portrait', *Harper's Bazaar*, March 1962.

vii   Jack Kerouac, introduction to Robert Frank's seminal photo-book *The Americans* (1955–1956).

viii   Guy Debord, *The Society of the Spectacle (La société du spectacle)*, 1967, Zone Books, 1995, translation by Donald Nicholson-Smith, p. 12.

ix   Ibid, p. 22.

FACE IN THE CROWD

(2013)

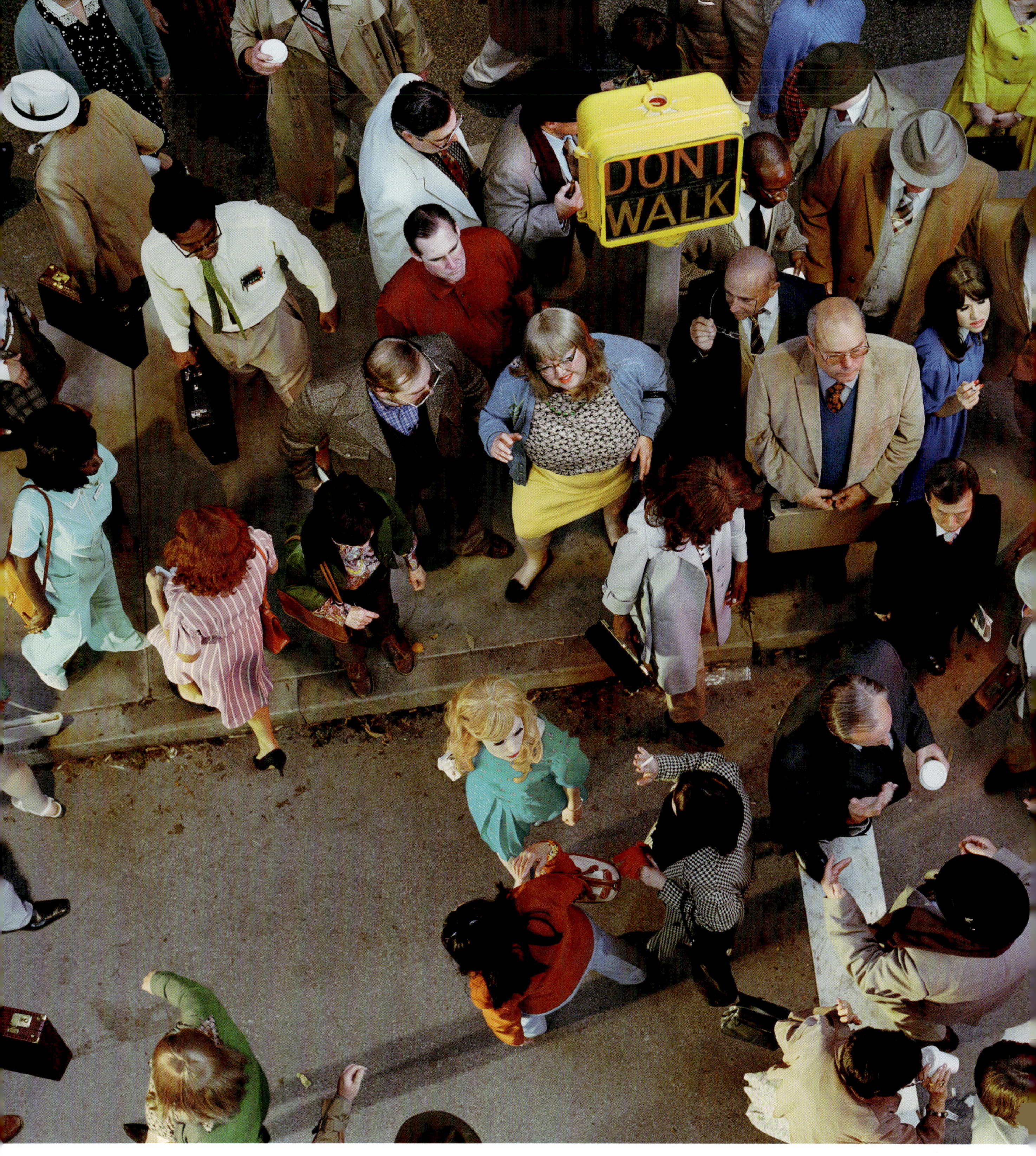
DONT
WALK

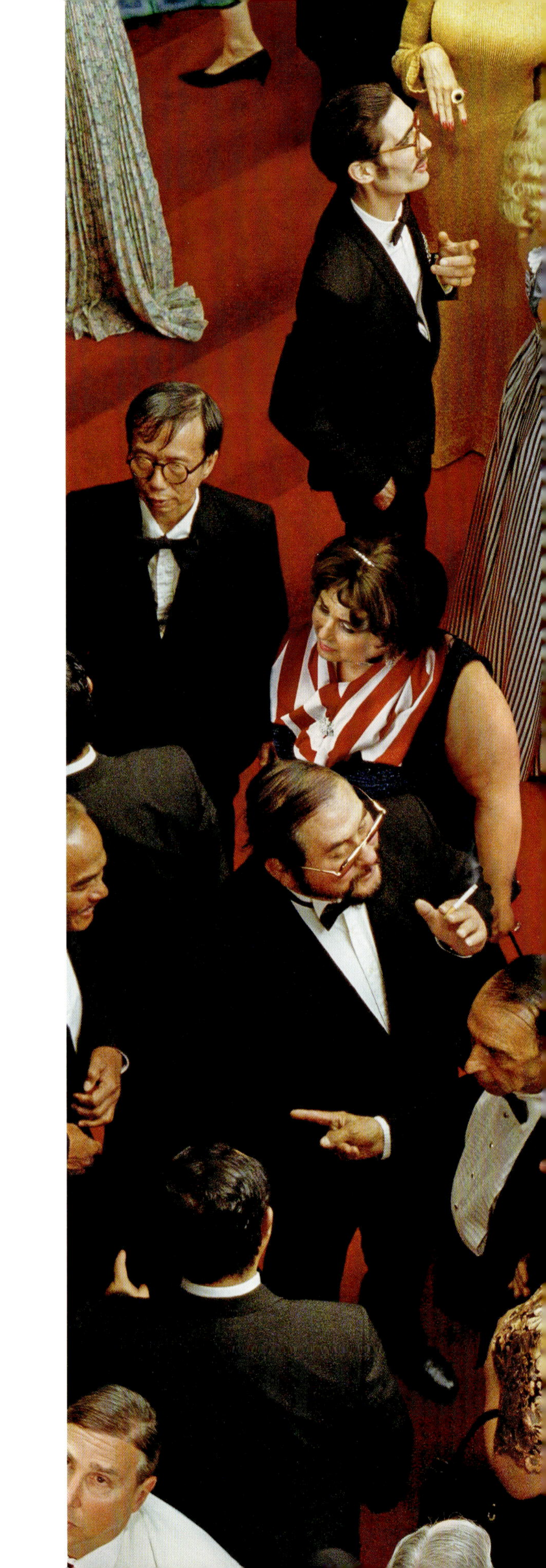

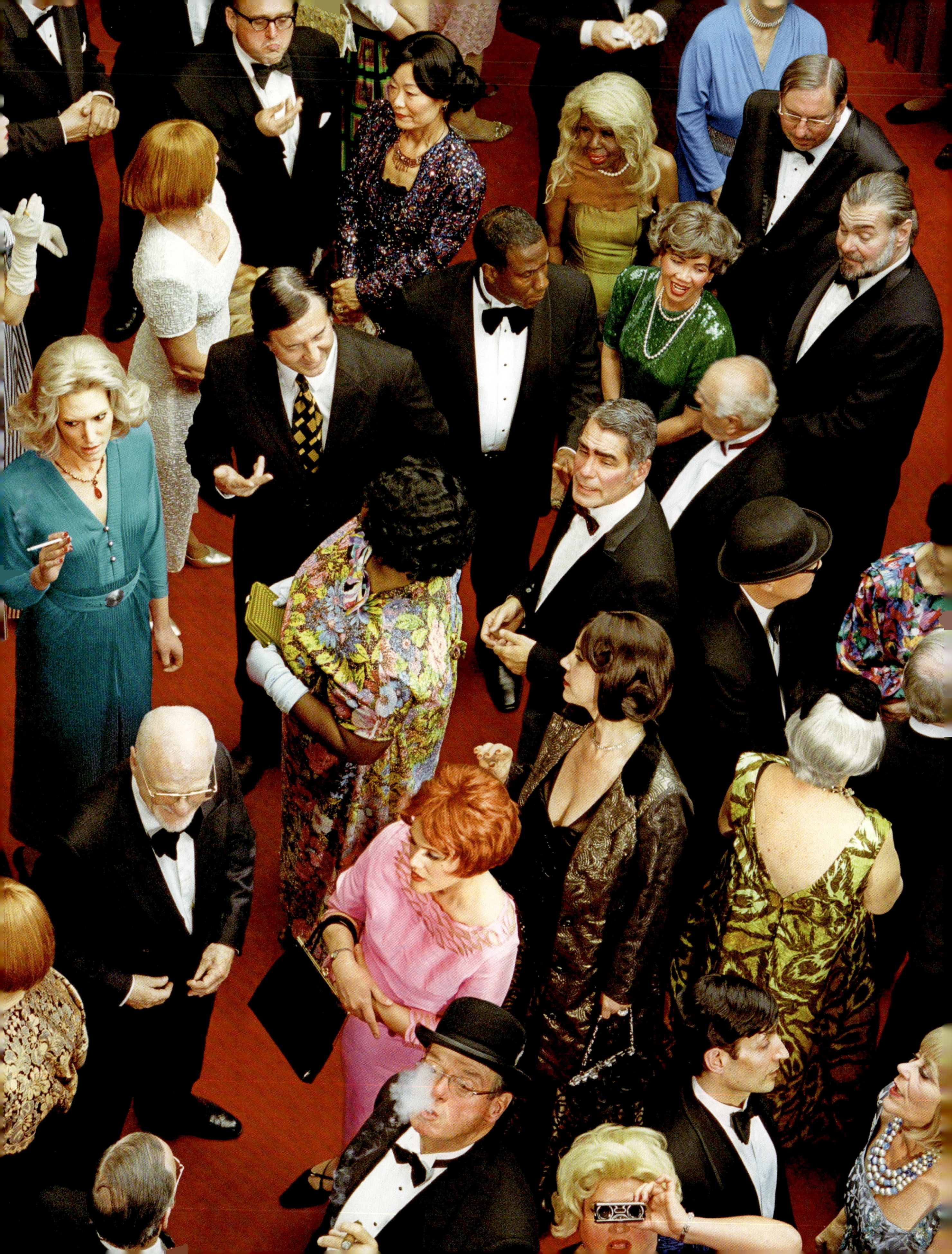

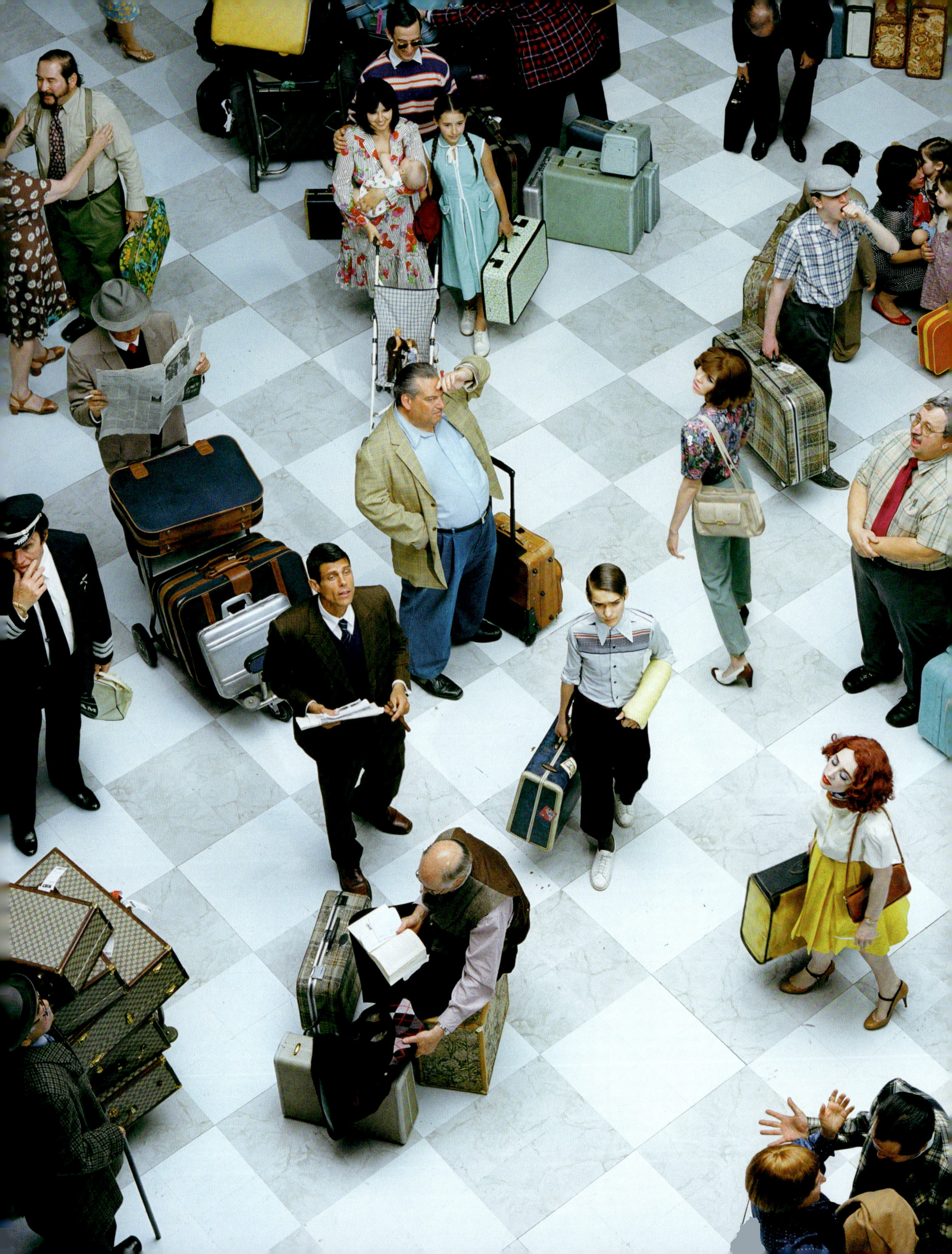

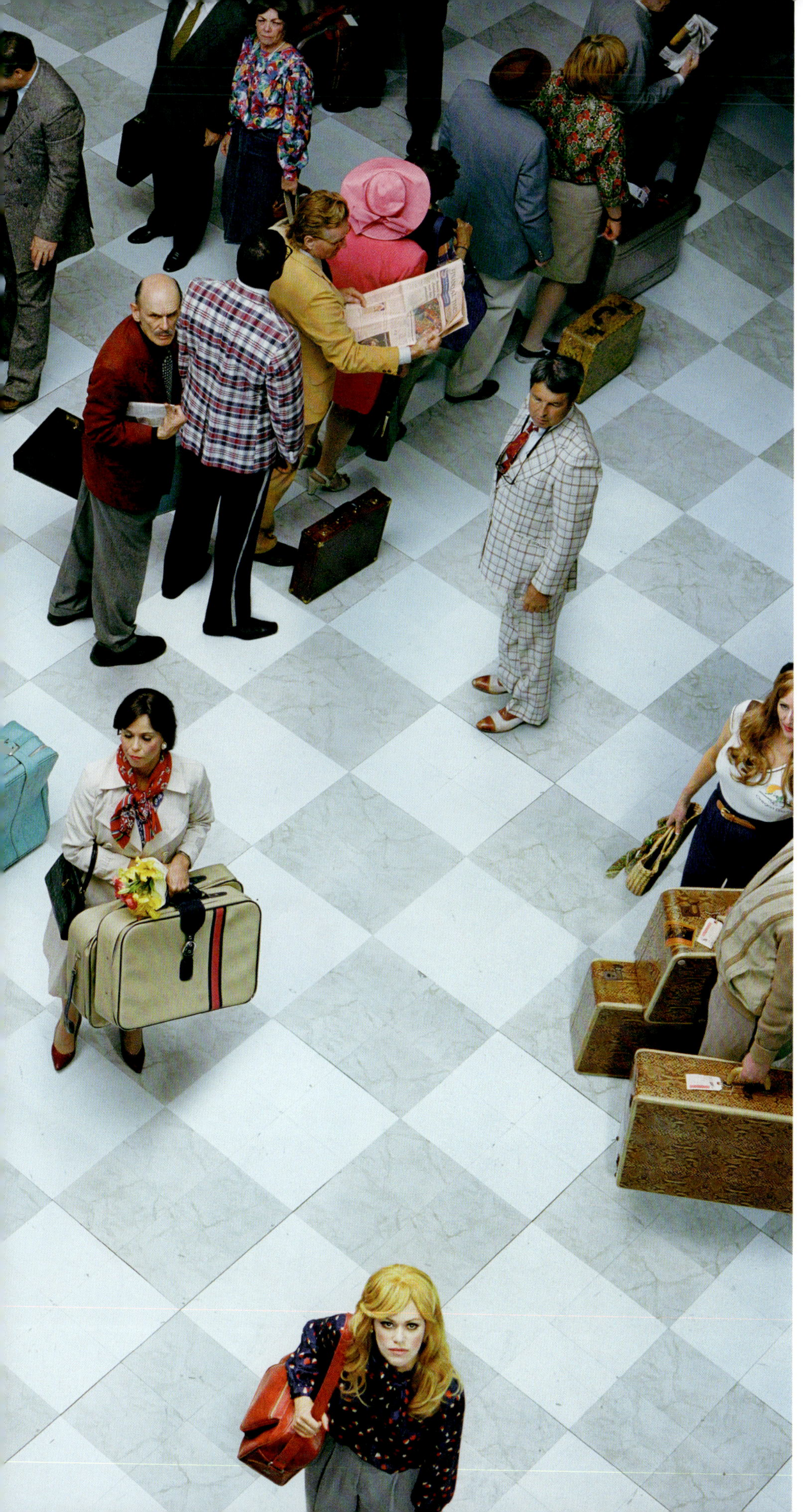

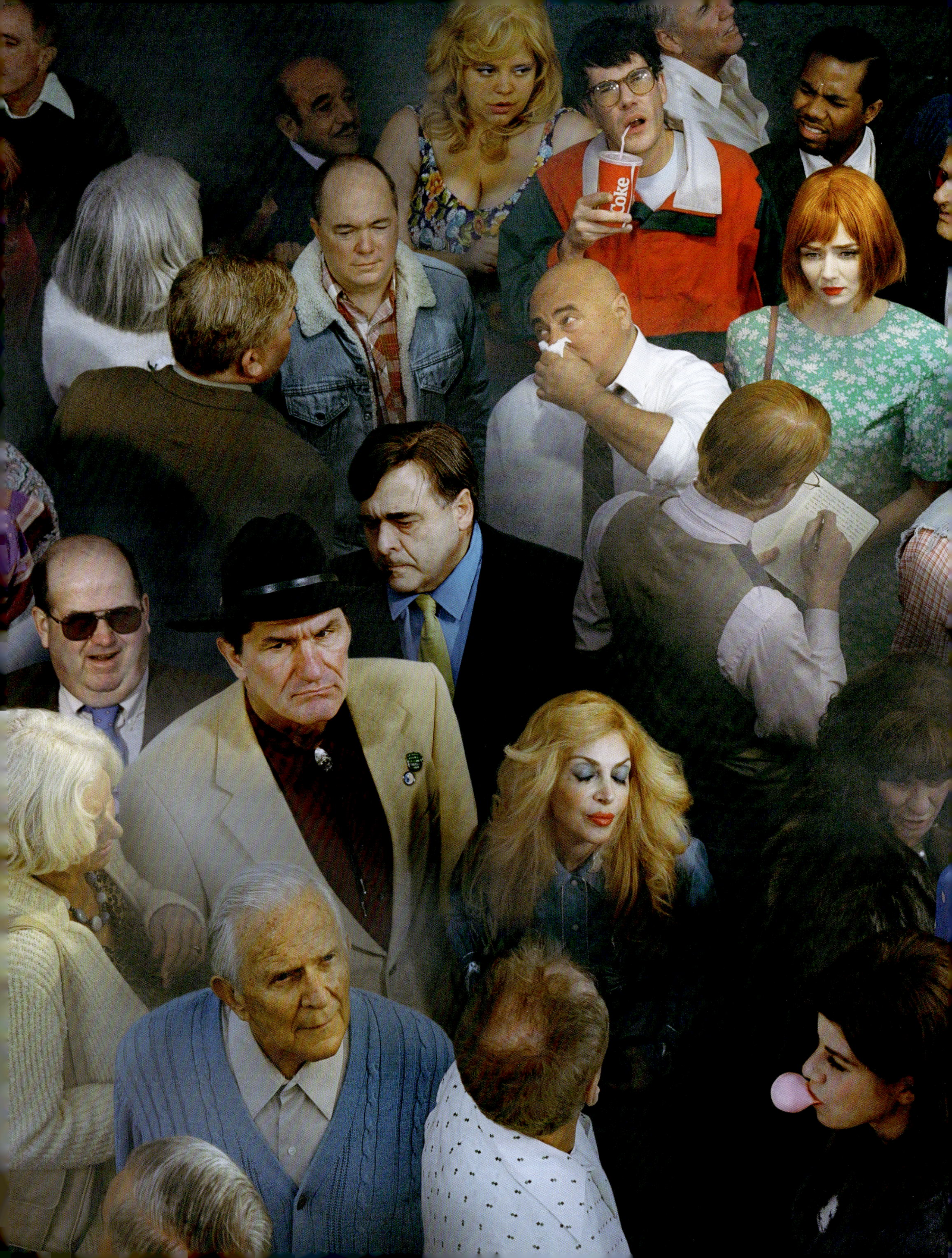

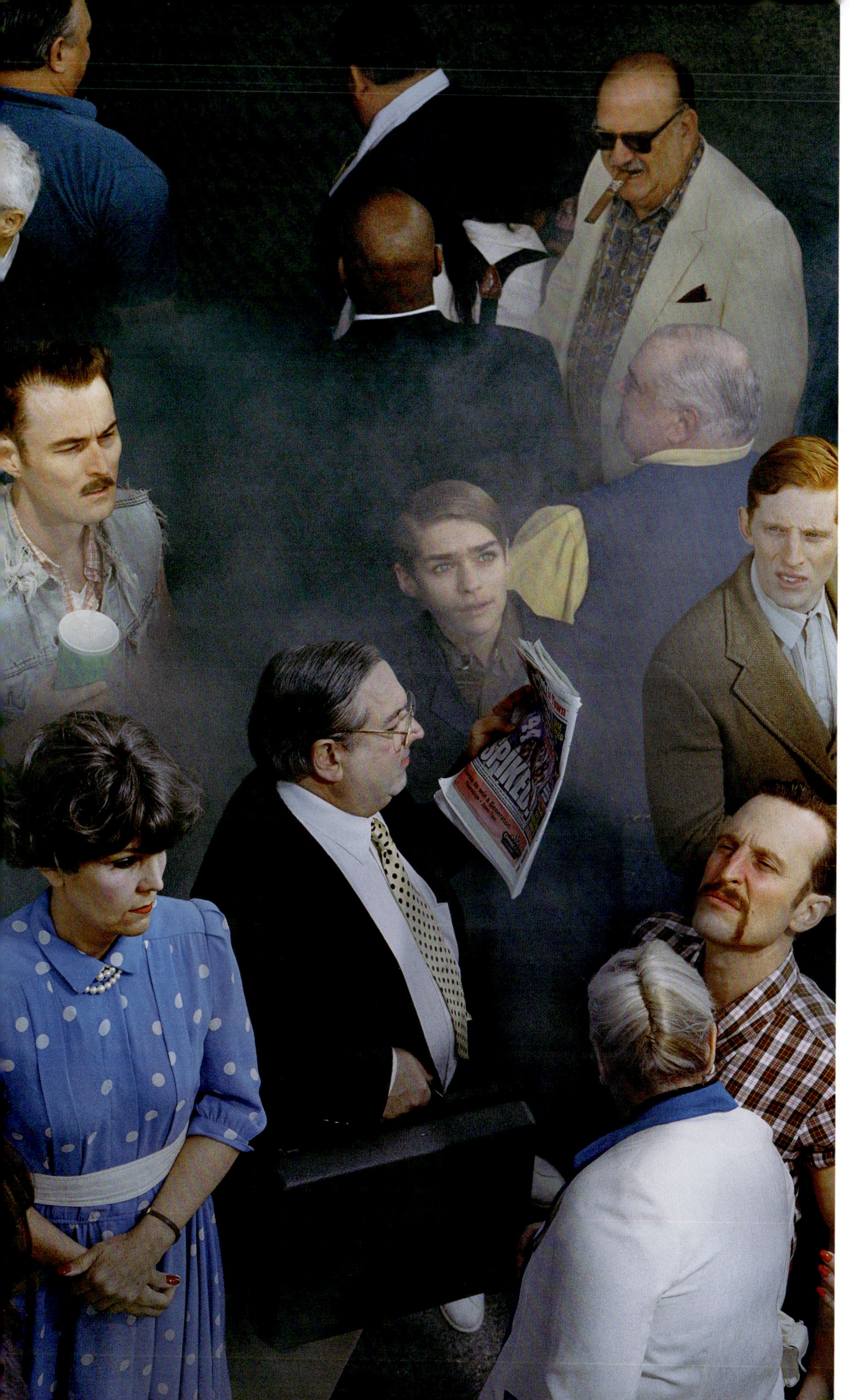

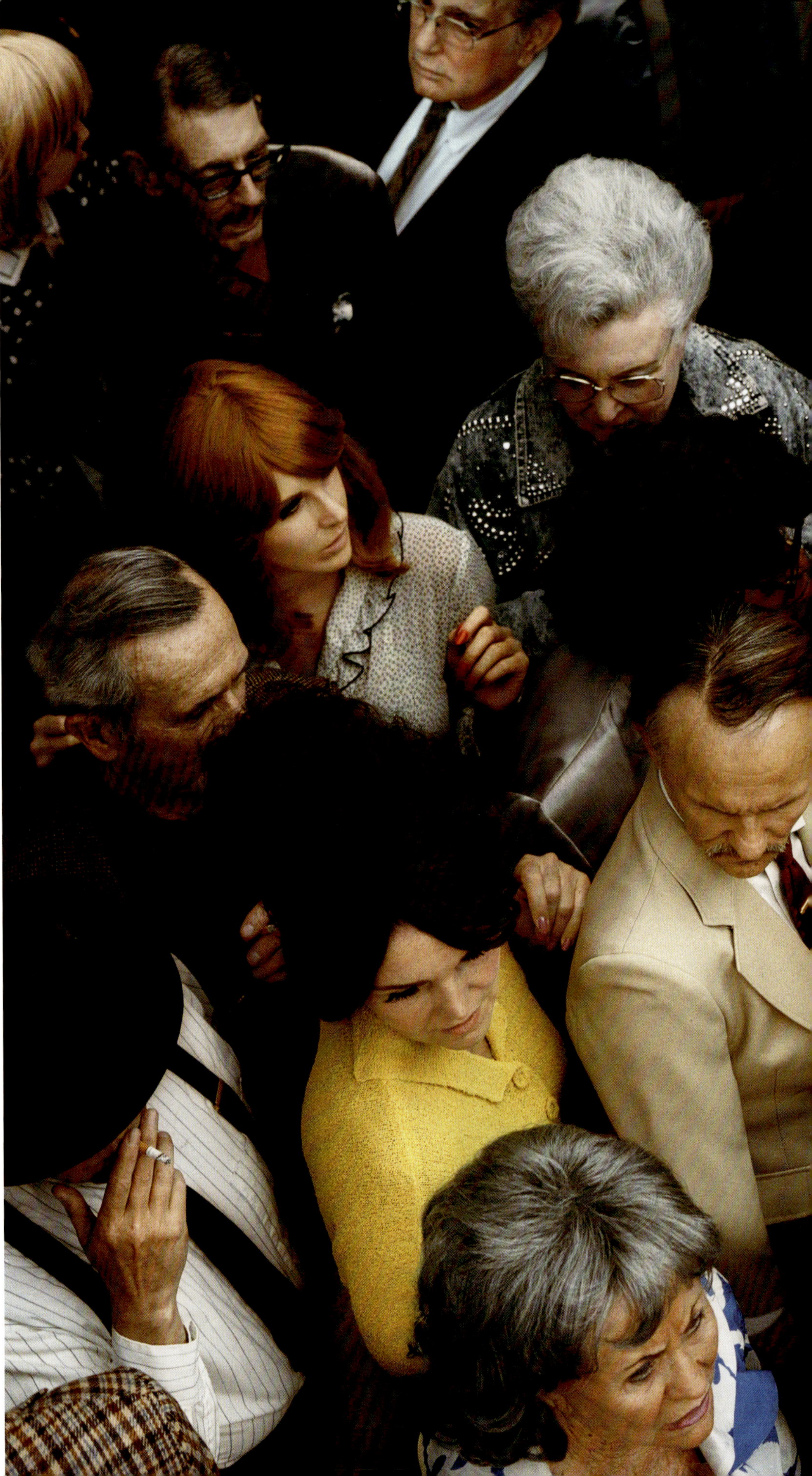

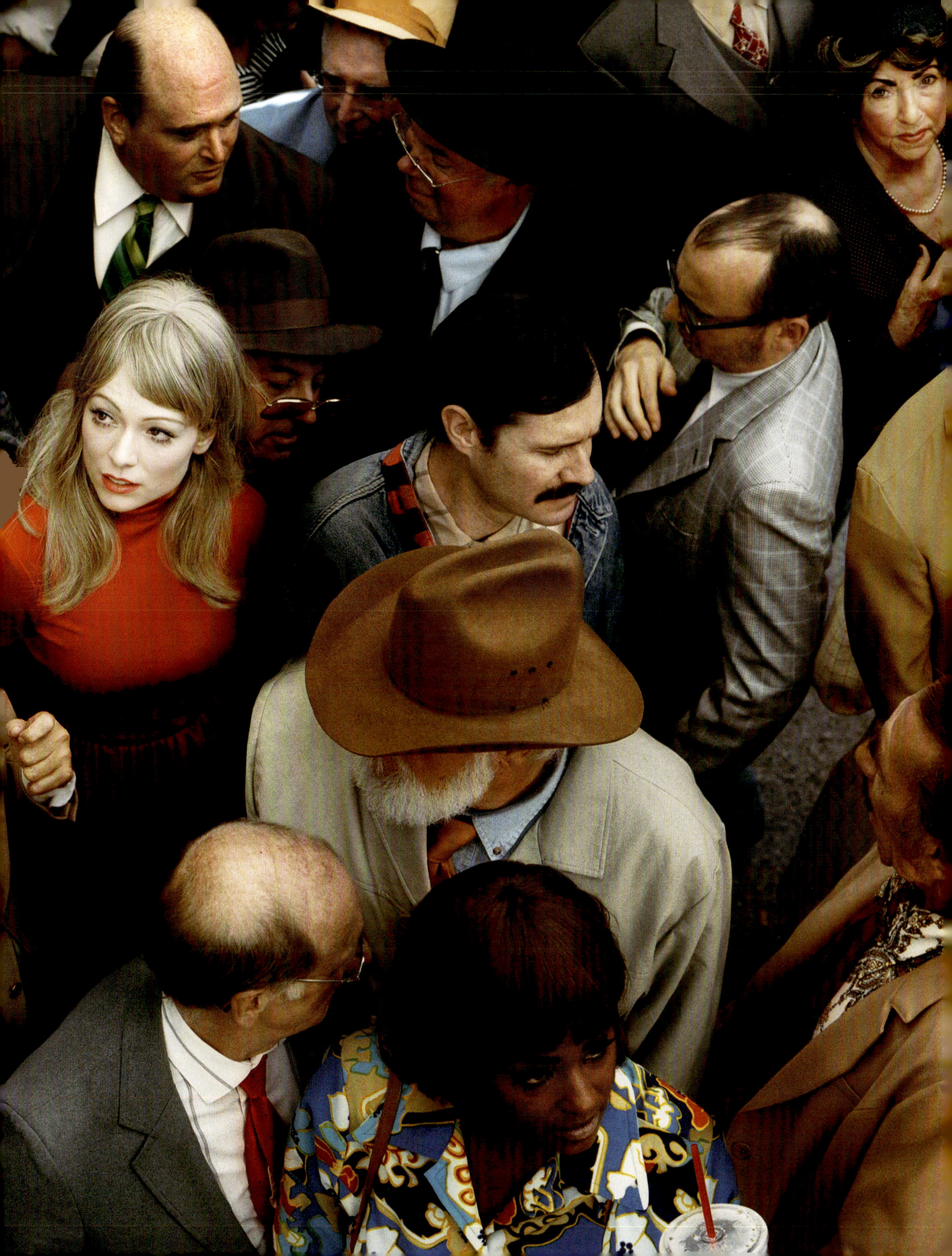

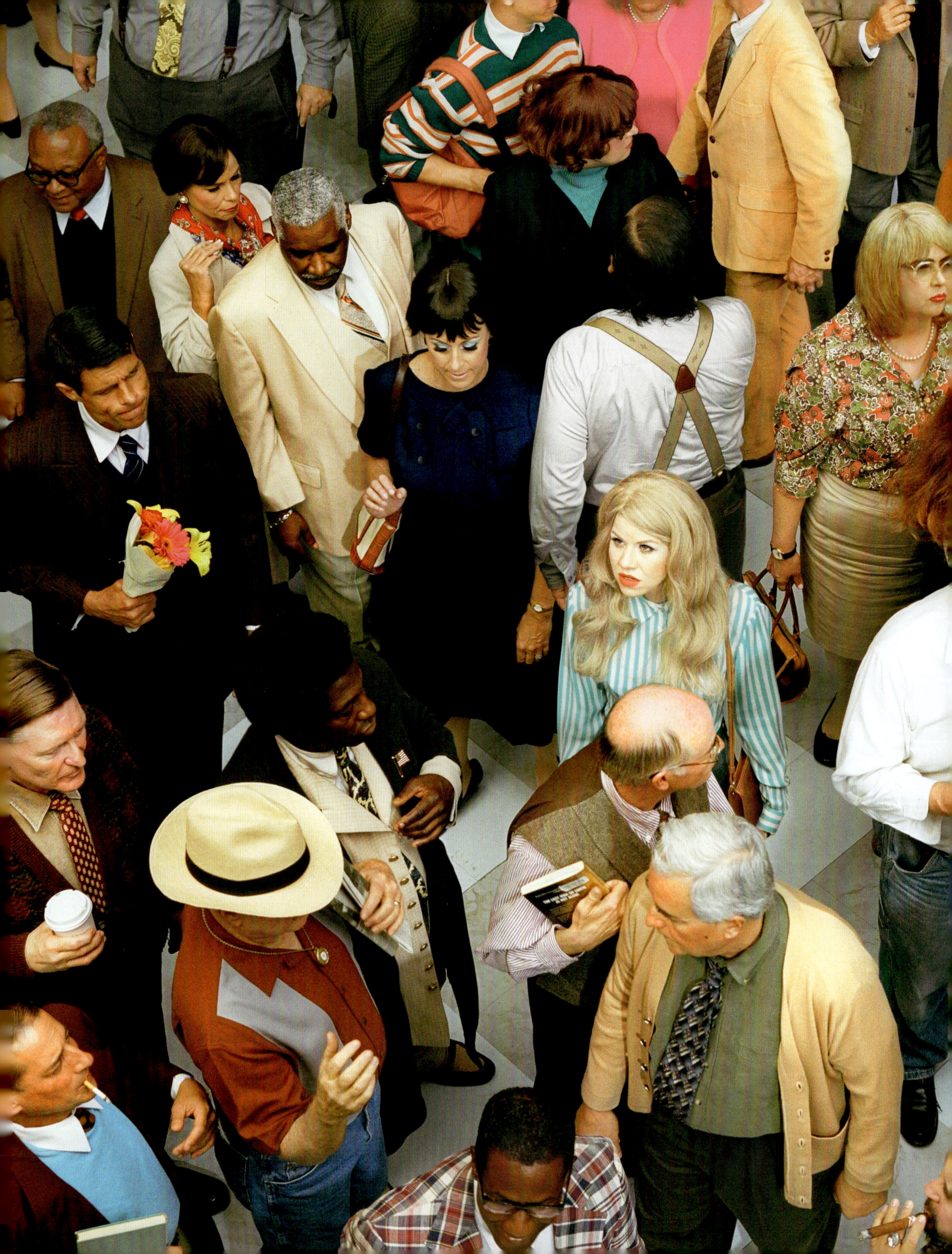

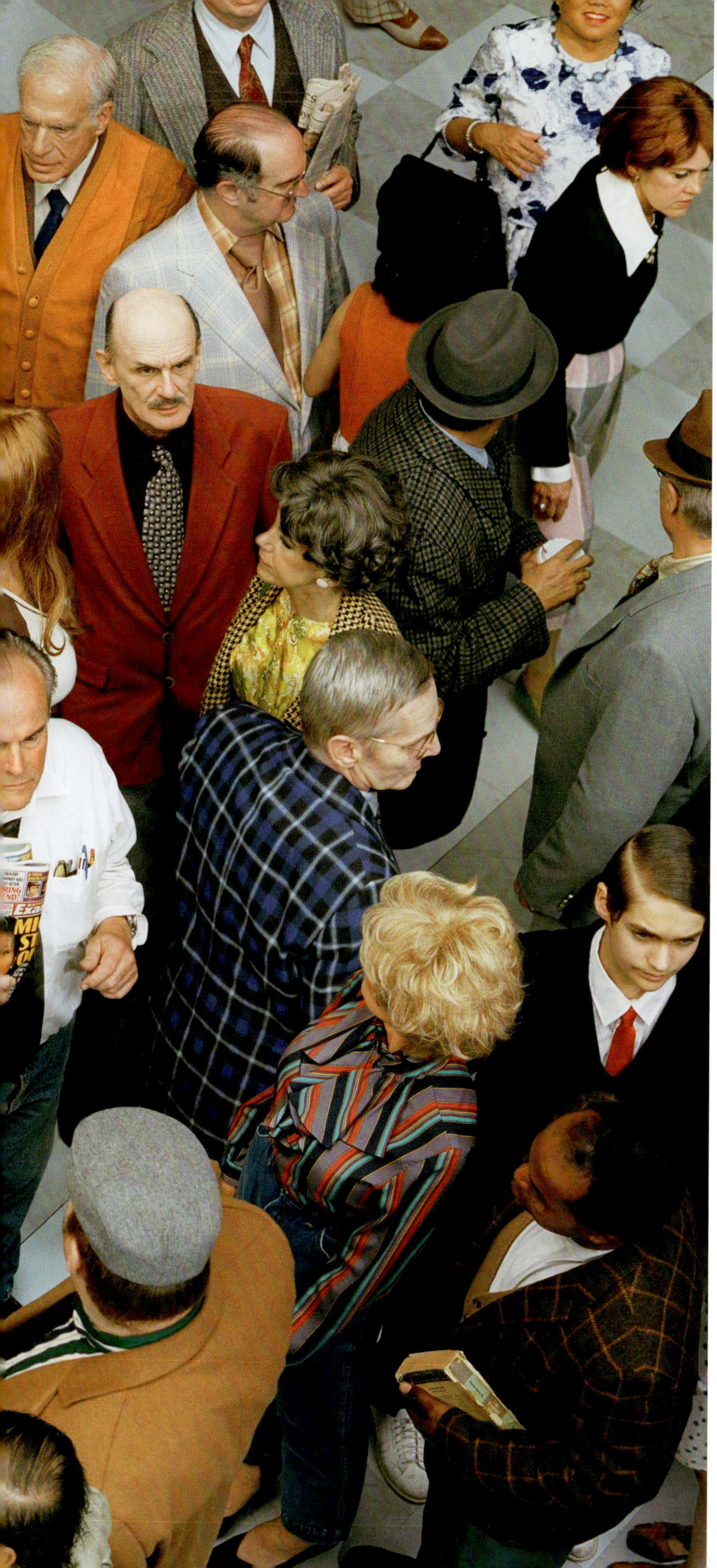

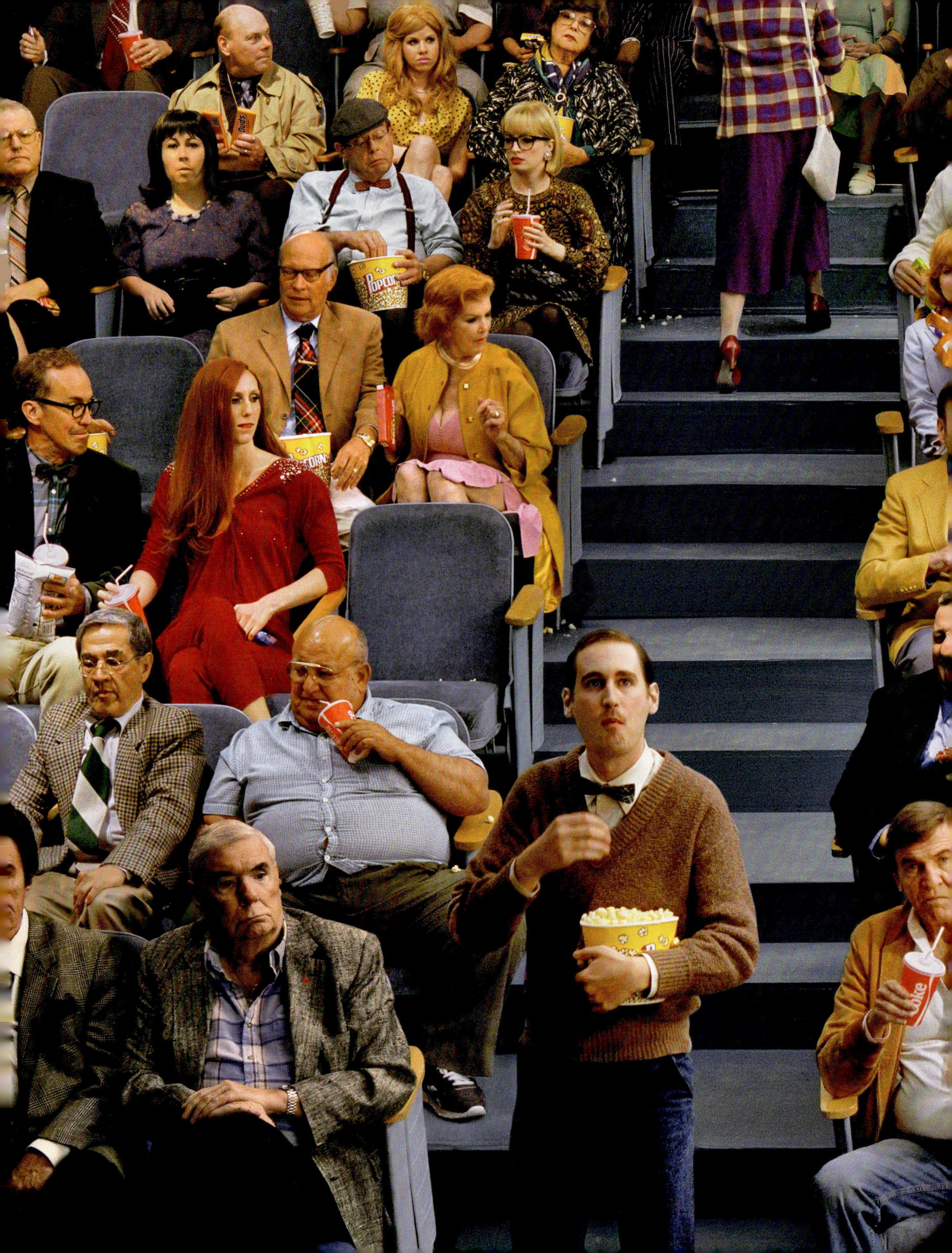

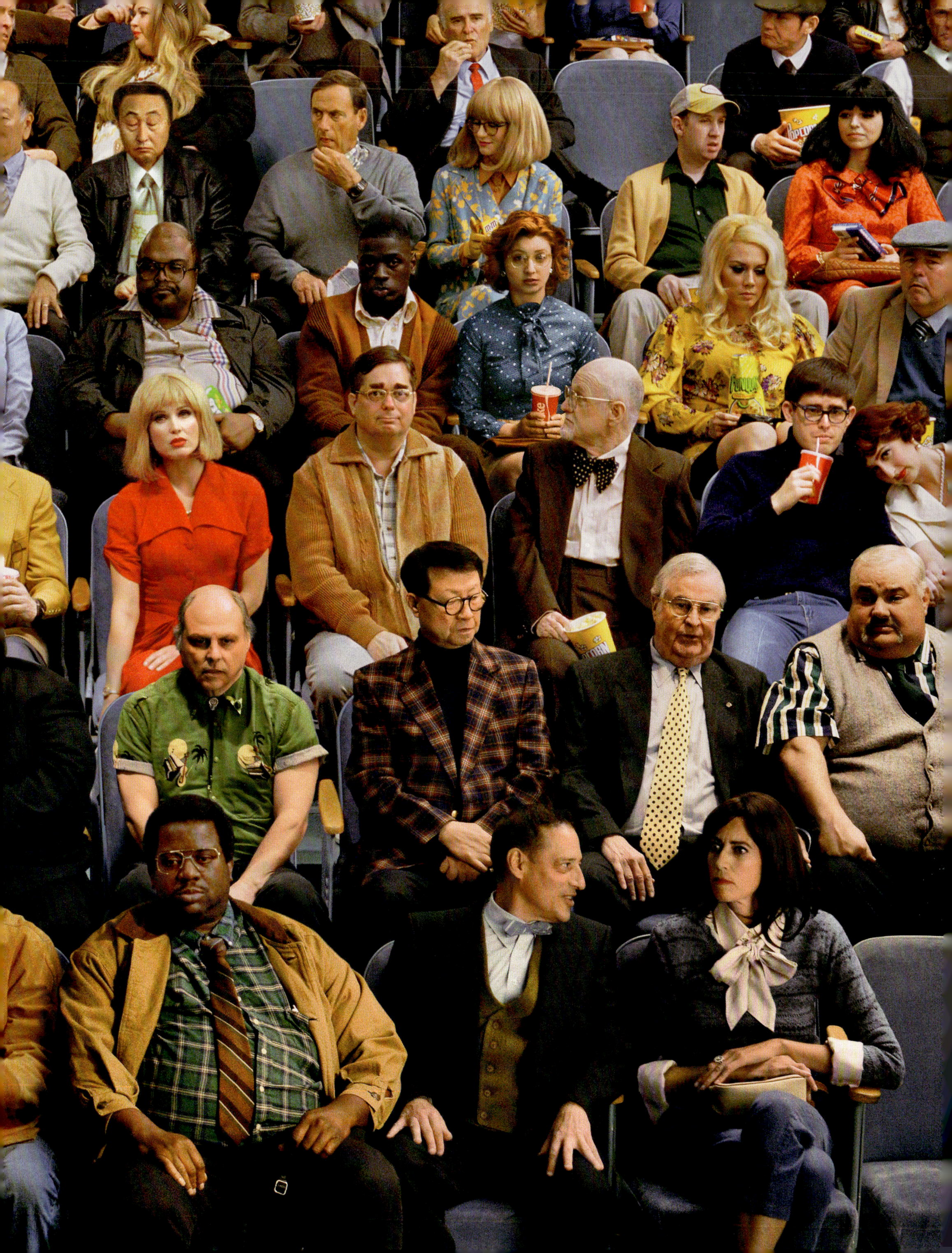

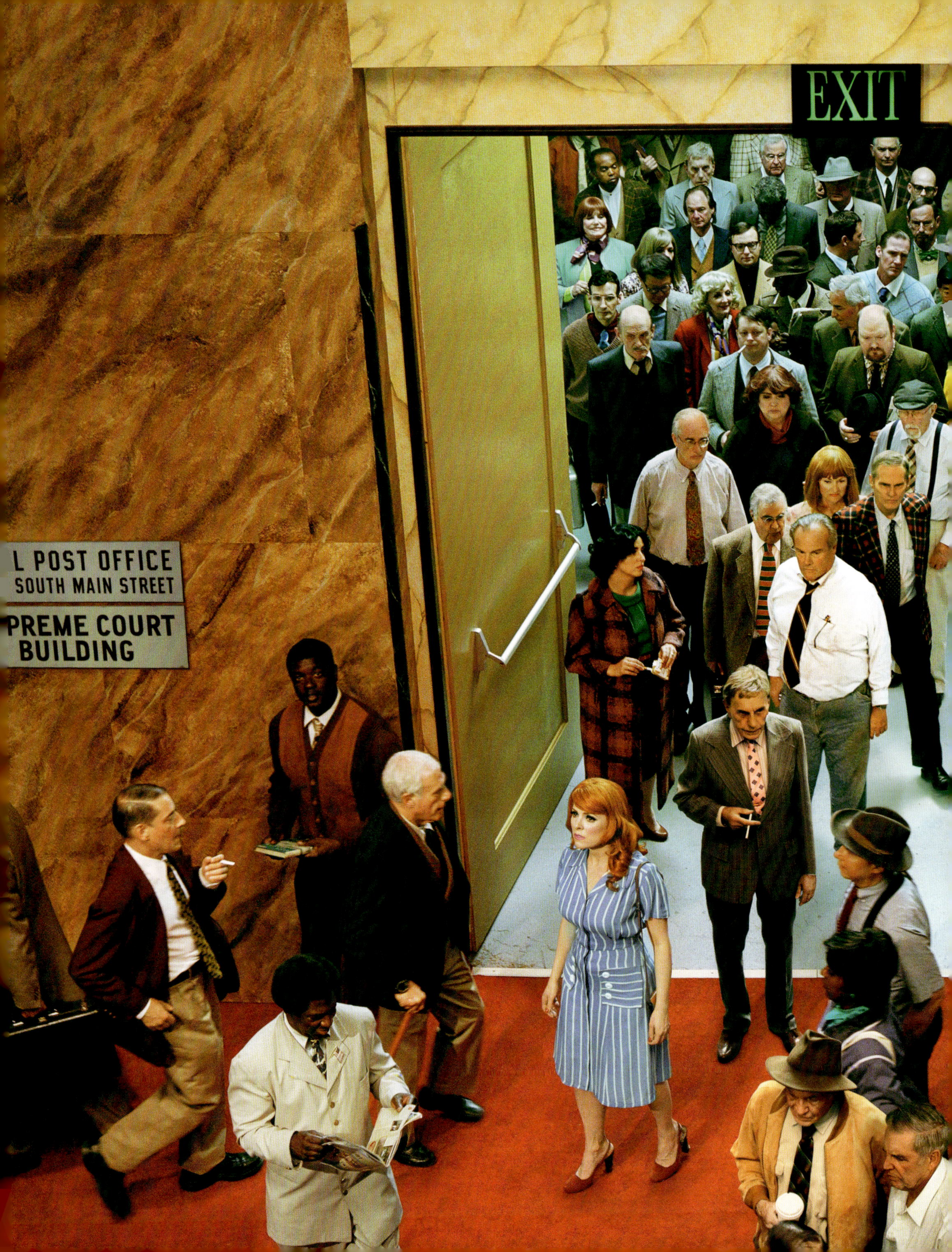

EXIT
L POST OFFICE
SOUTH MAIN STREET
PREME COURT
BUILDING

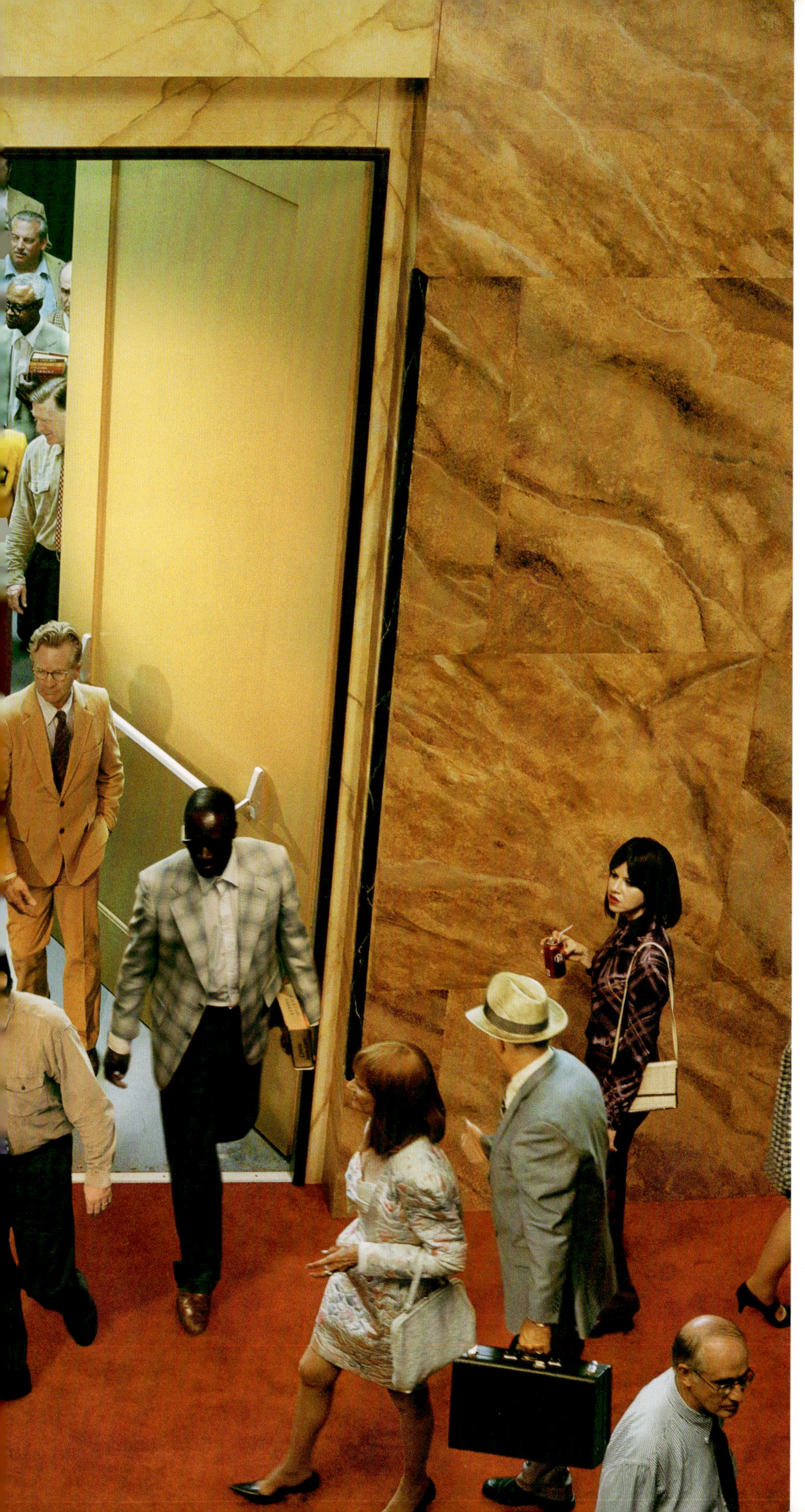

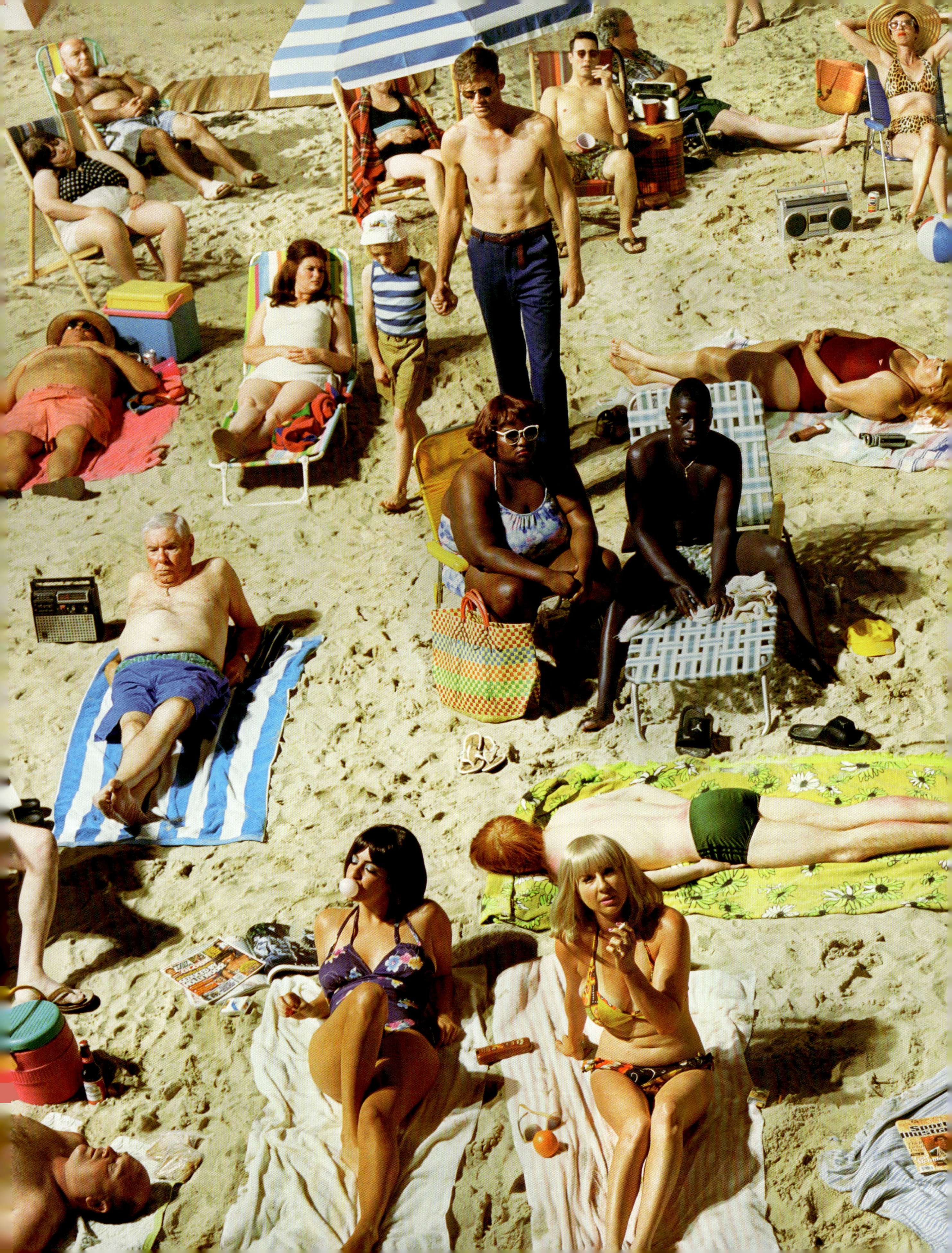

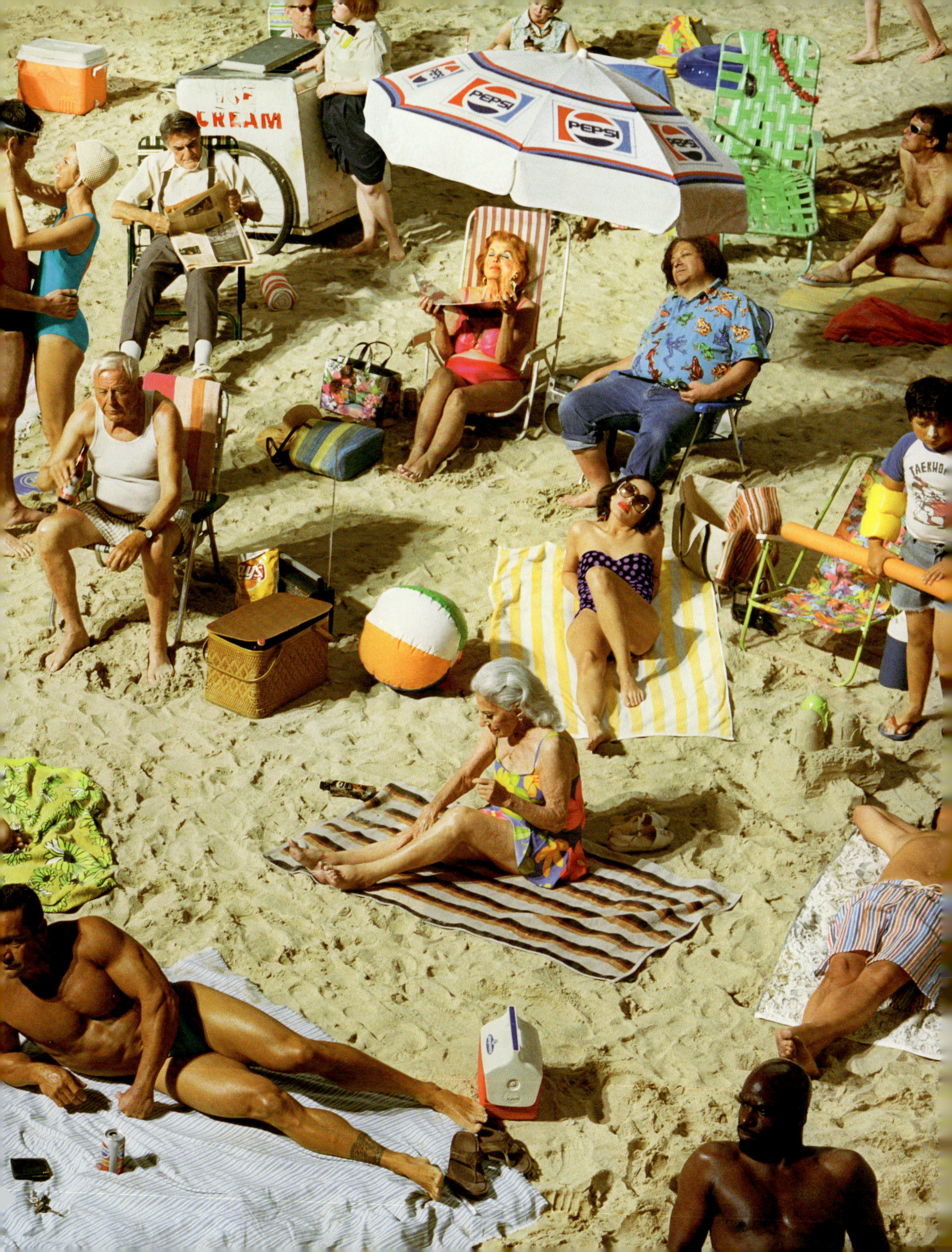

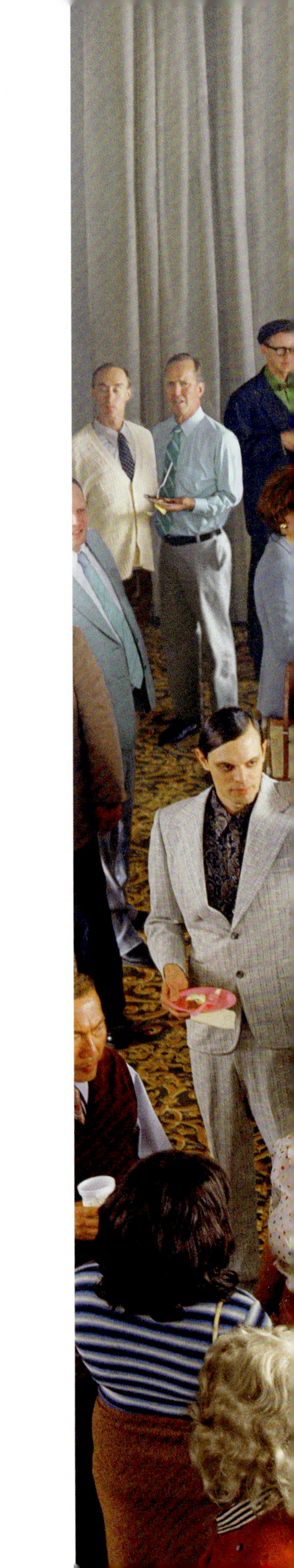

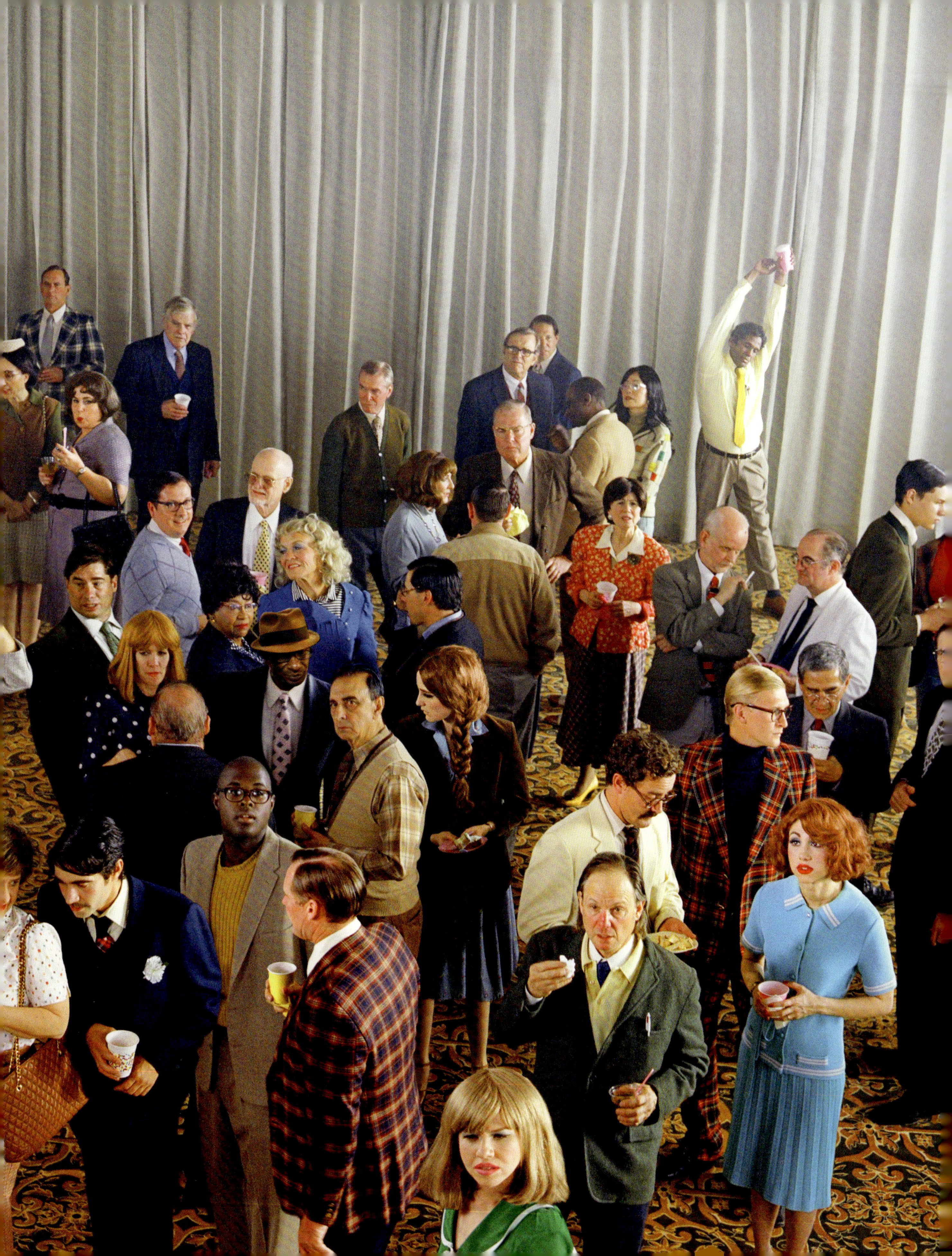

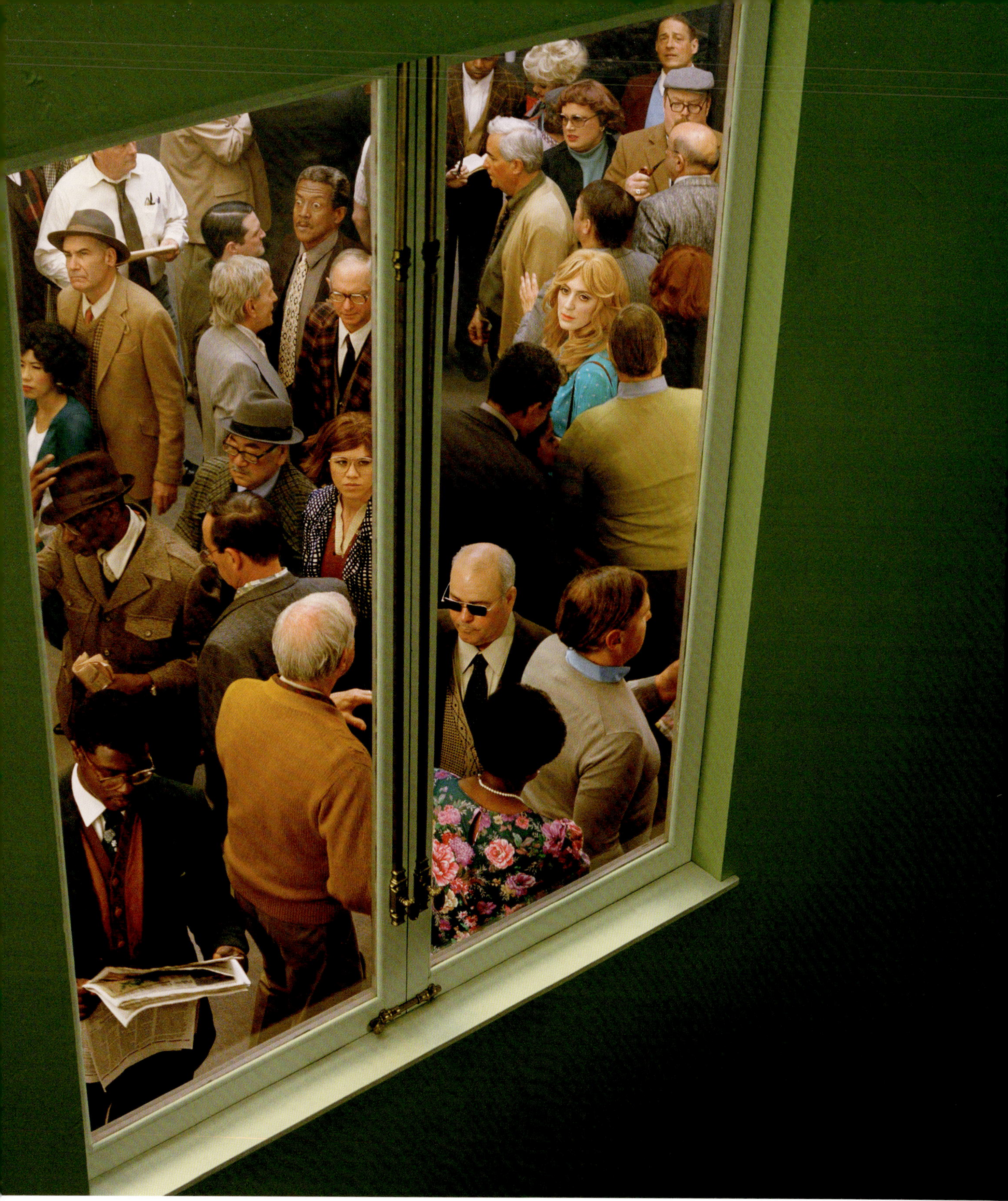

FILMS

Pretend to Pretend in the Art of Appearances

Michael Mansfield

'Emotions as such are deceiving. There are no specifically fake emotions
because, as Freud puts it literally, the only emotion which doesn't deceive
is anxiety. All other emotions are fake.

So, of course, the problem here is are we able to encounter in cinema the
emotion of anxiety, or is cinema as such a fake? Cinema, as the art of
appearances, tells us something about reality itself. It tells us something
about how reality constitutes itself.'[i]

Slavoj Zizek

From the opening frame, Alex Prager's films are spellbinding. They are bright, bold, electric. They are beguiling and morbidly seductive. They unfold in surprising ways to reveal perplexing incidents that linger with us long after their rolling credits.

And these films appear as if we have seen them before. The characters are nearly recognizable, their stories vaguely familiar. They are permanently stuck in another time. What is reflected on the big screen is at once uncertain and exact. They suggest a cinema we've visited in the past, but cannot quite place. The cast and the cadence are clearly leading us towards something we should already know. Yet, Prager's films don't fully reveal themselves scene by scene. They rather reintroduce us frame by frame and in every aspect of film.

Prager belongs to a generation of contemporary artists who fully own their media. She wields a camera and a director's chair with equal strength, and creates both movies and photographs in full view of their commercial influences and the complex politics of art-house avant-garde cinema. And she does so at full throttle without apology.

During the second half of the 20th century, artists were seeking to distance themselves from art-historical tradition. A generation, which included Bruce Nauman, Eleanor Antin, and John Baldessari, particularly in California, began to weave photography, film, and video with performance and sculpture. They engaged electronic technologies as a means to wrest the media of mass communication from commercial interests. Increased portability of 16mm cameras and video tape further liberated artists from the studio, giving them a new and independent voice where polished and well-financed productions were abandoned in favour of a low-fidelity, democratic avant-garde.[ii]

What followed in the late 1970s, and continued through to the end of the millennium, was a political and social reversal. As curator and scholar Douglas Eklund observes, artists were disillusioned that the utopian promise of an effective counterculture had 'devolved into a commercialized pastiche of rebellious stances prepackaged for consumption.'[iii] *The Pictures Generation, 1974–1984* exhibition at the Metropolitan Museum of Art in New York (2009) took authority and made way for globally conscious artists among a burgeoning universe of images, and eventually set the stage for immersive, virtual, and moving works of art.

Composing both motion pictures and two-dimensional photographs, Prager's artistic practice mirrors that of large-scale studio productions, from scripting, set design, casting, and wardrobe to lighting, choreography, sound design, and screening. Yet Prager distills the resulting components into a rich Hollywood concentrate. Each highly polished work presents a jewel-toned intensity[iv] littered with the parodied clichés of popular cinema and packed with melodramatic renderings of tension, anxiety, and suspense. But hers are not empty calories. For all of the familiar Hollywood glitz and vivid glamour of the finished films, Prager has shaped a novel artistic practice that mingles southern California-studio aesthetics with a distinctively informed vision. One aspect of her accomplishments in film, and one aspect of our sometimes guilty pleasure of consuming it, is that what screens as a cinematically pristine and signature style is collectively rendered from generations of cinematic and photographic influences, social currents and filmic intent. Consumed all together, they fulfil an imaginative and determined mode of production that gives the artist a voice.

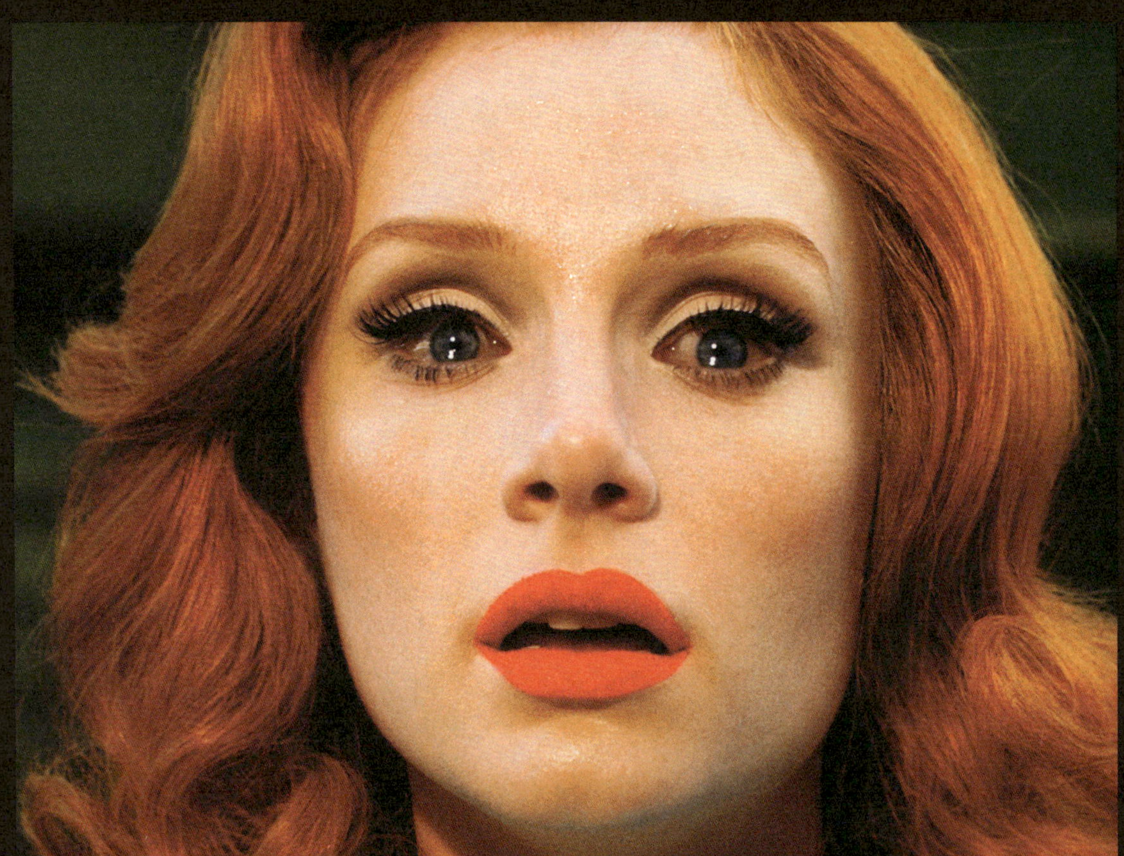

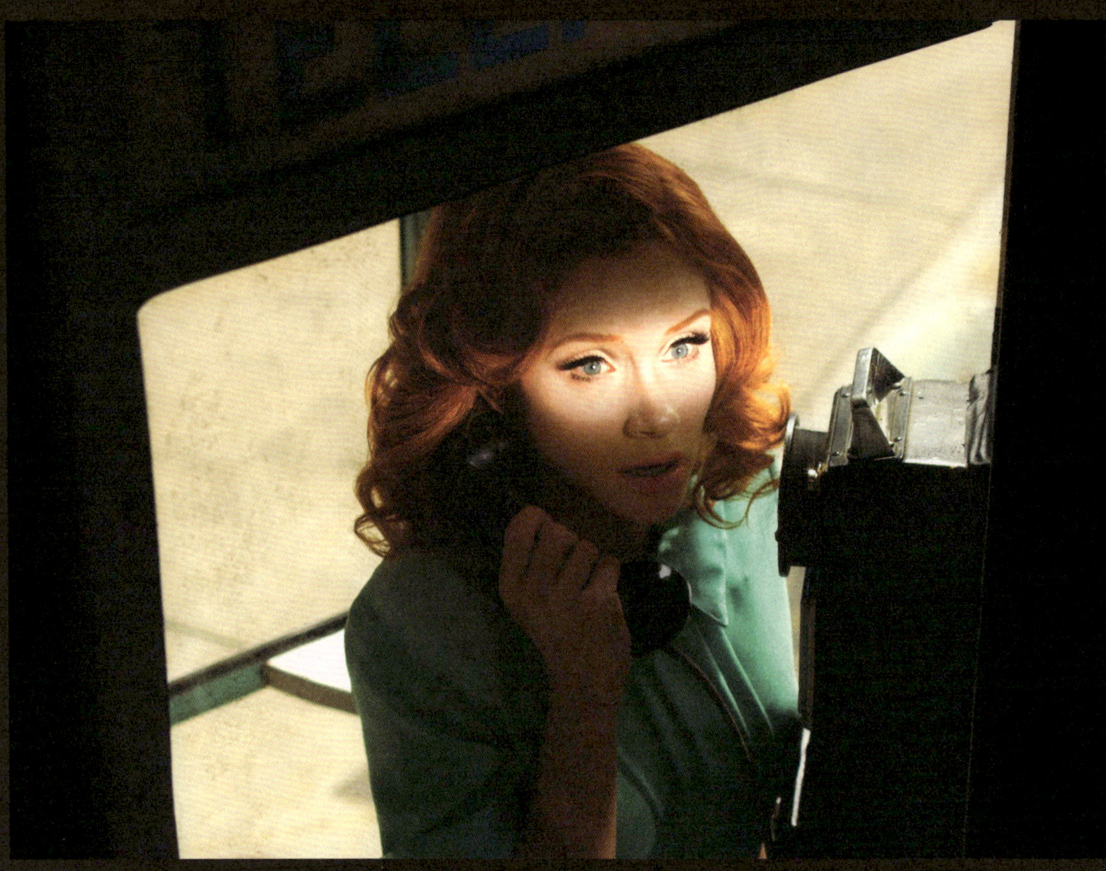

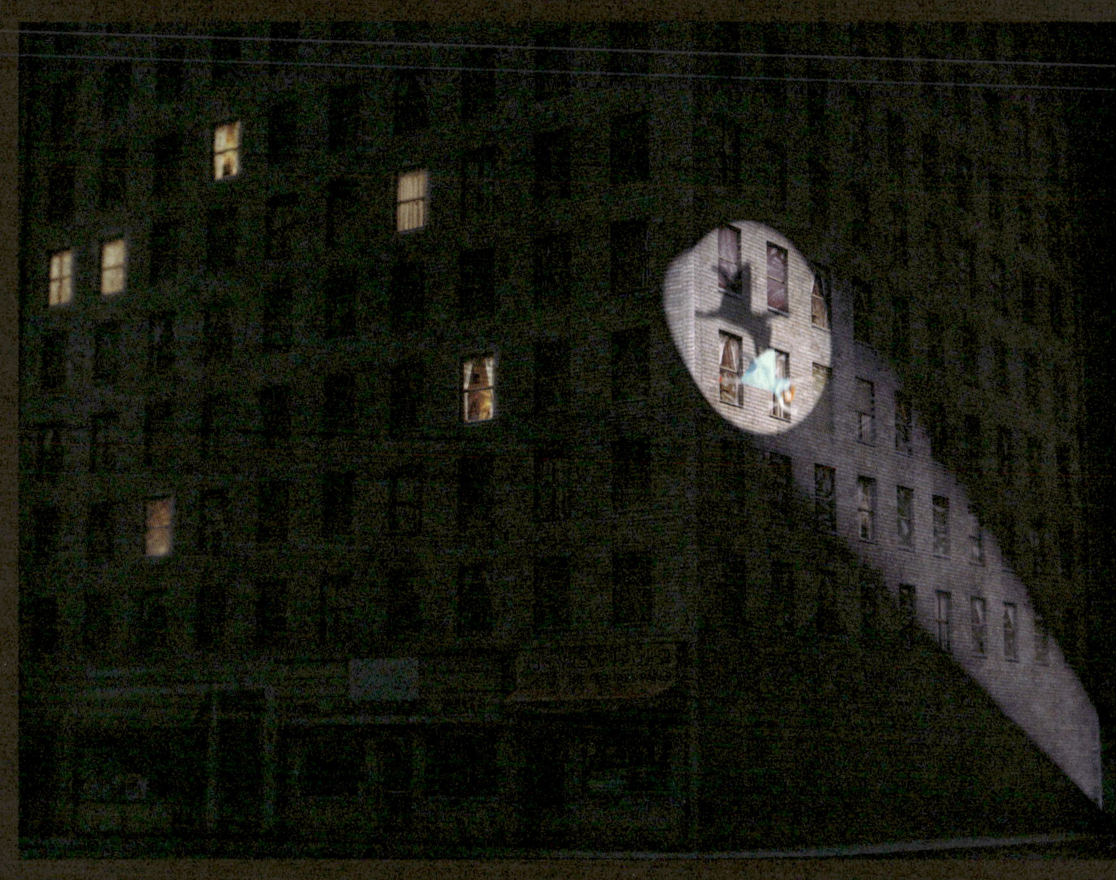

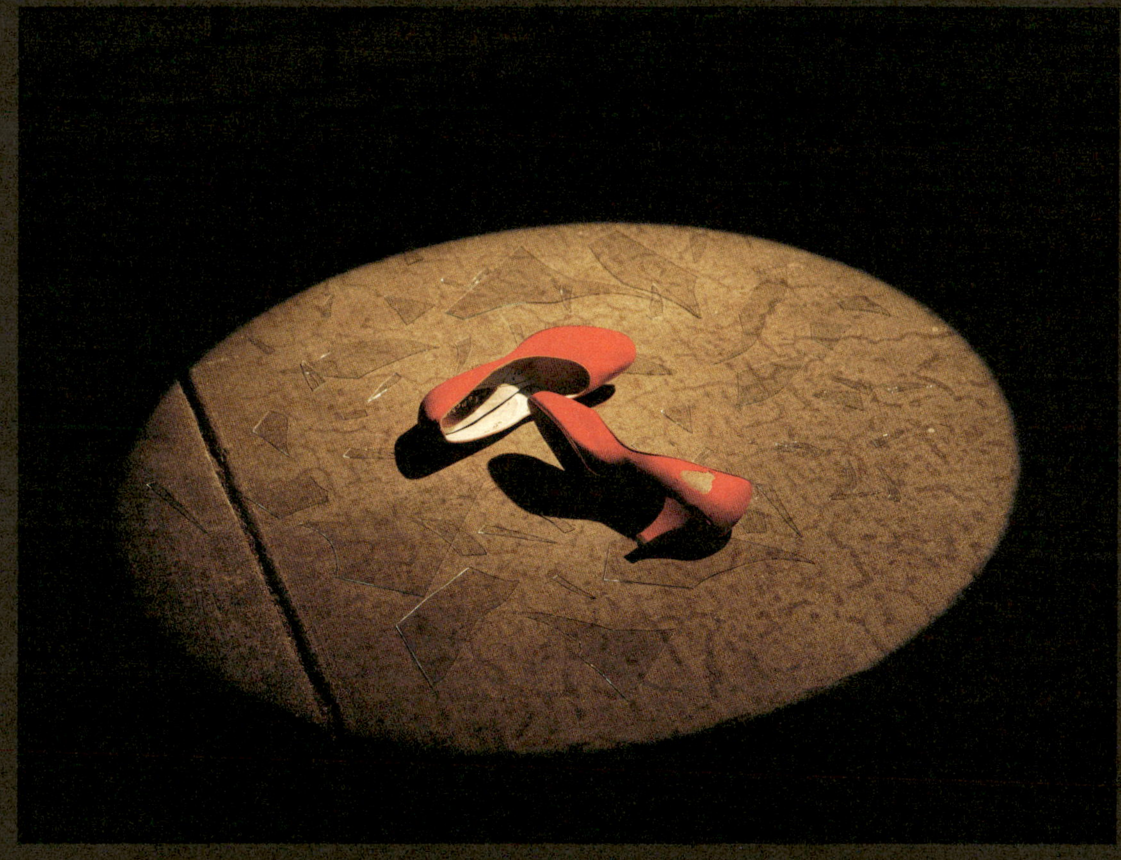

Prager's artistic practice, on the whole, identifies a sophisticated relationship between still photography and moving images. Often produced at the same time, her large-format photographs are exhibited alongside motion pictures intended for the big screen. For Prager, they are distinct modes of expression that, while technically and aesthetically tethered to one another, are realized independently. Her engagements evoke notions of storytelling and processes of interpretation, but underscore just how a picture is held together, be it moving or otherwise. They urge us to look at the symptoms of stories and storytelling, as well as the symptoms of watching stories unfold in time.

A photograph – whether motivated by social documentary, editorial, or high-art ambition – has no beginning and there is no end.[v] It is frozen in the moment, and a photograph is, of course, mute. Prager's early work in moving pictures expands photography to include the added dimension of time. For Prager, these single compositions reveal what happens 'just before, just now, and just after' her photographs.[vi]

Sunday, filmed in 2010, is built from that single scene. It unfolds in just over one minute, but was achieved with the full complement of actors, editors, and designers. In it, Prager draws from her own rich photographic practice, and builds a set of devices anew that she would return to in her later films. *Sunday* opens cinematically in stereo. Two nearly identical frames, playing side by side, unfold in what at first appears to be a single take. Upon closer scrutiny, each frame is composed with modestly different gestures, the actors altering their performances ever so subtly between takes. Screened concurrently, the sequences present an unbalanced timeline from beginning to end. They are a crowd at the track waiting for the action to begin. Anticipation resides just under the surface as we wait with them, sharing a cigarette with a companion, reading a paper, or peering through binoculars to adjust our view. The protagonist only emerges in the last tenth of the film. She is full of tension and acutely focused. As the starter pistol fires, she unifies the films in the closing frame just as her heart begins to race.

Fortunately for us, we never see the action that the spectators patiently await. In its place, Prager turns our attention to the individual characters that make up the audience and the stories they bring to the event. Each of them brings a reason for being in the moment. Theirs is a finite moment in time recorded to repeat indefinitely.

If Prager's early motion pictures were temporal expansions of her photography, *Despair* feels like a leap towards traditional cinema. Prager refers to *Despair* as her first film. It was a clearly ambitious production. The artist cast the accomplished actor Bryce Dallas Howard in the lead role, and commissioned an original score by composer Ali Helnwein. Under Prager's direction, it emerged as a fully formed film with all of a narrative arc's requisite parts – exposition, rising action, anticipation, climax, falling action, and resolution. And all in just over four minutes.

But *Despair* is unreal. It's Los Angeles circa 1960. There is a striking woman. She stands in a dramatically lit phone booth. Bright red lipstick with high heels to match, she is dressed to the nines but distraught. Her eyes well up with tears as she bolts out of the booth and down a sunlit street, her heels striking the pavement with a determined but somehow false staccato. She is surrounded by southern California perfection but is beset with emotion, nonetheless. Pure, cinematic melodrama. Our heroine finds her

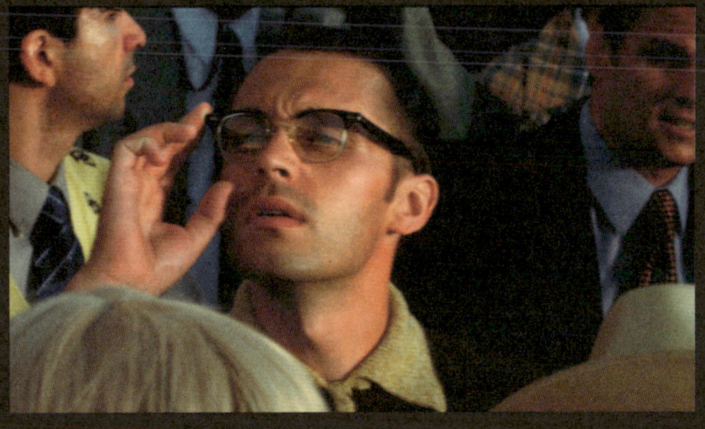
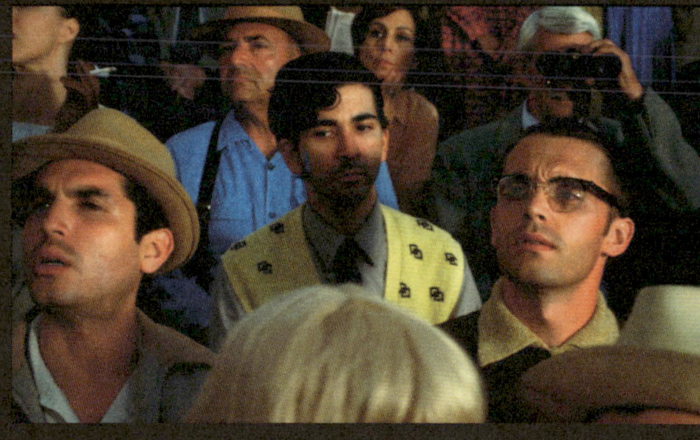
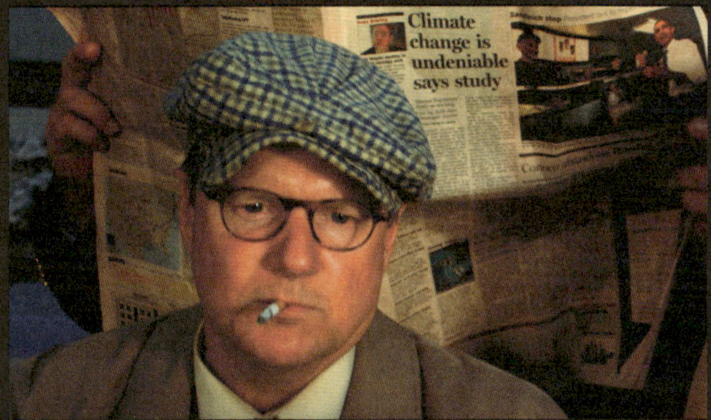
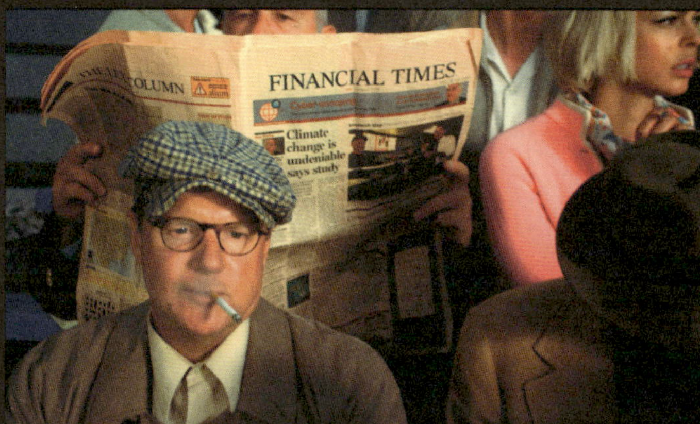
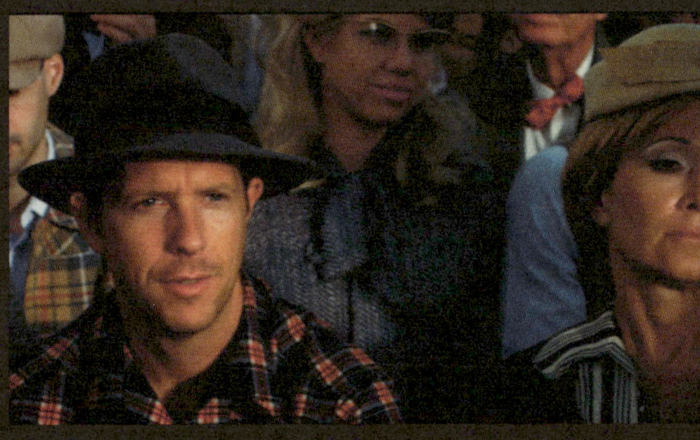
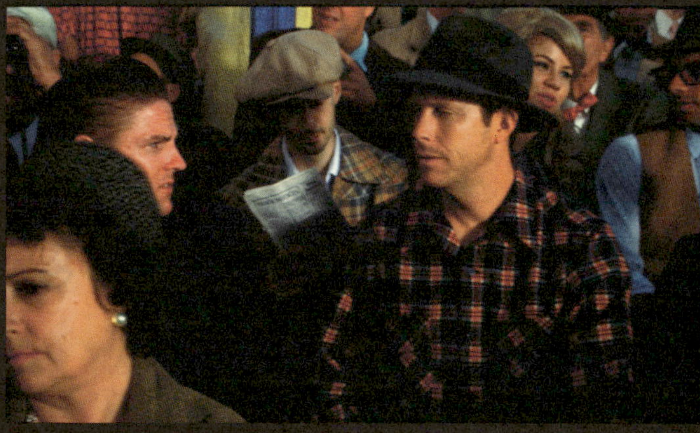
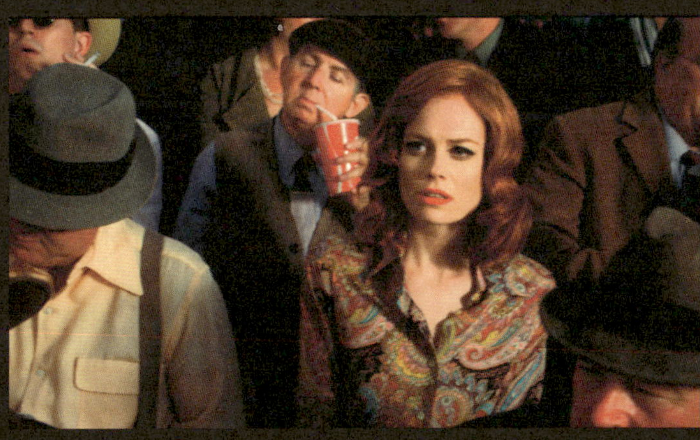
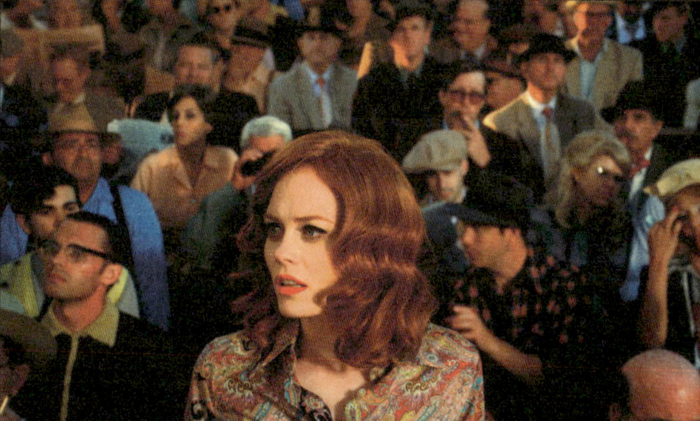

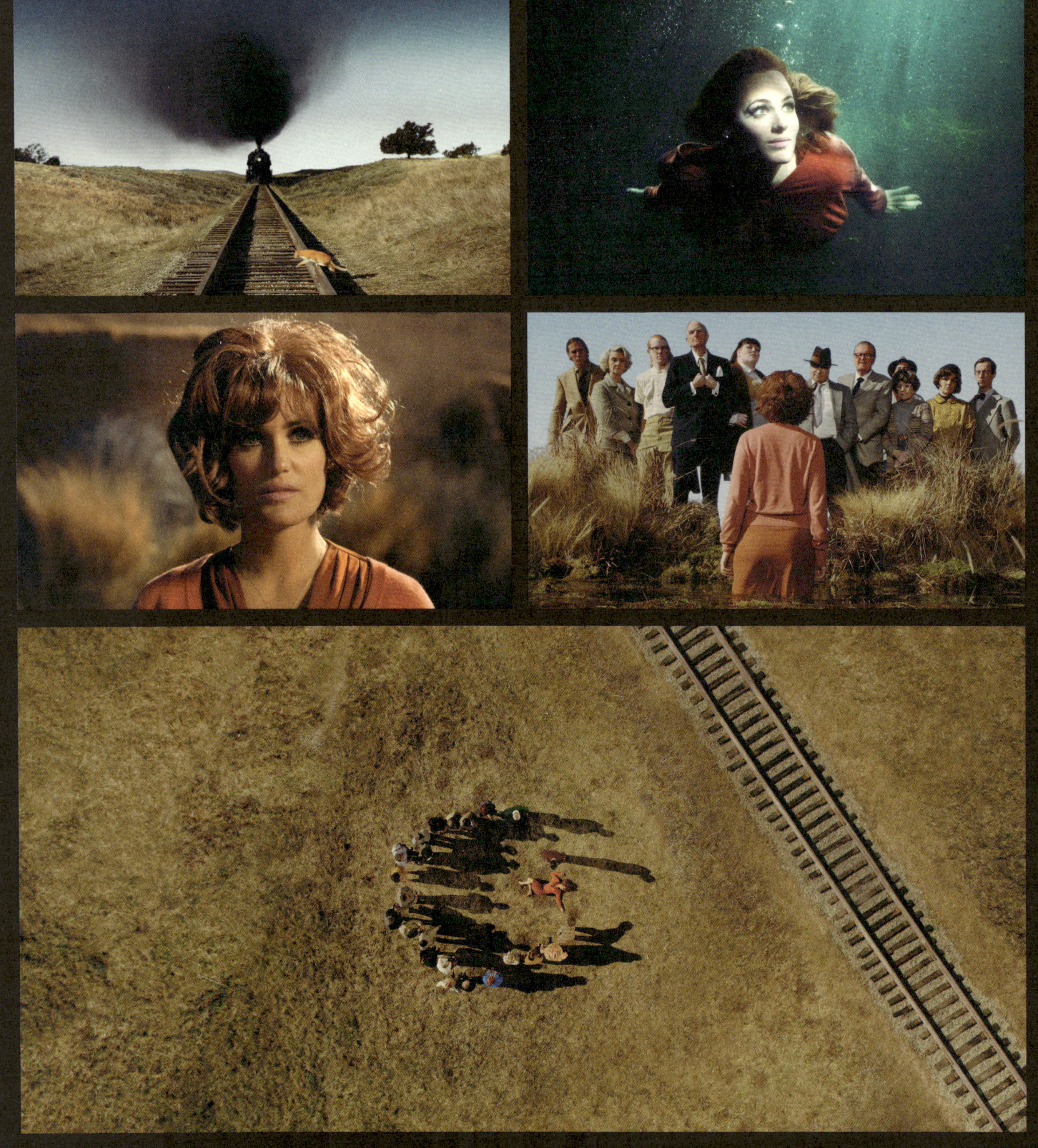

escape through a red door and eventually by leaping through a sugar-glass window. Her descent is not violent. Instead, she finds solace in the setting sun and the sky before her shoes alone land on the pavement below, spot-lit, suggesting the end. The casting is perfect. The costumes are perfect. The performance is perfect. The entire incident is idealized, but leaves us somehow unsettled and with a sense of anxiety.

Released in 2012, Prager's *La Petite Mort* also alludes to traditional cinema and to television's *The Twilight Zone*, but is decidedly more noir in delivery. A narrator and our finely composed protagonist – performed by French actor Judith Godrèche – contemplate the moment of death. She stands on the tracks and focuses longingly on an approaching train – the quintessential symbol for the relentless persistence of time. Briefly interrupted by a scampering kitty, the locomotive deals the final blow. As this heroine reemerges from the void, she is joined by characters from her story. They are emotionally complicit. Hapless as they are as witnesses, their silent judgment gives life to the tale. At the conclusion of the film, and as the credits roll, we are left with the train's tracks trailing off behind us. Among numerous not-so-subtle metaphors throughout Prager's work, this one brilliantly signals what is behind us and its influence on our futures.

Face in the Crowd (2013) represents a significant departure. Rather than showing in a traditional, single-screen theatre, it comprises three screens in a digital-cinema installation. The feature on each screen is independent, linked together only in the final moments of the film. A full sound-scape fills the room.

The work begins with a series of intimate monologues delivered by the extras in the film. Each one describes an array of personal experiences, fears, apprehensions, memories, and relationships. In an instant, the scenes change and their characters flood the screens surrounding the viewer. Bodies are packed together in hallways, on the beach, in movie theatres, or on the street. They push and shove their way to imaginary destinations, their voices drowning in the hustle. The central character – played by American actor Elizabeth Banks – peers through a windowpane at the endless parade. She anxiously meanders her way into the crowd, joining the fray. The chaos quickly overwhelms her and she becomes unable to move. Just as she might collapse from the crowd-phobic tension, the action halts. The throngs freeze. And in a moment of both confusion and relief, she directs herself through the motionless bodies and exits stage left.

The film traces a spectrum of concerns: a fear of crowds and the desire to stand out among them; voyeurism and exhibitionism; the spectator's gaze and the inability to live up to expectations. But it more acutely identifies the anxiety of being swept up by the masses while trying to create and maintain a sense of self; conditions long present in the physical world, but amplified yet again in the virtual spaces we inhabit today.

These concerns are paramount once more in the production *La Grande Sortie*. The film originates also with a crowd as they queue at the Opéra Bastille for a long-anticipated performance of a prima ballerina – a role performed by étoile Émilie Cozette. The orchestral score is Stravinsky's, although it is arranged by contemporary rock producer Nigel Godrich. From the beginning, the tension is thick. Is she nervous? Confident? Hopeful? Excited? Our ballerina grows ever more unsettled and off-balanced after each entanglement with the audience. Her anxiety is riveting, either real or imagined, until she makes her escape.

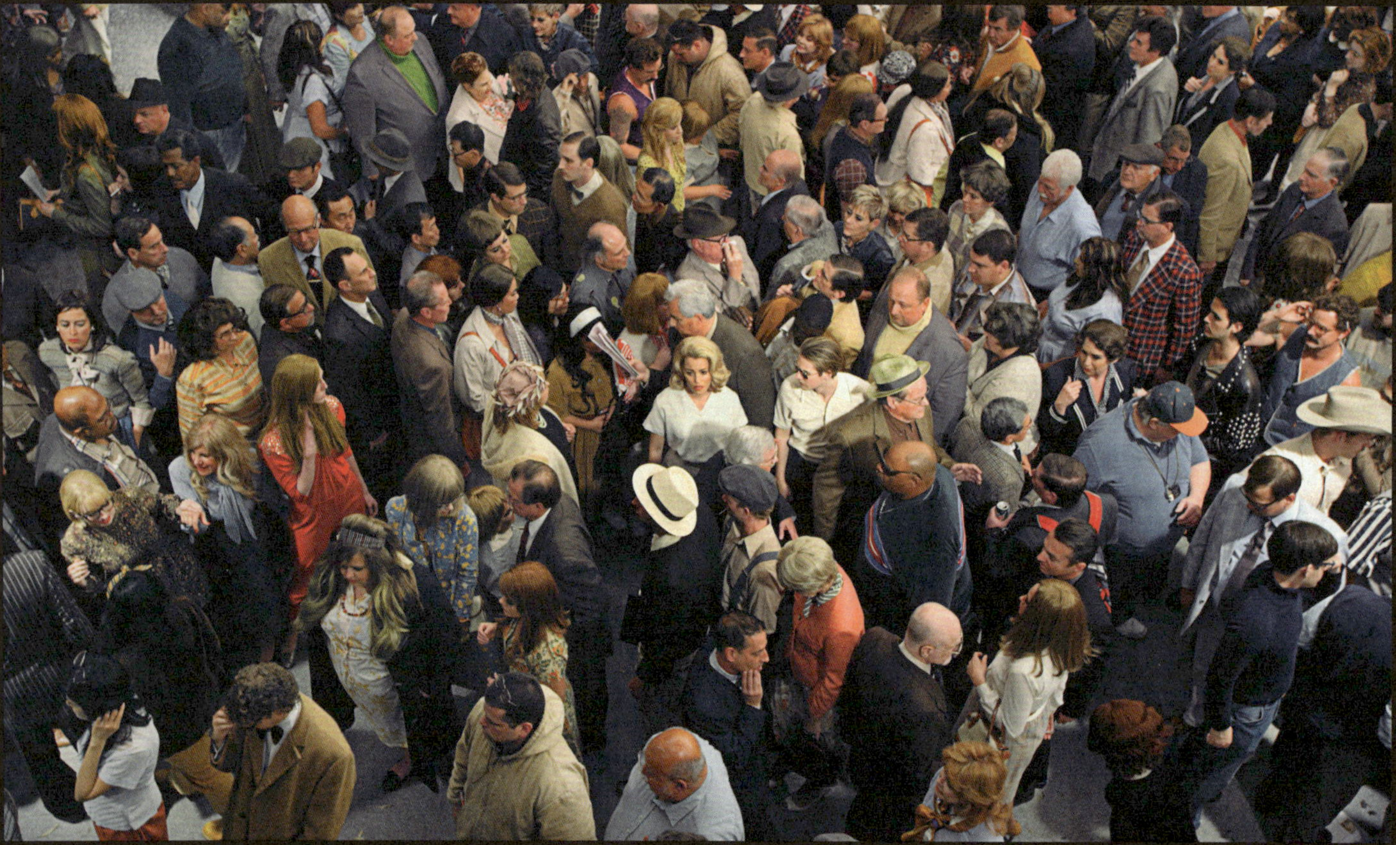

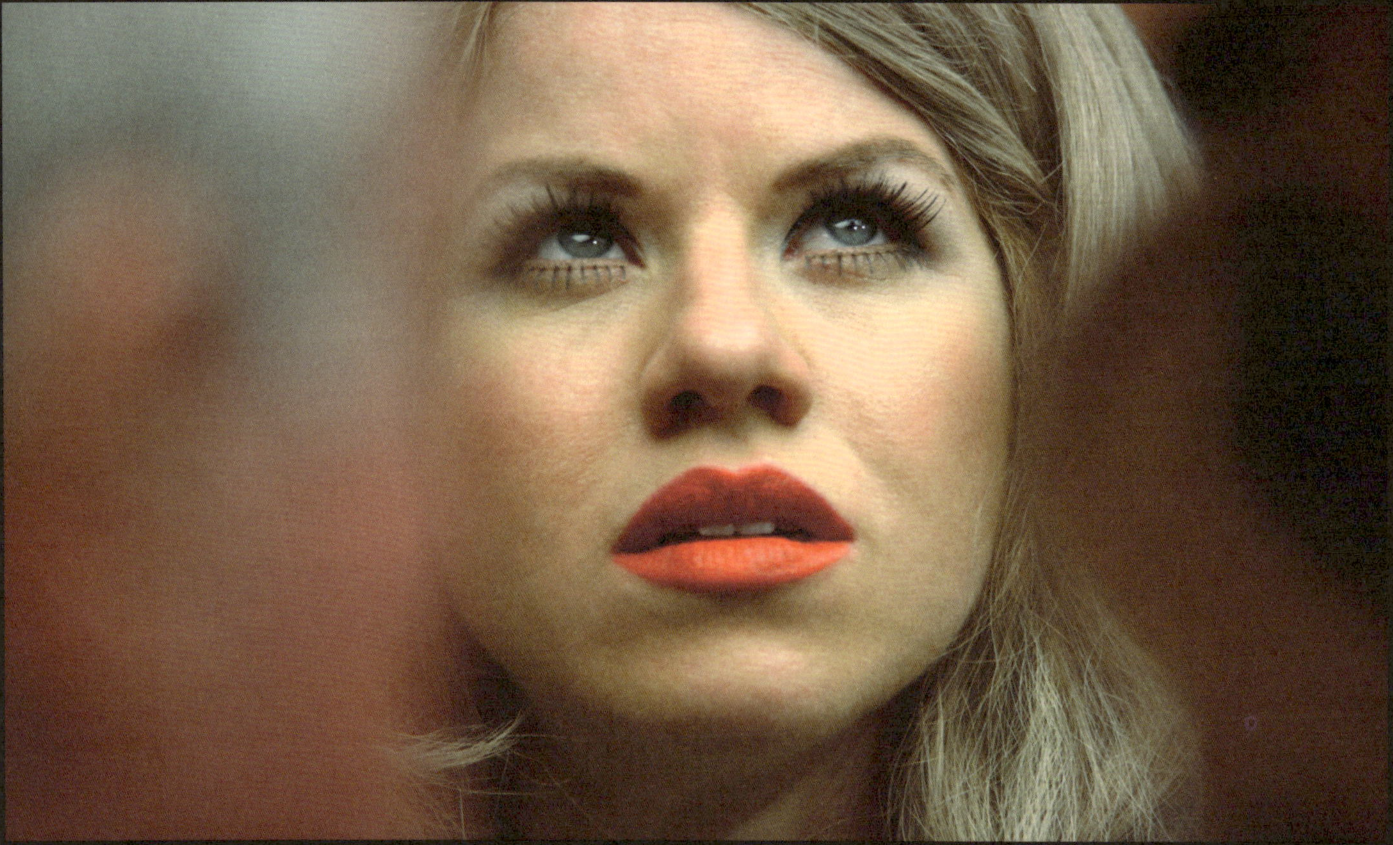

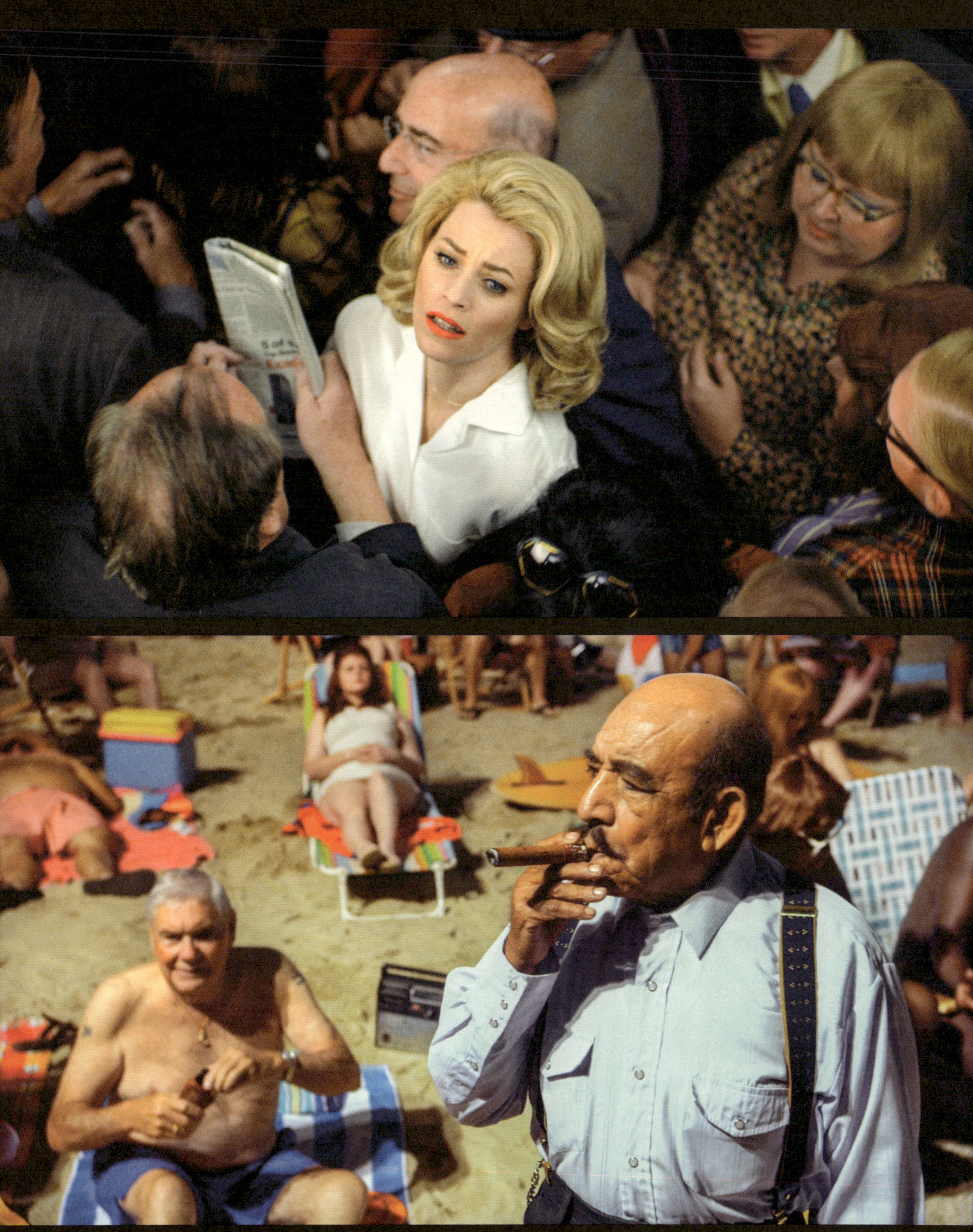

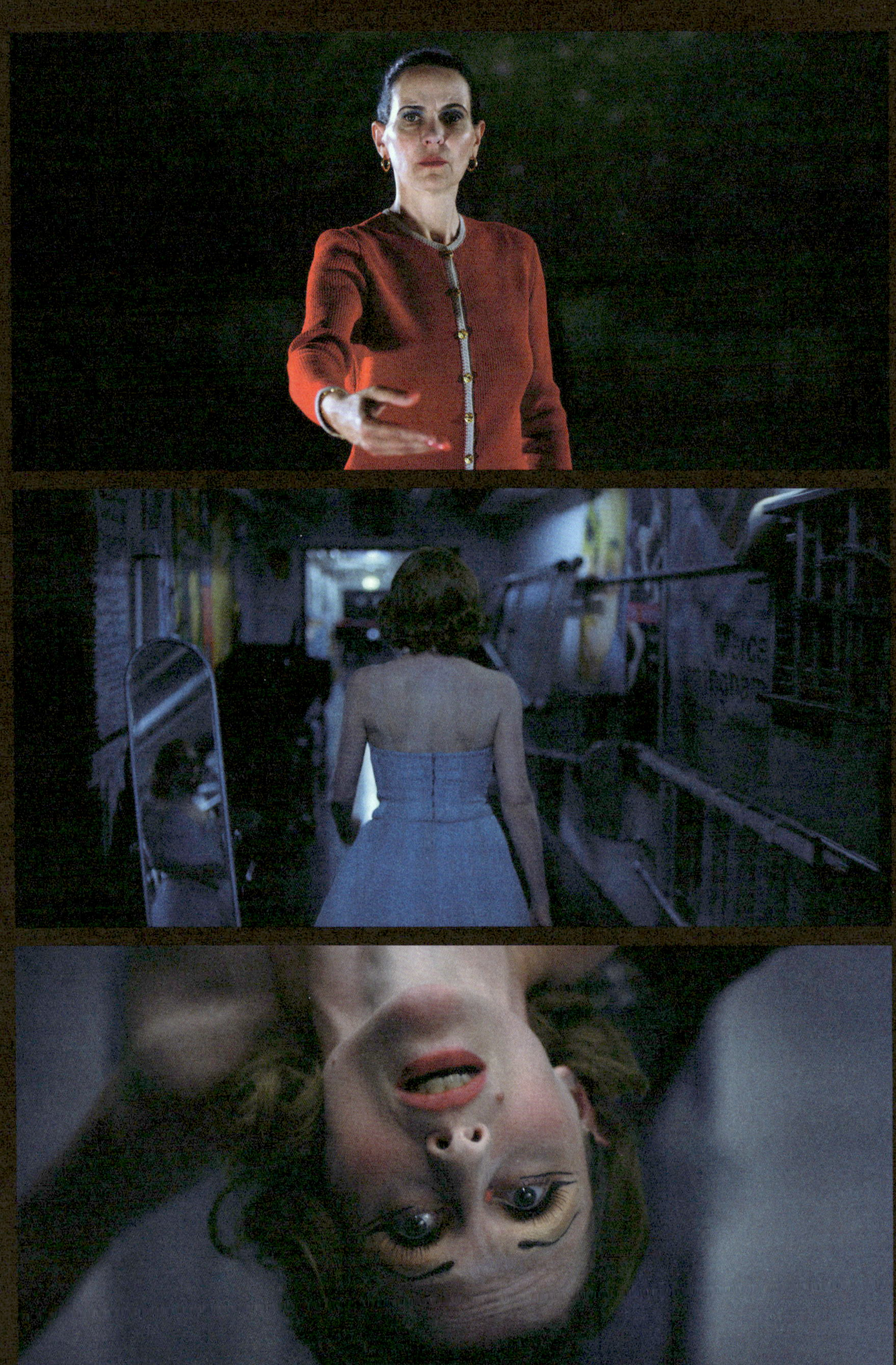

These stories may be as much autobiographical as they are fiction. In each film, women occupy the lead role, the centre of attention among prying eyes and in a sea of stories. The role Prager plays as film-maker is the same. She moves seamlessly between the emotional states rendered in her films, drawing sharp contrast from one to the next. Her films clearly reference Alfred Hitchcock and film noir, and owe debts of gratitude to Maya Deren or Alain Resnais, just as her photographic works remind us of William Eggleston, Enrique Metinides, Cindy Sherman, and Jeff Wall. In a nod to the noted French theorist Jacques Derrida, 'To pretend, I actually do the thing: I have therefore only pretended to pretend.'[vii] Part of our response rests upon Prager's masterful delivery and our recognition of these artistic pillars. The other depends upon our deferment to, or indulgence of, the power of their seduction.

But that parity is not necessarily a critique of cinema or Hollywood, but rather a likely and necessary companion. Prager's ability to distill pictures down to their most vivid parts is compelling. These devices of hyper-synthetic technicolour and hot stereotypes, amplified character actors in polyester wardrobes, are indeed the seductive play of special effects.[viii] They play to our personal tellings. The perceived shallow nature of these characters, even in brief, allows them an unmistakable dimension, placing the burden back upon us to imagine depth where there is none.

This visual language precedes us. Rather than challenging our assumptions, Prager invites us to participate in the story's making. In so doing, she exposes the fugitive nature of motion pictures. The coded symbolism and visual vocabularies authored during the golden age of movies continue to have a profound effect on how we interpret the characters we encounter today. With this hermetic view of cinema, films perhaps refer to other films as much as their making. And at this moment in Hollywood, as we are each taking stock of personal interactions, social codes and conduct with one another, Prager's achievements draw focus. These are films that manage to be precisely of their time and utterly timeless.

i   Slavoj Zizek, *The Pervert's Guide to Cinema*, directed by Sophie Fiennes, 2006, ICA Projects UK.

ii   'Video Art', *Art Journal*, Winter 1995, vol. 54, no. 4, edited by John G. Hanhardt and Maria-Christina Villasenor.

iii   Douglas Eklund, *Heilbrunn Timeline of Art History*, Department of Photographs, The Metropolitan Museum of Art, New York, October 2004.

iv   Leslie Camhi, 'L.A. Noir: Alex Prager's "Compulsion"', *Vogue*, March 2012.

v   Interview with Gregory Crewdson, *Art Forum Magazine*, 26 January 2016.

vi   Interview with Alex Prager, https://www.nowness.com/story/bryce-dallas-howard-in-despair, retrieved August 2017.

vii   Vincent Descombes, *Modern French Philosophy*, Cambridge University Press, Cambridge, 1980, p. 137.

viii   Norman M. Klein, *From the Vatican to Vegas: A History of Special Effects*, The New Press, New York, 2004, p. 512.

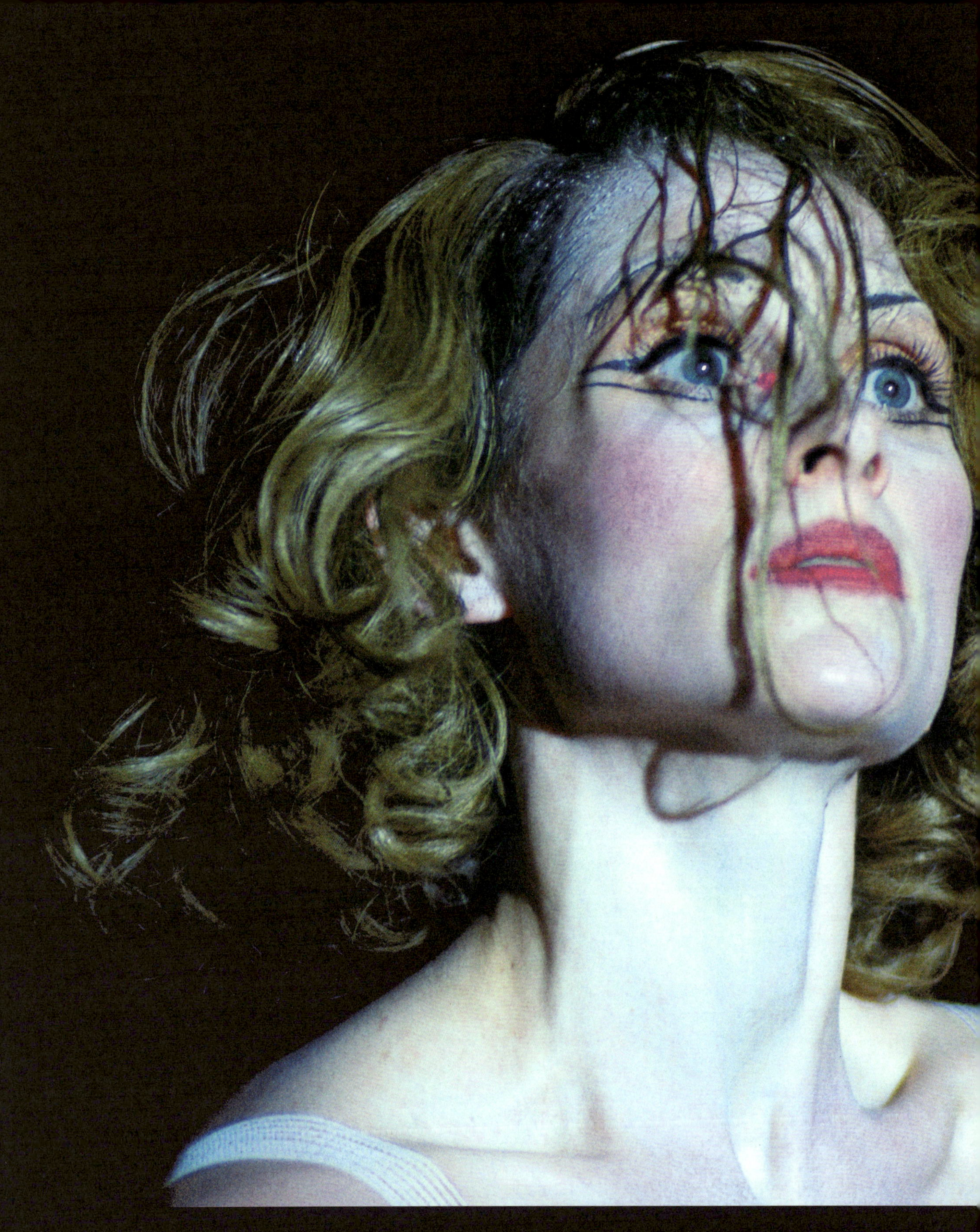

LA GRANDE SORTIE (2016)

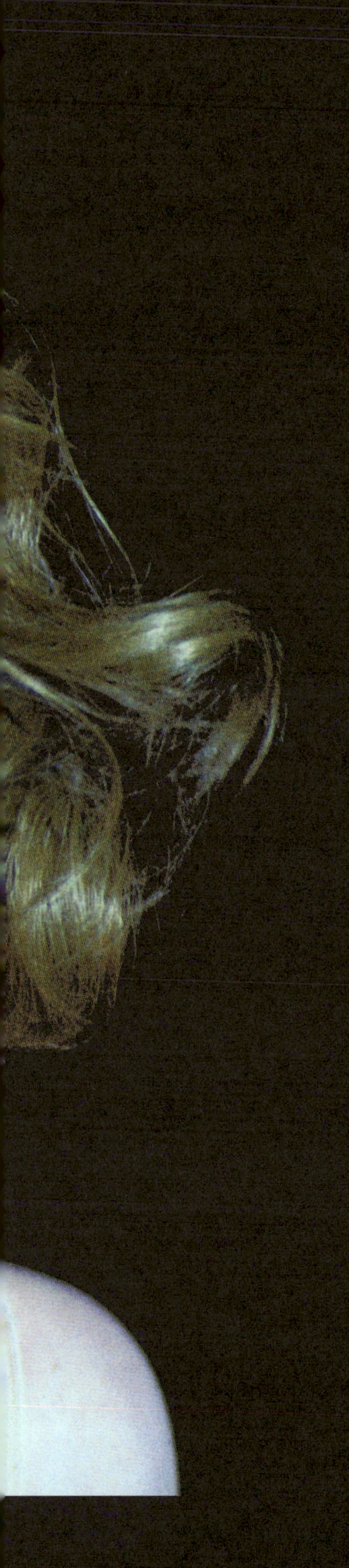

PART 3

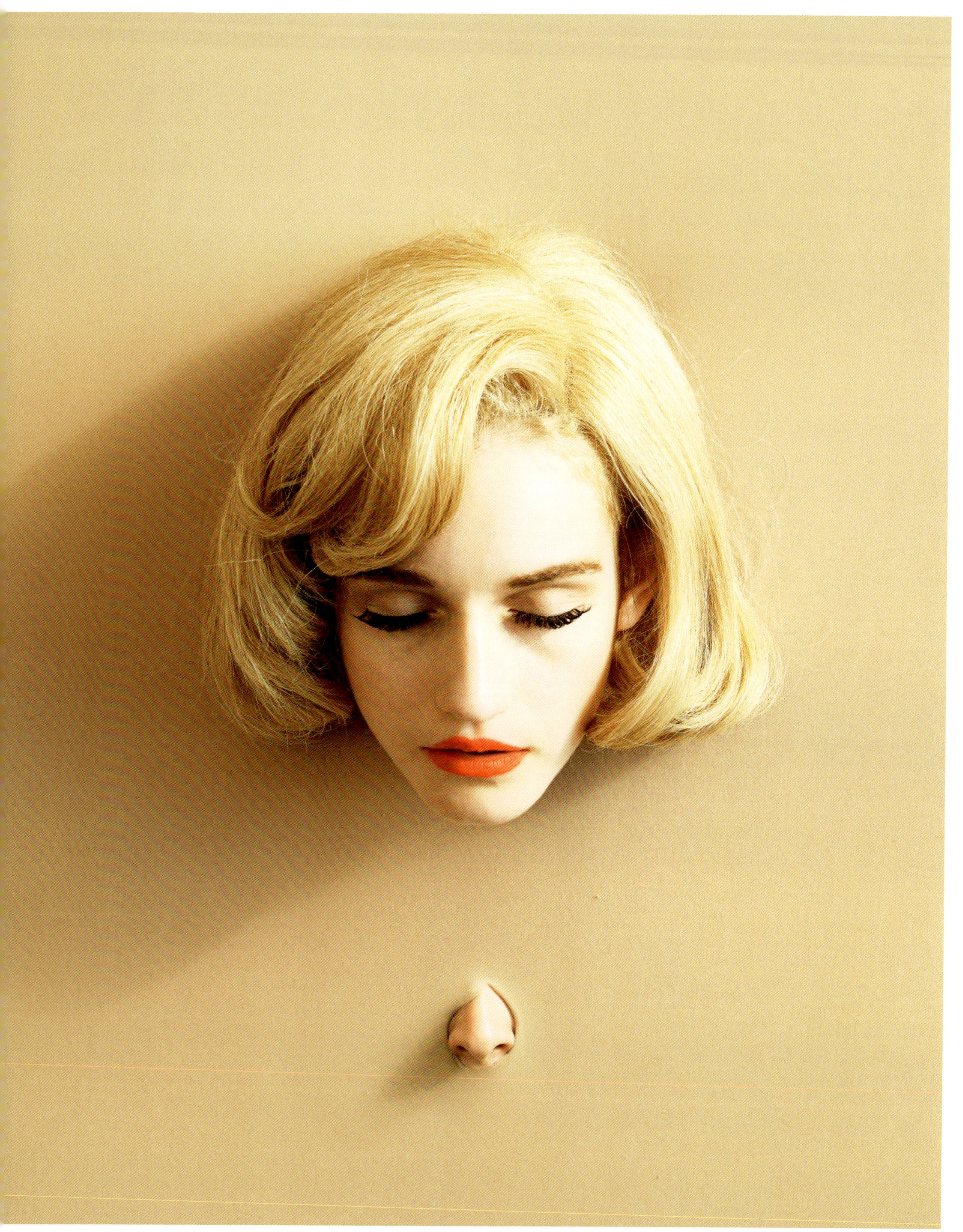

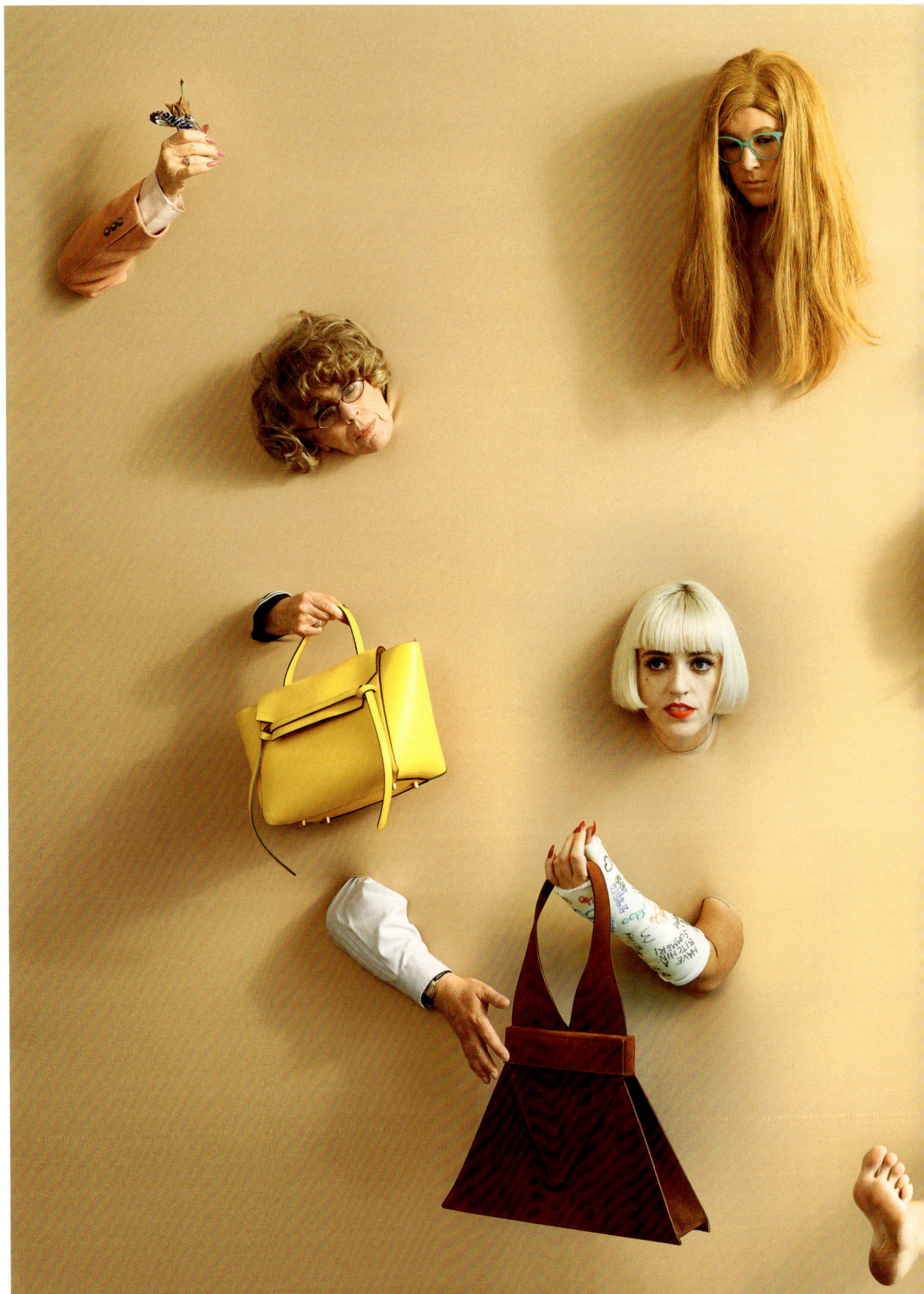
HAVE A BITCHIN' SUMMER!

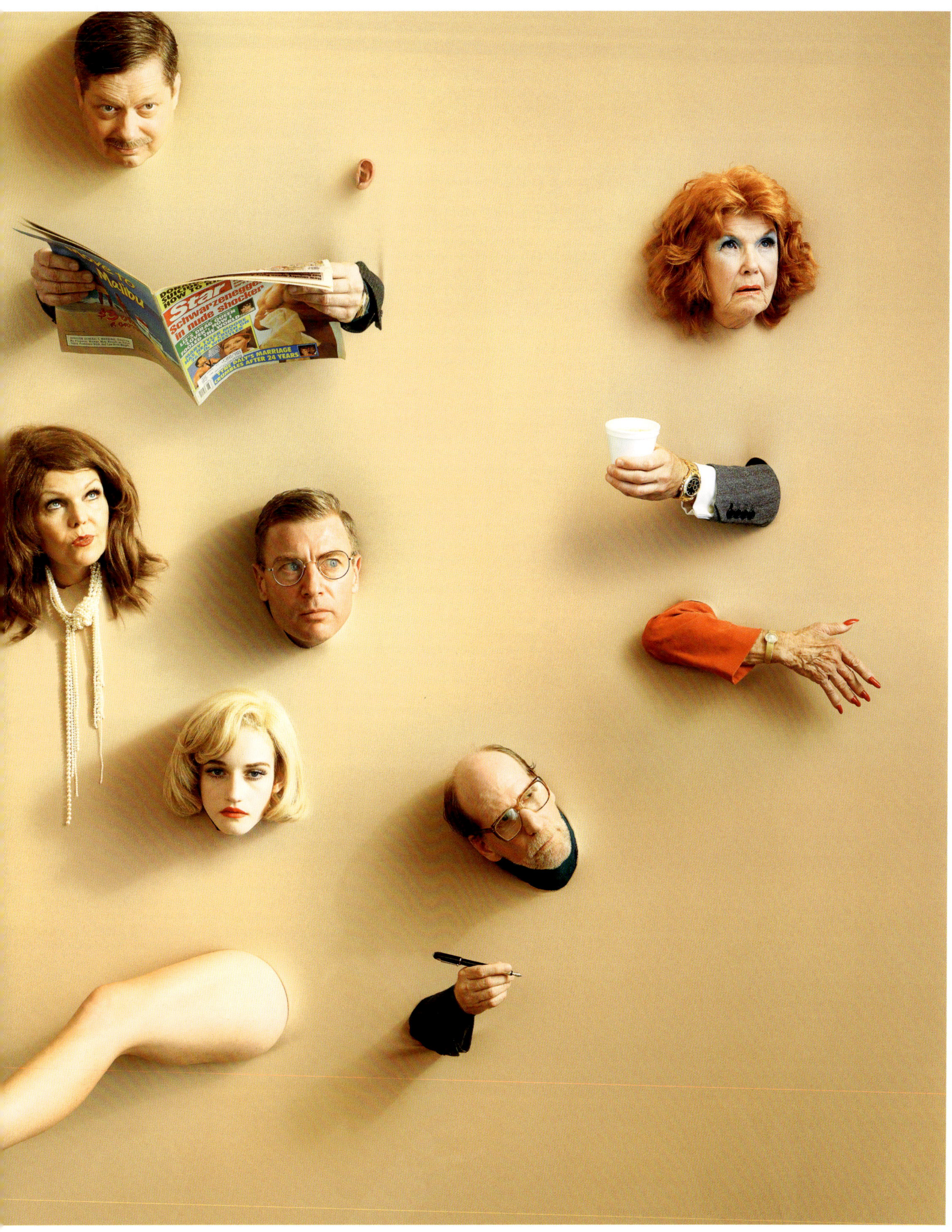

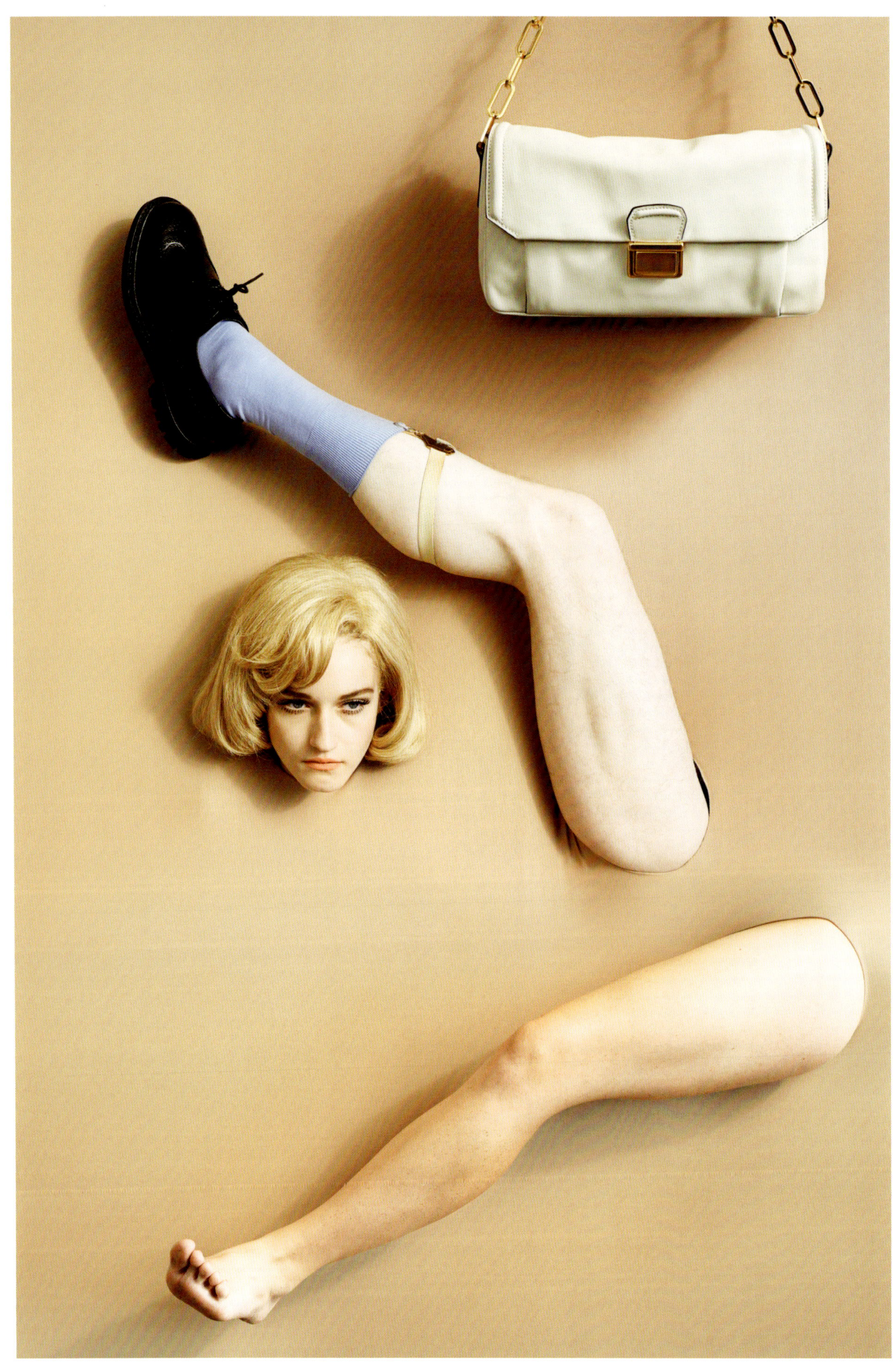

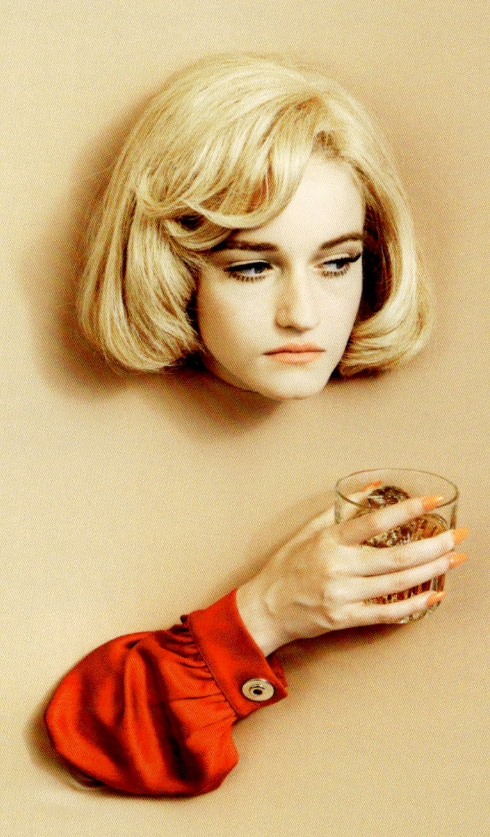
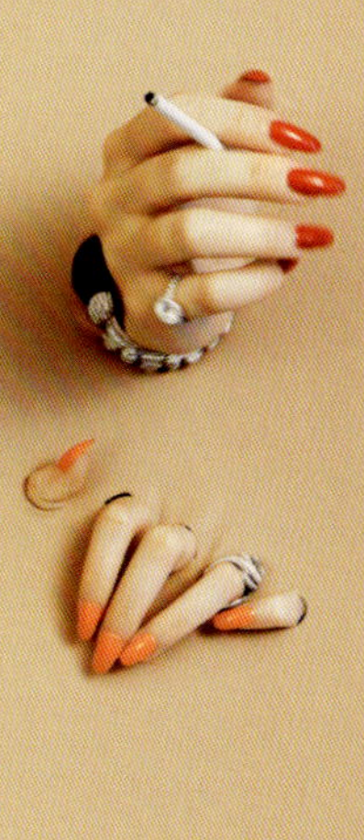

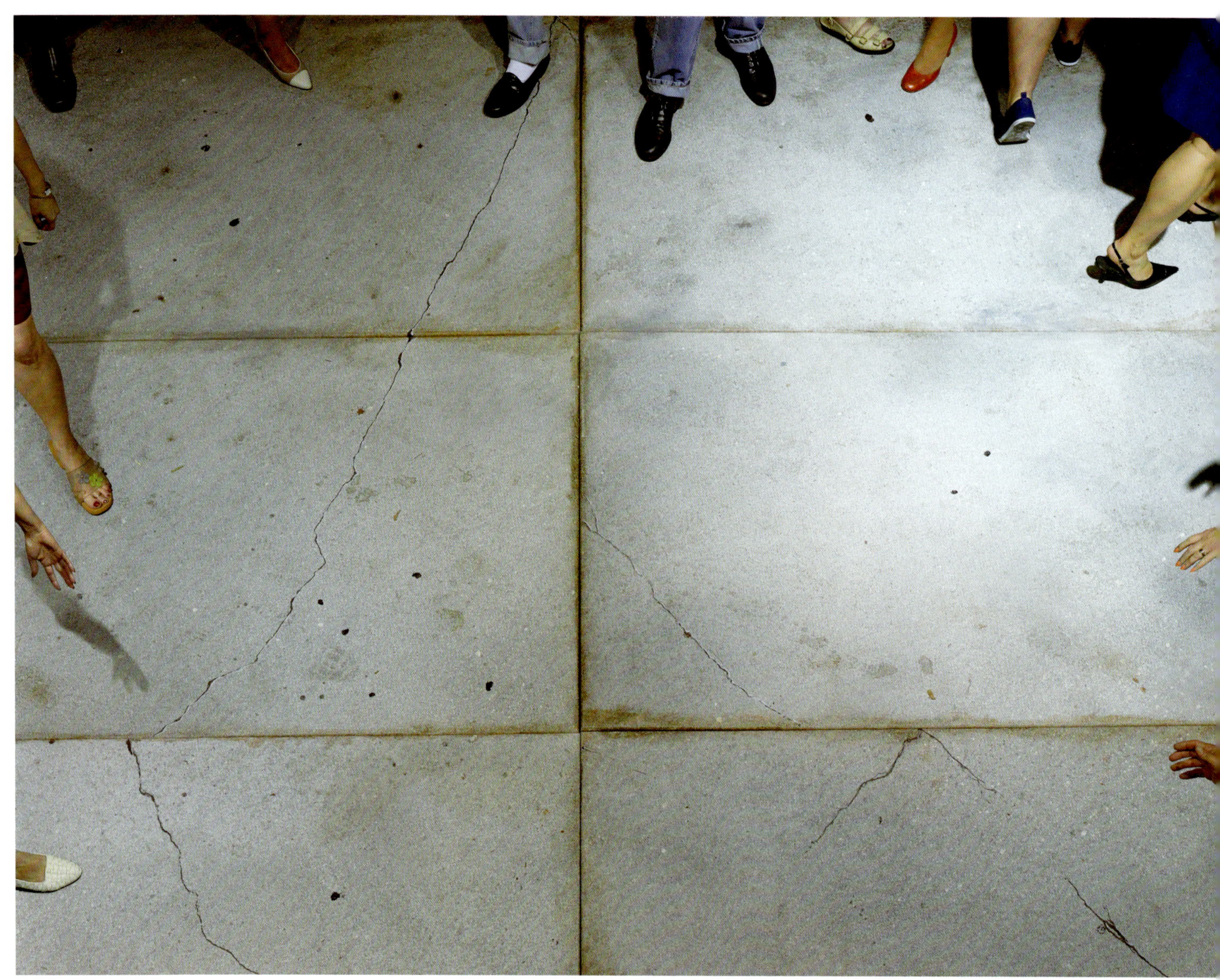

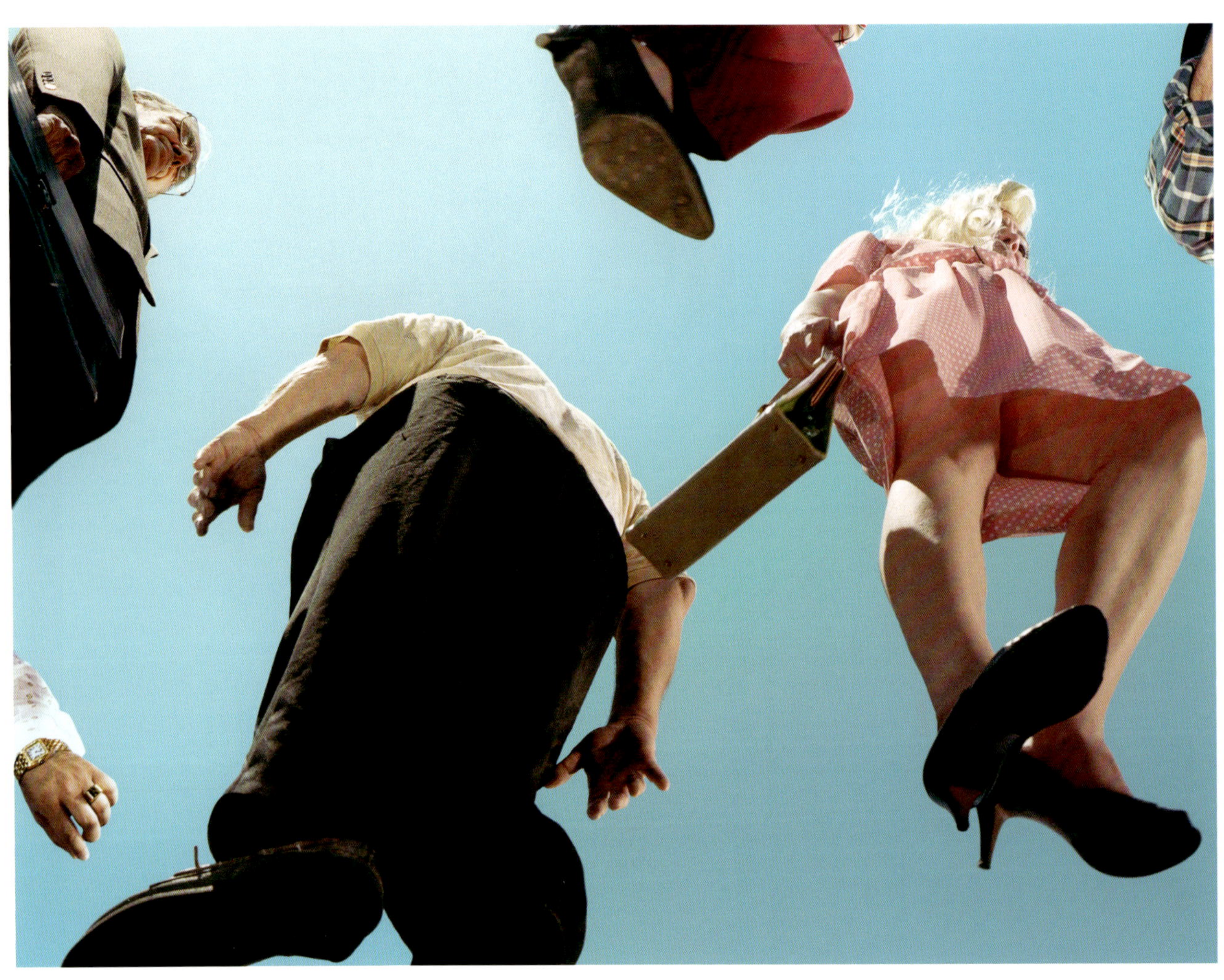

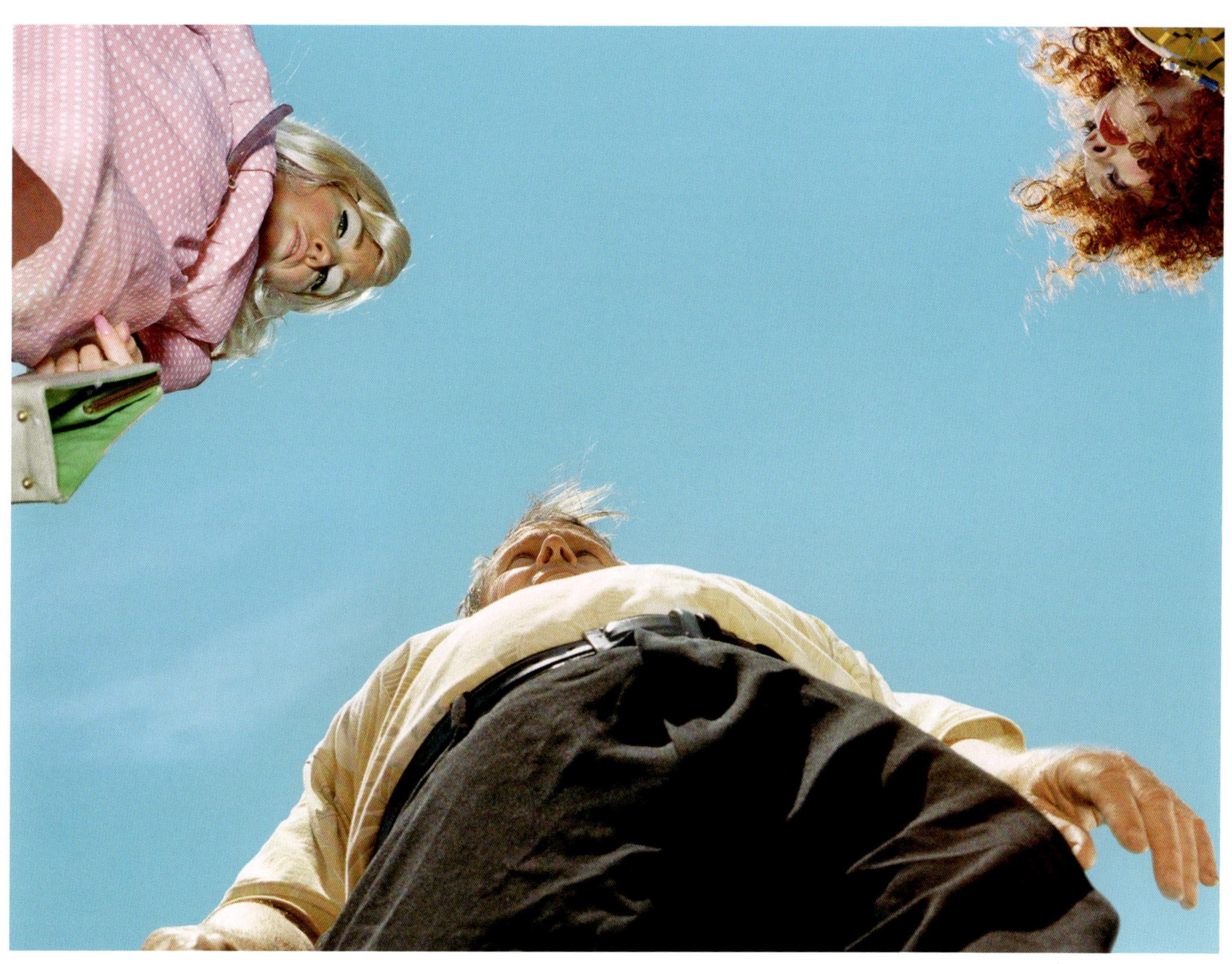

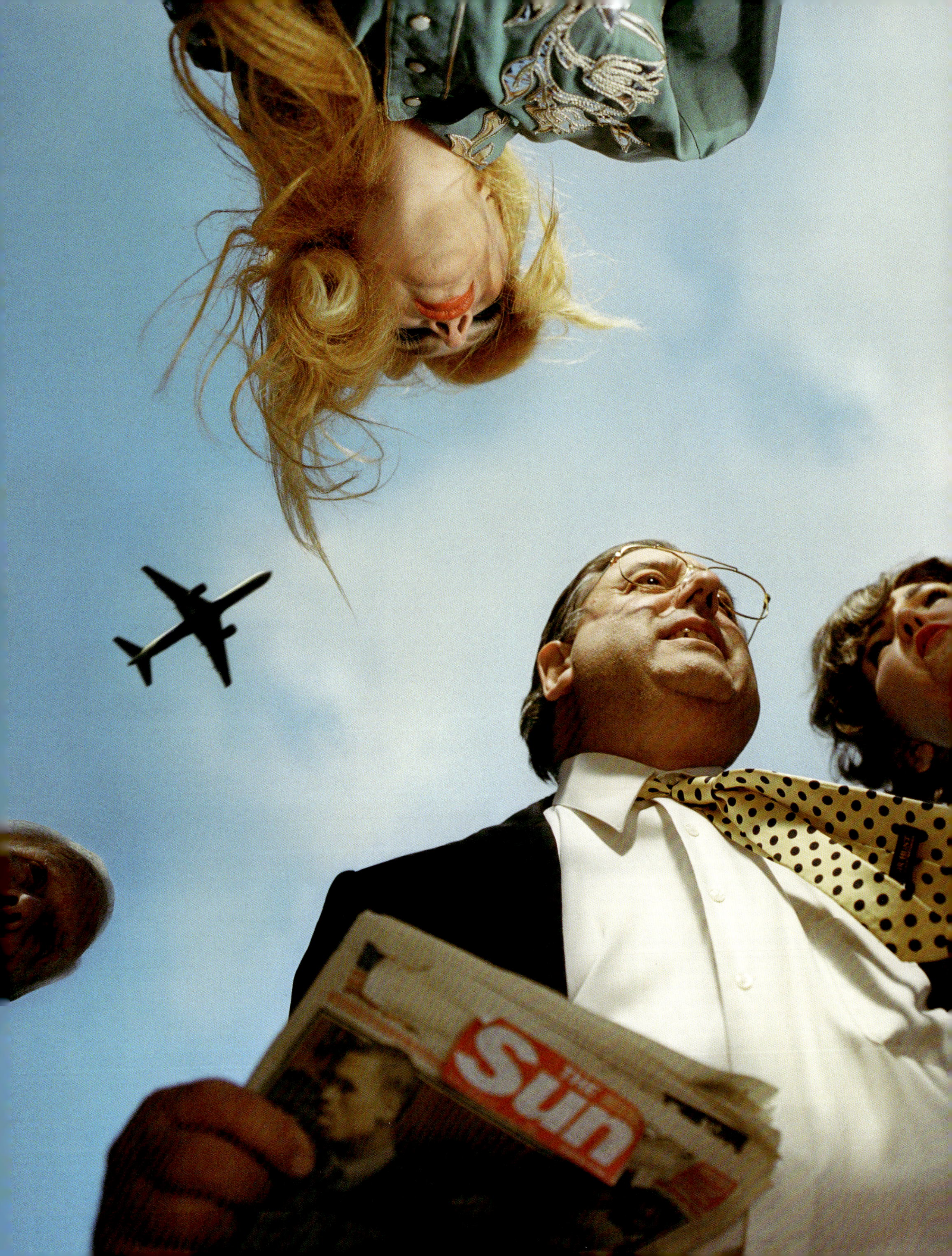
the sun

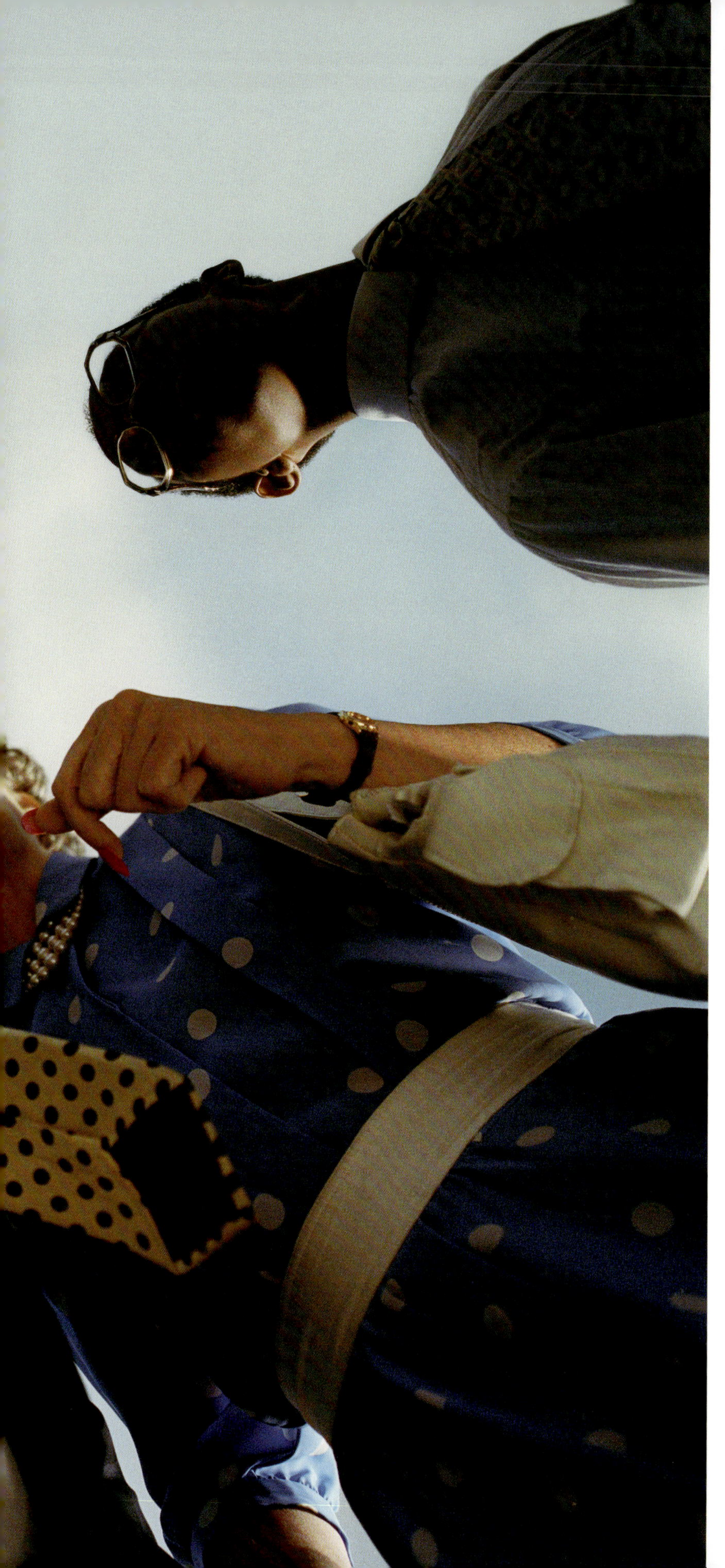

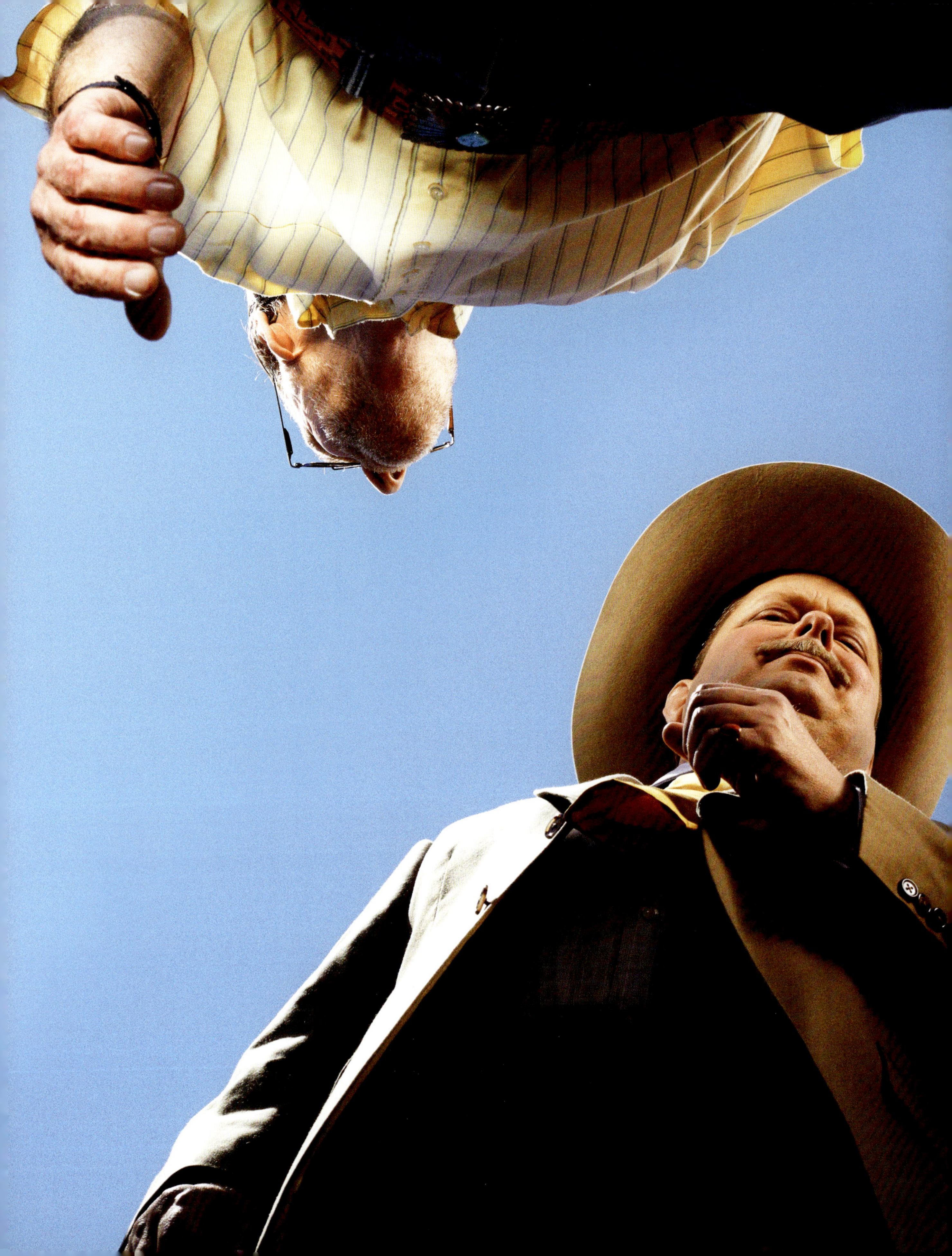

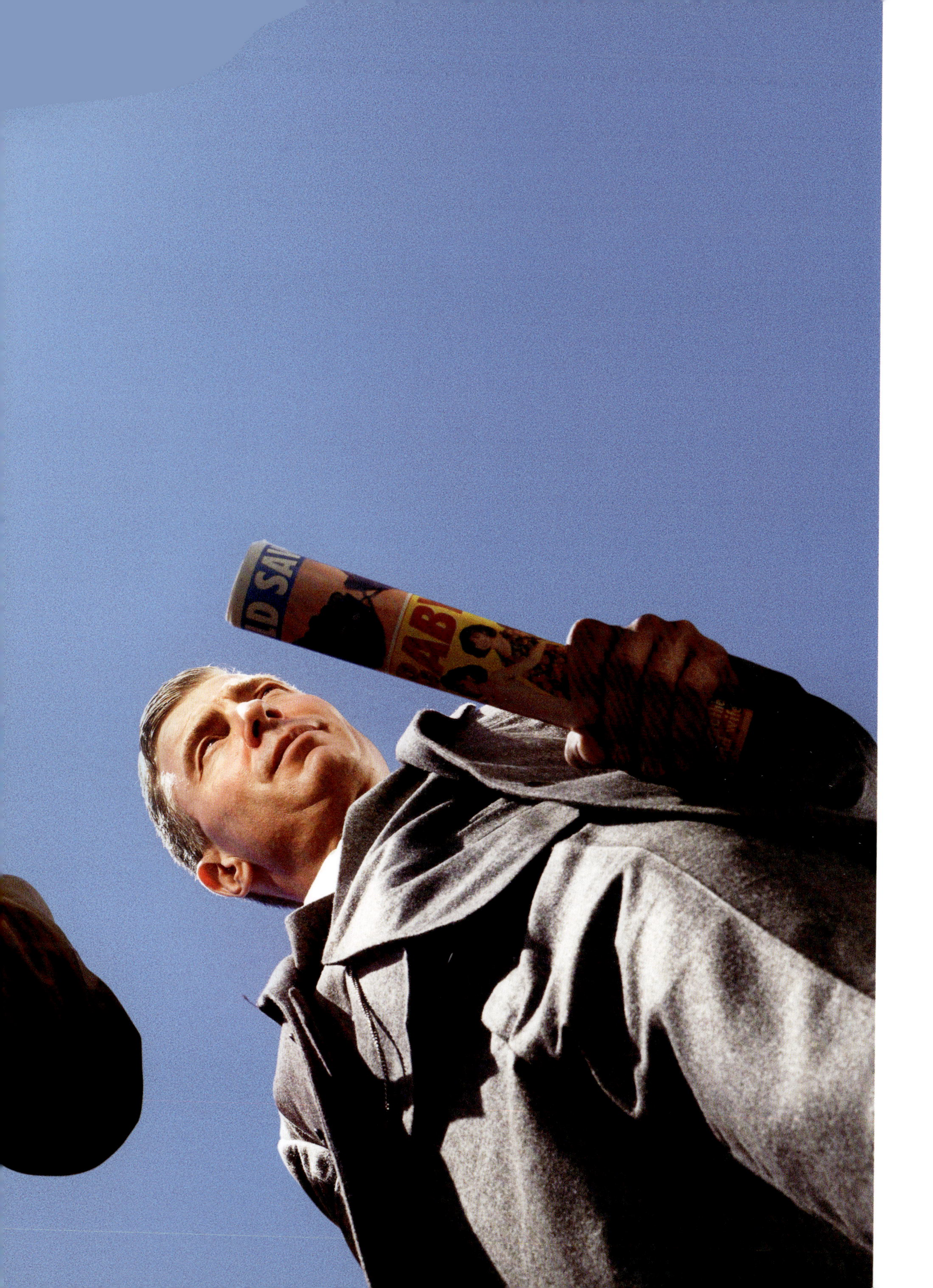

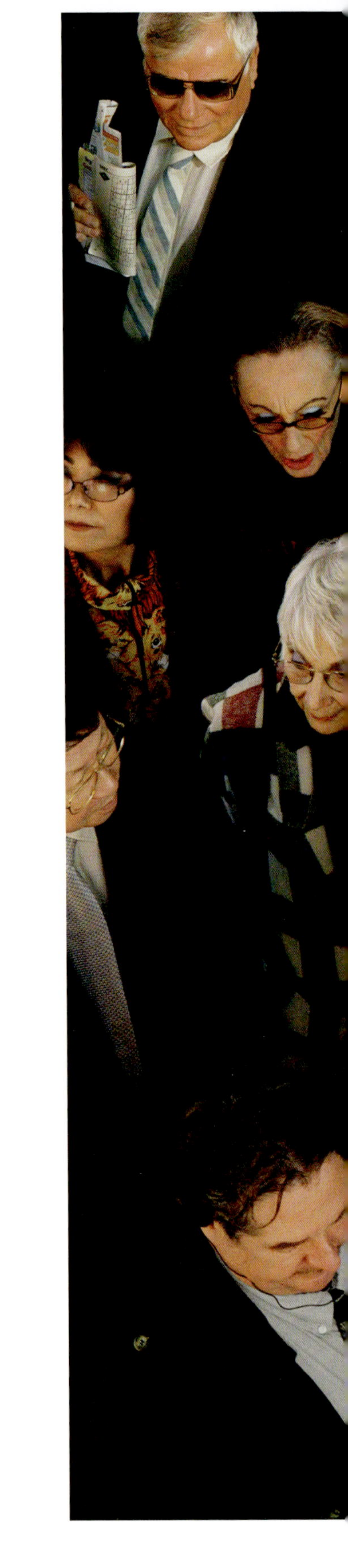

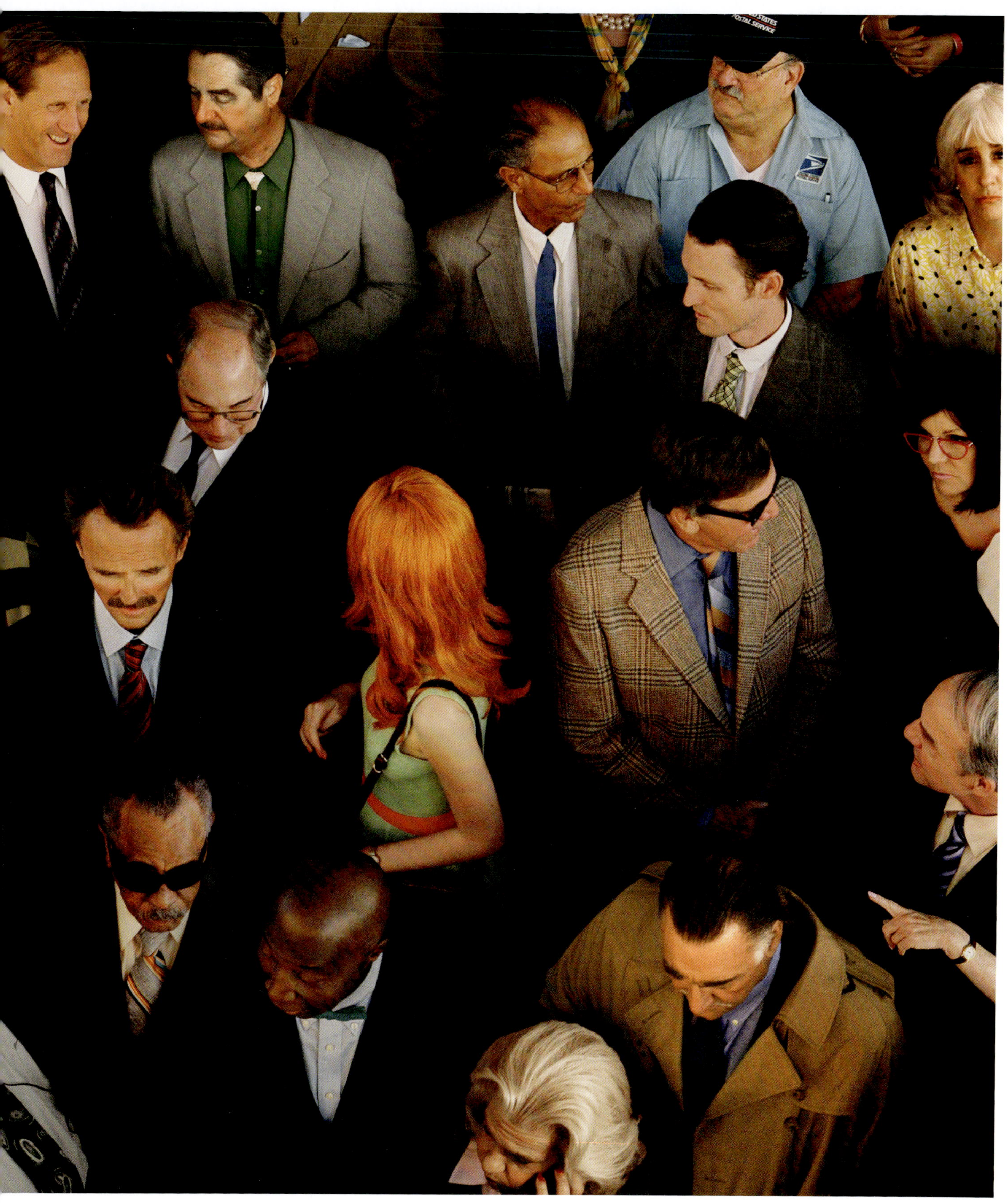

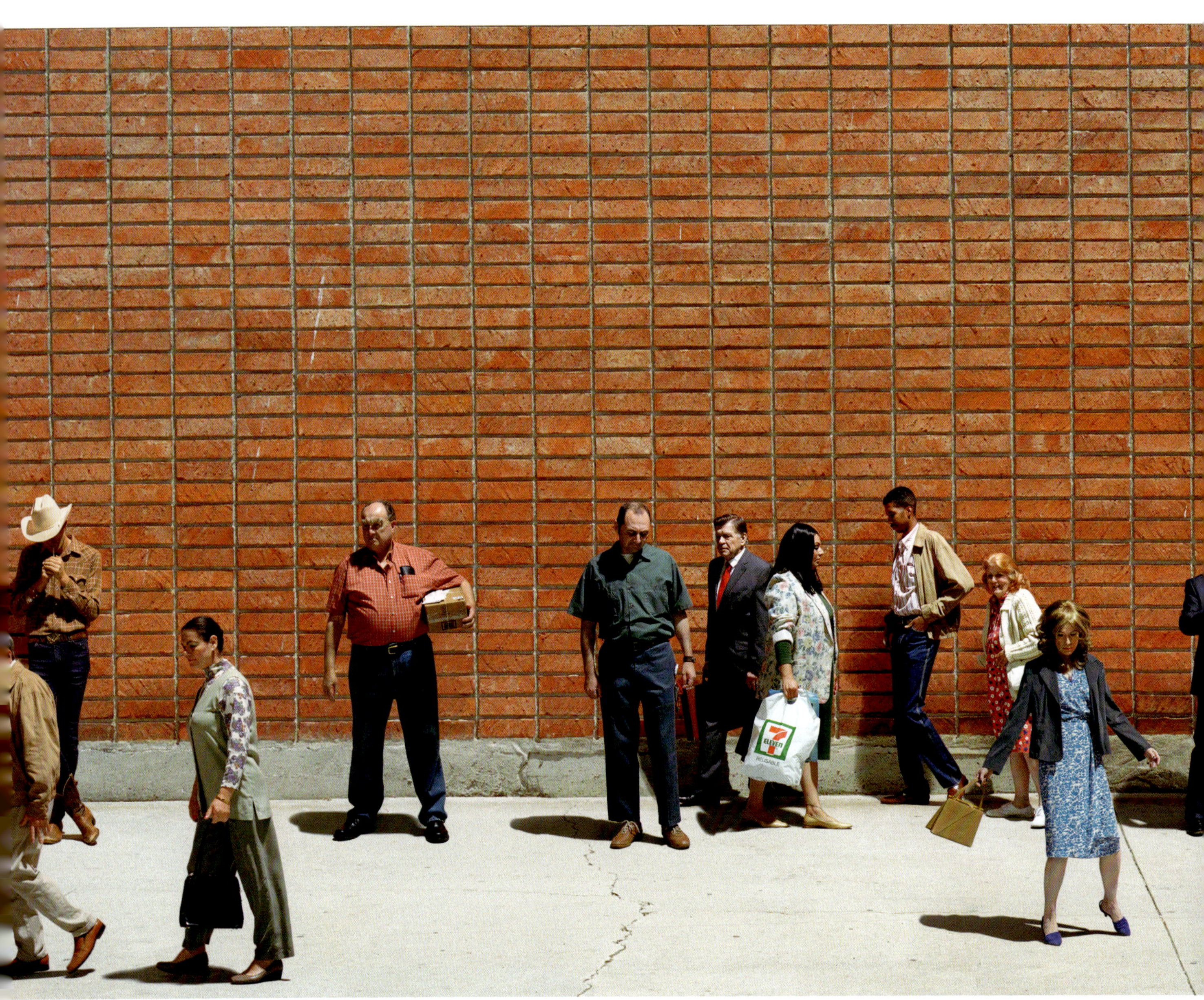

7-ELEVEN
REUSABLE

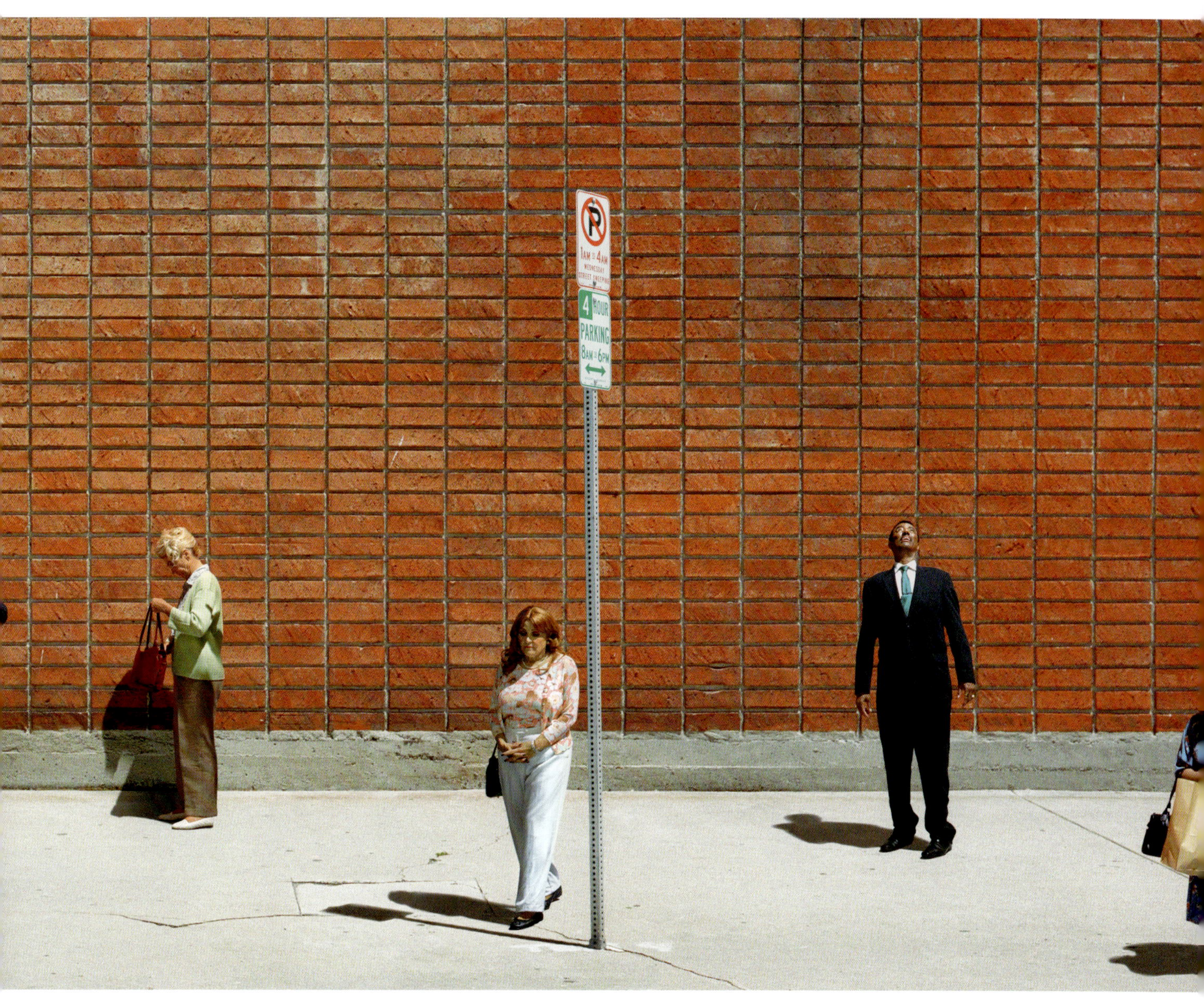

1AM to 4AM
WEDNESDAY
STREET SWEEPING
4 HOUR
PARKING
8AM to 6PM

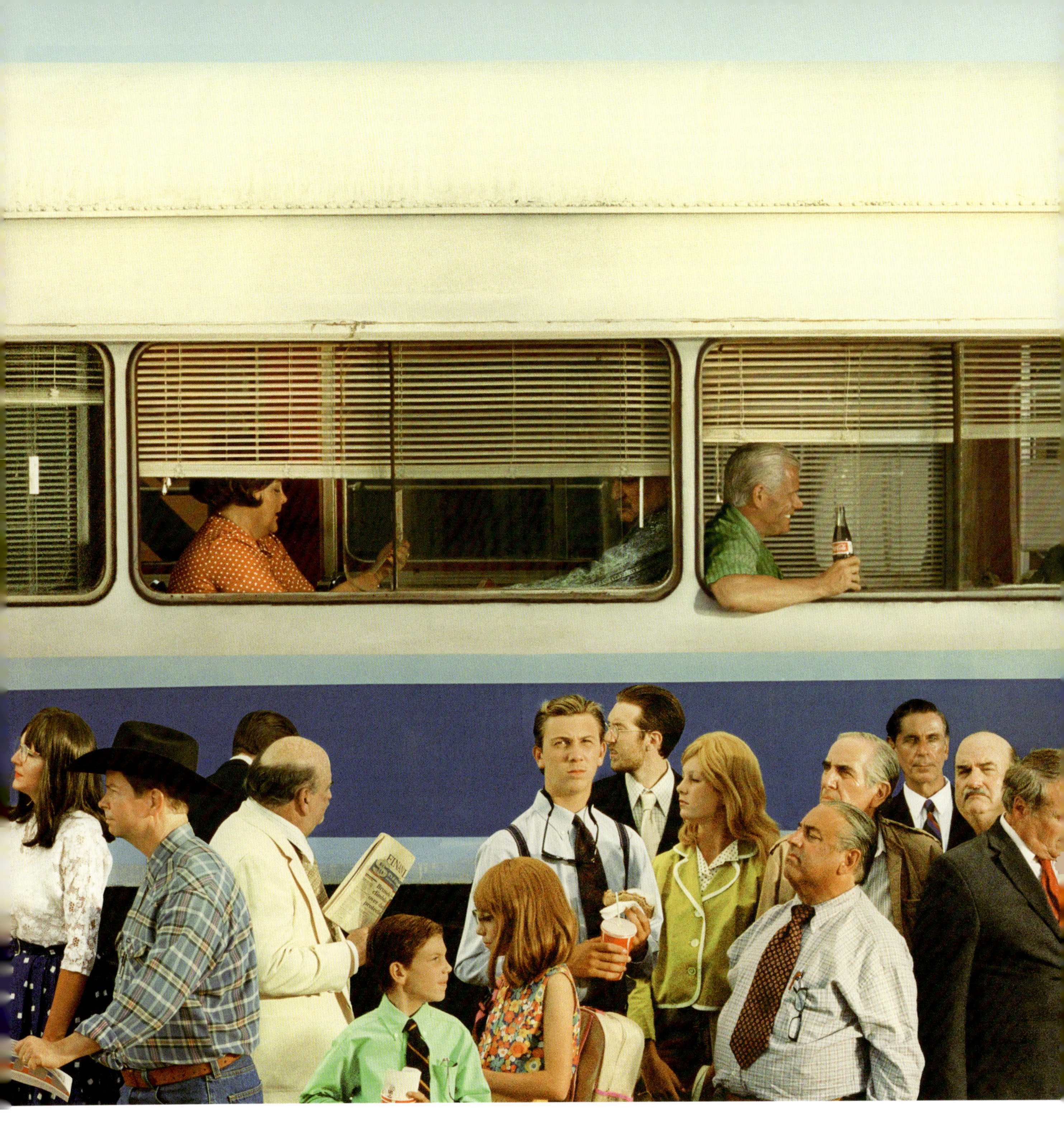

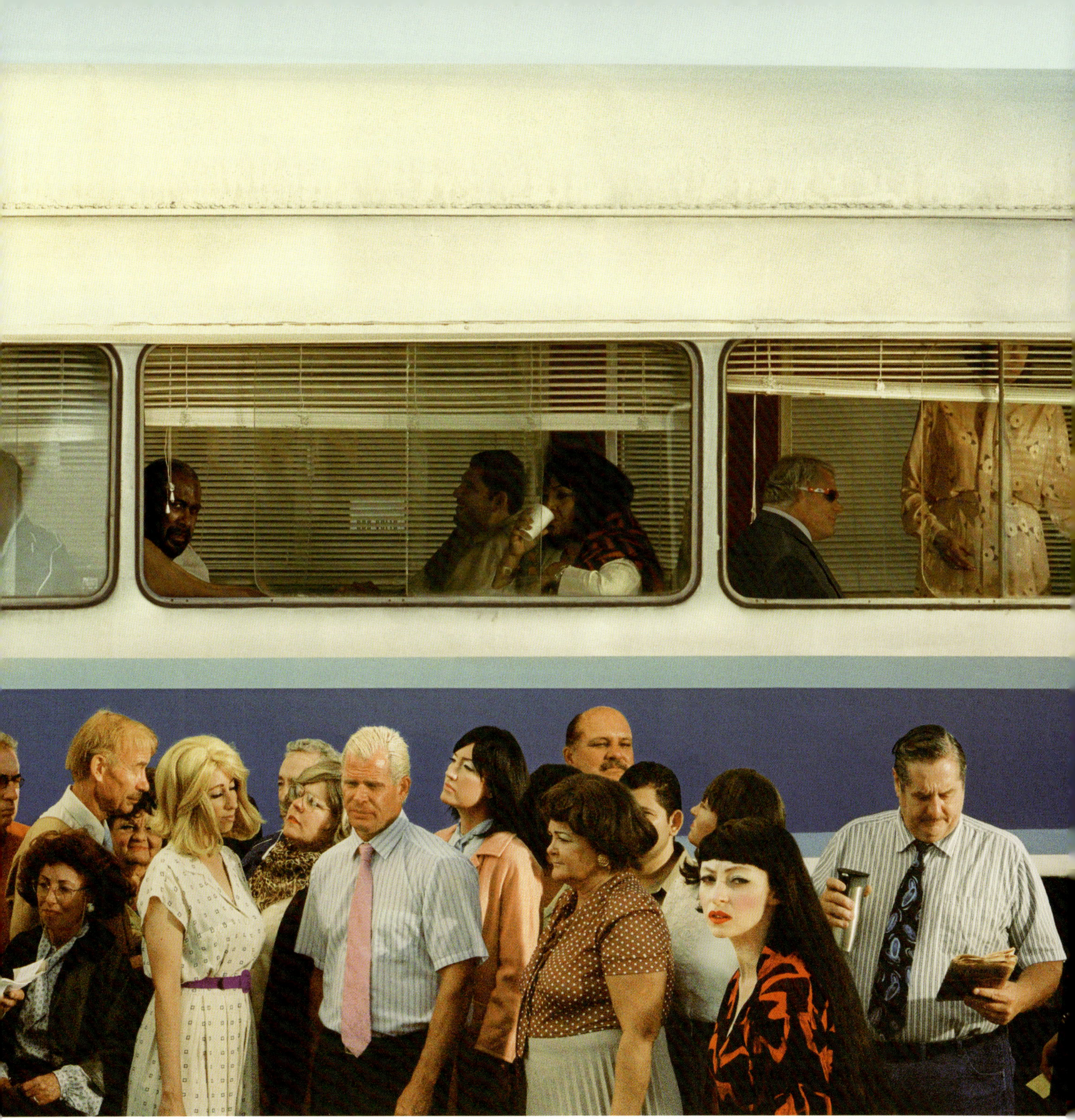

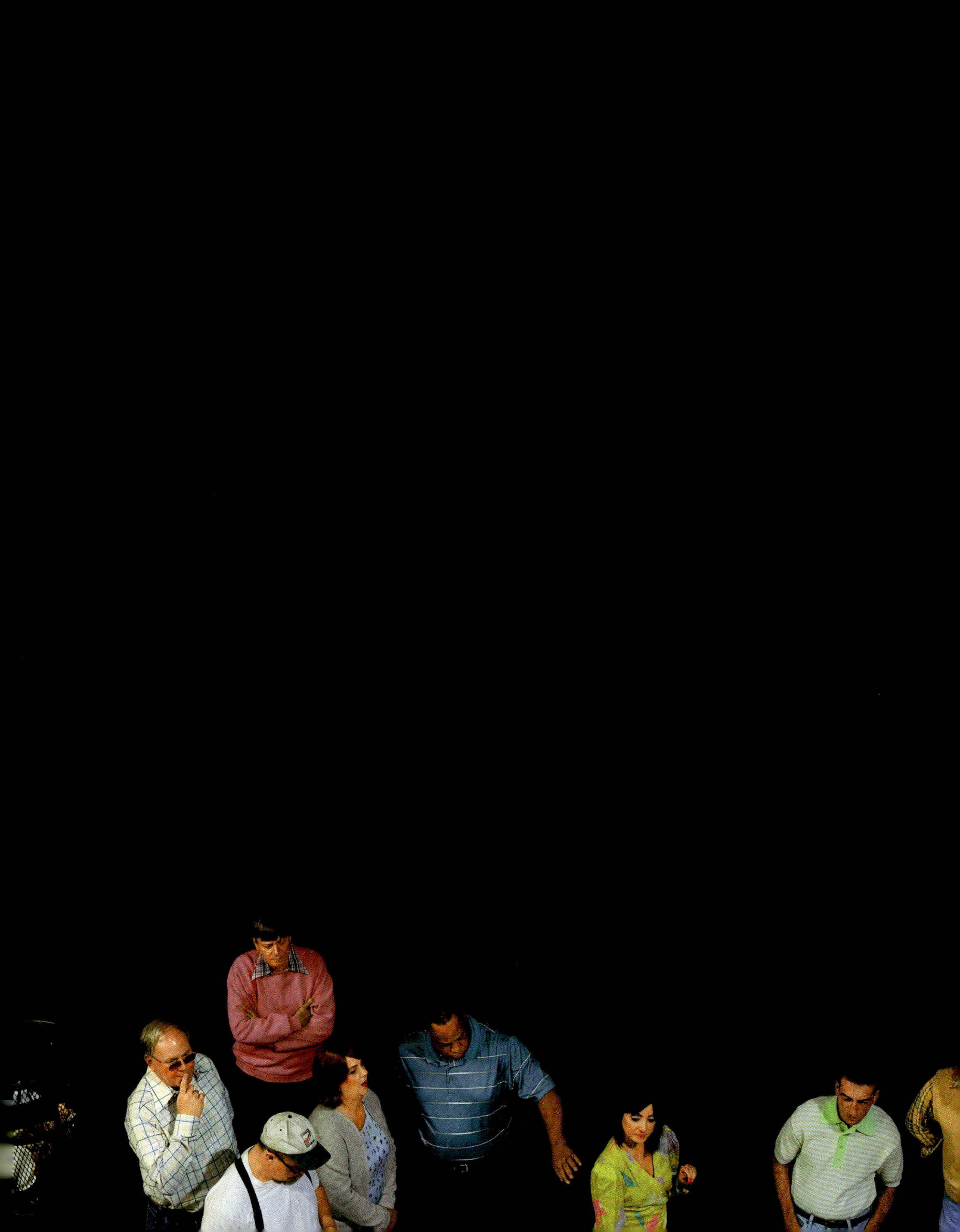

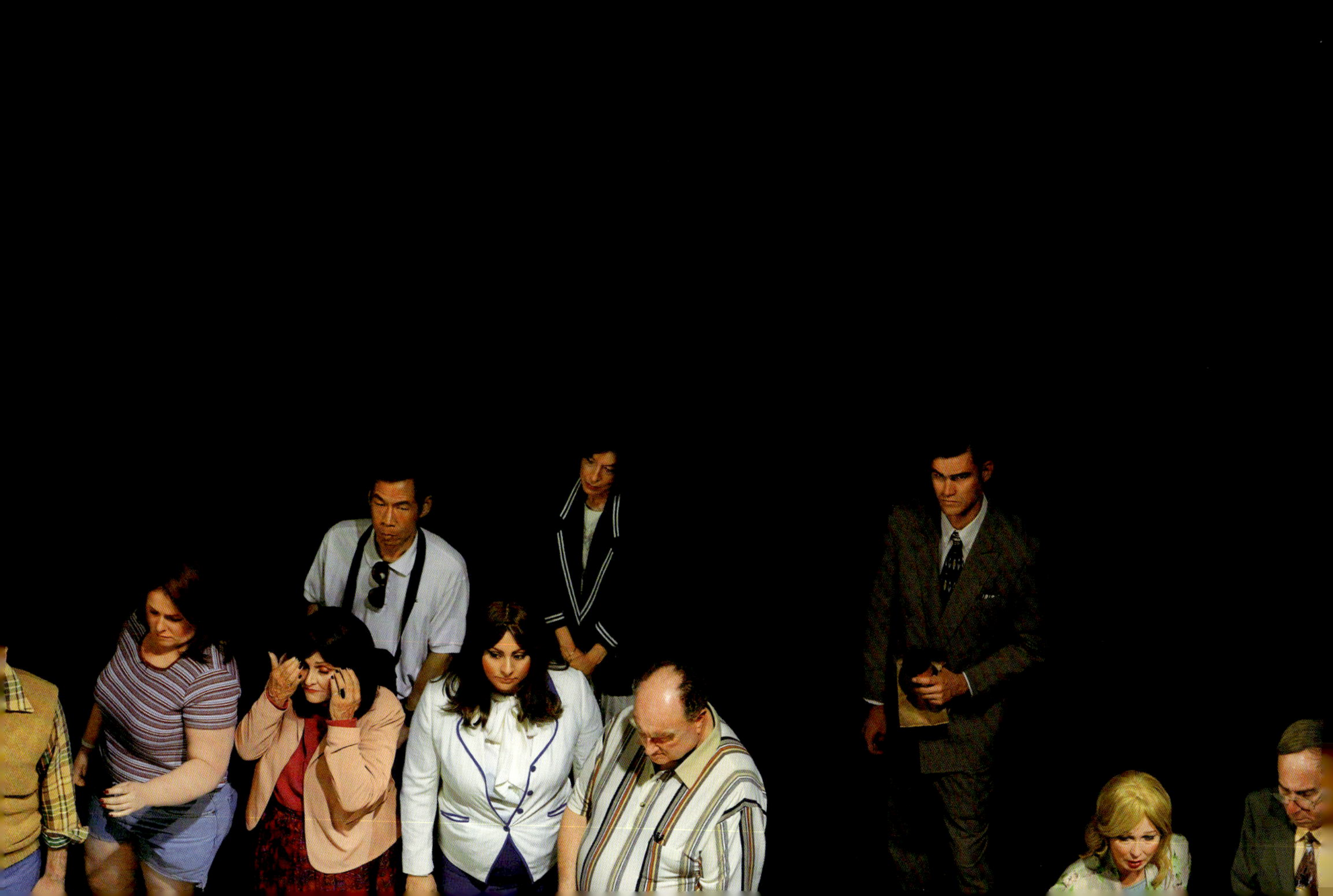

LA GRANDE SORTIE

(2016)

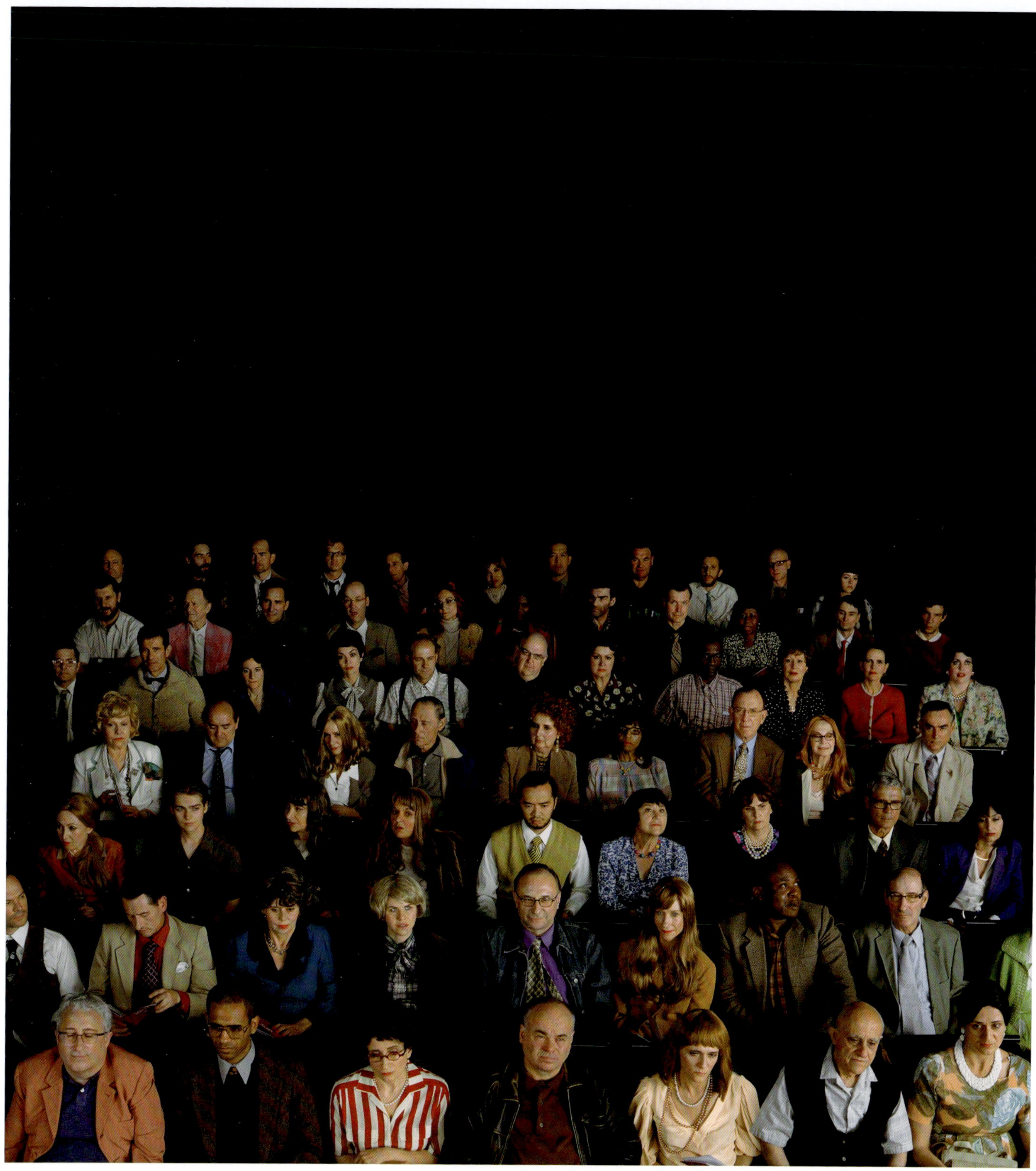

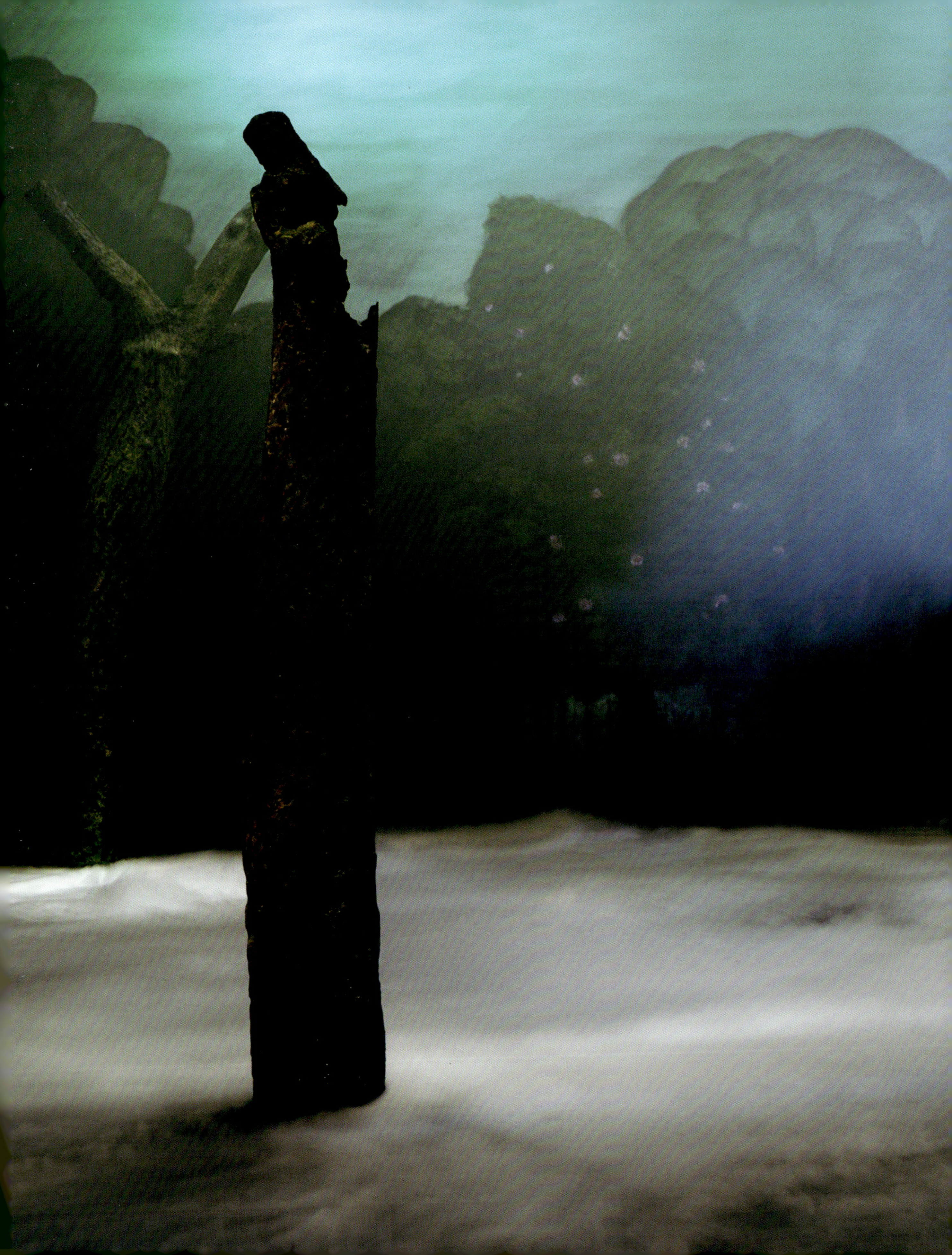

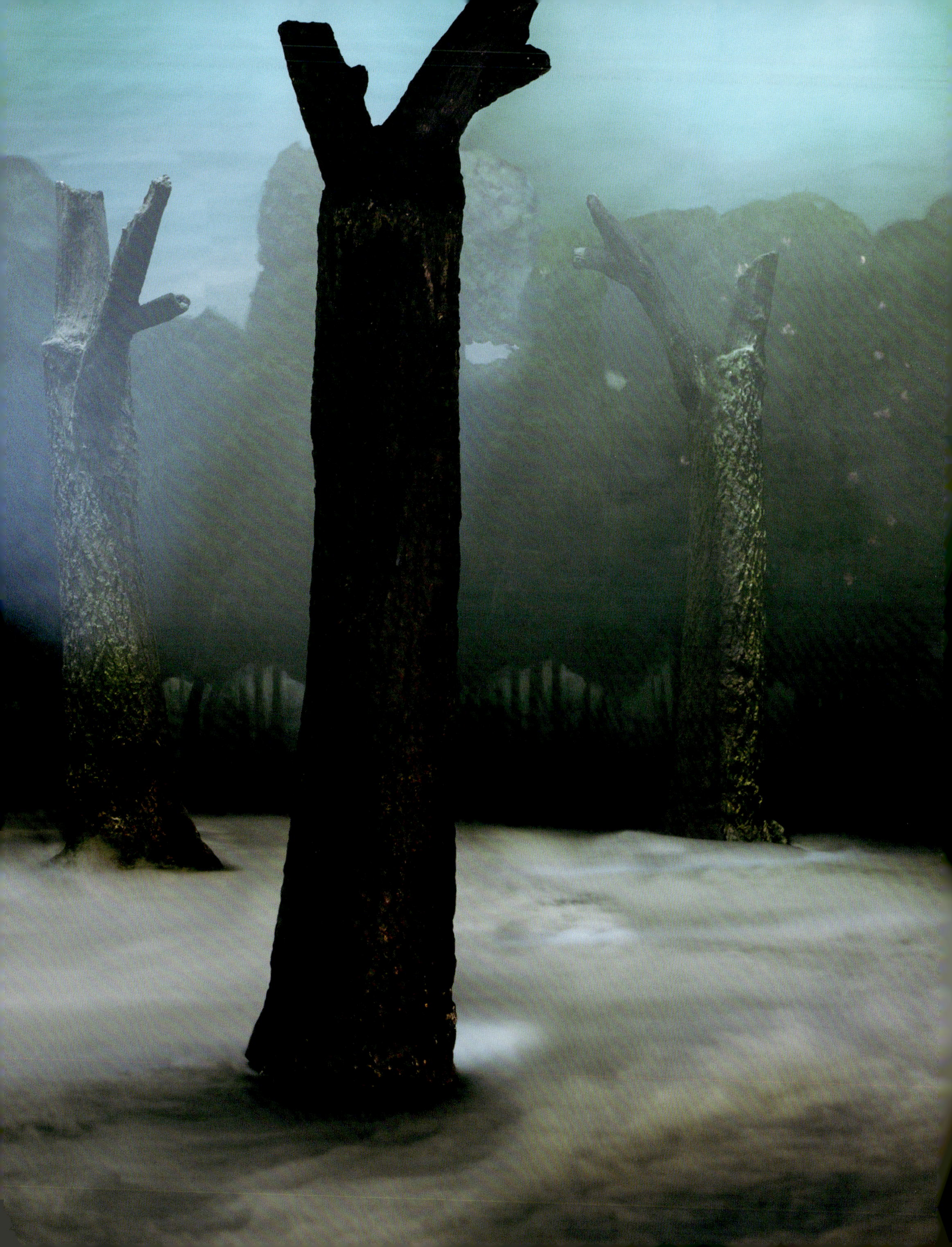

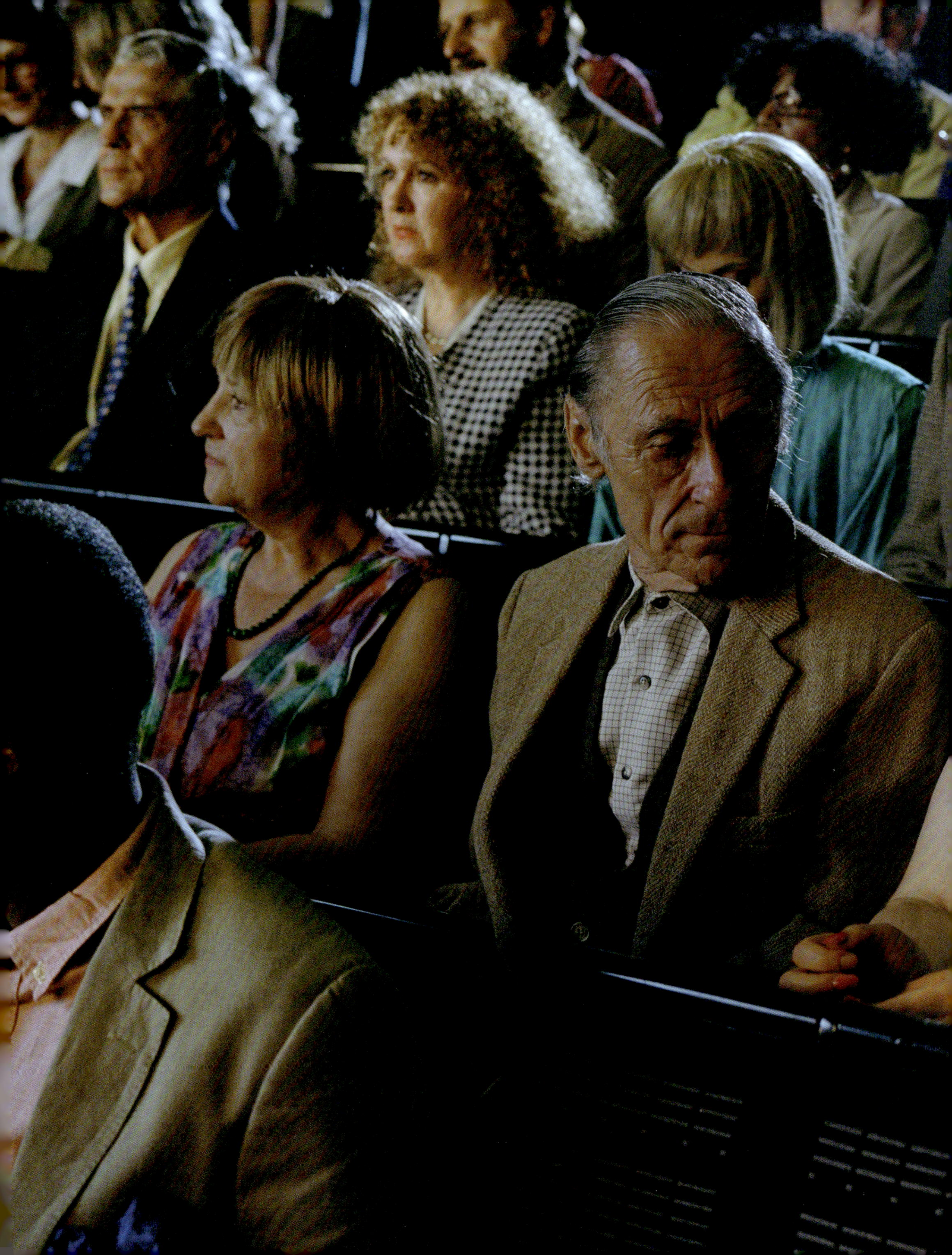

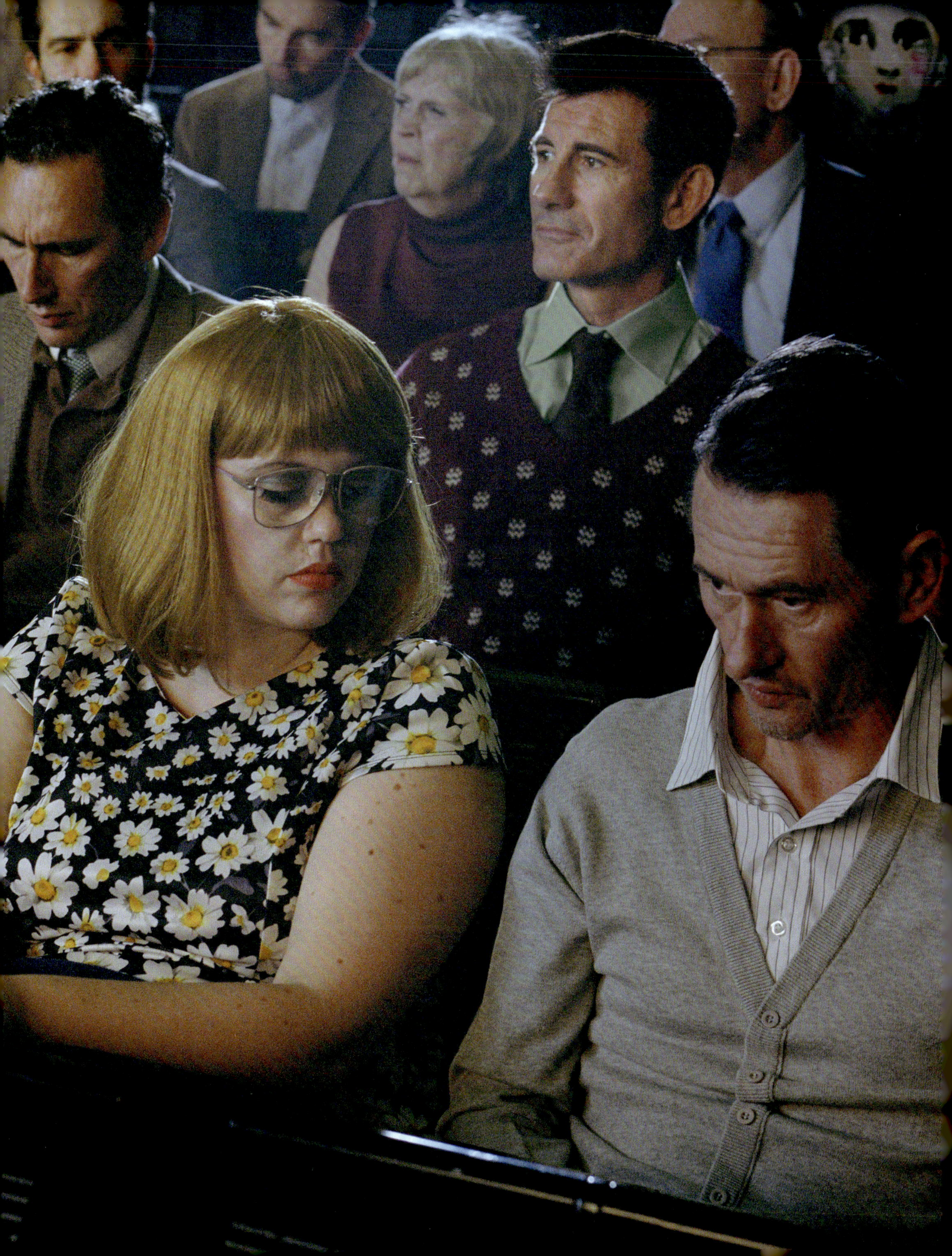

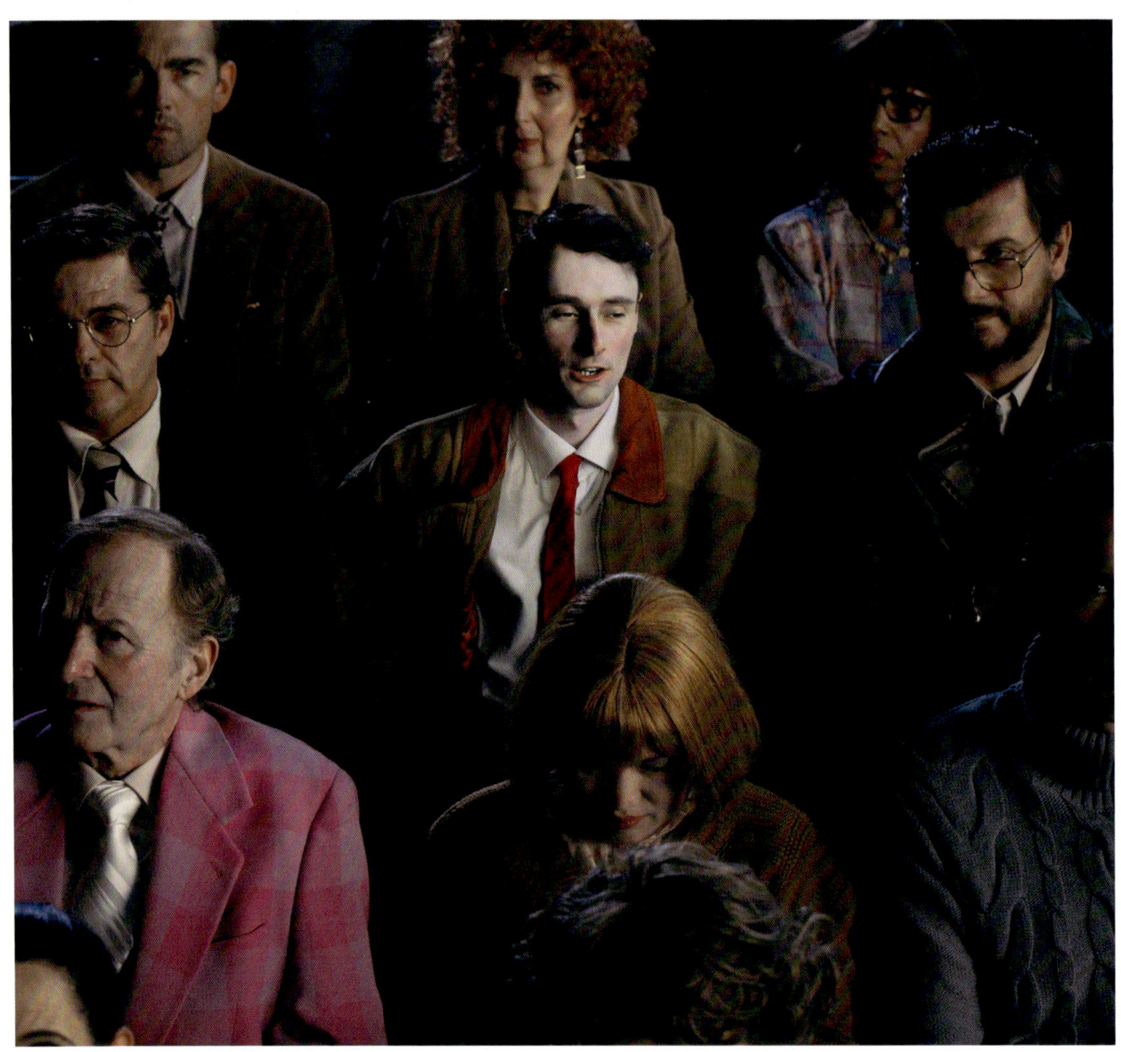

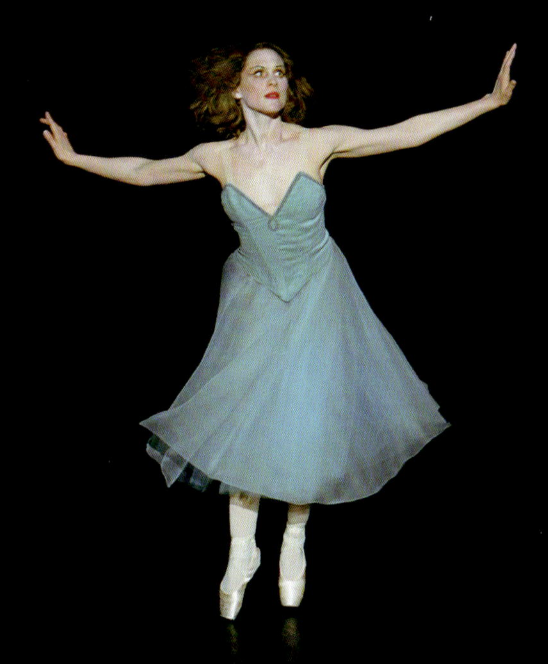

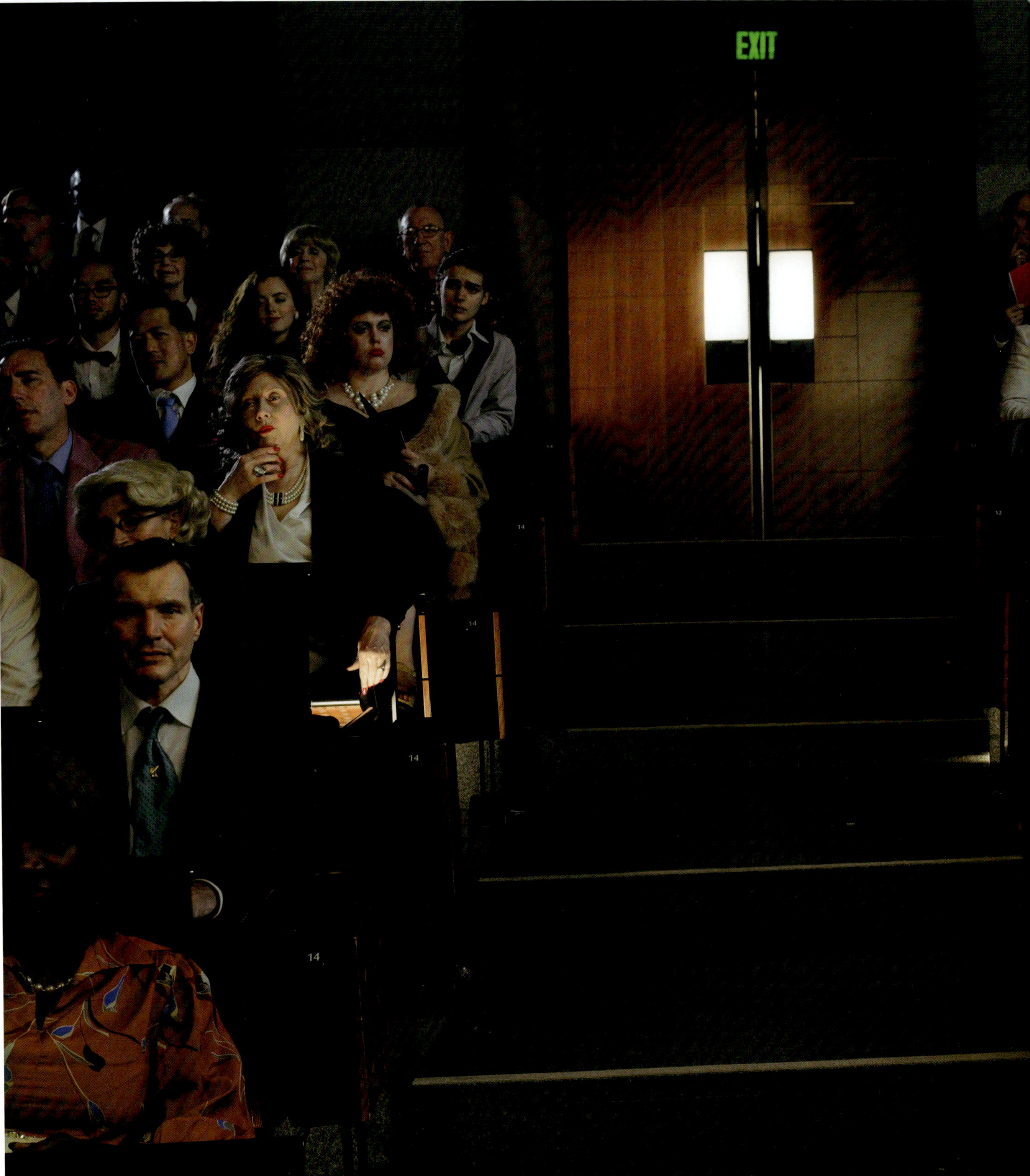
EXIT

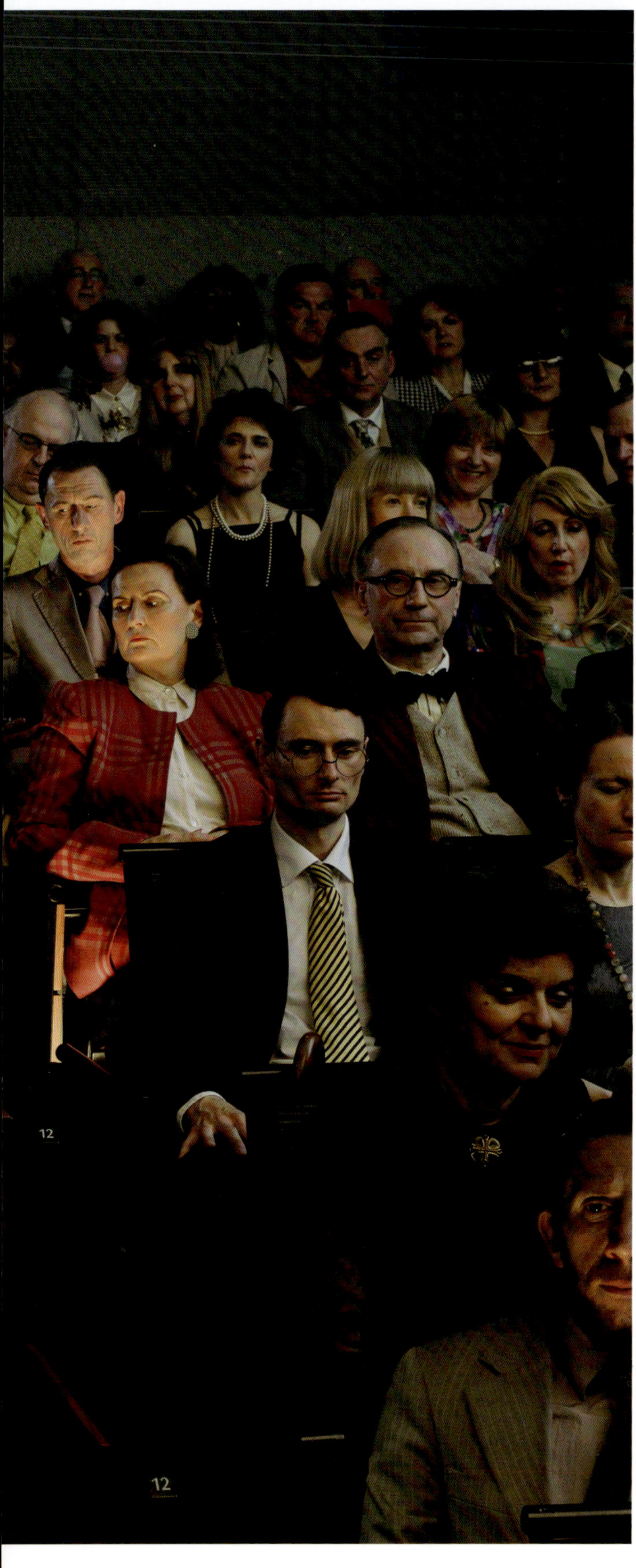

12
12

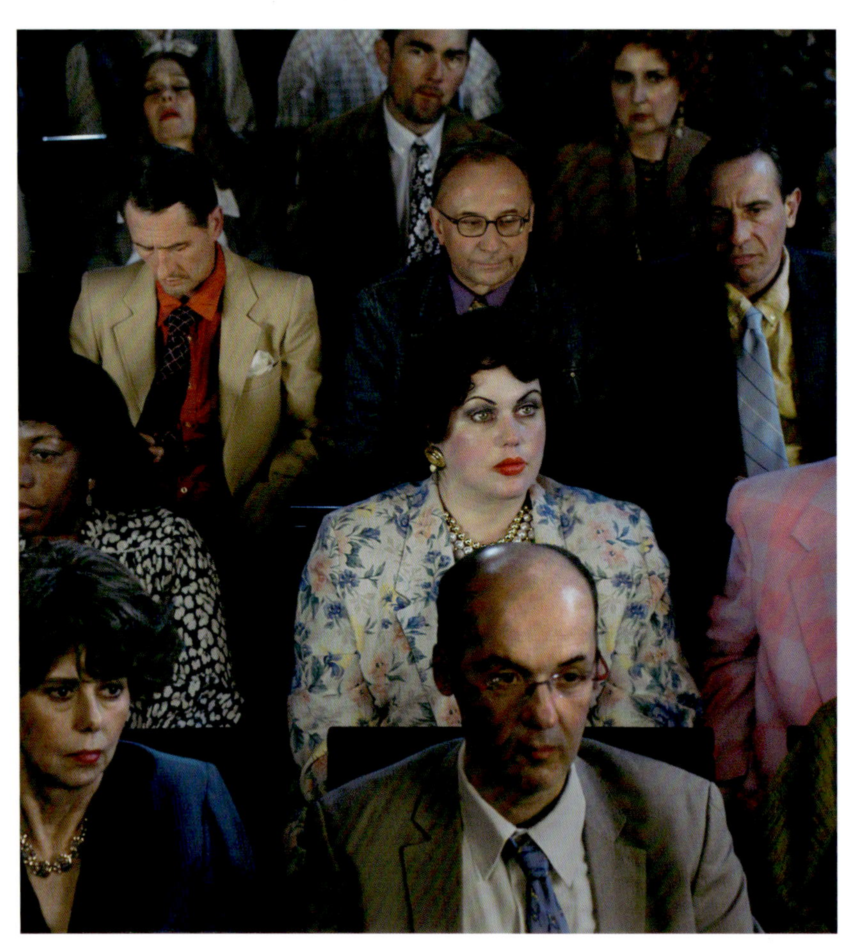

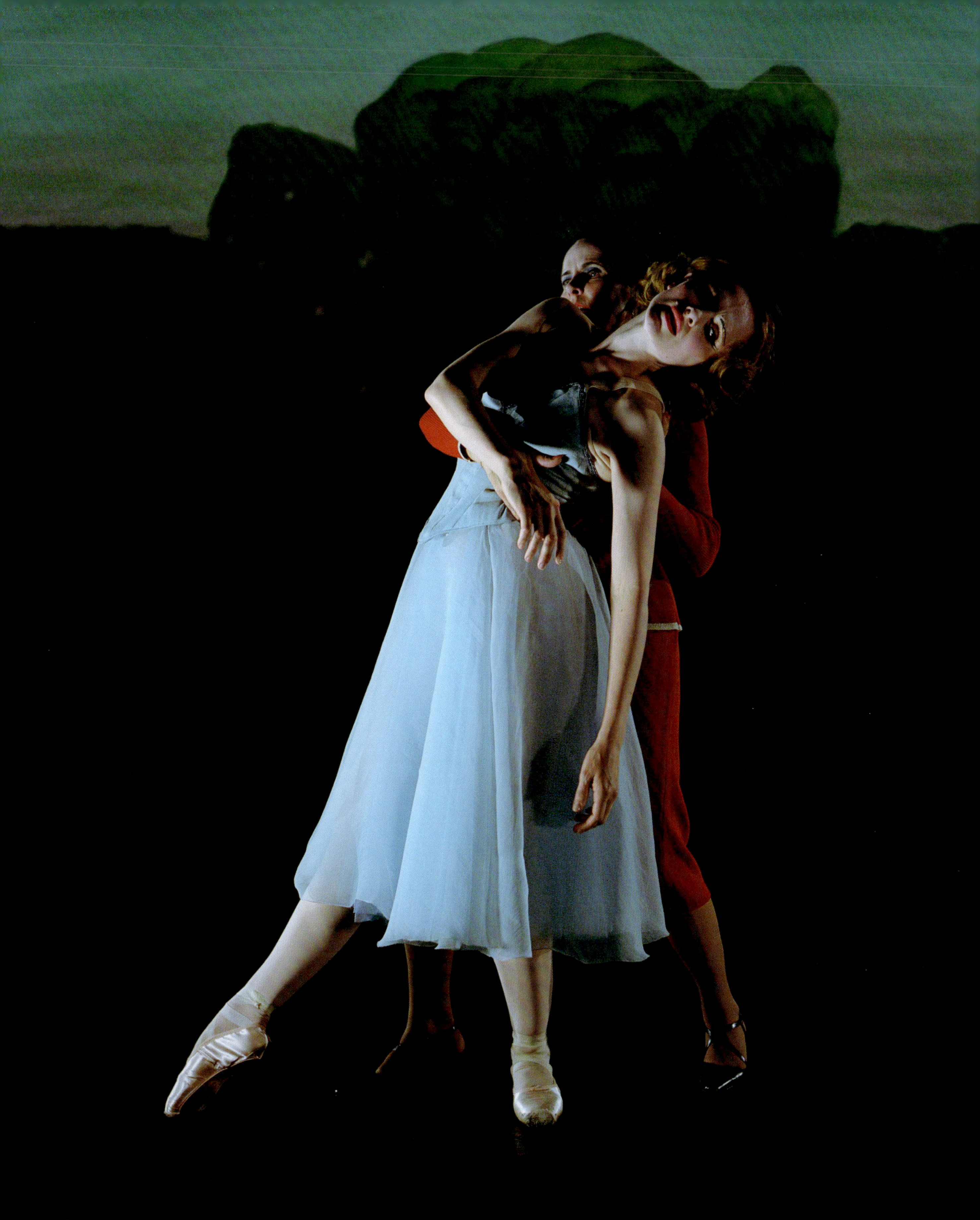

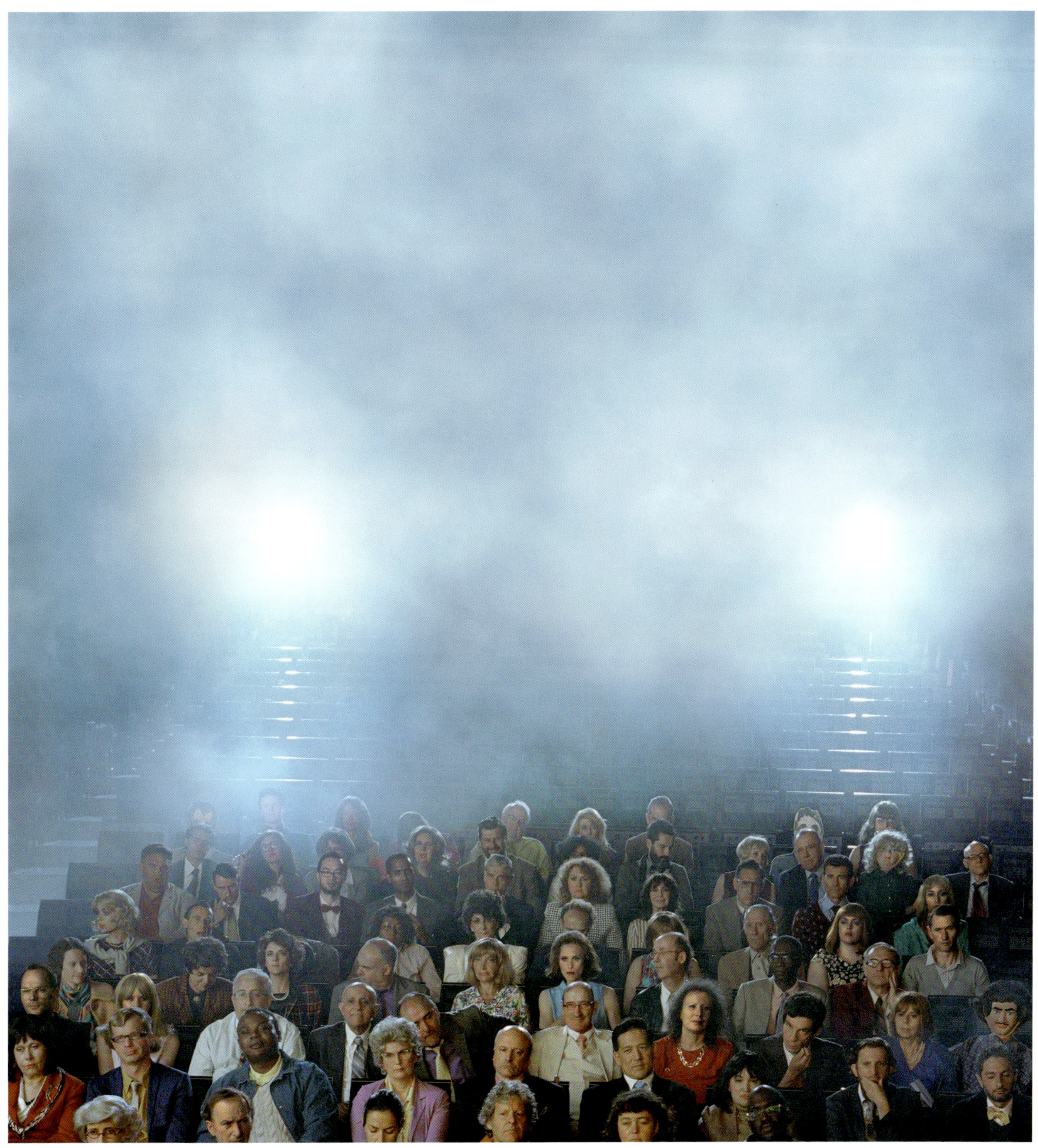

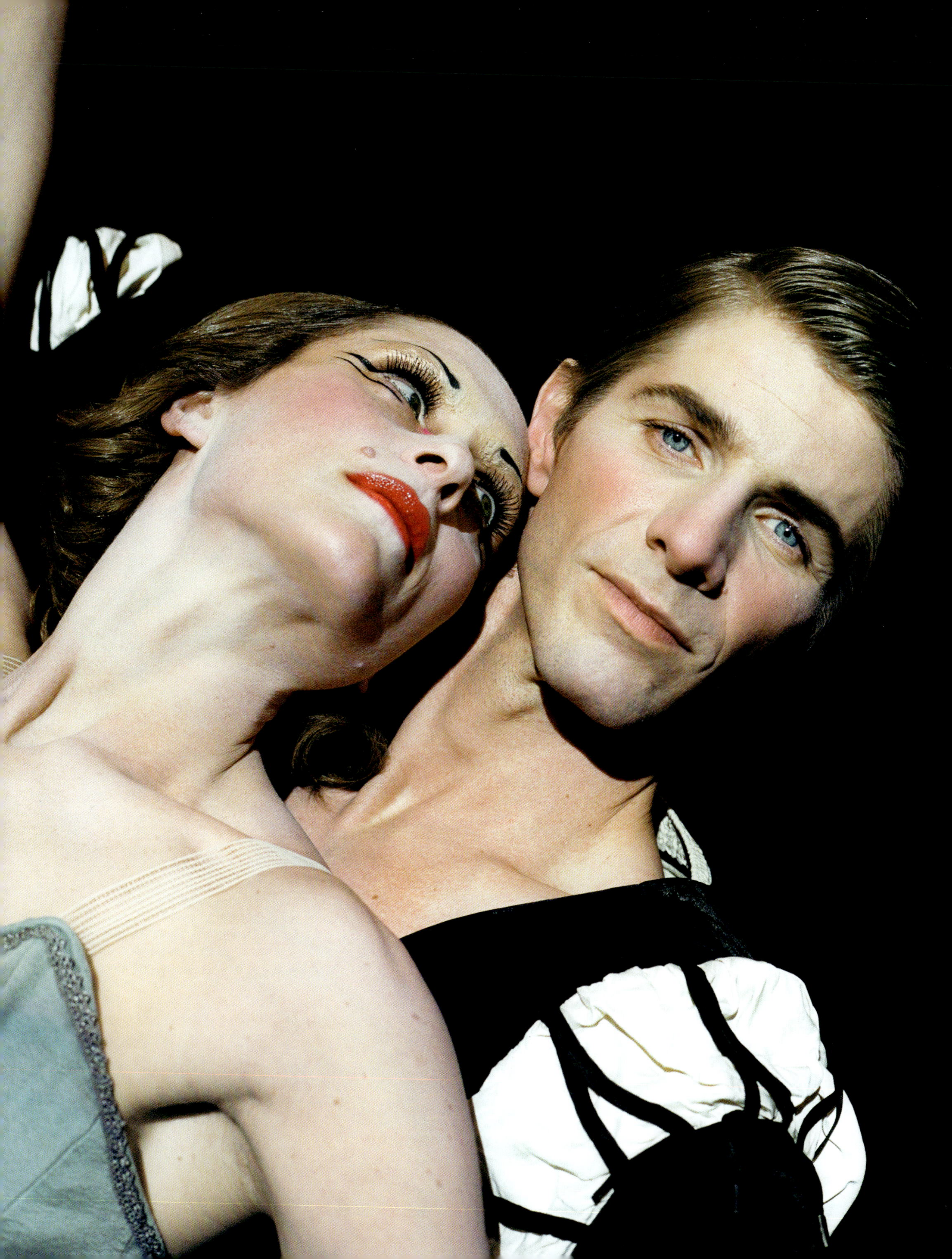

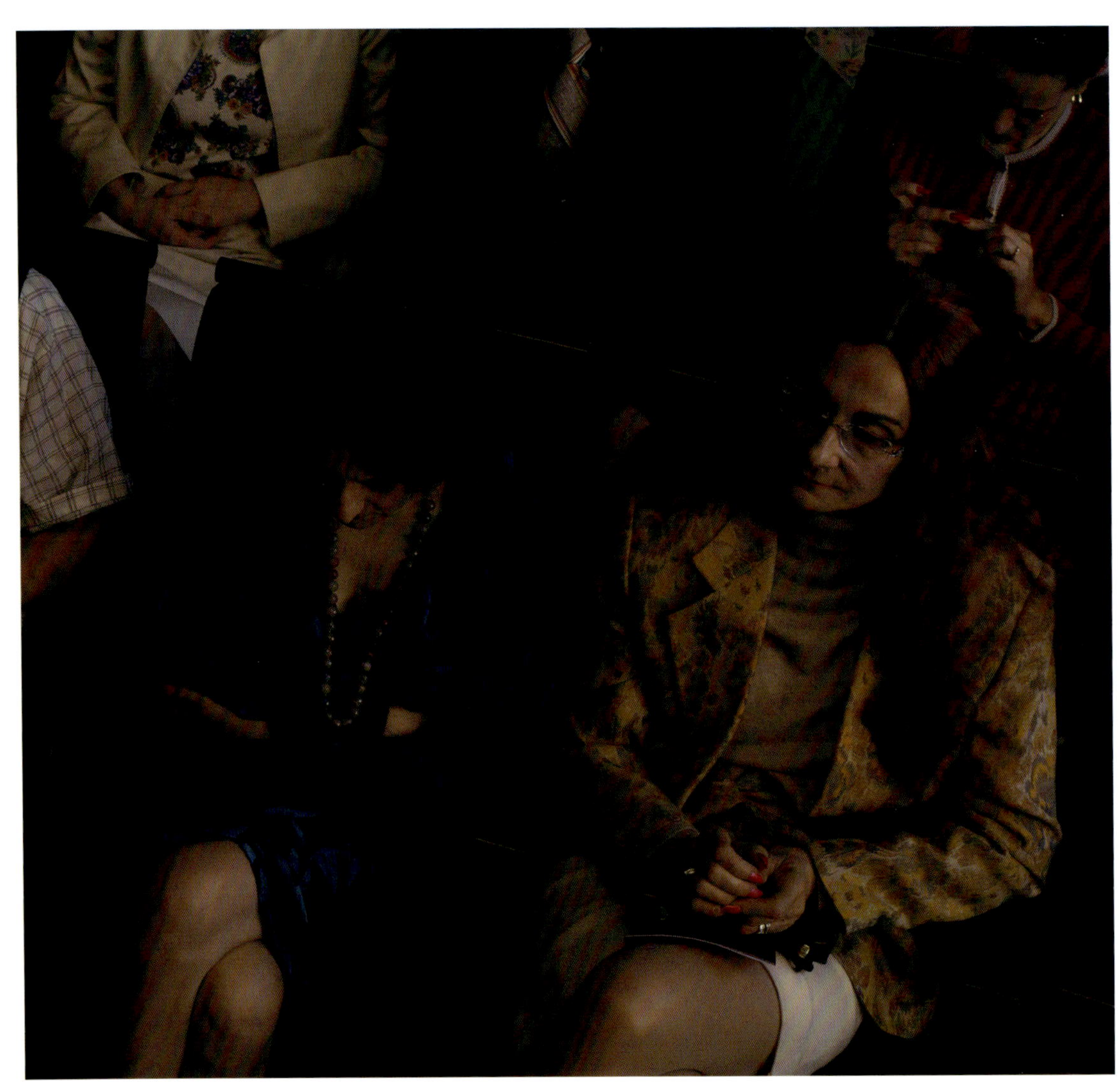

BEHIND THE SCENES

Behind the scenes of *La Grande Sortie*, 2016

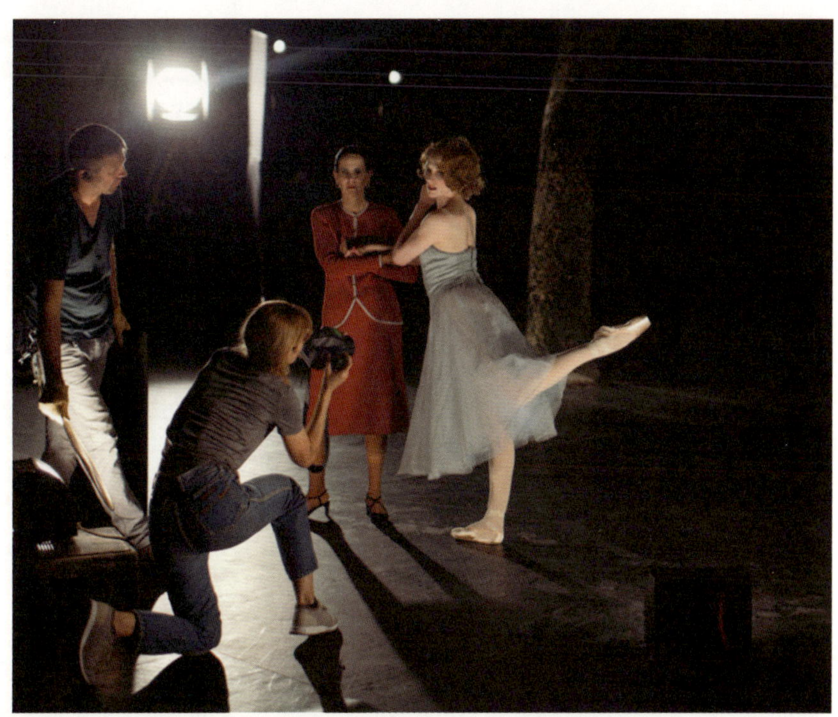

Behind the scenes of *La Grande Sortie*, 2016

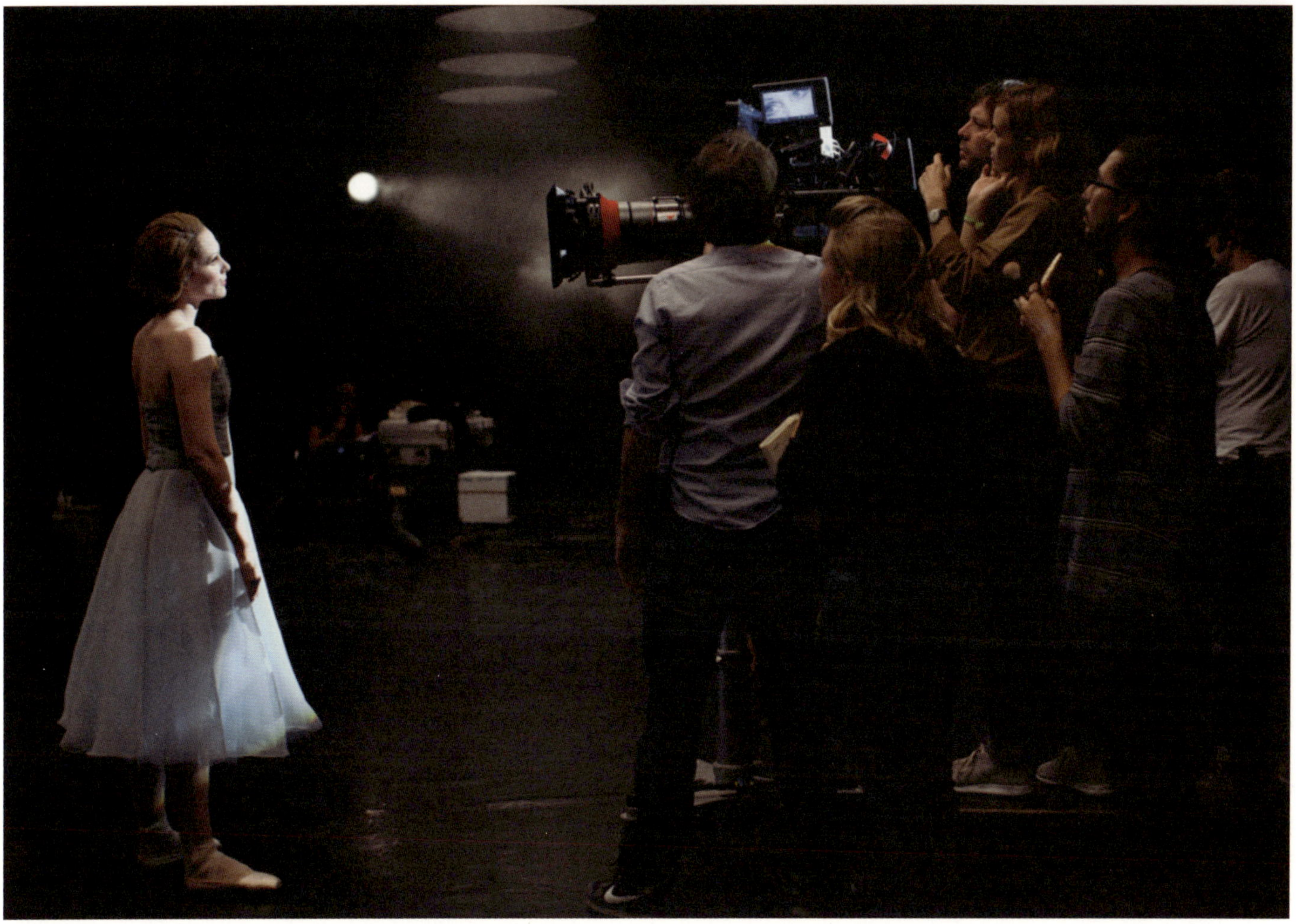

Behind the scenes of *Face in the Crowd*, 2013.
Courtesy of Jeff Vespa

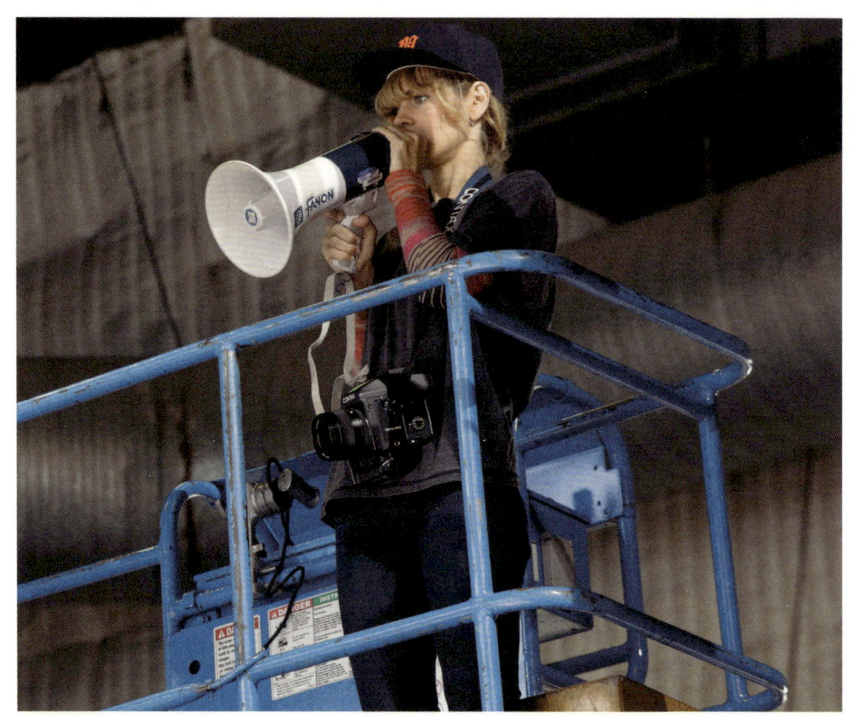

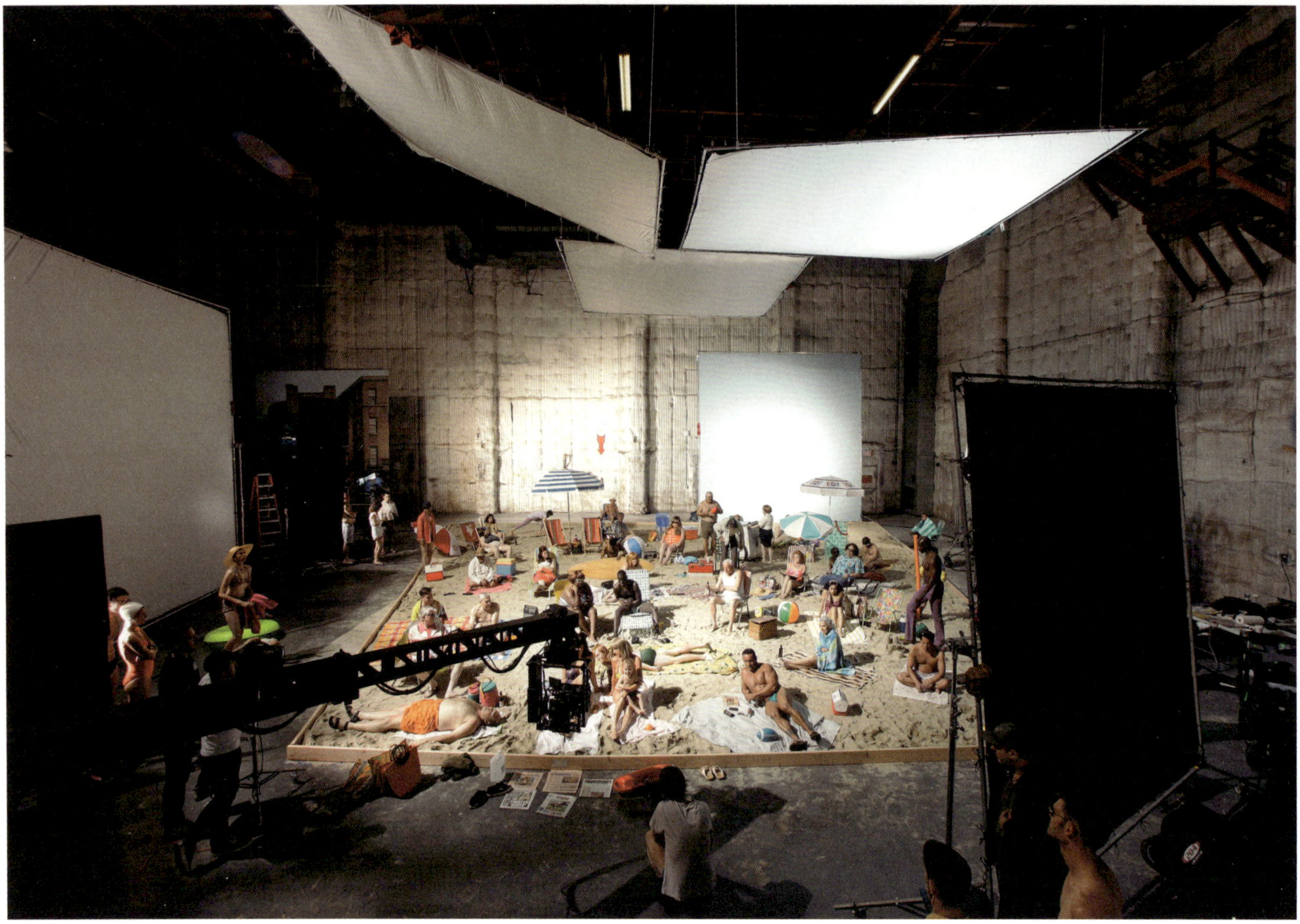

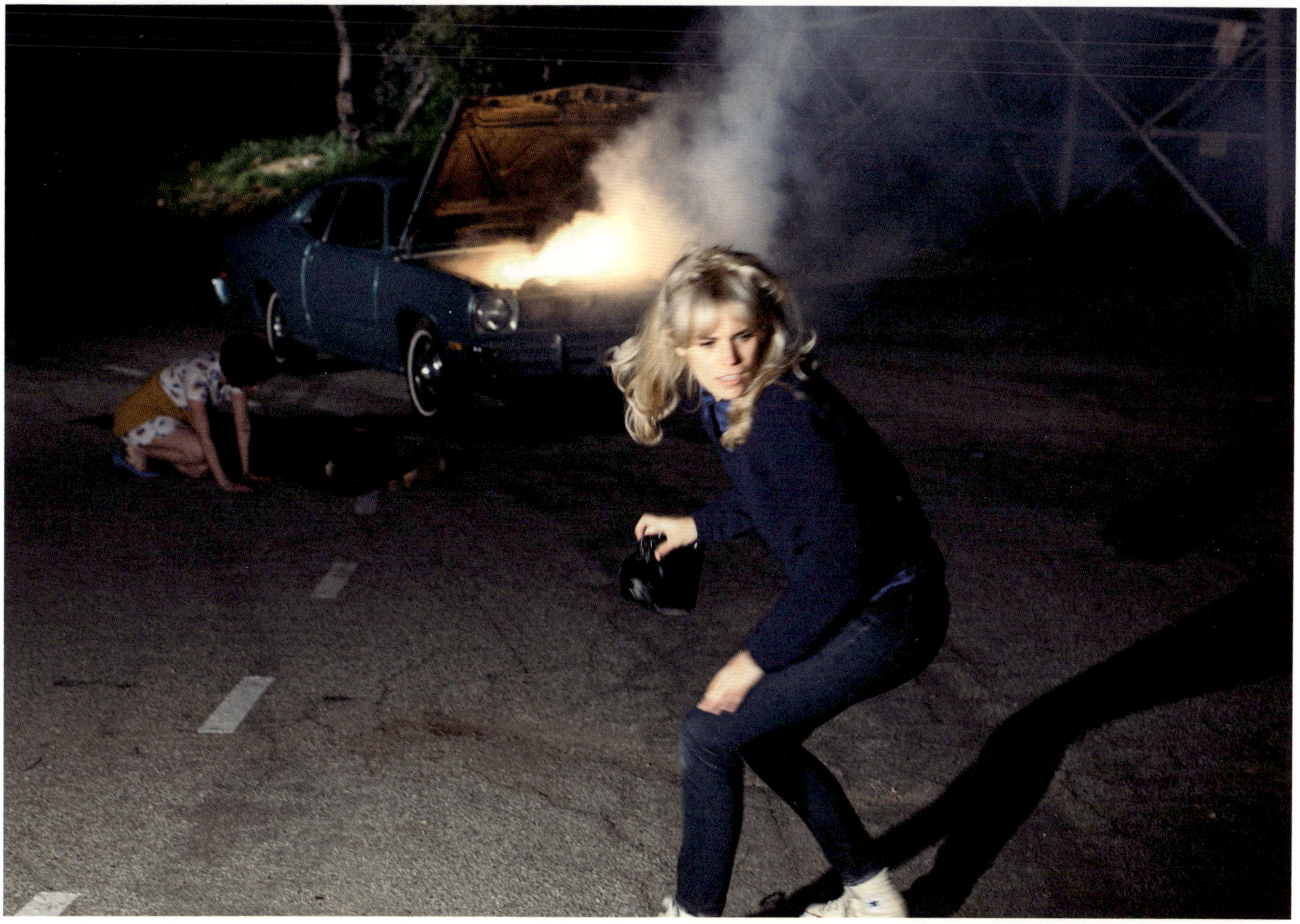

Behind the scenes of *Compulsion*, 2012.
Courtesy of Jeff Vespa

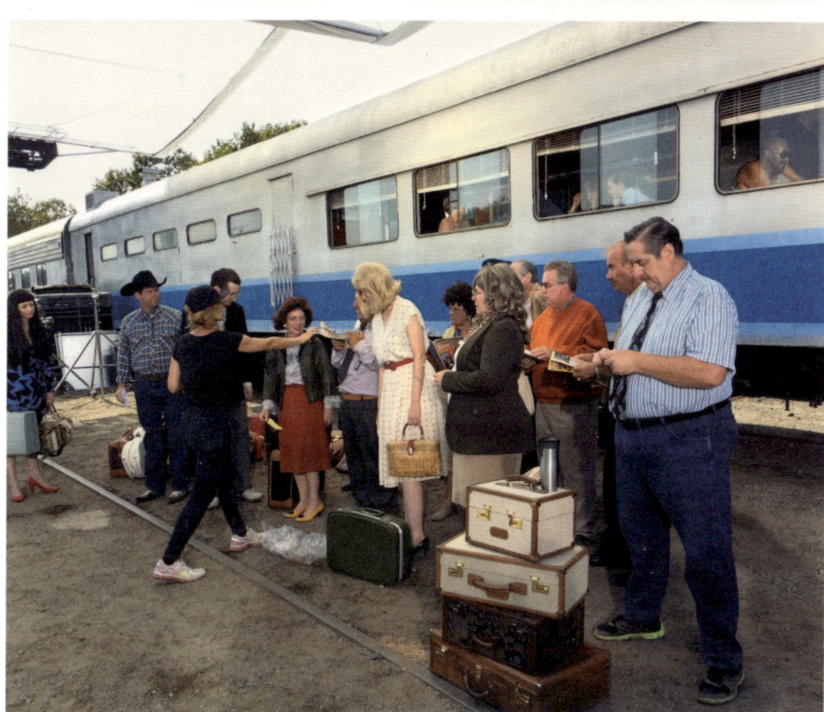

Behind the scenes of *Simi Valley*, 2014.
Courtesy of Callan Stokes

SELECTED WORKS

POLYESTER

(2007)

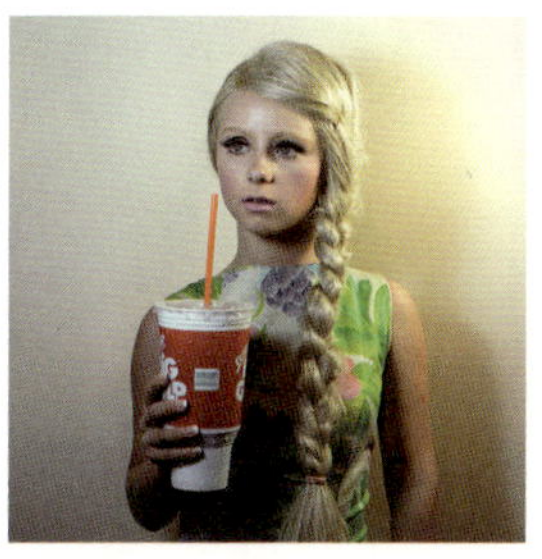

* Ellen, 2007
48 × 43.5 inches
121.9 × 110.5 cm

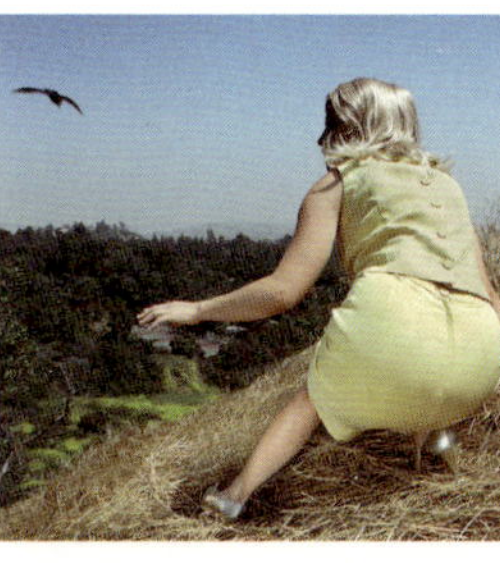

* Julie, 2007
48 × 63 inches
121.9 × 160 cm

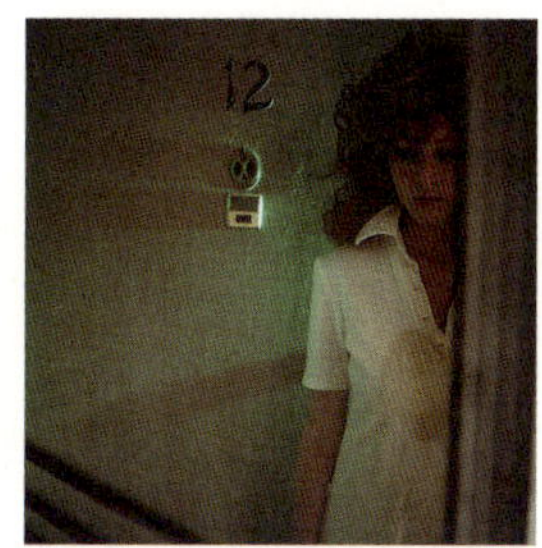

Jessica, 2007
48 × 64 inches
121.9 × 162.6 cm

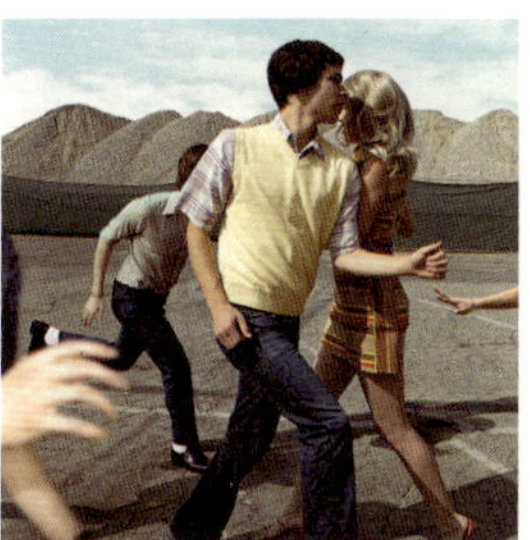

* Crowd, 2007
48 × 43.5 inches
121.9 × 110.5 cm

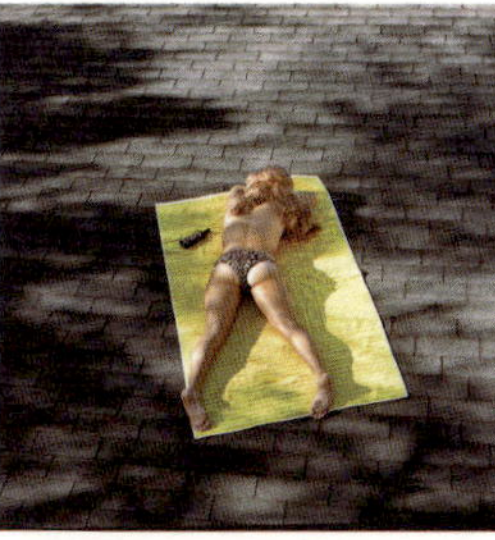

* Crystal, 2007
48 × 62.5 inches
121.9 × 158.8 cm

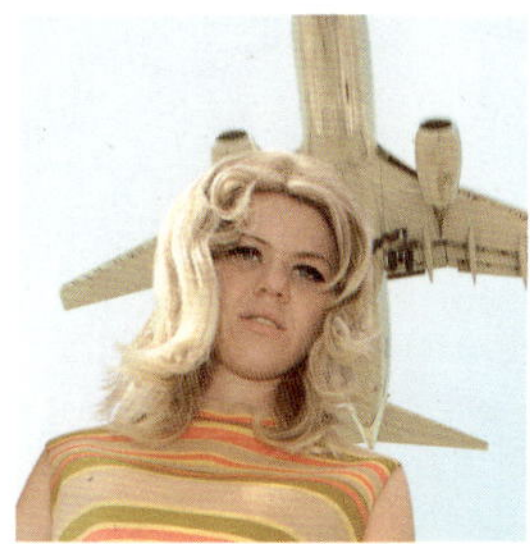

* Alexandra, 2007
48 × 62.5 inches
121.9 × 158.6 cm

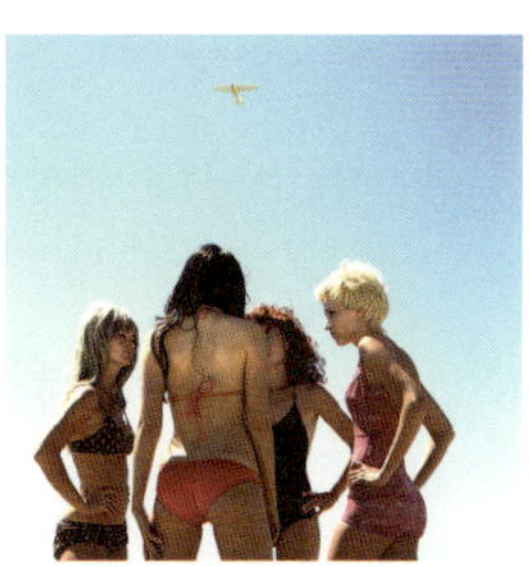

* Four Girls, 2007
48 × 55.4 inches
121.9 × 140.7 cm

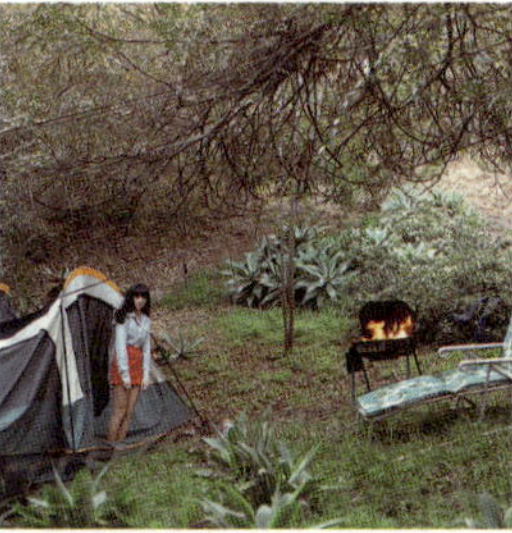

Joan, 2007
48 × 63 inches
121.9 × 160 cm

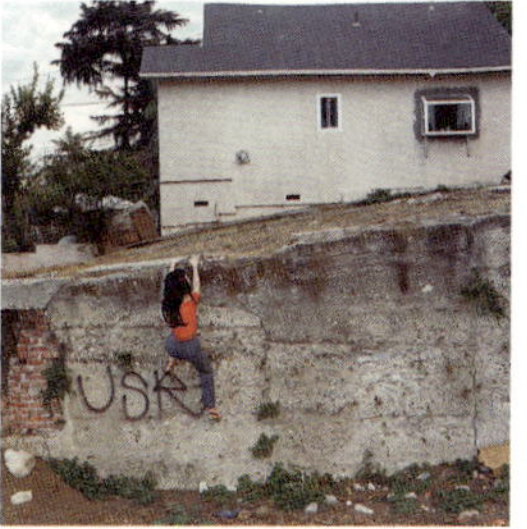

Diana, 2007
48 × 63 inches
121.9 × 160 cm

** Images marked with an asterisk are reproduced in full in the book.*

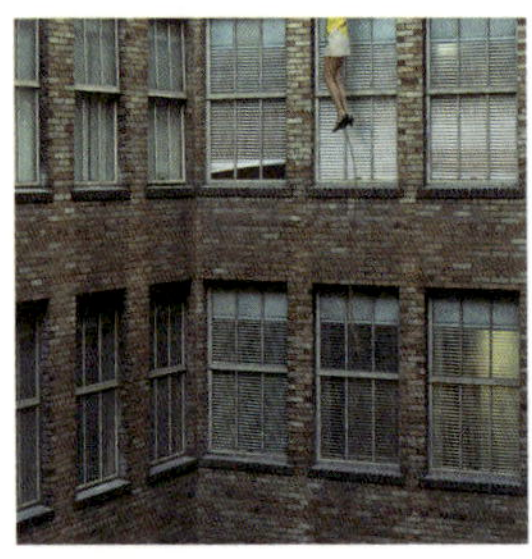

* Emily, 2007
48 × 78.5 inches
121.9 × 199.4 cm

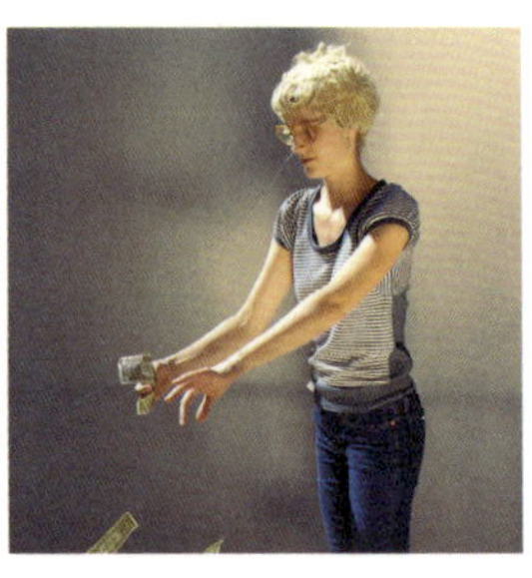

Jenny, 2007
48 × 36.5 inches
121.9 × 92.7 cm

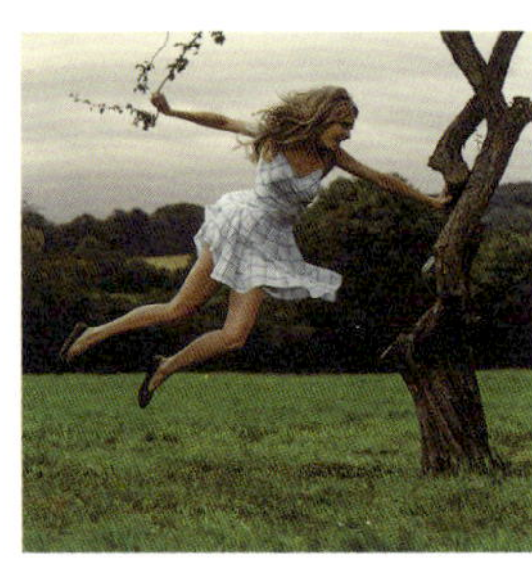

Sarah, 2007
48 × 81 inches
121.9 × 205.7 cm

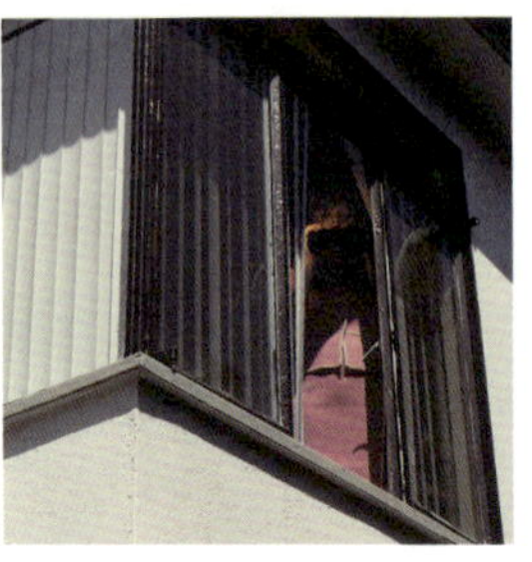

* Megan, 2007
48 × 23 inches
121.9 × 58.4 cm

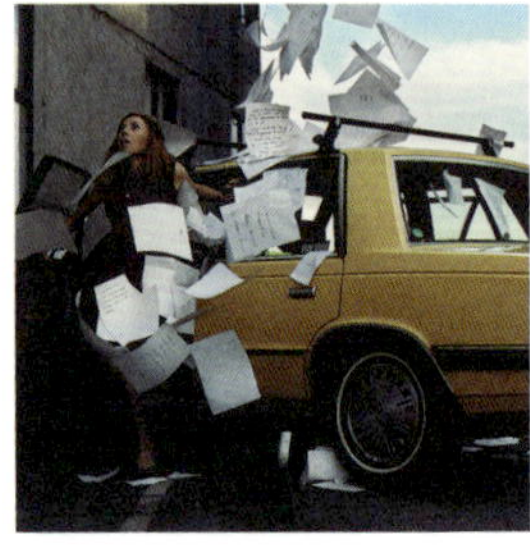

Caroline, 2007
48 × 27 inches
121.9 × 68.6 cm

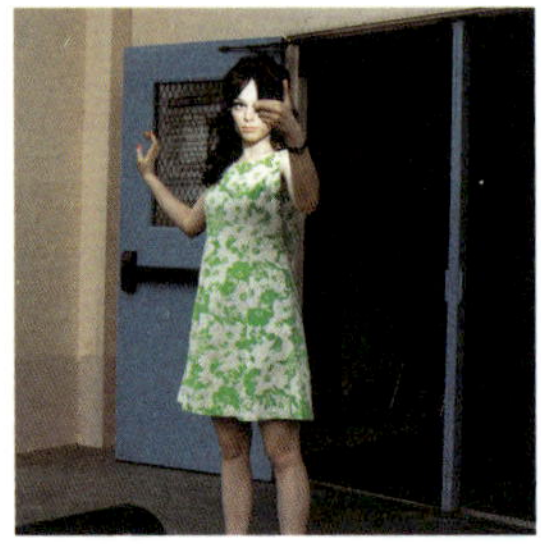

* Hannah, 2007
48 × 53 inches
121.9 × 134.6 cm

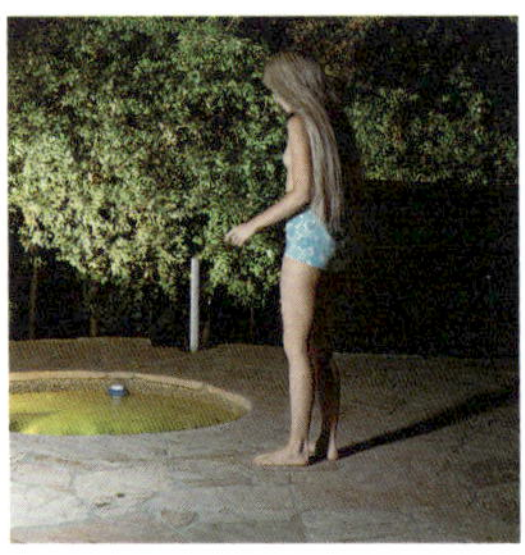

Lucy, 2007
48 × 48.5 inches
121.9 × 123.2 cm

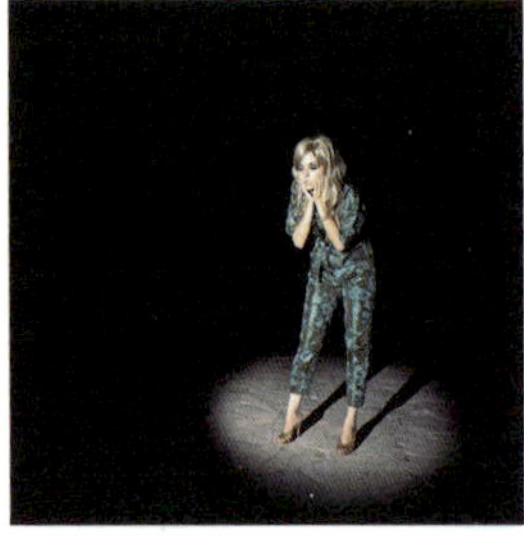

* Jackie, 2007
48 × 63 inches
121.9 × 160 cm

THE BIG VALLEY
(2008)

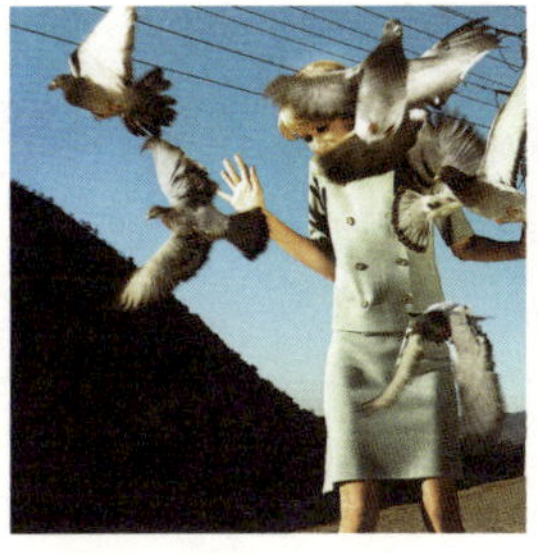

* Eve, 2008
48 × 60 inches
121.9 × 152.4 cm

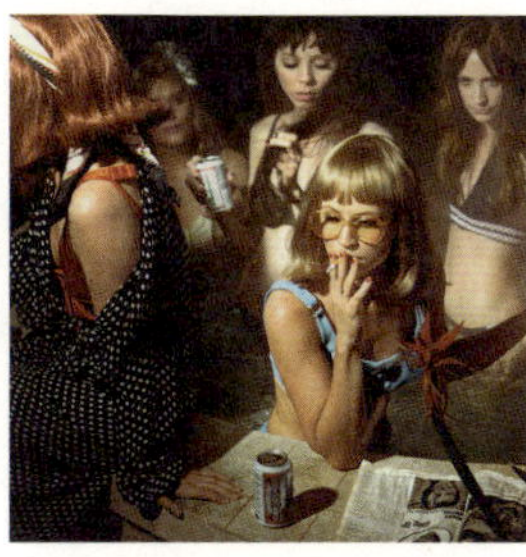

* Susie and Friends, 2008
48 × 76.5 inches
121.9 × 194.3 cm

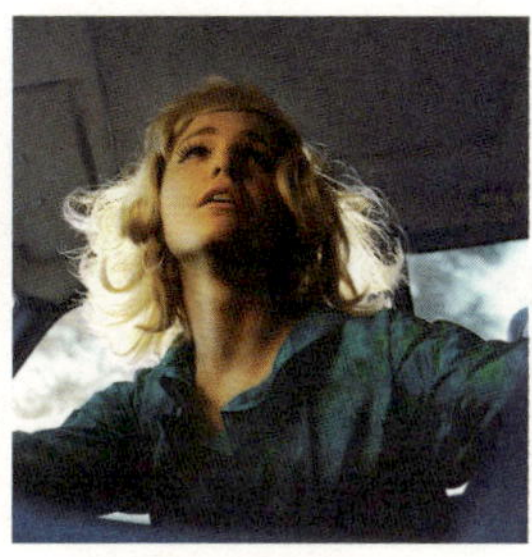

* Virginia, 2008
48 × 68 inches
121.9 × 172.7 cm

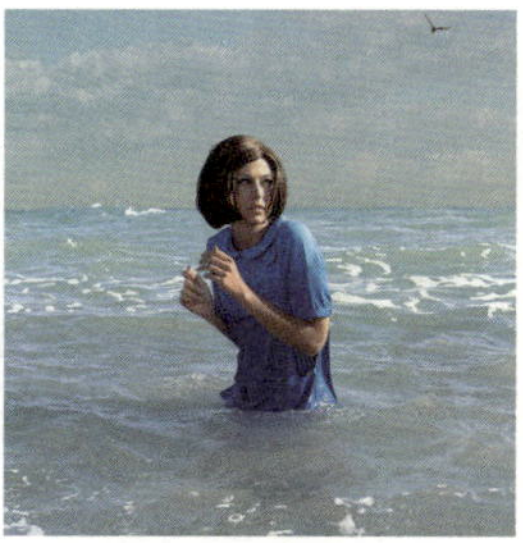

* Annie, 2008
48 × 63.5 inches
121.9 × 161.3 cm

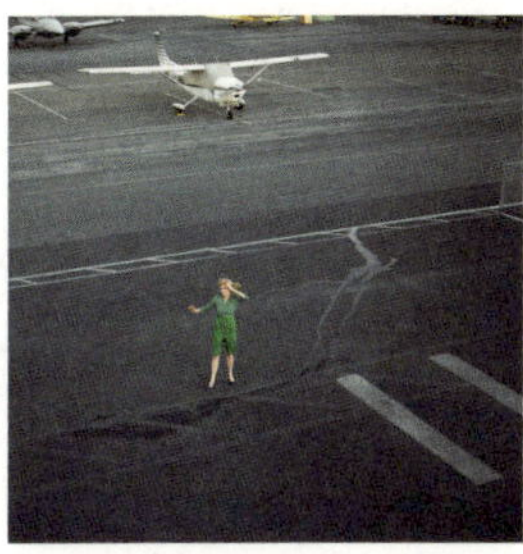

* Kimberly, 2008
48 × 62.75 inches
121.9 × 159.4 cm

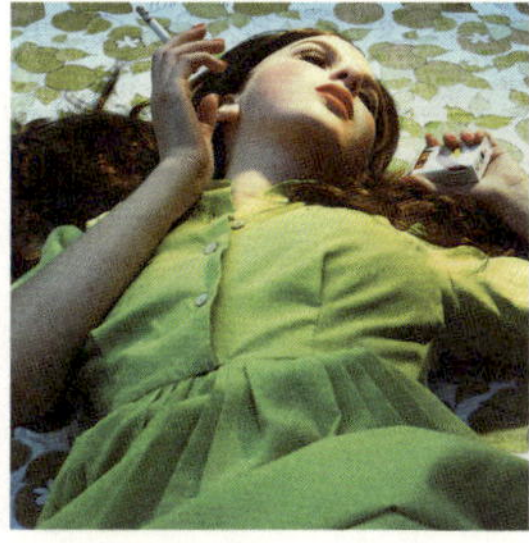

* Desiree, 2008
48 × 65 inches
121.9 × 165.1 cm

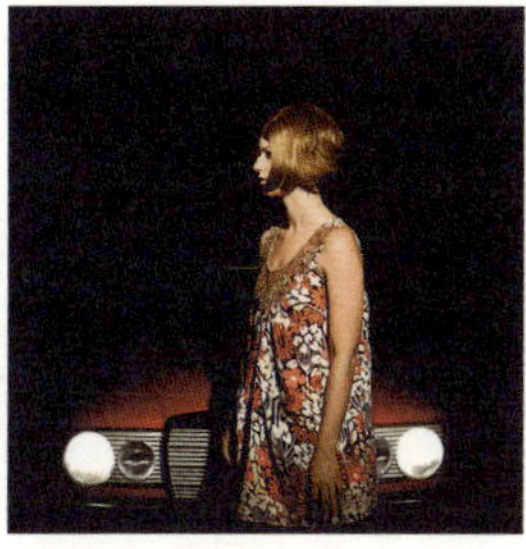

Cindy, 2008
48 × 98.5 inches
121.9 × 250.2 cm

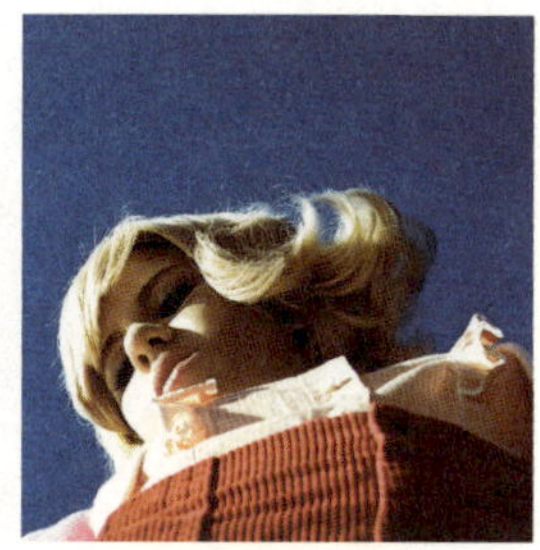

* Helen, 2008
48 × 83 inches
121.9 × 210.8 cm

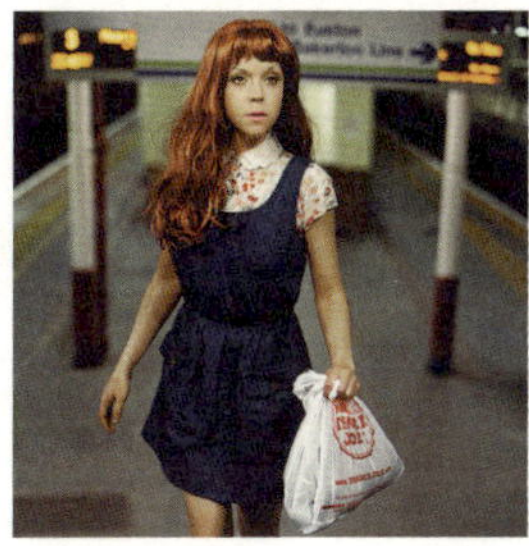

Kate, 2008
48 × 35.5 inches
121.9 × 90.2 cm

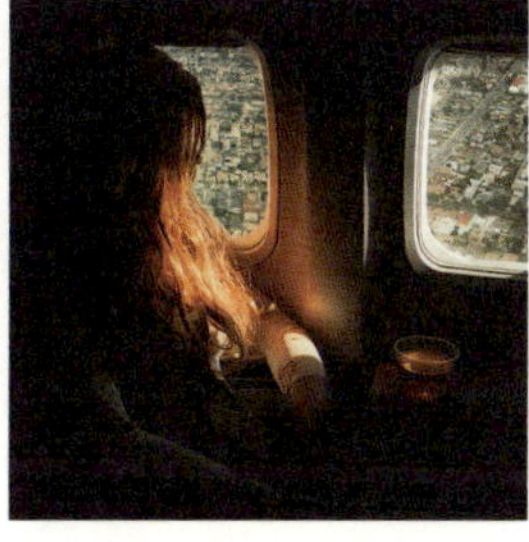

* Nancy, 2008
48 × 49.5 inches
121.9 × 125.7 cm

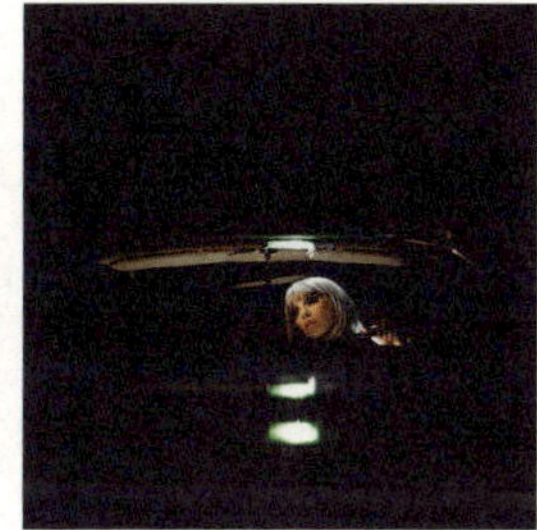

Gloria, 2008
48 × 48 inches
121.9 × 121.9 cm

WEEK-END & THE LONG WEEKEND
(2009—2012)

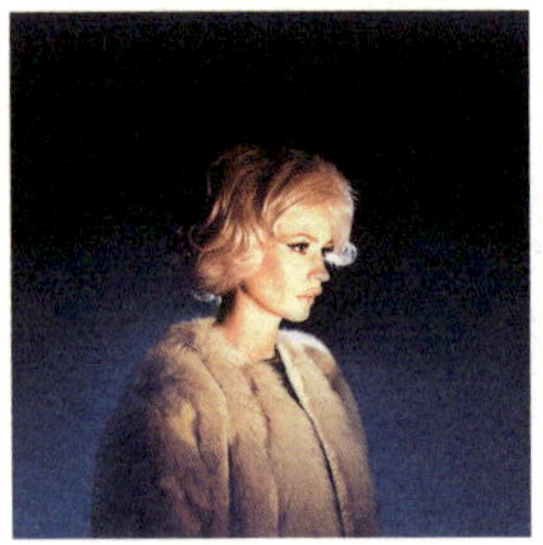

* Barbara, 2009
36 × 48 inches
91.4 × 121.9 cm

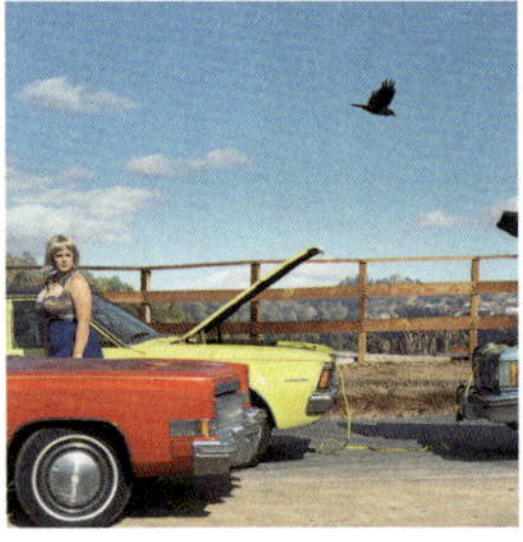

* Lois, 2009
48 × 70 inches
121.9 × 177.8 cm

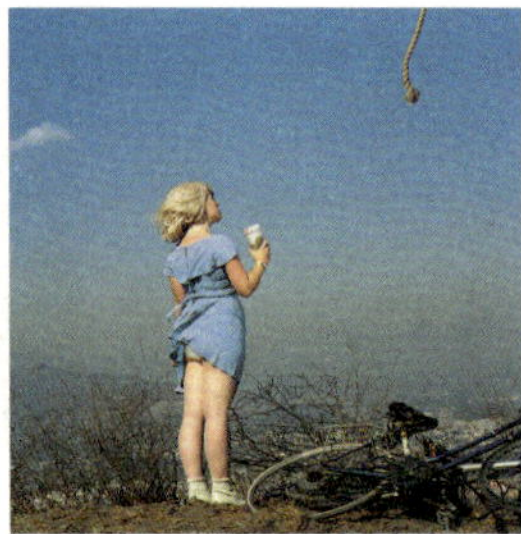

* Molly, 2009
48 × 63.5 inches
121.9 × 161.3 cm

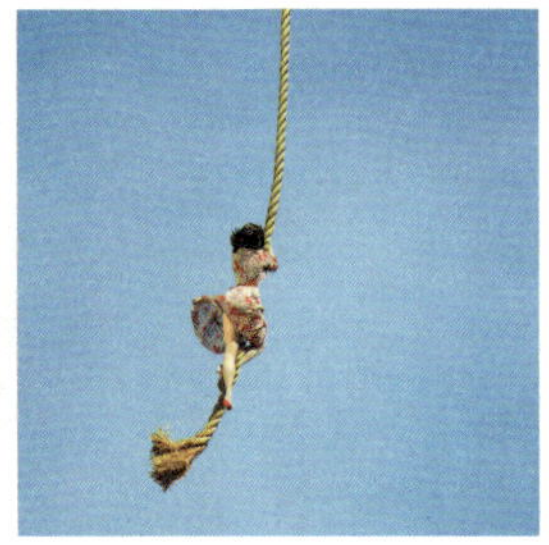

* Judith, 2012
48 × 35 inches
121.9 × 88.9 cm

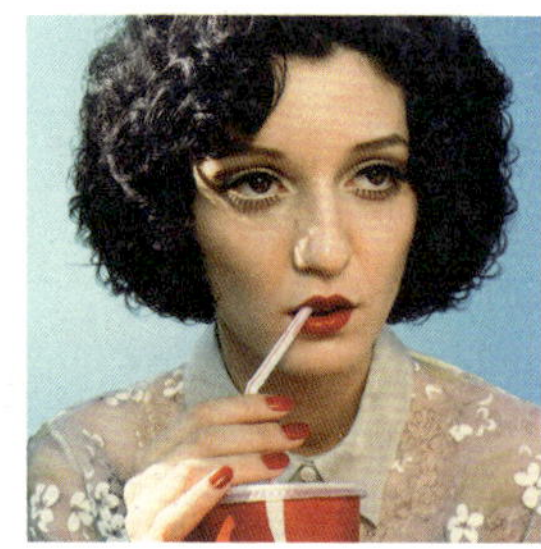

Isabelle, 2010
48 × 36 inches
121.9 × 91.4 cm

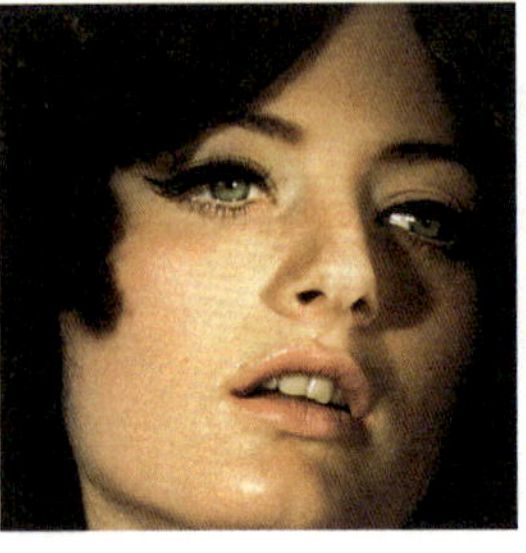

* Wendy, 2009
48 × 59.5 inches
121.9 × 151.1 cm

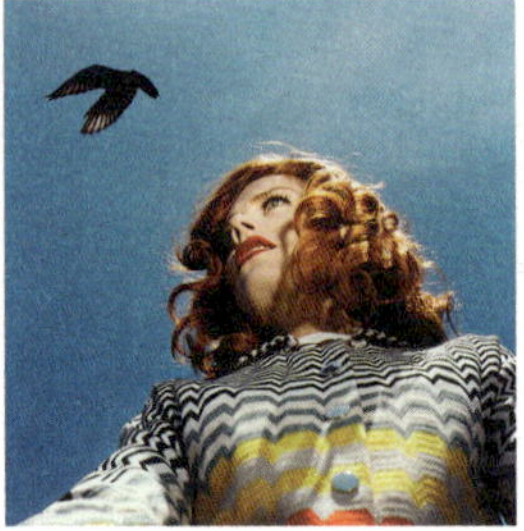

Renee, 2010
36 × 27 inches
91.4 × 68.6 cm

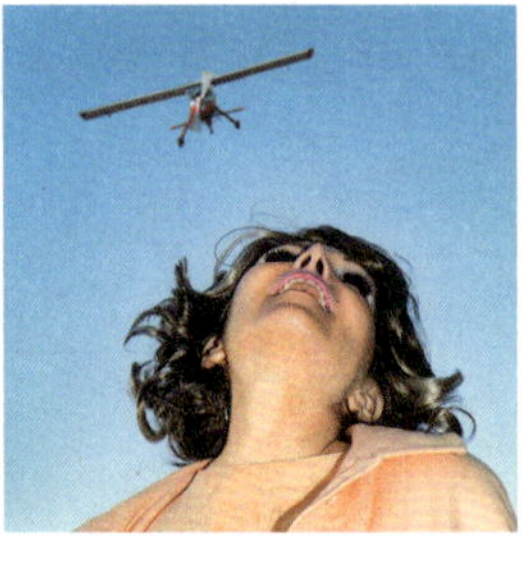

* Beverly, 2010
48 × 39.5
121.9 × 100.3 cm

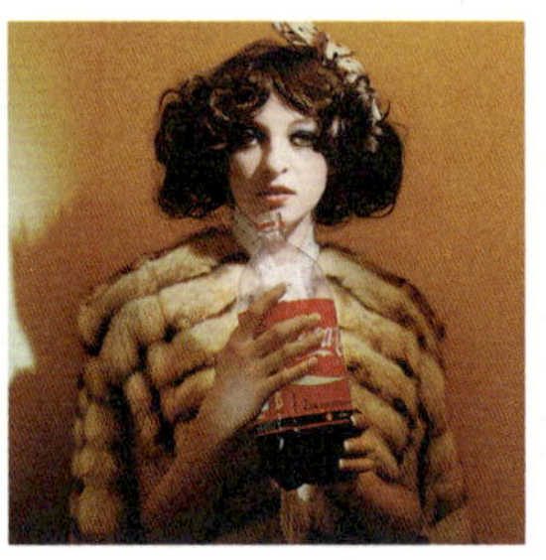

Jane, 2009
48 × 42 inches
121.9 × 106.7 cm

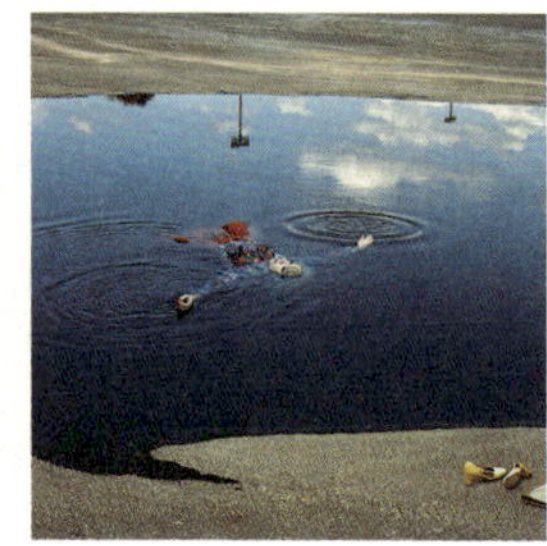

* Maggie, 2009
48 × 64.5 inches
121.9 × 163.8 cm

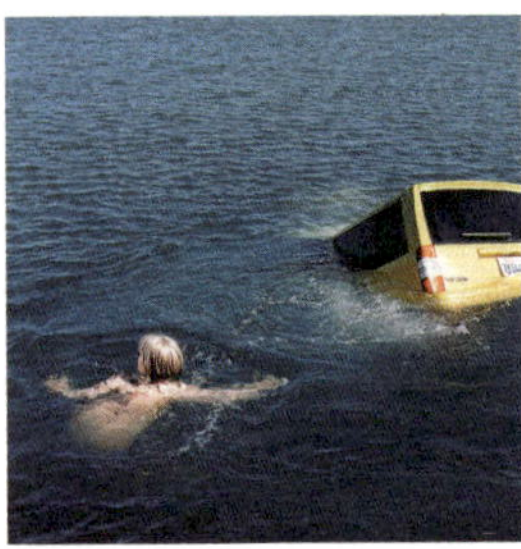

* Cathy, 2009
48 × 63 inches
121.9 × 160 cm

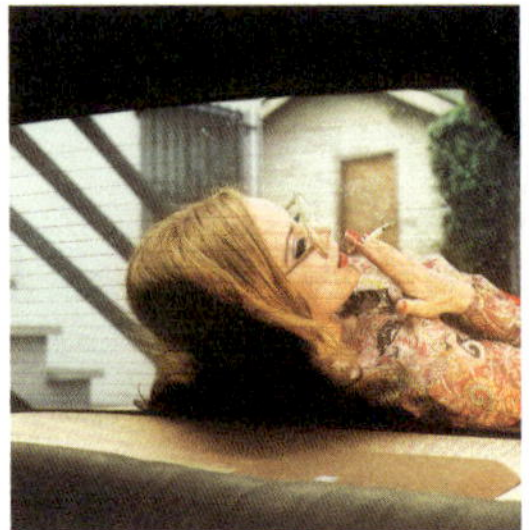

* Deborah, 2009
48 × 66 inches
121.9 × 167.6 cm

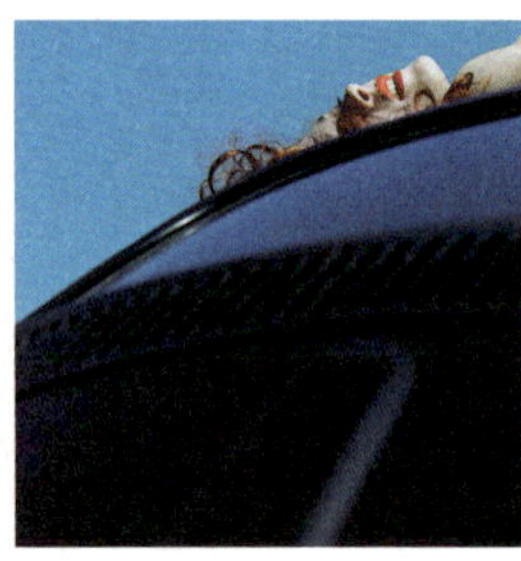

* Anne, 2009
48 × 48 inches
121.9 × 121.9 cm

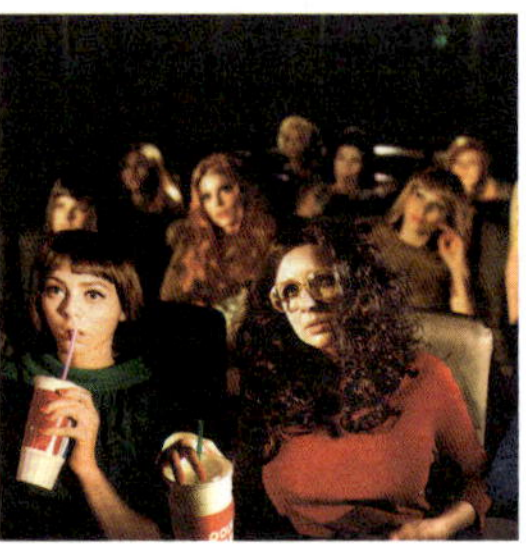

* Rachel and Friends, 2009
48 × 62 inches
121.9 × 157.5 cm

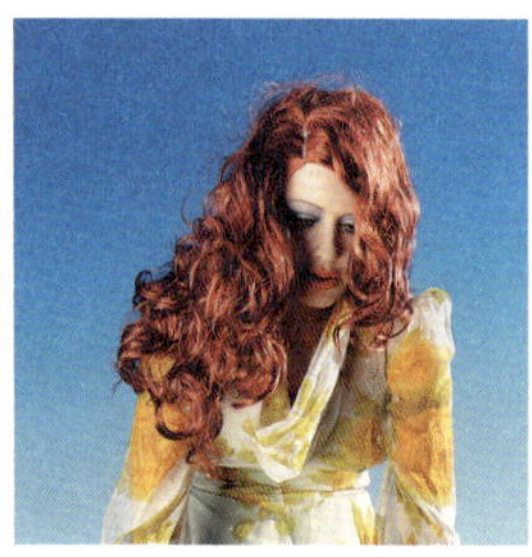

Rita, 2009
48 × 64 inches
121.9 × 162.6 cm

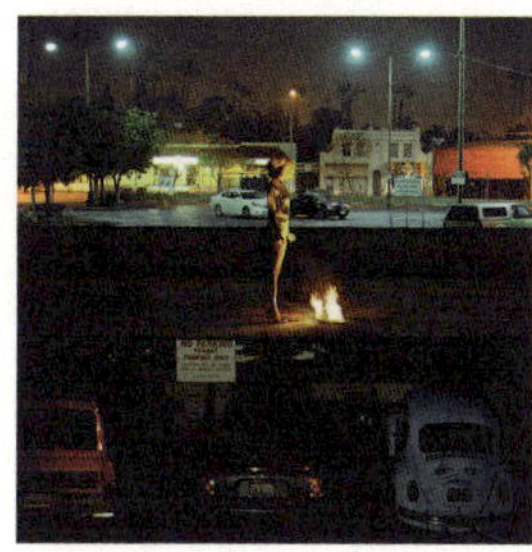

Beth, 2009
48 × 60.5 inches
121.9 × 153.7 cm

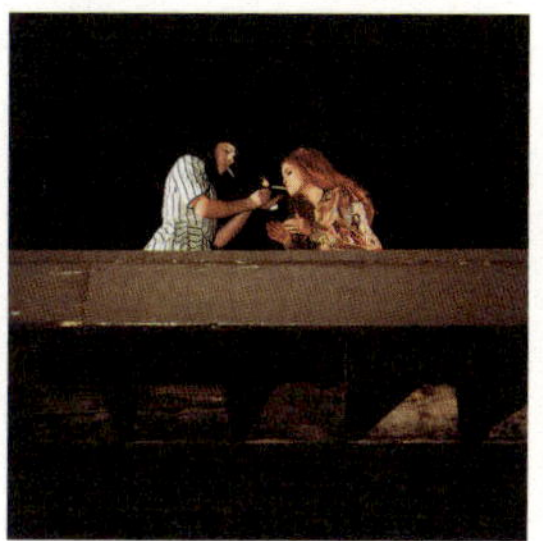

* Amy and Michelle, 2009
48 × 72.5 inches
121.9 × 184.2 cm

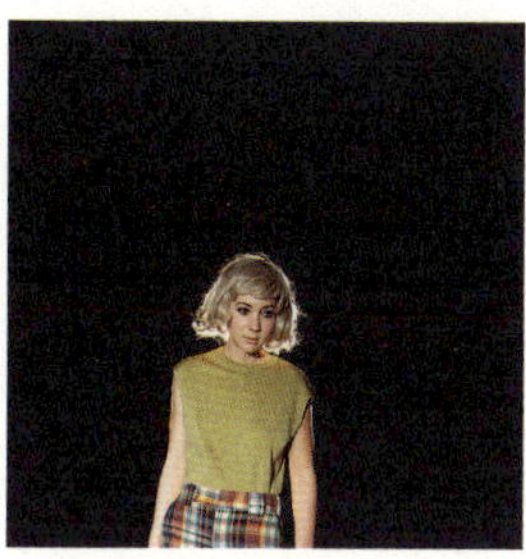

Sophie, 2009
48 × 62 inches
121.9 × 157.5 cm

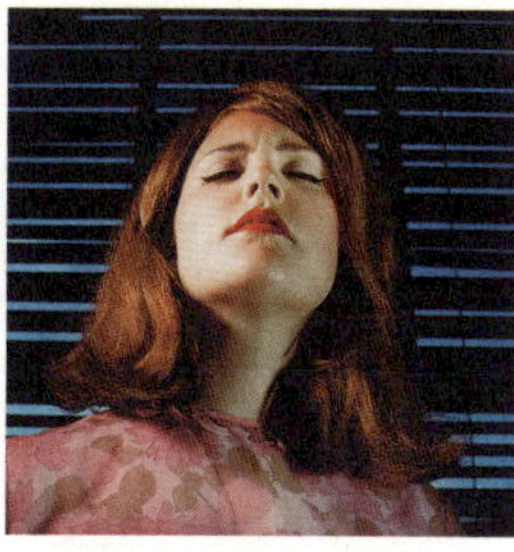

Eva, 2009
48 × 63 inches
121.9 × 160 cm

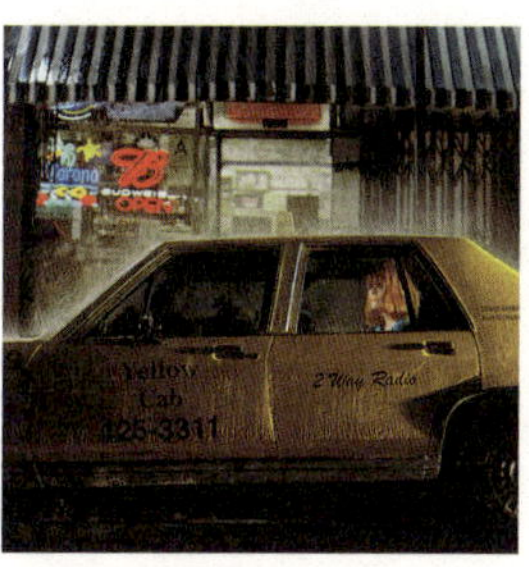

* Irene, 2010
48 × 70 inches
121.9 × 177.8 cm

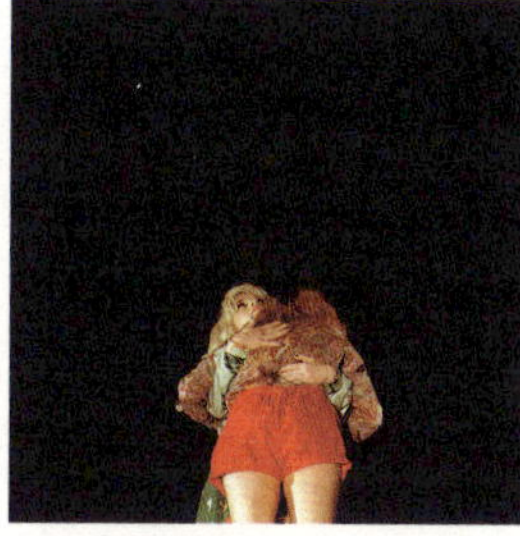

Becky and Jill, 2009
48 × 74 inches
121.9 × 188 cm

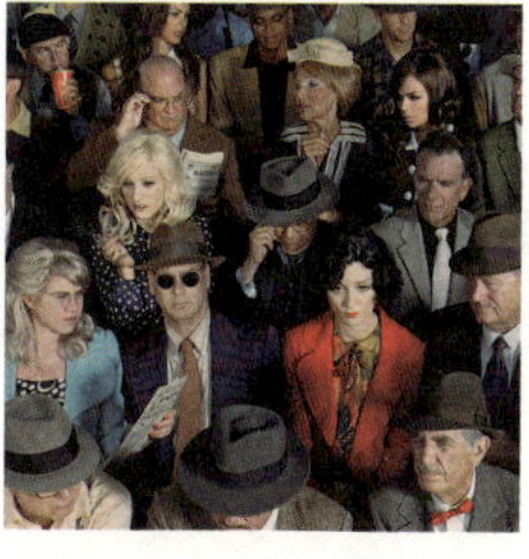

* Crowd #1 (Stan Douglas),
2010
48 × 80.75 inches
121.9 × 205.1 cm

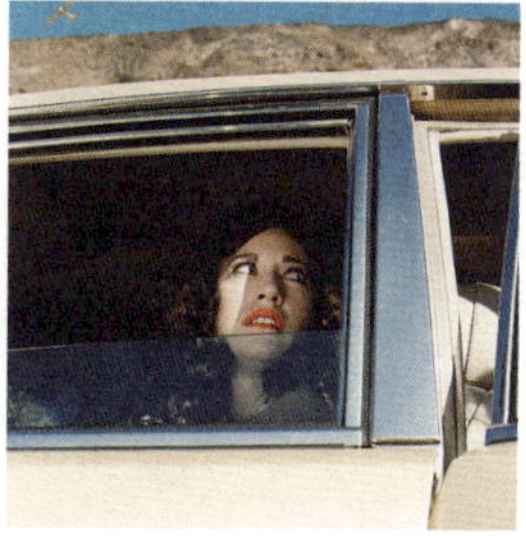

Sheryl, 2009
48 × 36 inches
121.9 × 91.4 cm

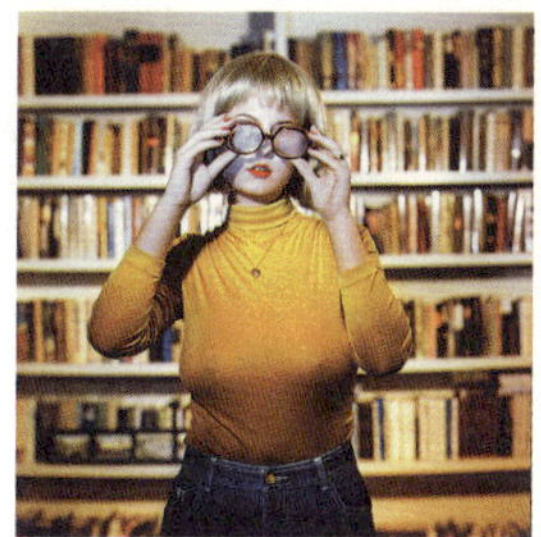

Tiffany, 2009
48 × 36.5 inches
121.9 × 92.7 cm

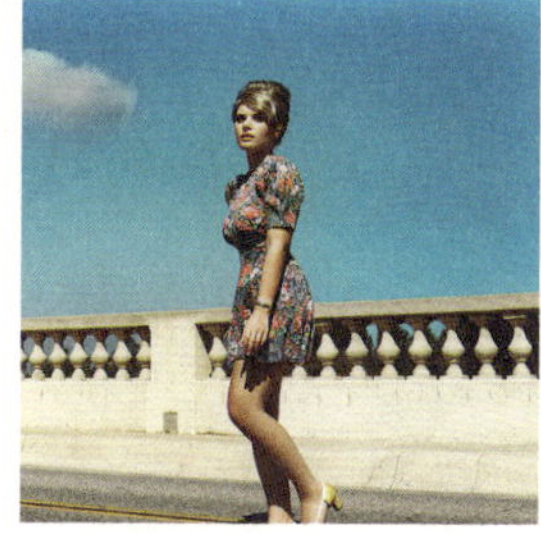

June, 2010
48 × 65 inches
121.9 × 165.1 cm

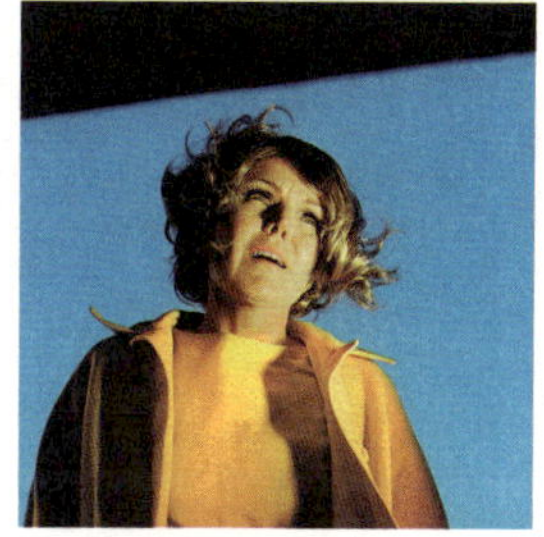

* Marilyn, 2010
48 × 63 inches
121.9 × 160 cm

COMPULSION

(2012)

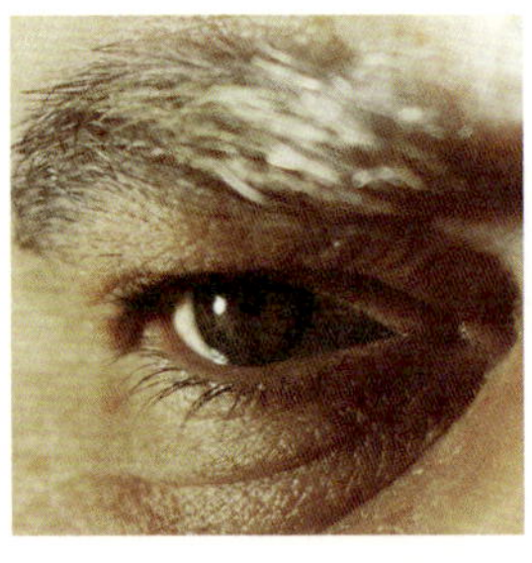 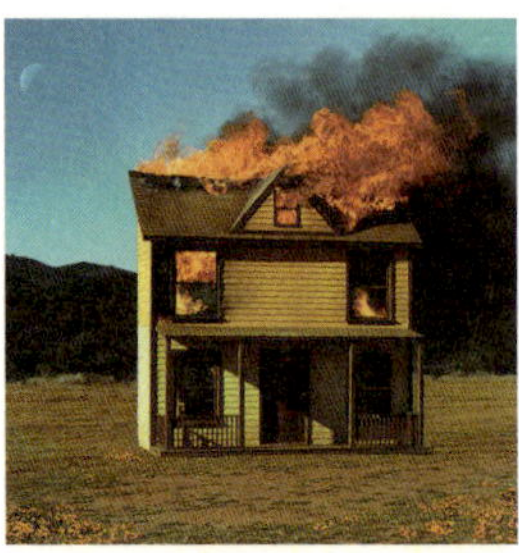 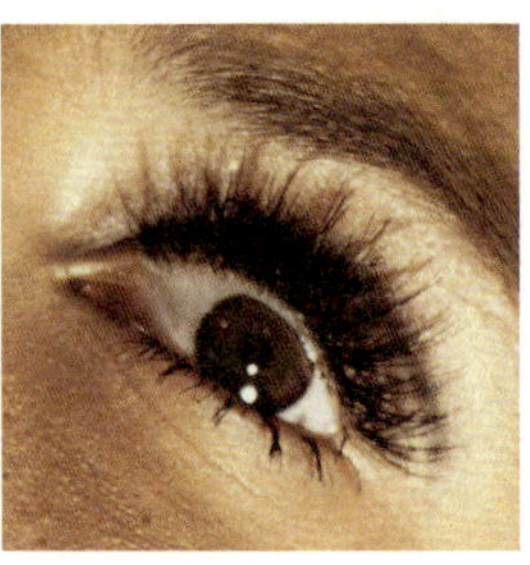 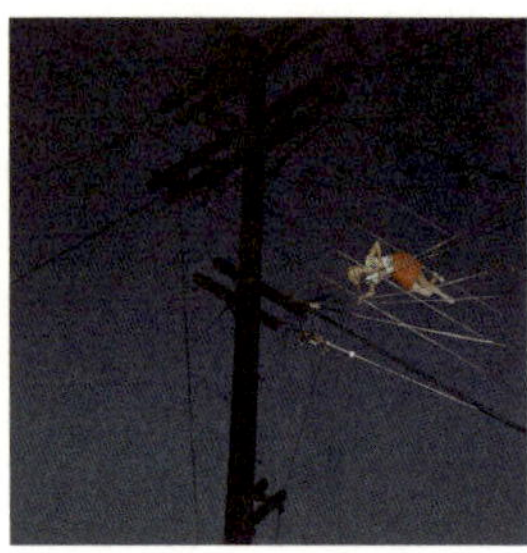

* Eye #3 (House Fire), 2012
16.25 × 18.75 inches
41.3 × 47.6 cm

* 4:01 pm, Sun Valley, 2012
48 × 60.18 inches
121.9 × 152.9 cm

* Eye #10 (Telephone
Wires), 2012
16.25 × 18.75 inches
41.3 × 47.6 cm

* 7:12 pm, Redcliff Ave,
2012
36 × 24.5 inches
9.14 × 62.2 cm

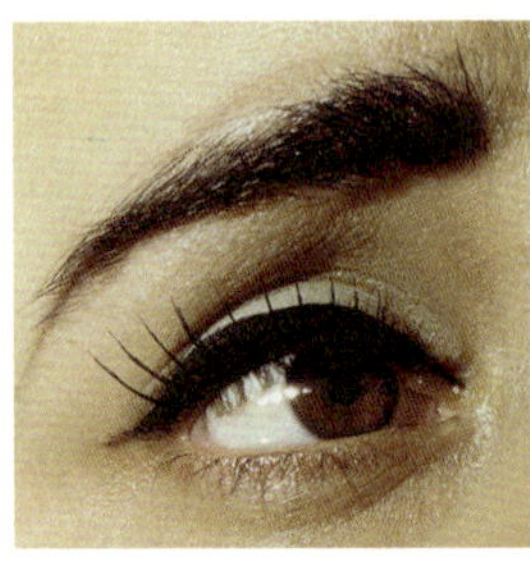 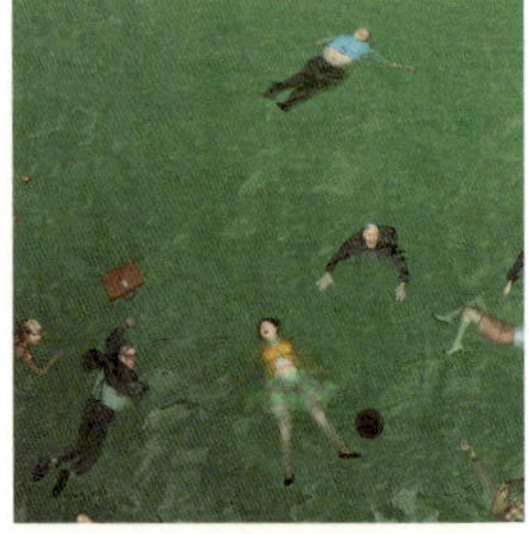 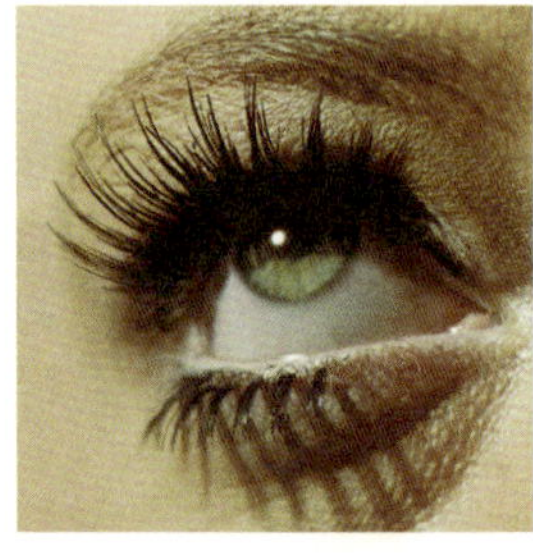 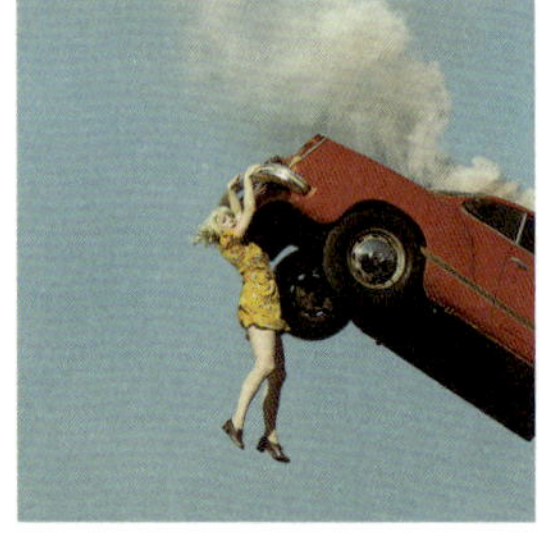

* Eye #9 (Passenger
Casualties), 2012
16.25 × 18.75 inches
41.3 × 47.6 cm

* 3:14 pm, Pacific Ocean,
2012
48 × 45.13 inches
121.9 × 114.6 cm

* Eye #5 (Automobile
Accident), 2012
16.25 × 18.75 inches
41.3 × 47.6 cm

* 3:32 pm, Coldwater
Canyon, 2012
36 × 14.8 inches
91. 4 × 37.6 cm

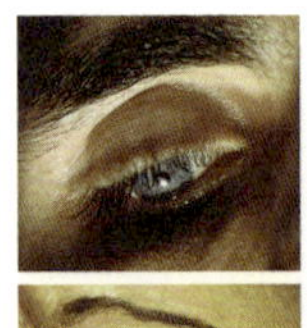 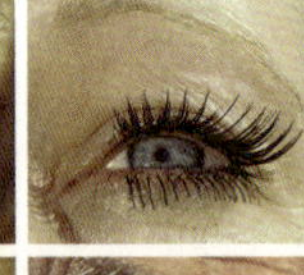 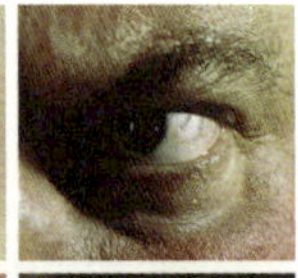 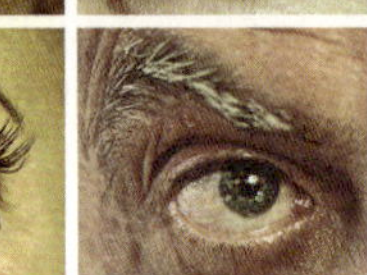 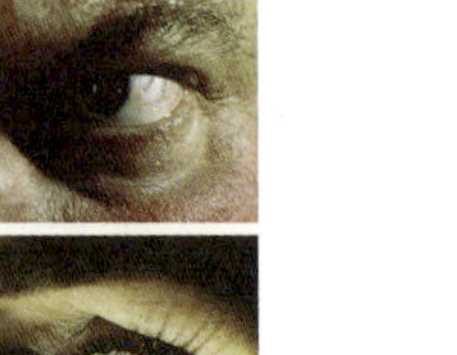 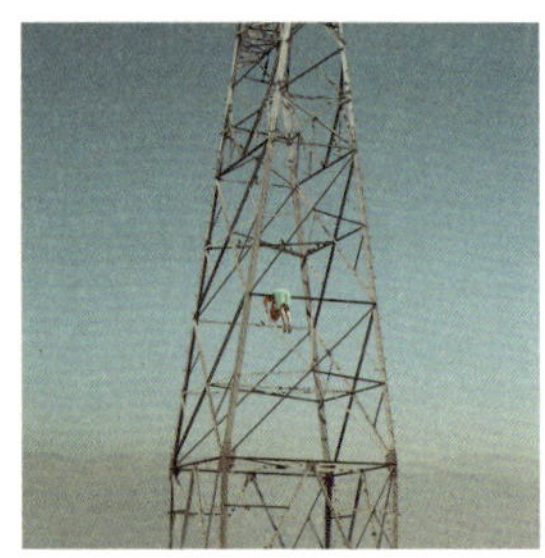

* Compulsion #1, 2012
43 × 73 inches
109.2 × 185.4 cm

* Eye #8 (Electric Tower),
2012
16.25 × 18.75 inches
41.3 × 47.6 cm

* 4:29 pm, Van Nuys, 2012
36 × 36.5 inches
91.4 × 92.7 cm

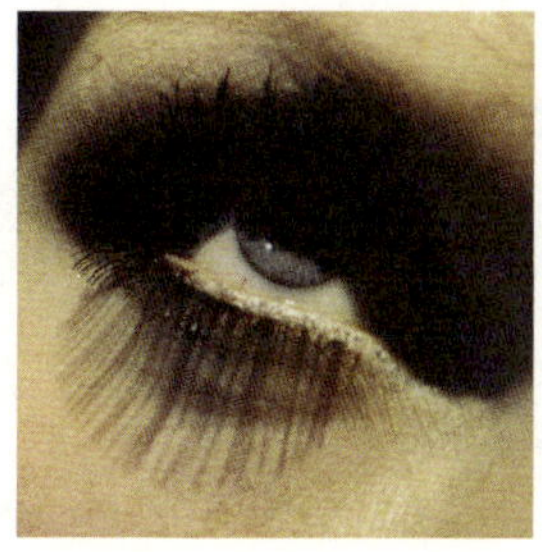

* Eye #7 (Suicide), 2012
16.25 × 18.75 inches
41.3 × 47.6 cm

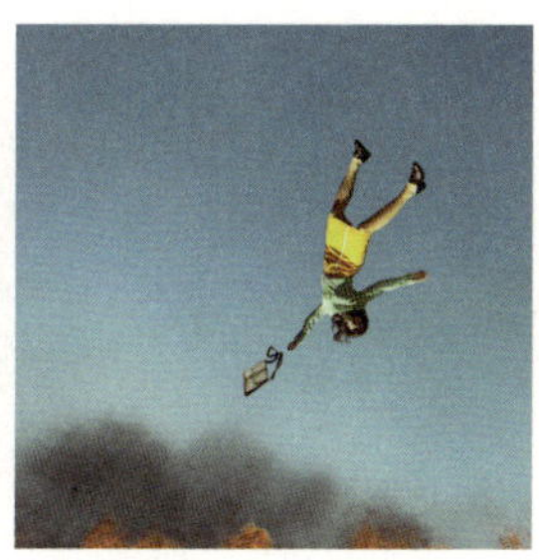

* 10:58 am, Bunker Hill,
2012
36 × 25.2 inches
91.4 × 64 cm

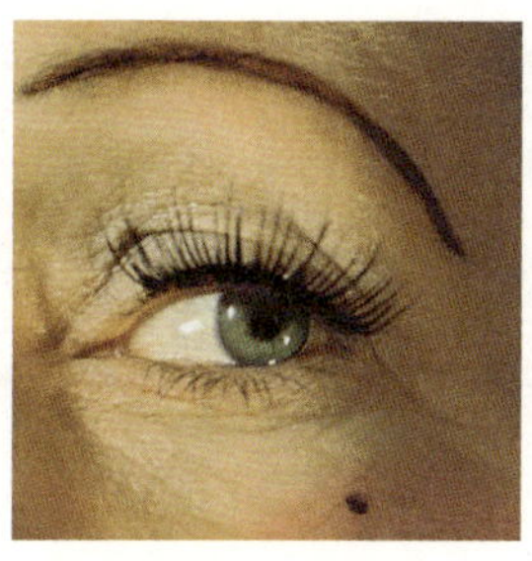

* Eye #6 (Sinkhole), 2012
16.25 × 18.75 inches
41.3 × 47.6 cm

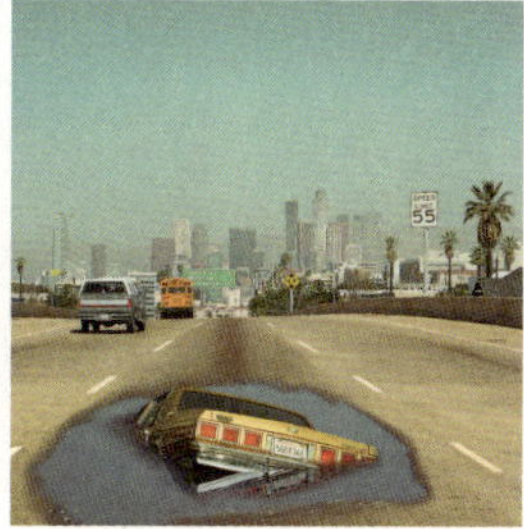

* 2:00 pm, Interstate 110,
2012
48 × 40.5 inches
121.9 × 102.9 cm

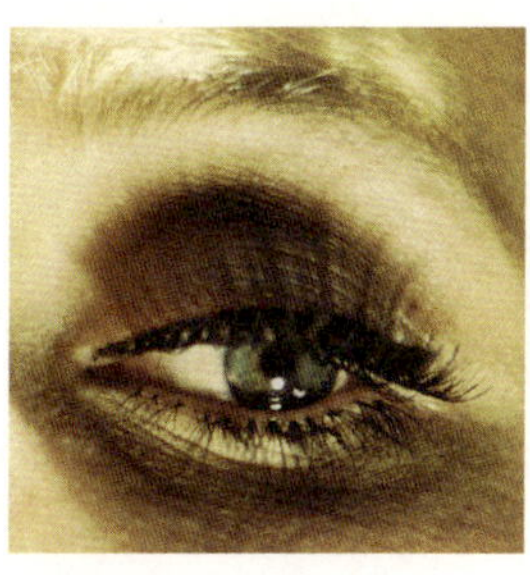

* Eye #1 (Flood), 2012
16.25 × 18.75 inches
41.3 × 47.6 cm

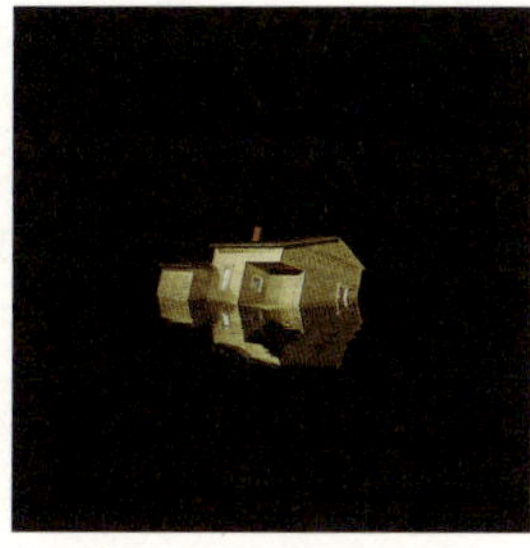

* 3:56 am, Milwood Ave,
2012
49 × 56 inches
124.46 × 142.24 cm

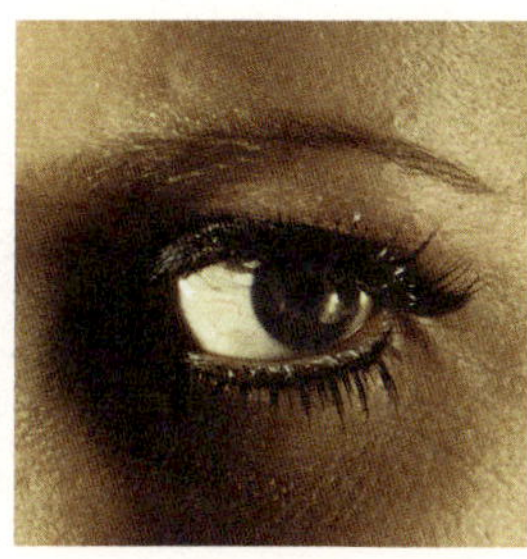

* Eye #2 (Boulder), 2012
16.25 × 18.75 inches
41.3 × 47.6 cm

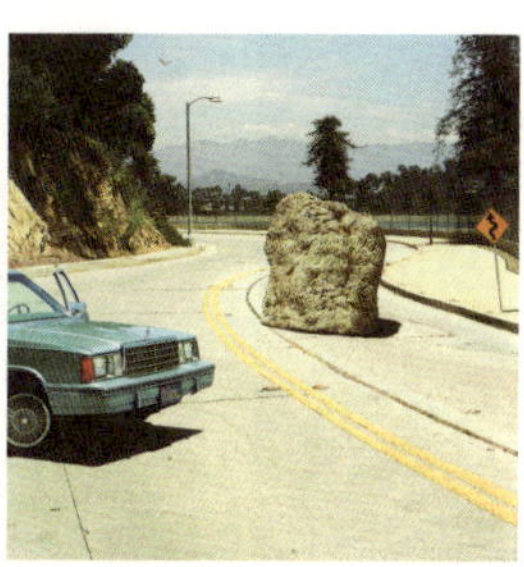

* 1:18 pm, Silverlake Drive,
2012
48 × 52.61 inches
121.9 × 133.6 cm

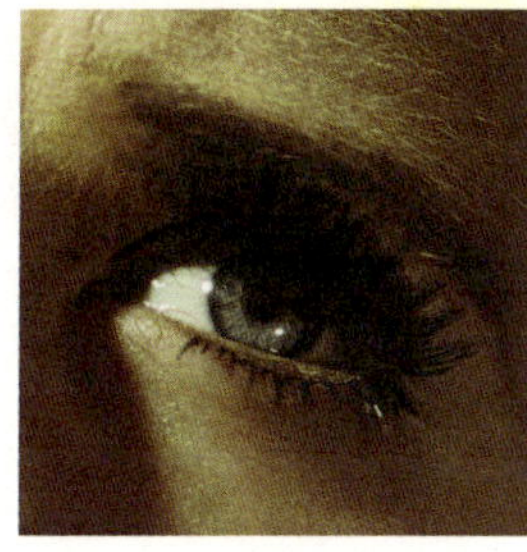

* Eye #4 (Roadside Victim),
2012
16.25 × 18.75 inches
41.3 × 47.6 cm

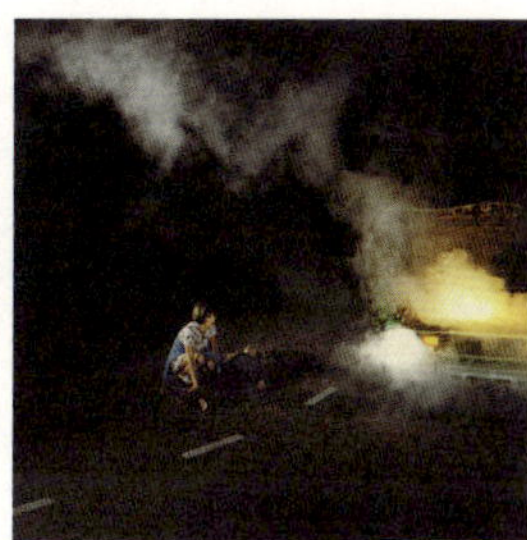

* 11:45 pm, Griffith Park,
2012
36 × 47 inches
91.4 × 119.4 cm

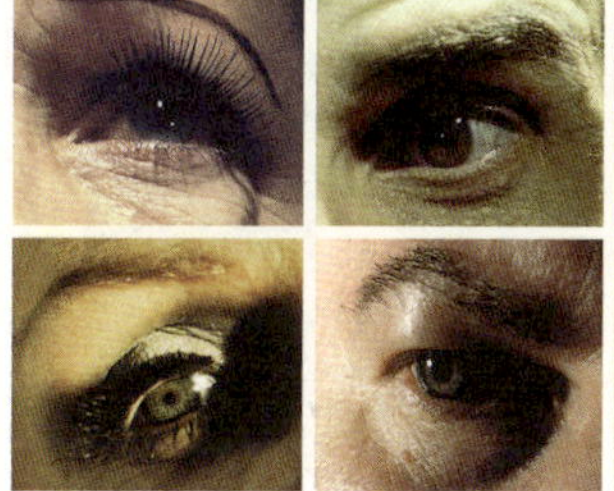

* Compulsion #2, 2012
43 × 73 inches
109.2 × 185.4 cm

FACE IN THE CROWD
(2013)

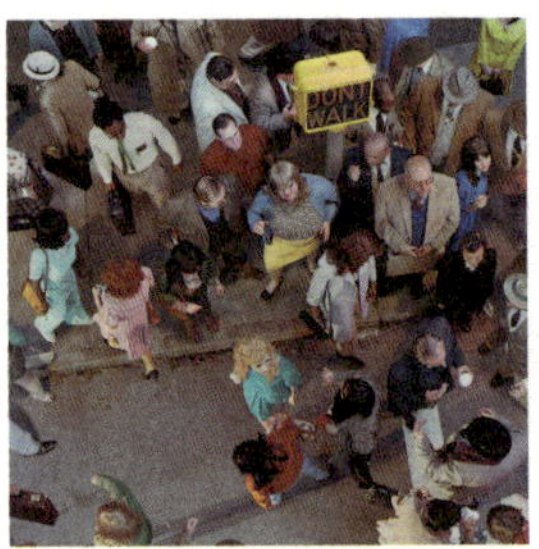

* Crowd #11 (Cedar and Broad Street), 2013
59.5 × 56.5 inches
151.1 × 143.5 cm

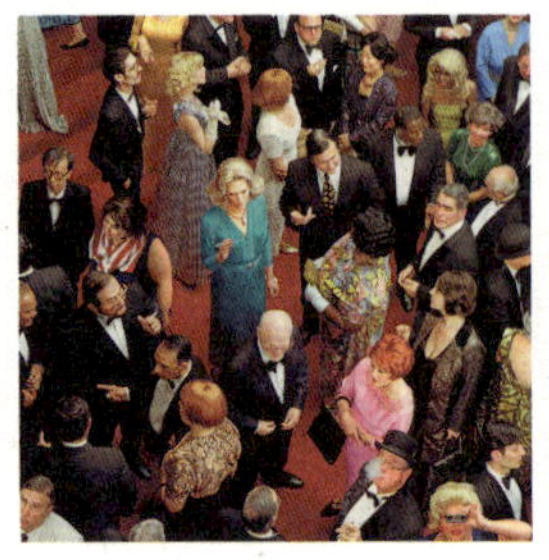

* Crowd #10 (Imperial Theatre), 2013
59.5 × 67.5 inches
151.1 × 171.5 cm

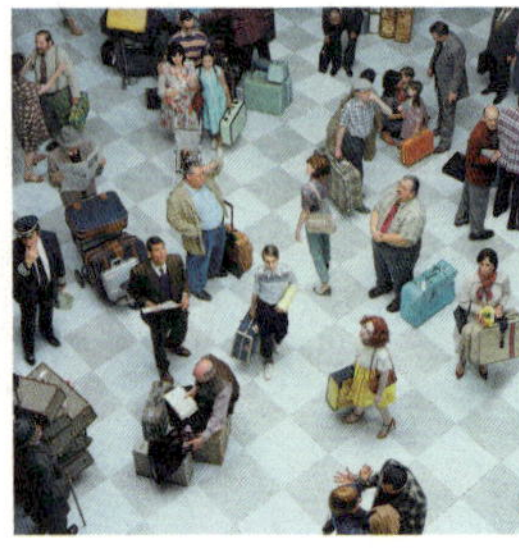

* Crowd #7 (Bob Hope Airport), 2013
59.5 × 79 inches
151.1 × 200.7 cm

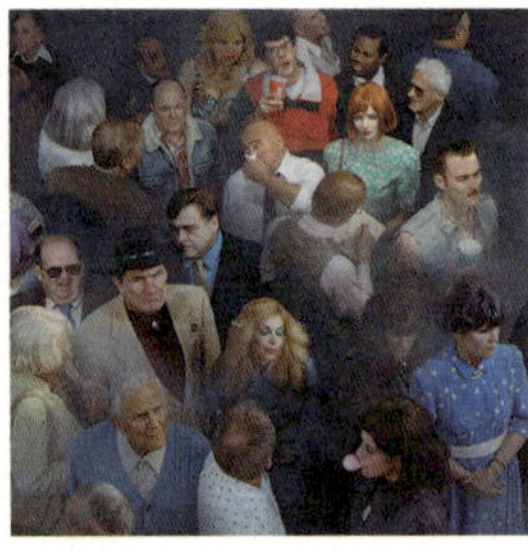

* Crowd #6 (Hazelwood), 2013
59.5 × 85 inches
151.1 × 215.9 cm

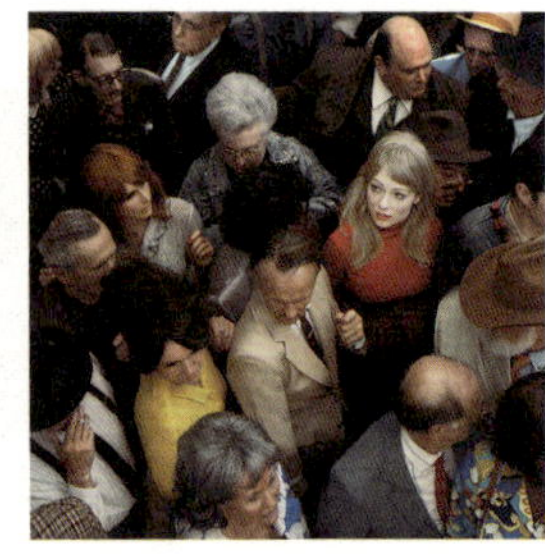

* Crowd #2 (Emma), 2012
59 × 80.7 inches
149.7 × 205 cm

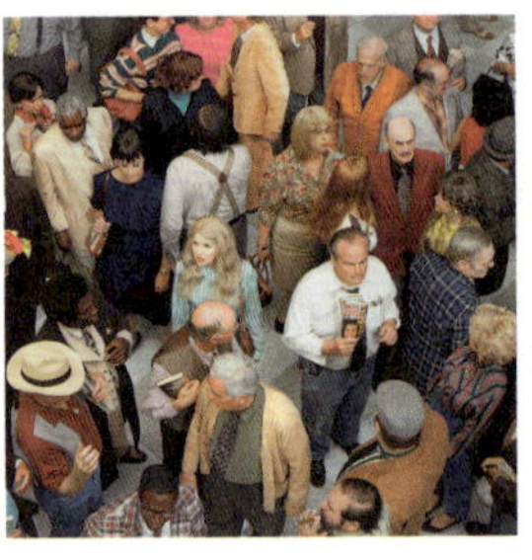

* Crowd #4 (New Haven), 2013
59.5 × 75 inches
151.1 × 190.5 cm

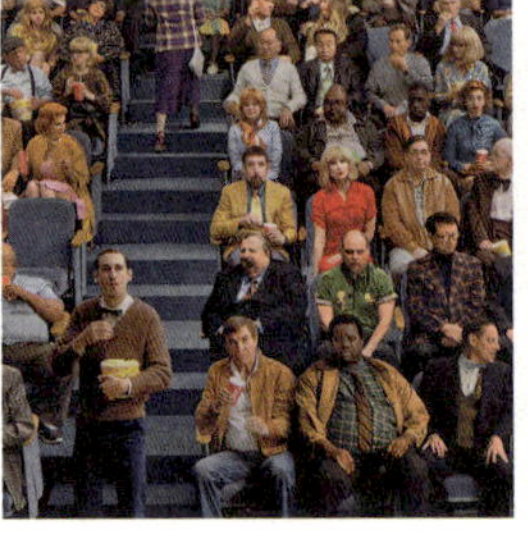

* Crowd #9 (Sunset Five), 2013
59.5 × 91.5 inches
151.1 × 232.4 cm

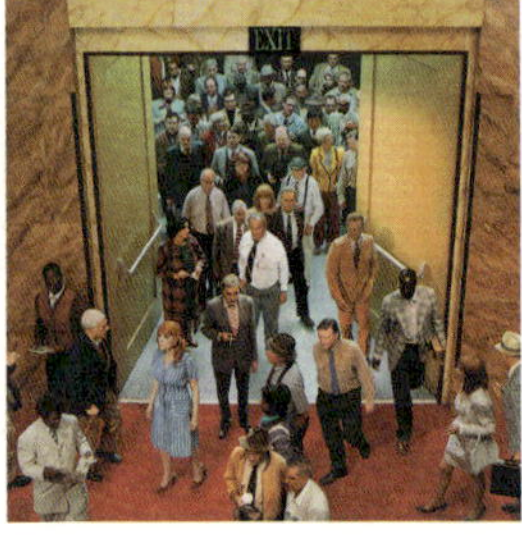

* Crowd #8 (City Hall), 2013
59.5 × 80.5 inches
151.1 × 204.5 cm

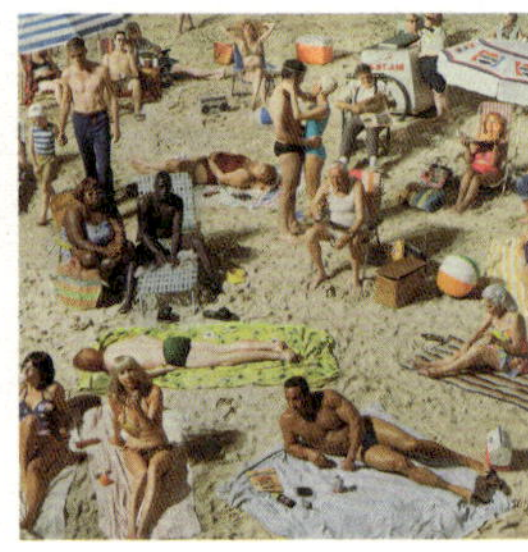

* Crowd #3 (Pelican Beach), 2013
59.5 × 92.85 inches
151.1 × 235.8 cm

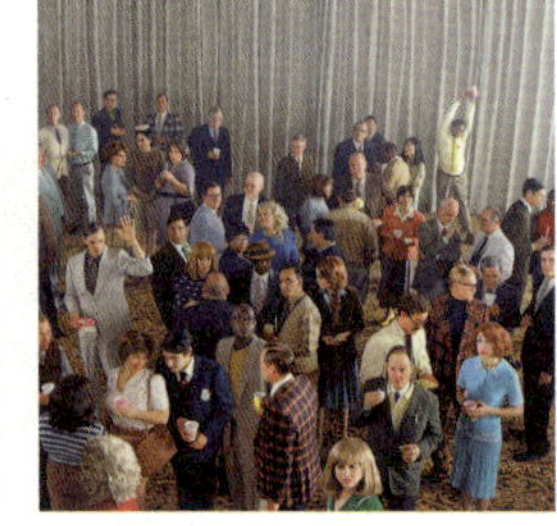

* Crowd #12 (speedy-click.com), 2013
59.5 × 56 inches
151.1 × 142.2 cm

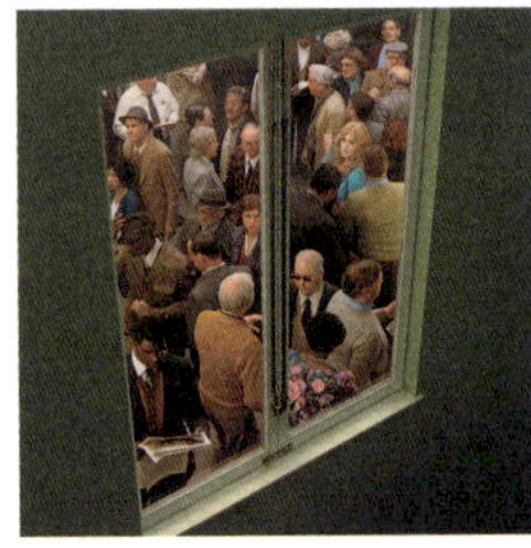

* Crowd #5 (Washington Square West), 2013
59.5 × 72 inches
151.1 × 182.9 cm

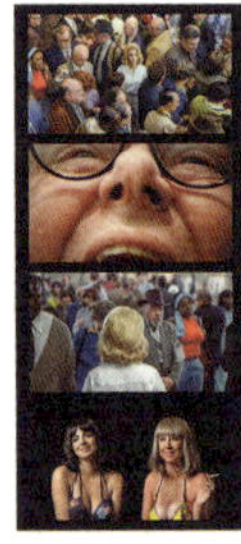

Film Strip #1, 2013
48 × 23 inches
121.9 × 58.4 cm

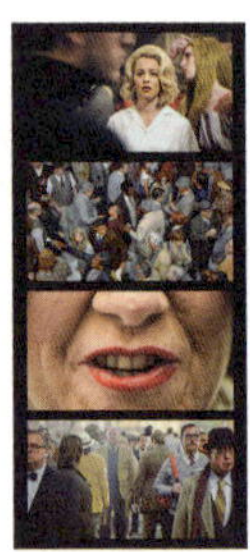

Film Strip #2, 2013
48 × 23 inches
121.9 × 58.4 cm

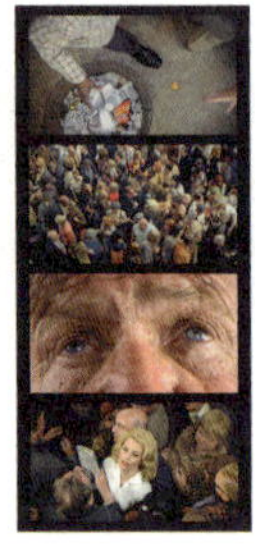

Film Strip #3, 2013
48 × 23 inches
121.9 × 58.4 cm

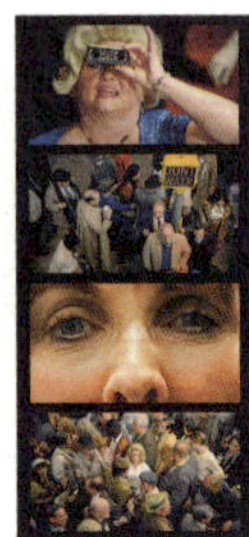

Film Strip #4, 2013
48 × 23 inches
121.9 × 58.4 cm

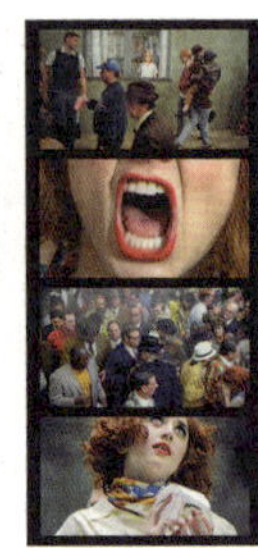

Film Strip #5, 2013
48 × 23 inches
121.9 × 58.4 cm

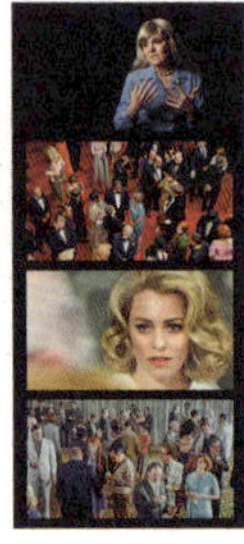

Film Strip #6, 2013
48 × 23 inches
121.9 × 58.4 cm

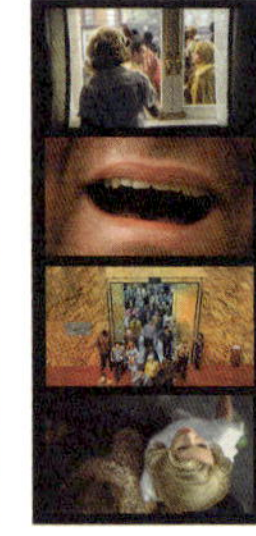

Film Strip #7, 2013
48 × 23 inches
121.9 × 58.4 cm

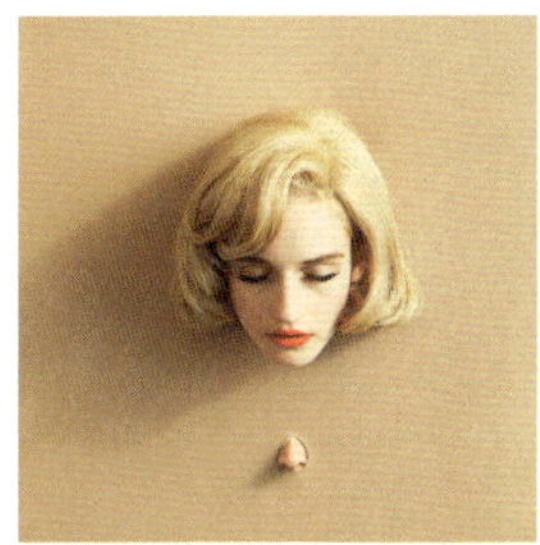

* Untitled (Parts 1), 2014
48 × 50 inches
121.9 × 127 cm

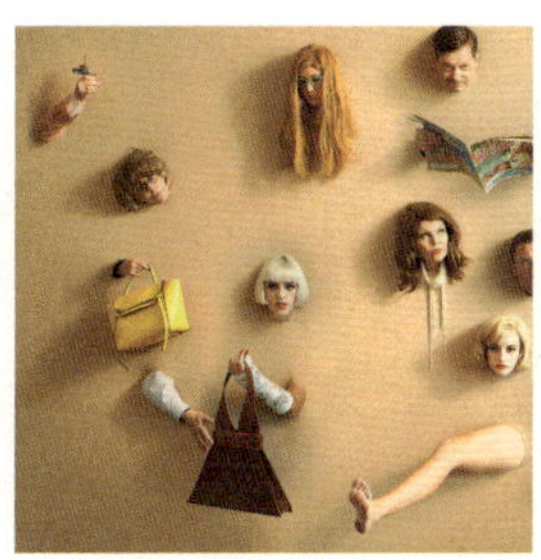

* Untitled (Parts 3), 2014
48 × 74.5 inches
121.9 × 189.2 cm

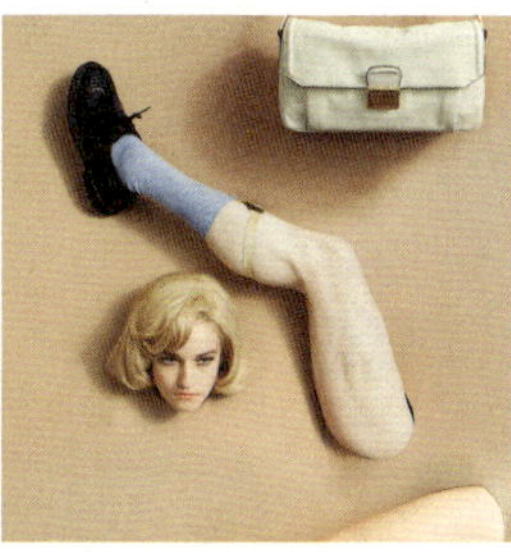

* Untitled (Parts 4), 2014
48 × 32 inches
121.9 × 81.3 cm

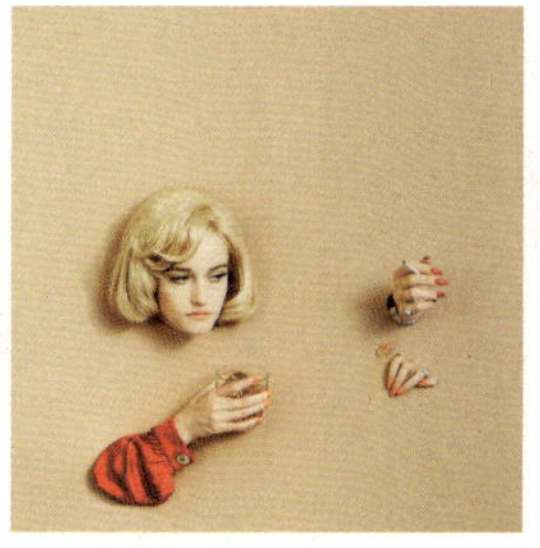

* Untitled (Parts 2), 2014
48 × 32 inches
121.9 × 81.3 cm

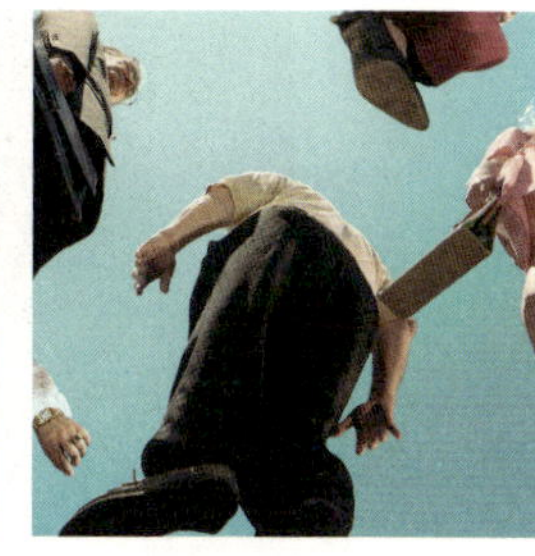

* Glendale, 2014
59 × 77 inches
149.9 × 195.6 cm

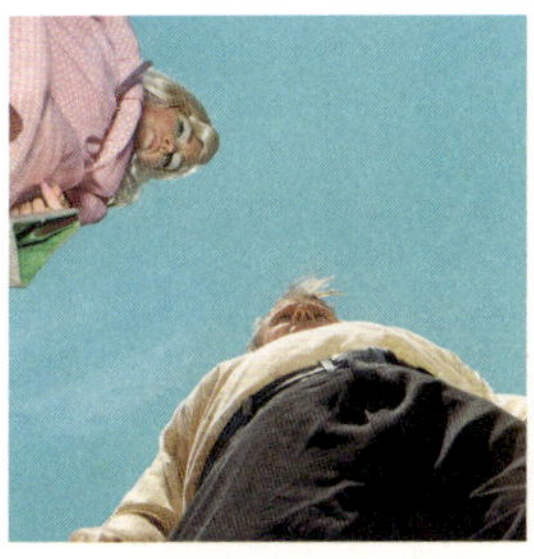

* Burbank, 2014
59 × 78.58 inches
149.9 × 199.6 cm

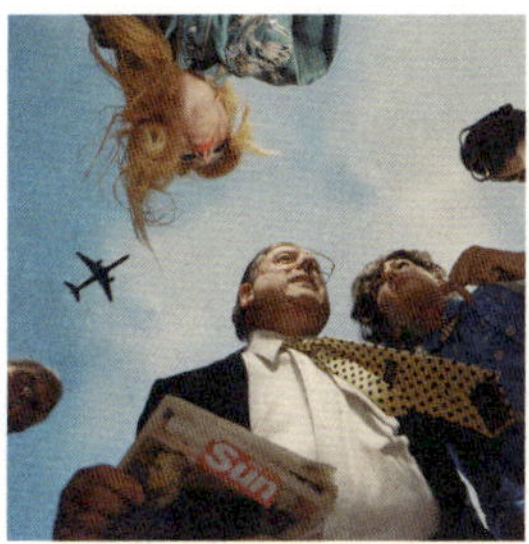

* Hazelwood #2 (after
Steven Siegel), 2014
59 × 75 inches
149.9 × 190.5 cm

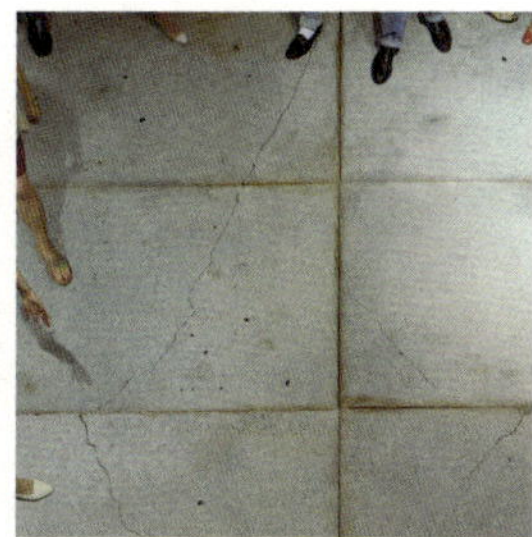

* Shopping Plaza 2, 2015
59 × 77.3 inches
149.9 × 196.3 cm

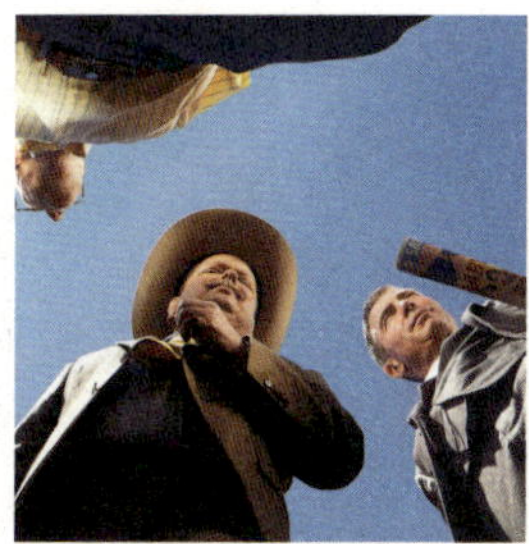

* Culver City, 2014
59 × 88.5 inches
149.9 × 224.8 cm

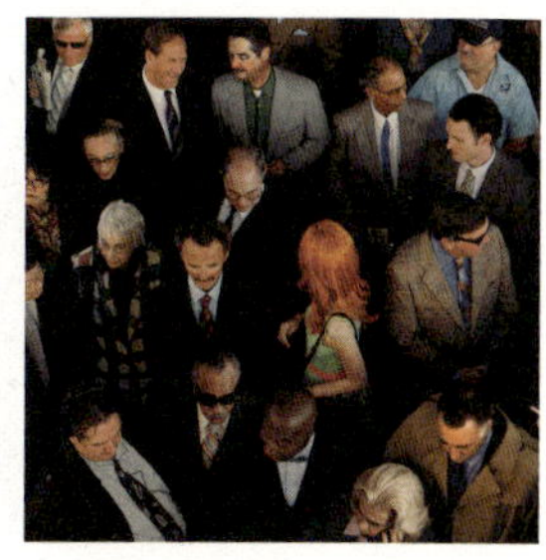

* Hollywood and Vine, 2014
59 × 64.5 inches
149.9 × 163.8 cm

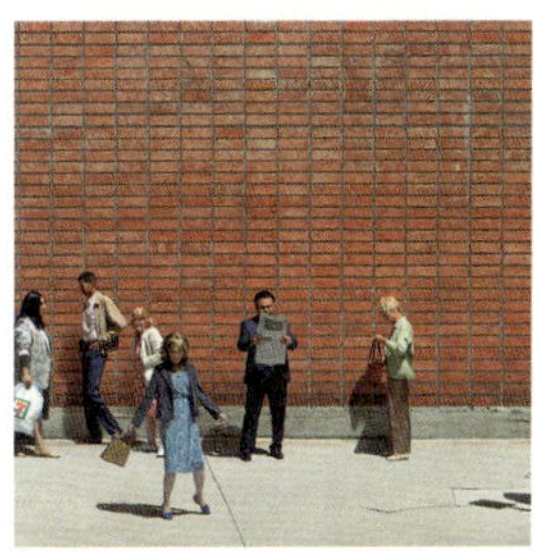

* See's Candies, Payless,
Supercuts 1, 2015
48 × 127.45 inches
121.9 × 323.7 cm

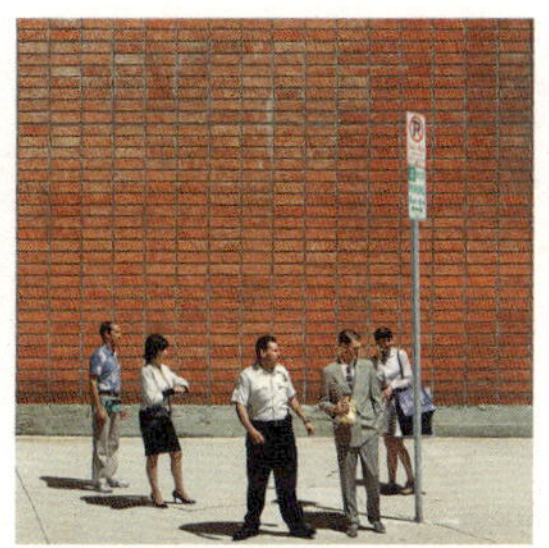

See's Candies, Payless,
Supercuts 2, 2015
48 × 127.45 inches
121.9 × 323.7 cm

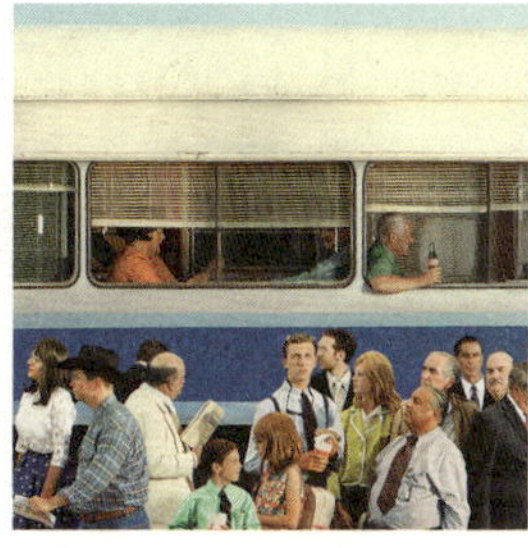

* Simi Valley, 2014
47 × 96 inches
119.4 × 243.8 cm

* Shopping Plaza 1, 2015
59 × 90 inches
149.9 × 228.6 cm

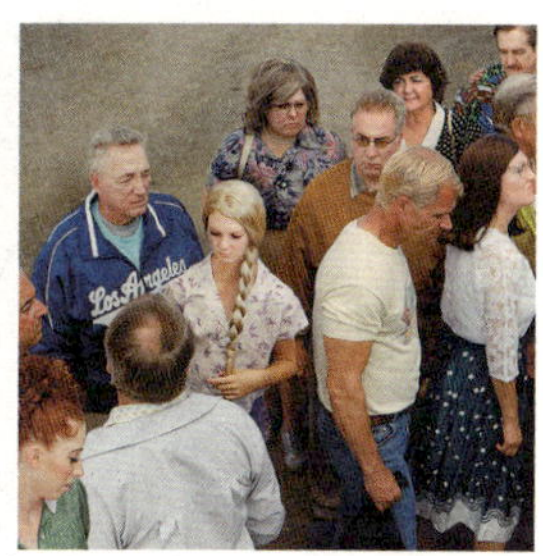

Hollywood Park, 2014
59 × 67.75 inches
149.9 × 172.1 cm

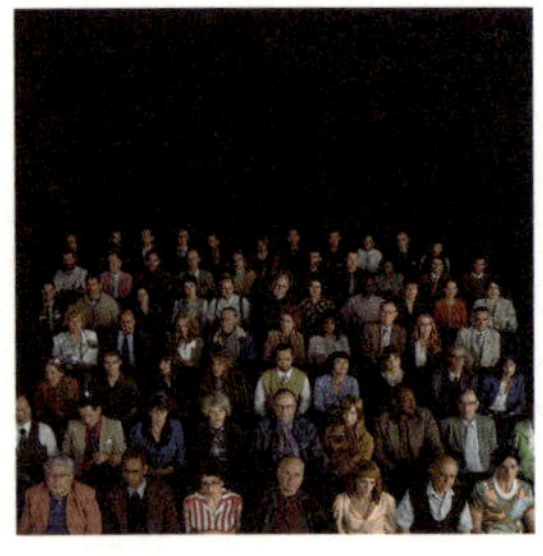

* Orchestra Center
(Intermission), 2016
51.95 × 48 inches
132.4 × 121.9 cm

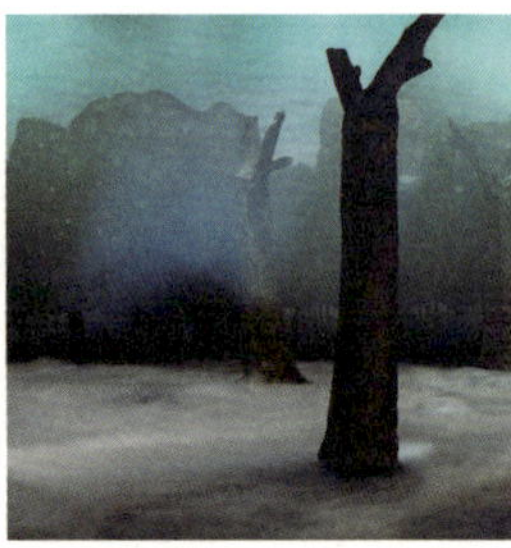

* Stage (Intermission), 2016
59 × 98.1 inches
149.9 × 249.2 cm

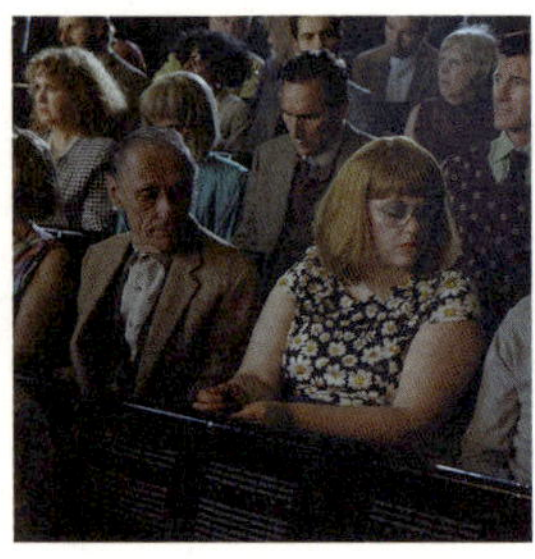

* Orchestra East, Section B,
2016
59 × 89.8 inches
149.9 × 228.1 cm

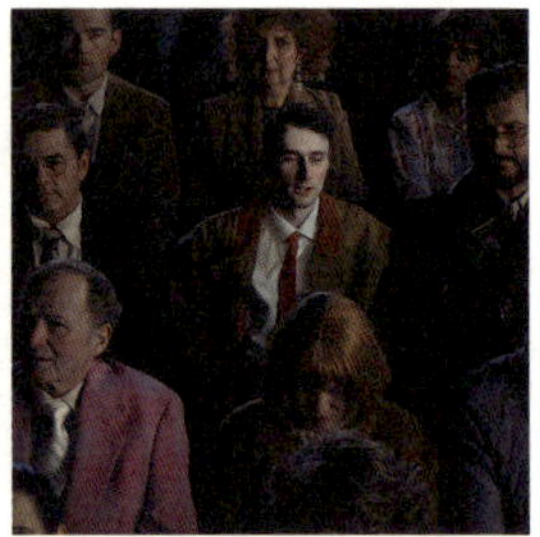

* Mezzanine East, 2016
40 × 43.88 inches
101.6 × 111.5 cm

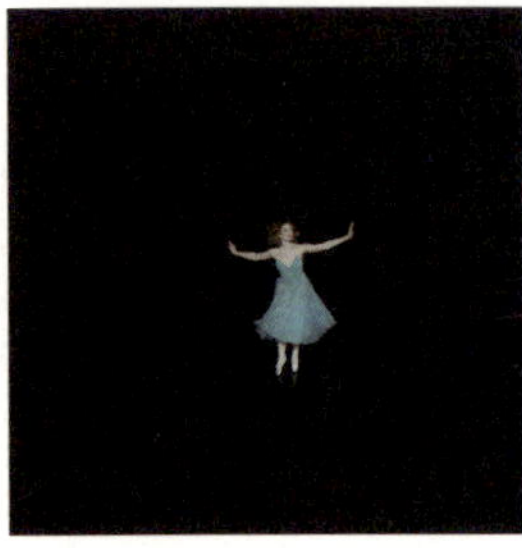

* Act III, Scene 2, 2016
59 × 59 inches
149.9 × 149.9 cm

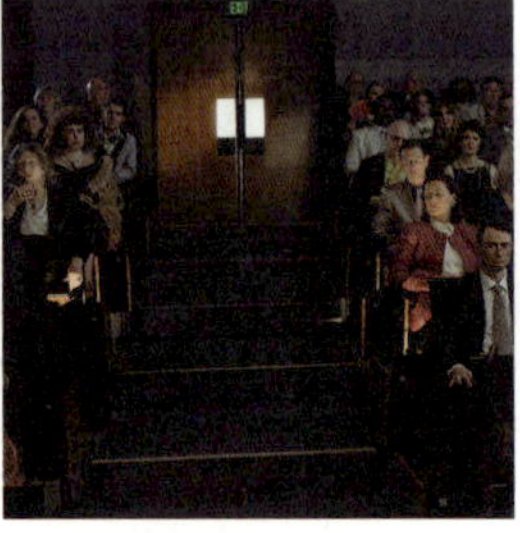

* Lower Level, Door 2, 2016
59 × 78.67 inches
149.9 × 199.8 cm

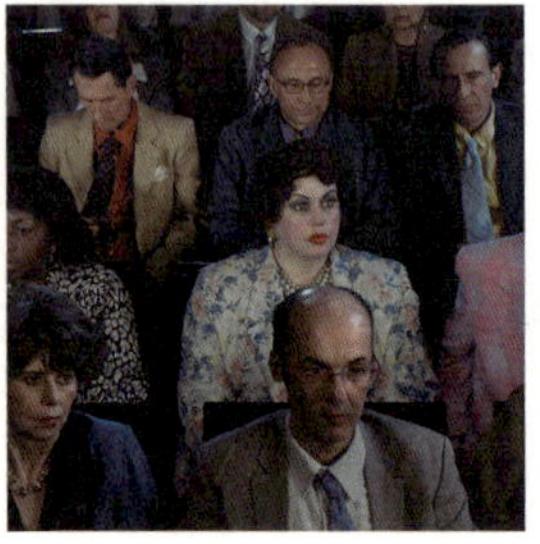

* Mezzanine West, 2016
40 × 37 inches
101.6 × 94 cm

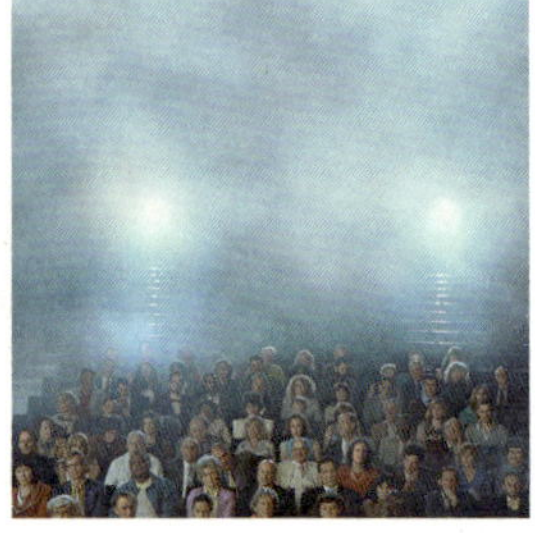

* Orchestra Center (Stage),
2016
52 × 48 inches
132.1 × 121.9 cm

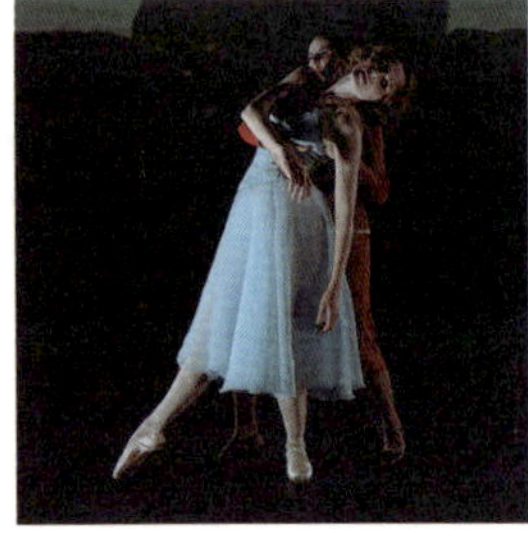

* Act II, Scene 2, 2016
36 × 27.4 inches
91.4 × 69.6 cm

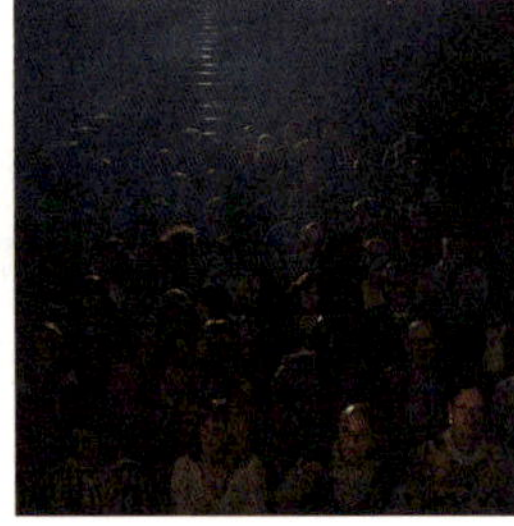

* Orchestra Center
(Curtain), 2016
51.95 × 43 inches
132.4 × 109.2 cm

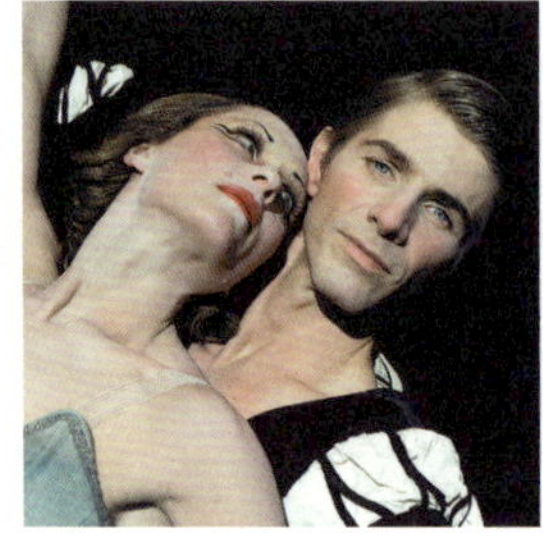

* Étoiles, 2016
48 × 39.2 inches
121.9 × 99.6 cm

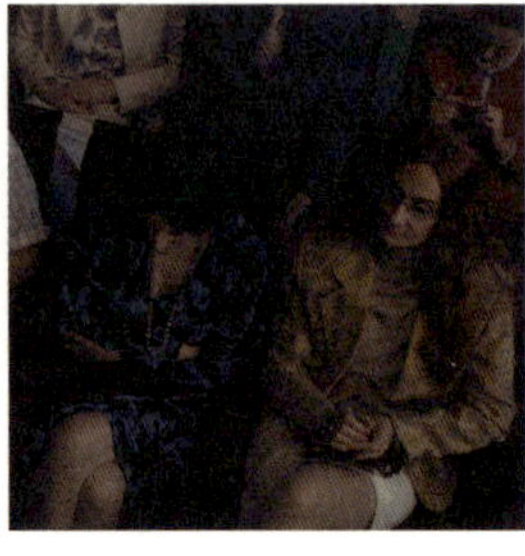

* Orchestra East, Section E,
2016
48 × 51 inches
121.9 × 129.5 cm

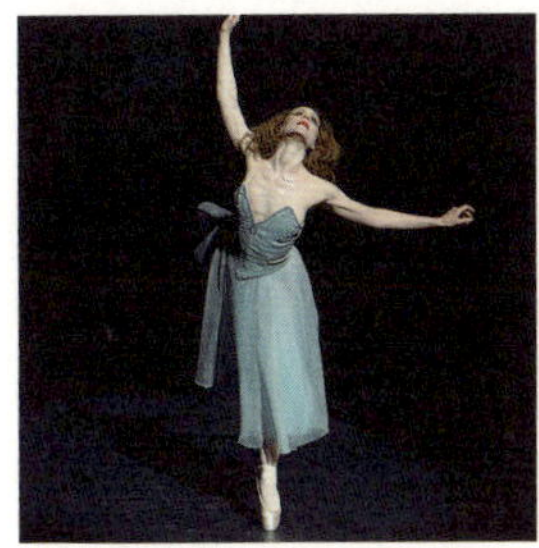

Act III, Scene 1, 2016
36 × 27 inches
91.4 × 68.6 cm

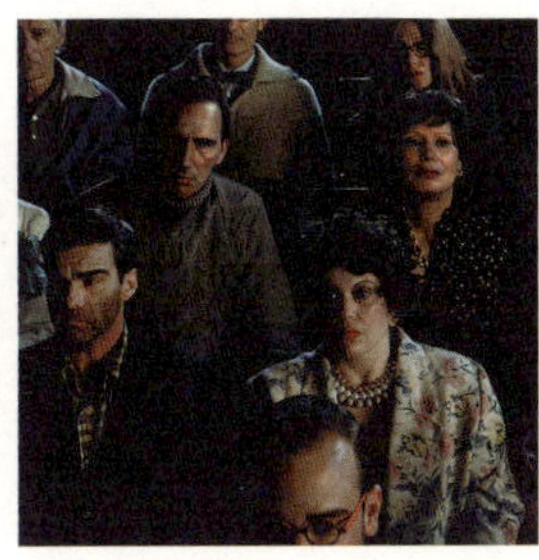

Mezzanine Center, 2016
24 × 39.3 inches
61 × 99.8 cm

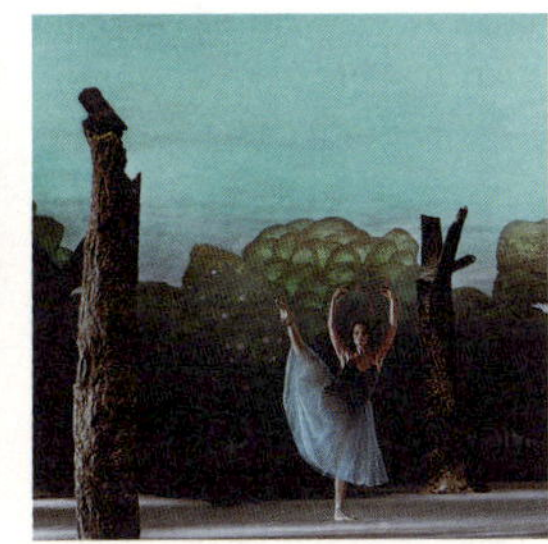

Act I, Scene 1, 2016
24 × 41.3 inches
61 × 104.9 cm

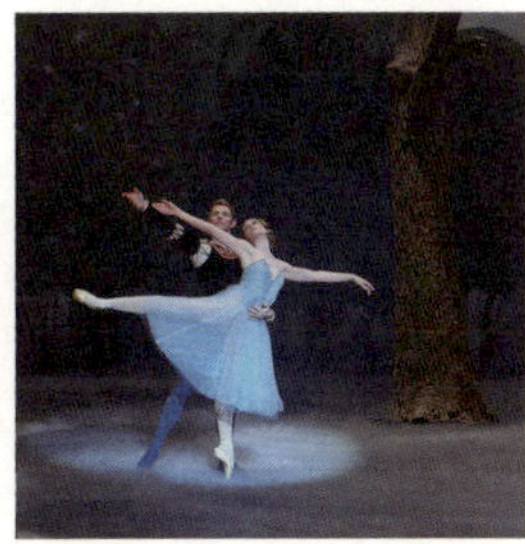

Film Still #9 (La Grande
Sortie), 2016
11 × 21 inches
27.9 × 53.3 cm

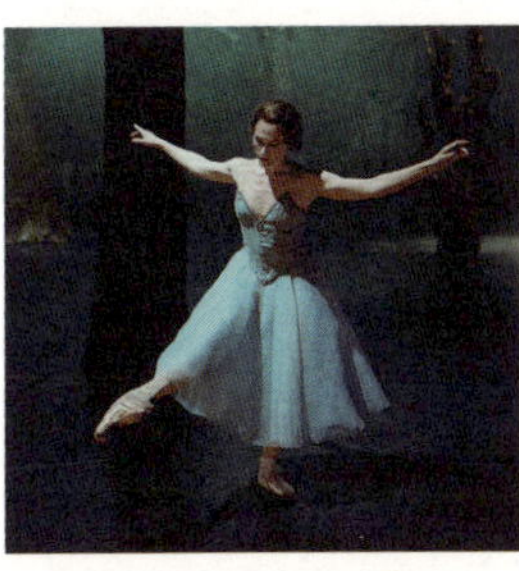

Act I, Scene 2, 2016
48 × 64.38 inches
121.9 × 163.5 cm

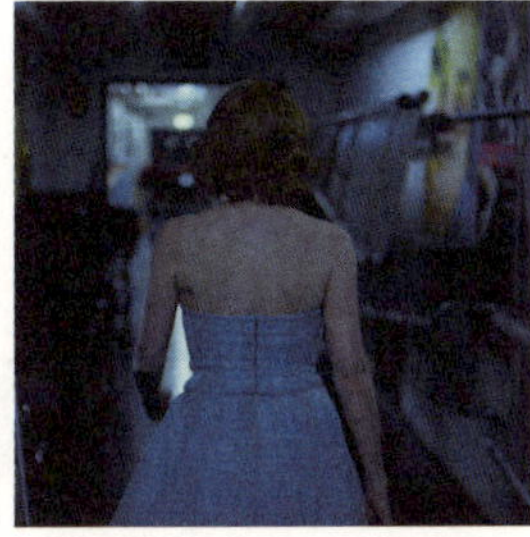

Film Still #7 (La Grande
Sortie), 2016
11 × 21 inches
27.9 × 53.3 cm

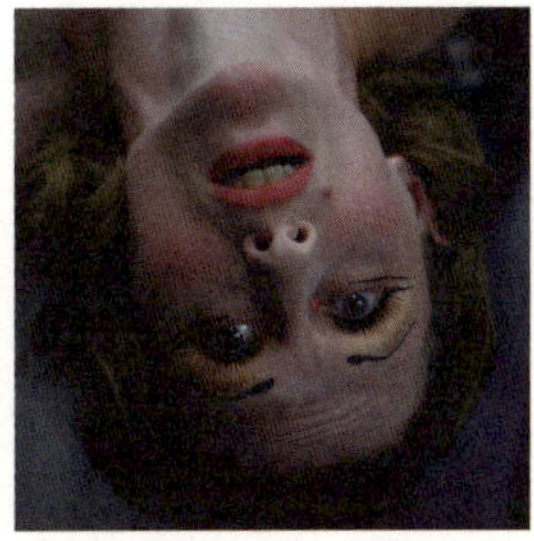

Film Still #8 (La Grande
Sortie), 2016
11 × 21 inches
27.9 × 53.3 cm

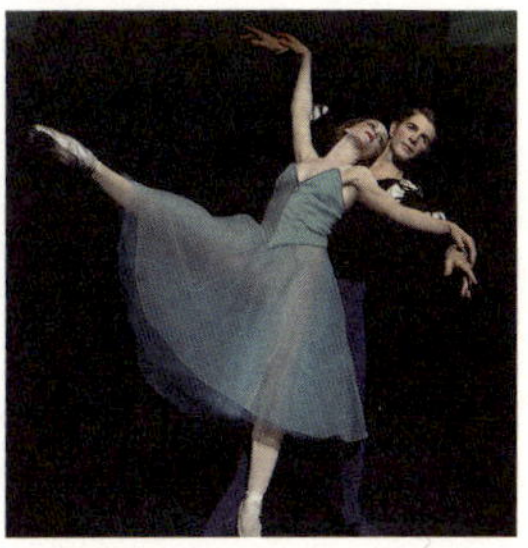

Act I, Scene 3, 2016
36 × 25.12 inches
91.4 × 63.8 cm

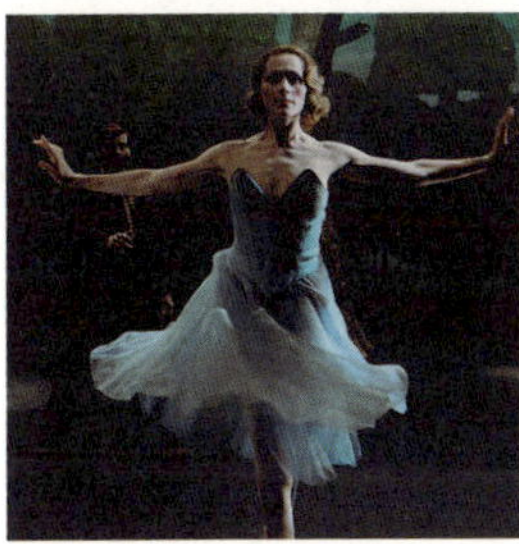

Act II, Scene 1, 2016
30 × 38 inches (print)
76.2 × 96.5 cm

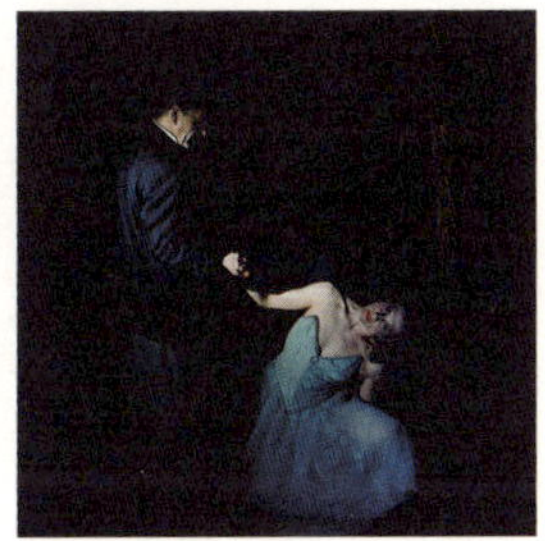

Act II, Scene 3, 2016
36 × 28.1 inches
91.4 × 71.4 cm

CURRICULUM VITAE

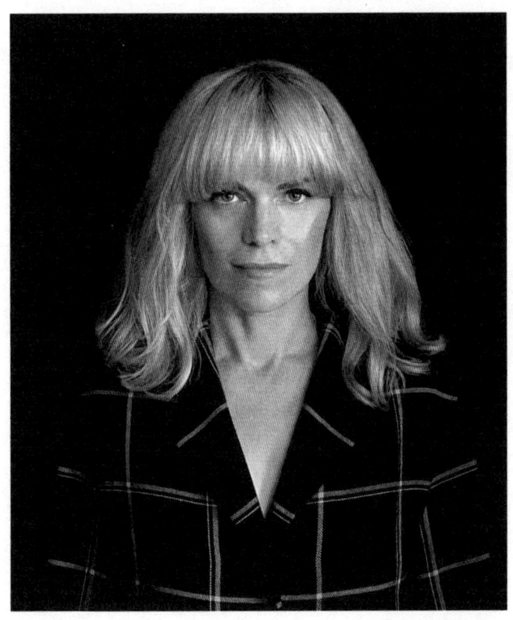

Courtesy of Simon Dargan, 2022

ALEX PRAGER

1979   Born in Los Angeles; lives and works in
Los Angeles

SOLO EXHIBITIONS

2022   *Alex Prager: Big West*, Lotte Museum of Art, Seoul, South Korea
—   *Part One: The Mountain*, Lehmann Maupin, London
2020   *Alex Prager: Farewell, Work Holiday Parties*, Los Angeles County
Museum of Art (LACMA), Los Angeles
—   *Welcome Home*, Fotografiska, Tallinn
2019   *Welcome Home*, Fotografiska, Stockholm
—   *Play the Wind*, Lehmann Maupin, New York
—   *Alex Prager: Silver Lake Drive*, Fondazione Sozzani, Milan
—   *Alex Prager: Silver Lake Drive*, Foam, Amsterdam
—   *Alex Prager: Compulsion*, Multimedia Art Museum, Moscow
2018   Musée des Beaux-Arts Le Locle, Switzerland
—   The Photographers' Gallery, London
—   Lehmann Maupin, Hong Kong

2017	*Journeys into Peripheral Worlds*, Des Moines Art Center, Des Moines
—	*Applause*, Times Square Arts: Midnight Moment, New York
2016	*La Grande Sortie*, Lehmann Maupin, New York
2015	*Alex Prager*, Galerie des Galeries, Paris
—	*Alex Prager: Face in the Crowd*, Saint Louis Art Museum, Saint Louis
—	*Alex Prager*, Lehmann Maupin, Hong Kong
—	*Alex Prager*, Istanbul '74, Beyoglu, Istanbul
—	*Alex Prager*, Goss-Michael Foundation, Dallas
2014	*Alex Prager*, The National Gallery of Victoria, Melbourne
—	*Face in the Crowd*, The Arts Club, London
—	*Face in the Crowd*, M+B Gallery, Los Angeles
—	*Face in the Crowd*, Lehmann Maupin, New York
2013	*Face in the Crowd*, Corcoran Gallery of Art, Washington, D.C.
—	*Mise-en-scène*, Savannah Museum of Art, Savannah
2012	*Compulsion*, M+B Gallery, Los Angeles
—	*Compulsion*, Yancey Richardson Gallery, New York
—	*Compulsion*, Michael Hoppen Gallery, London
—	*Compulsion*, Foam Museum, Amsterdam
2010	*Week-End*, Michael Hoppen Gallery, London
—	*Week-End*, Ring Cube Gallery, Tokyo
—	*Week-End*, M+B Gallery, Los Angeles
—	*Week-End*, Yancey Richardson Gallery, New York
2009	*The Big Valley*, Yancey Richardson Gallery, New York
2008	*The Big Valley*, Michael Hoppen Gallery, London
2007	*Polyester*, Robert Berman Gallery, Santa Monica

COMMISSIONS AND SPECIAL PROJECTS

2020	Hyundai Card Music Library, Seoul
2017	*Applause*, 2017, Times Square Arts: Midnight Moment, New York
2016	*Orchestra Center (Intermission)*, The Billboard Creative, Los Angeles
2015	*La Grande Sortie*, Paris National Opera
2011	*A Touch of Evil*, *The New York Times Magazine*, 6 December

AWARDS

2012	Emmy Award, *Touch of Evil*, video portfolio for *The New York Times Magazine*, Director
—	Culture for *Touch of Evil* (*The New York Times Magazine*)
—	FOAM Paul Huf Award, Foam Museum, Amsterdam
2010	PDN's 30 New and Emerging Photographers to Watch
2009	Vevey International Photography Award
—	Lucie Award
2006	London Photographic Award

PUBLIC COLLECTIONS

Amon Carter Museum of American Art, Fort Worth
Cincinnati Art Museum, Cincinnati
Elgiz Museum of Contemporary Art, Istanbul
Fondation Carmignac Gestion, Paris
High Museum of Art, Atlanta
Hood Museum of Art, Hanover
Igal Ahouvi Art Collection, Tel Aviv
K11 Art Foundation, Hong Kong
Kunsthaus Zürich, Zurich
Los Angeles County Museum of Art, Los Angeles
Metropolitan Museum of Art, New York
Moderna Museet, Stockholm
The Museum of Modern Art, New York
National Gallery of Victoria, Melbourne
North Carolina Museum of Art, Raleigh
Princeton University Art Museum, Princeton
Queensland Gallery of Modern Art, Queensland
San Francisco Museum of Modern Art, San Francisco
The Sir Elton John Photography Collection, London
Smithsonian American Art Museum, Washington, D.C.
Whitney Museum of American Art, New York

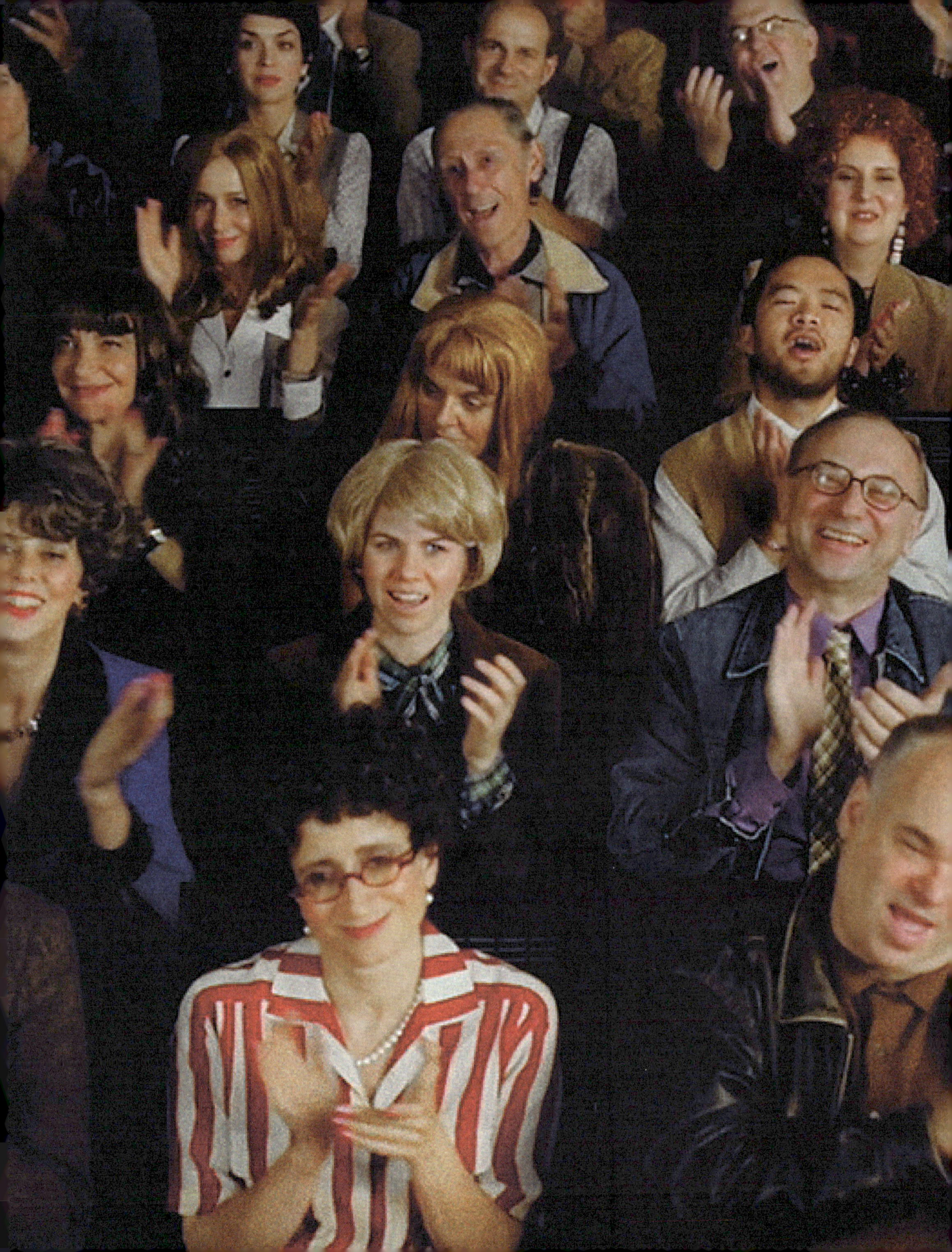

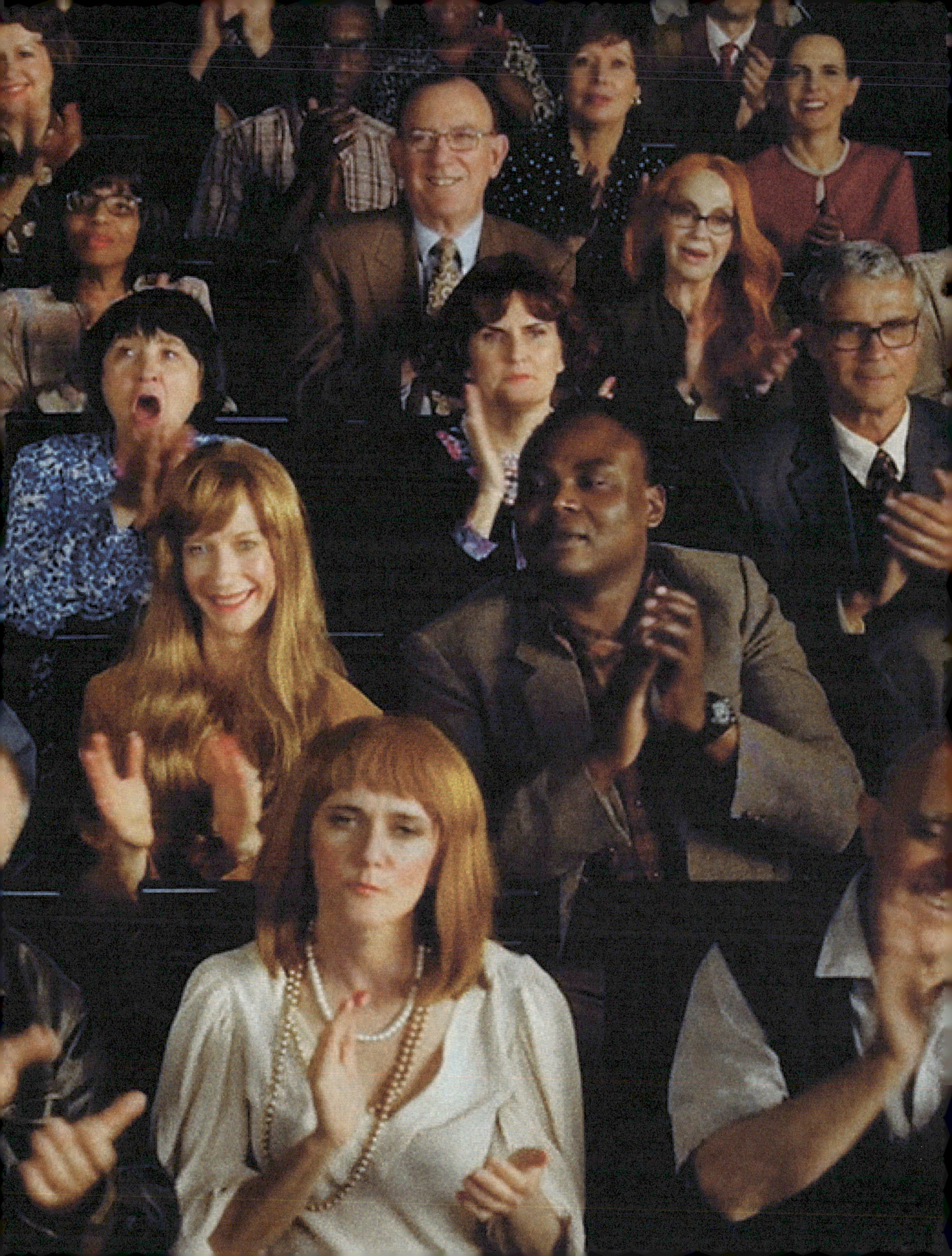

ACKNOWLEDGMENTS

I would especially like to thank Andrew Sanigar, Sadie Butler, and Sam Palfreyman at Thames & Hudson for their confidence in this project, and their patience and guidance, as well as Clare Grafik and The Photographers' Gallery, Michael Govan, Michael Mansfield and Nathalie Herschdorfer for being so generous with their time and sharing their distinctive and stimulating insights into my work.

I would also like to thank Adriaan Mellegers for his persistence, even temper, and striking creativity.

And thanks to my family and their passion for life. You are the best school and also happen to be my favourite muses: Ennis, Mom and Dad, Nana, Simon Dargan, Francis Prager-Dargan, and Vanessa Prager.

A special acknowledgment to my team for always being extraordinary, courageous, and going along with any idea I've had even when it doesn't seem sensible: Ali Helnwein, Amy Chance, Amy Cosier, Ariana Govan, Callan Stokes, Chip and Lara Leavitt at Lumiere, Chris McElrath at Contact, Chris Wadhams, Christopher Warren, Darin Friedman, David Maupin and Rachel Lehmann from Lehmann Maupin, Ebony Dee Cheyne, Erin Thompson, Evans Wittenberg at Figures on a Landscape, Felix Firth, Fionna Flaherty, Gary Oldman, Gene Warren, Gina Ribisi, Giovanni Ribisi, Henrik Fett, Jeff Vespa, Jeremy Dawson, Jessie Cohen, Josie Dichter, Katy McClintock, Len Levine, Lisa Ziven, Lottie Stannard, Matt Chessé, Matty Libatique, Marie Ramos, Nichole Servin, Nigel Godrich, Paul Rizzo, Red Studios, Ross Richardson, Shea Spencer, and Tyler William Parker.

Also a big thank you to those of you who have helped me and given me advice and wisdom time and time again throughout my career; your support and encouragement has been invaluable. Benjamin Millepied, Benjamin Trigano, David and Sayoko Teitelbaum, Jody Quon, Kathy Ryan, Michael Hoppen, Nion McEvoy, Roxana Marcoci, Stefano Tonchi, Yancey Richardson, Bryce Dallas Howard, Elizabeth Banks, Émilie Cozette, and Judith Godreche.

And a very special thanks to all of my friends and background artists who have helped me immensely by being in my films and photographs over the past ten years.

Dedicated to Francis

First published in the United Kingdom in 2018 by Thames & Hudson Ltd, 181A High Holborn, London WC1V 7QX

This compact paperback edition published in 2022.

Alex Prager: Silver Lake Drive
© 2018 Thames & Hudson Ltd, London

Photographs © 2018 Alex Prager

Photographs and films courtesy of Alex Prager Studio and Lehmann Maupin, New York and Hong Kong unless otherwise stated in the captions

Alex Prager, Double Take © 2018 Michael Govan

Interview with Alex Prager © 2018 Nathalie Herschdorfer

Face in the Crowd © 2018 Clare Grafik

Pretend to Pretend in the Art of Appearances © 2018 Michael Mansfield

Designed by Adriaan Mellegers

On the cover: *Simi Valley*, 2014

British Library Cataloguing-in-Publication Data A catalogue record for this book is available from the British Library

ISBN 978-0-500-02535-2

Printed and bound in China by Artron Art (Group) Co. Ltd

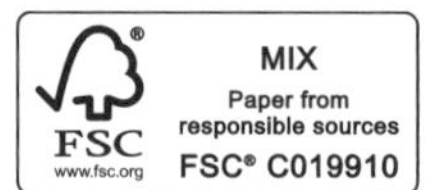